A DICTIONARY OF THE SUSSEX DIALECT

A DICTIONARY

OF THE

SUSSEX DIALECT

AND

COLLECTION OF PROVINCIALISMS

IN USE IN THE

COUNTY OF SUSSEX

BY

THE REV. W. D. PARISH

VICAR OF SELMESTON, SUSSEX

(ORIGINALLY PUBLISHED BY FARNCOMBE & CO., LEWES, 1875)

NOW PUBLISHED BY GARDNER'S OF BEXHILL LTD.

•

EXPANDED, AUGMENTED and ILLUSTRATED

BY

HELENA HALL

TOGETHER WITH

SOME SUSSEX SAYINGS and CRAFTS

GARDNER'S of Bexhill Ltd.

Published by Gardners of Bexhill Ltd.,
Providence Way, Eastwood Road, Bexhill on Sea, Sussex.

A NEW DICTIONARY OF KENT DIALECT
by W. D. Parish and W. F. Shaw,
augmented and illustrated by Alan Major, is published in a uniform edition with this book by Meresborough Books.

First published 1875
Augmented edition 1957
Reprinted 1967, 1981

ISBN 0 900 390 01 8

Printed and bound by Mackays of Chatham Ltd.

CONTENTS

FOREWORD

I am glad to have this opportunity of paying tribute to Miss Helena Hall for preserving, and making available to scholars, this immense collection of words and phrases which are, or were, used within the borders of her native Sussex. Miss Hall has long passed her eightieth birthday, and for sixty-seven years she has been accumulating the material which she now prints as a memorial to her elder brother and former collaborator, John Henry Sussex Hall, who died in 1949.

Miss Hall and her brother were keen and accurate observers and listeners. The present work is the result of their industry. They followed in the footsteps of that other East Sussex antiquary, William Douglas Parish, whose book on Sussex dialect has served for over three-quarters of a century. Miss Hall has reprinted Parish's book in its entirety, thereby ensuring that this pioneer work will not be forgotten.

With the cinema, wireless and television has come a change in the use and meaning of many English words, a change not altogether welcome. The advances in our educational system have resulted in almost everyone alive today being able to read and write, but in the process local dialects have been almost obliterated, Americanisms have been introduced, and there is a marked lack of good pronunciation. As a nation we are becoming standardized in our speech (as in other things), and before many years are past there will be no one left who will have heard terms which were expressive, picturesque, and often of great antiquity and were once not only peculiar to, but used daily in, various localities. It is, therefore, essential to preserve by the tape-recorder, by the written word, by photographs or drawings, and by exhibits in our museums, the recollection of sayings and objects relating to this branch of history for which the evidence is disappearing rapidly and can never be recovered once it is lost.

Miss Hall has done for Sussex what ought to be done for every county while there is yet time. There is, however, one aspect of such work which needs to be emphasized. It is impossible to compile a dictionary of words which are restricted to any one county: Sussex words may occur in Hampshire or Surrey, Surrey words may occur in Kent or Sussex, and who is to say in which county they originated? Neither must it be forgotten that with the development of communications, fresh words and sayings have been introduced into every county and become absorbed into the daily speech of the inhabitants. In some cases these imported words have been corrupted and a new word thus come into being. Miss Hall's dictionary includes many examples of words and phrases which are strictly provincialisms rather than of undisputed Sussex origin, but it is important that these provincialisms, heard in Sussex, should be recorded.

Miss Hall's book is a major contribution to the study of etymology, philology and local history, and I warmly commend it not only to the experts in these subjects but especially to Sussex people and students of its history. The debt which Sussex owes to Miss Hall is a heavy one, and it is my hope that the book she has now produced will meet with the success and welcome it so richly deserves.

FRANCIS W. STEER.
County Archivist of East and West Sussex.

DECEMBER, 1957

ORIGINAL PREFACE

THE march of education must sooner or later trample down and stamp out anything like distinctive provincial dialect in England; but when this result shall have been effected, much that is really valuable will be lost to our language, unless an effort is promptly made to collect and record words which, together with the ideas which first rendered them necessary, are rapidly falling into disuse.

Although in all such collections there will be a large proportion of words and phrases which are mere curiosities of expression, utterly useless to the science of language, yet there will remain a considerable number well worthy of being retained, and if possible revived.

Every year new words are being imported into the English language and gradually coming into general use amongst us. Too many of these are selected from the ghastly compounds of illiterate advertizers, and many more are of the most offensive type of slang—the sweepings of the music-hall, the leavings of the prize-ring and the worst specimens of Americanisms, selected to the exclusion of many good old English words which are to this day more frequently used in the United States of America than in our own country.

The English Dialect Society, which has lately been formed, will soon become the centre of a very valuable influence, by encouraging and uniting many word-collectors who have been quietly working for some time past in different parts of the country, and by giving a right direction to their labours.

To the Rev. W. W. Skeat, as the representative of that Society, I owe more than I am able to express for the guidance that he has given me, and the pains that he has taken to render this work as free as possible from imperfections. Without his assistance I could never have presented it to the reader in the form it now assumes.

Professor Bosworth also, although busily engaged (in his 87th year) in bringing out a new quarto Anglo-Saxon dictionary, found time to encourage me in my work, and set me in the right track by correcting the first pages of my proof. To him and many others my best thanks are due. Such a work could never have been done single-handed, and volunteers have come forward on all sides to help me.

The Rev. W. de St. Croix, late editor of the Sussex Archæological Society's Collections, has for many years given me valuable assistance. Miss Bessie C. Curteis, of Leasam, near Rye, has contributed at least 200 words, with conversational illustrations and legends from the East Sussex district. The Rev. J. C. Egerton, of Burwash, has also placed at my disposal his collection of upwards of 100 words in use in his section of the county; and when I add that the Rev. C. Swainson has helped me in my folk-lore, and Mr. James Britten, of the British Museum, has corrected my botanical definitions, the reader will understand how much kindly effort has been made to render my work successful, and how little its success (if it shall be attained) is due to myself.

W. D. PARISH.

While my Dictionary was in the press, I received the following words from the Rev. A. F. Kirkpatrick, Trinity College, Cambridge and Edgar Sharpe, Esq., Carshalton. They came too late to be placed in their alphabetical order, but were too interesting to be omitted. [They are marked †.]

The following words[1] *(kindly sent to me by Frederick E. Sawyer, Esq., of Brighton), are from the Brighton "Costumal,"* (custumal) *1580; i.e., a book of certain customs, chiefly relating to fishing, which received Royal confirmation at that date.* [They are marked §.]

[1] In the present edition I have correctly indexed these words as well as all other words which were out of place in the Dictionary.

H. H.

Biographical Sketch

OF

WILLIAM DOUGLAS PARISH

The Revd. William Douglas Parish, m.a., was born on 16 December, 1833. He was the son of Sir Woodbine Parish, F.R.S., the diplomatist and naturalist who did much to establish British relations with the South American republics; he also discovered the fossils of the megatherium, mylodon and glyptodon, and the Treaty of Peace signed at Paris, 20 November, 1815, on the conclusion of the Napoleonic war, was in his handwriting.

William was educated at Charterhouse and Trinity College, Oxford. He was ordained in 1859 and after four years as curate at Firle, was preferred to the vicarage of Selmeston with Alciston.

At that time the names of these places were pronounced Simpson and Ahson, and it was as Vicar of Simpson that he was always known. In 1866 he superintended the rebuilding of Selmeston church, having each stone marked and reset in its place. As curate he was an inspector of schools and his own school at Selmston was considered a model for the county.

In 1877 Bishop Durnford appointed him Chancellor of the Cathedral of Chichester. In 1886 he was elected a member of the Council of the Sussex Archæological Society, and in 1895 became the first chairman of that body, a function for which he showed the necessity and which he exercised until his death.

In literature Parish is most generally known as the author of this dictionary, but his other publications covered a wide field. His educational works range from poetry for elementary classes to a manual of instruction on the electric telegraph. With W. F. Shaw, vicar of Eastry, he published a dictionary of the Kentish dialect; but his most important work was editing the Sussex Doomsday for the Archæological Society. In that work a facsimile of the original record is printed, with a literal extension of the Latin text and an English translation in parallel, together with a list of tenants, historical notes and an explanation of the terms.

He died on 23 September, 1904, and is buried in his own churchyard among the people he loved and whose speech he knew so well.

PREFACE

TO THE

AUGMENTED EDITION

SO long ago as 1890 my late elder brother, John Henry Sussex Hall, and I began noting any Sussex Dialect words we heard other than those given by the Revd. W. D. Parish, Vicar of Selmeston, in his DICTIONARY OF THE SUSSEX DIALECT, published in 1875.

Some of the words he records are not now peculiar to the County, although they may have been in his day, some ninety years ago; many of those now added are used not only in Sussex, but are dialect words not widely known. All will be appreciated by those readers interested in rural subjects, especially in the tools of the old hand craftsmen. The much greater mobility of the population generally makes localisation of words a very different matter from its exactitude in Parish's time.

I have accordingly gathered together all the words and phrases my brother and I collected, and have combined them with those already in his dictionary. In this collection, the words of the Revd. W. D. Parish are printed in Monotype Baskerville italic type; those of ours in Monotype Baskerville roman type, in order that the additions may clearly be seen AS additions.

It is thought by some people that dialect words were used only by rustics and the so-called " working classes "—that such words were their property as it were. But this attitude towards dialect is not true, for cultured people in the last century, and to a less extent even in the present, used and use words and phrases which are definitely local in character, and, although less usual now, were ordinary enough in their time, and as common in hall as in cottage. Also several like expressions may be noticed today in the parlance of older people Sussex born and bred. All dialects are beautiful to those who use them, and in this county expecially to those who still find beauty in the voice of a Sussex countryman.

The dictionary of 1875 has been out of print for many years; accordingly it is hoped that this reprint including the supplementary part, of 67 year's collection, will be welcomed by the many who are interested in the sayings, often amusing and generally rather apt, of Sussex country men and women of two or more generations ago; and that it will preserve some of those delightful old-fashioned words of the common speech of our forefathers. Dialect words seem to me part of the treasure of English Literature.

There is, in the library of the Sussex Archæological Society at Barbican House, Lewes, an interleaved copy of Parish, formerly the property of the Revd. Jas. Fraser, of Chichester. It contains many notes of his own, and those of his friends in various handwritings, many by Parish himself and some signed and dated. Fraser had a factotum, one Howard who came from the Lavants, he was used as the dog to try Parish's words on, some of his comments are illuminating. I have found this book a most useful source, and words incorporated, for which I have no other authority, are marked‡.

Mr. E. R. Burder, of Wadhurst, who knew the Downland between Brighton, Lewes and Eastbourne before 1914 has suggested to me that as well as the vertical division of the County adopted by Parish, there is at any rate, in East Sussex a division between Downland and Wealden dialect, the Wealden dialect extending into the adjoining parishes in West Kent. He has cited Kipling's REWARDS AND FAIRIES, (Macmillan 1910) at p. 19 where he writes:

> " They made friends with an old shepherd, called Mr. Dudeney, who had known their father when their father was little. He did not talk like their own people in the Weald of Sussex, and he used different names for farm things, but he understood how they felt, and let them go with him."

Kipling is presumably contrasting Burwash with Rottingdean.

I owe very many thanks to my nephew Henry Warneford Bassano Hall for help and information given as well as for proof reading. Thanks are also due to my friends Evan Gill—a younger brother of Eric Gill, to Charles Butt of Littlehampton, and to Stanley Godman of Lewes, for help and advice; to Mr. Bentham Stevens, secretary, and the Council of the Sussex Archæological Society, particularly Mr. Steer our County Archivist: to my cousin Miss Valentine Bassano and to Mrs. Charles Wilson of Hove for typing the manuscript. Nor can I conclude my acknowledgements without thanking the kind curator of the Curtis Museum, at Alton, Hampshire, where I made, from their most interesting collection, a number of the sketches for the illustrations of tools and appliances.

HELENA HALL.

Blue Gate,
Lindfield, Sussex.
1957

LIST OF AUTHORITIES

W. Durrant Cooper's Sussex Glossary.

Halliwell's Dictionary of Archaic and Provincial Words.

W. Holloway's General Dictionary of Provincialisms.

Bosworth's Anglo-Saxon Dictionary.

Sussex Archæological Collections.

Ayscough's Shakespeare.

Brand's Popular Antiquities.

R. Chambers' Book of Days.

Notes and Queries.

M. A. Lower, Contributions to Literature, etc., etc.

Professor Lèo's Treatise on the Local Nomenclature of the Anglo-Saxons.

Stratmann's Old English Dictionary.

Wedgwood's Dictionary of English Etymology.

Ray's Collection of Local Words.

Bosham Manor Customs, and the old books of the Manor of Arundel (kindly lent by R. G. Raper, Esq.).

Various Inventories of Farm and Household Goods of the last three Centuries.

Mawer and Stenton, The Place-Names of Sussex.

Skeat's Etymological Dictionary of the English Language.

Johnson's Dictionary.

Sussex County Magazine.

Webb and Wilson, Elizabethan Brighton.

The Sussex Dialect

IN almost every establishment in the country there is to be found some old groom, or gardener, bailiff, or factotum, whose odd expressions and quaint sayings and apparently outlandish words afford a never-failing source of amusement to the older as well as to the younger members of the household, who are not aware that many of the words and expressions which raise the laugh are purer specimens of the English language than the words which are used to tell the story in which they are introduced.

Every schoolboy home for the holidays at Christmas knows that the London cabman who drives him to the Theātre accentuates the word much more classically than the young gentleman who sits inside, who, if he had the audacity to pronounce Theatron with a short a *in his next construe at school, would send a shudder through the Form amid which he would soon find himself in a lower place. So it is with our Sussex words; they sound strange to ears that are not accustomed to them; and by some persons they may be supposed to be mere slang expressions, not worthy of attention; but when they are examined, many of them will be found to be derived from the purest sources of our language, and to contain in themselves a clear reflection of the history of the county in which they are used.*

Every page of this dictionary will show how distinctly the British, Roman, Saxon and Norman elements are to be traced in the words in every day use among our labouring people, who retain among them many of the oldest forms of old words which although they have long ago become obsolete among their superiors in education, are nevertheless still worthy of our respect and attention. Like the old coins which he so often turns up with his plough, the words of the Sussex labourer bear a clear stamp of days long past and gone and tell a story of their own.

The fact that I have lived for several years in a village spelt Selmeston and pronounced Simpson; within reach of Brighthelmston, pronounced Brighton, and next to the village of Chalvington, called Charnton, will, I think, be considered sufficient excuse for the direction my studies have taken. My daily intercourse with persons speaking the purest Sussex dialect has enabled me to add from time to time many fresh words to the excellent list published by Mr. Durrant Cooper in his "Glossary" (which must always be the guide book for all who take an interest in the subject); and when I found that I had added as many as a thousand words to those which he had already published, I thought I might venture to take the next step forward in making known the Sussex dialect among Sussex people by the publication of this book. I had called it a dictionary of the Sussex dialect before I was aware that my friend Mr. M. A. Lower had stated in an article published in the Sussex Archæological Collections that there is no such thing as a Sussex dialect at all. I should be sorry to appear to set up my opinion in opposition to one whose authority on all matters connected with the antiquities of our county is so generally recognized; but I am sure that he will allow me the use of the word to indicate a form of speech, which in words and pronounciation is strictly defined by geographical boundaries, and frequently proves completely unintelligible to strangers who hear it for the first time.

So far as a distinct collection of words can be called a dialect, it may be said that there are three dialects in use in the County of Sussex, the East Sussex, Mid Sussex and West Sussex; and it will be observed that I have marked this distinction in the following pages by affixing to most of the words the initial of the district in which they are used. But besides these, there are many words which, as far as I can ascertain, are common to the whole county, and to these no distinctive letter is annexed.

I should (roughly) define the East Sussex district as the part of the county lying east of a line drawn northward from Hastings; the West Sussex district would be bounded by a line running northward from Shoreham; and the Mid Sussex district would, of course, be found between the two. I must request the reader to bear in mind these geographical distinctions, because few persons except word-collectors are acquainted with provincial expressions beyond their own district; and without this explanation it might be supposed that many words which occur in my list are not Sussex words at all.

The sources from which our Sussex words are derived will naturally have a special interest for many of my readers. All who collect or study strange words are anxious to know where they come from; and I confess that I was much surprised when I found that one of the first pieces of advice which was circulated among the members of the English Dialect Society was to abstain from etymology. It seemed to me that to encourage people to collect words, and at the same time to forbid them to attempt to give their derivations, was very like presenting a boy with a pair of skates and then desiring him on no account to go upon the ice. I little knew how treacherous was the element from which this humane society warns us off, till I was myself involved in its dangers, and only just rescued by the untiring efforts of the secretary, Mr. Skeat, from the consequences of rashness which might have been fatal to the success of my work.

Etymology is for many reasons surrounded with dangers and difficulties, not only on account of the prevalence and perpetuation of erroneous derivations already existing, on the authority of persons who knew nothing whatever of the subject, but also because there are so few works published on the subject which are reliable.

Besides this, every amateur etymologist, who fancies he has made a fresh discovery, is led to make a series of wild shots at derivations, forgetting that it is the history *of a word, and* not the similarity *of it to another in form or sound, which determines the source from which it is derived; so one mistake leads to others, and the confusion becomes every day worse confounded.*

Still, I am aware that after all that can be said, word collectors will never be satisfied with merely collecting without deriving, and many of them will be at first inclined to resent any restriction of their liberties; therefore I hope that the English Dialect Society will take an early opportunity of buoying the dangerous channels of etymology, and give a few clear and distinct directions whereby we may be able to steer a safe course within certain defined limits.

The dialect of the Sussex people has been affected by the geographical position and the history of the county. It may be traced chiefly to Anglo-Saxon, Old Dutch, Old Welsh (or British), with a dash of 14th century French, and a little Scandinavian, the latter due to the sea-coast, which has for many generations invited hosts of friendly invaders to our shores, and has twice witnessed the landing of armies destined to influence the history and language of the whole country.

When the Roman legions landed on our coast they left an evidence of their appreciation of the Pevensey shrimps, which remains to this day in the word pandle, *derived from the Latin* pandulas, *which is in constant use in this part of the county.*

The arrival of the Normans, and the foundation of their large monastic establishments marks a very distinct phase in the history of our vocabulary.

But it will be observed that most of our words now in common use, denoting agricultural and domestic implements, are either to be traced to an Anglo-Saxon derivation, or actually retain their original Anglo-Saxon names in all purity of spelling and pronunciation. From this source also nearly all the Sussex surnames and names of villages and farms (noticed in the Appendix) are derived. Nor must I forget to remark that when the Sussex peasant speaks of the sun as she, *he uses an expression which clearly asserts his German origin.*

As might be expected, many words are due to our proximity to the coast. The Sussex fishermen, in their constant intercourse with their Dutch and French brethren, although finding much difficulty in parleying to their satisfaction, have nevertheless for many generations adapted and introduced so many foreign words into common use among themselves, that their vocabulary is almost worthy of being called a fourth branch of the dialect.

Other circumstances, too, have tended to the increase of the French influence. Between 1562 and 1572 no less than 1,400 refugees from France settled themselves in Sussex, and many of their names may be still traced among our labouring people in the eastern division of the county. Besides this, the establishment of French prisoners in later times, and the custom which still prevails, though not so much as it did, of shopkeepers and townsfolk exchanging children with French families in order that each might learn enough of the other's language to be useful in after life, has kept the French element alive amongst us, and accounts for the existence of many words which are not so much derived from as positive corruptions of modern French.

But besides those words in the Sussex dialect which are really valuable as having been derived from authentic sources, there are a great many which are very puzzling to the etymologist, from the fact of their having been either actually invented without any reference to the laws of language, or adapted and corrupted from other words. A Sussex man has a great facility for inventing words. If he has any difficulty in expressing himself, he has no hesitation about forming a word for the occasion. This he does on the phonetic principle (if it can be said to be done on any principle at all), and as he prefers a long word, the result of his invention is generally very curious indeed; and whether or not the word serves the purpose for which it was intended, it is sure to be caught up by some one else, and, especially if it is a long one, is very soon incorporated among the words available for general use in the village.

There are also many words which are used to convey meanings totally different to their original intention. These may be called words of substitution. They are introduced in this way—a person hears a word which he does not quite understand; he does not take the trouble to ascertain either the meaning or pronunciation of it, but he uses a word something like it. *This is specially the case with the names of complaints, such as will be found incidentally mentioned in some of the illustrations which I have given of the use of Sussex words, as, for instance, browncrisis for bronchitis, and rebellious for bilious, etc. The names of any but the most common trees and shrubs are also strangely perverted. A friend of mine had a gardener who persisted in calling an acacia the Circassian, and after much pains had been taken to point out the mistake, never got nearer than calling it the cash-tree. I have heard chrysanthemums called Christy anthems, and China asters Chaney oysters; but that was by the same man who also once enquired how I made out with " them Scotch-Chaney fowls " of mine.*

It is also surprising how little trouble people will take to ascertain correctly even the names of their neighbours, and I know an instance of a man who lost sight of his own name altogether, from having been accustomed for many years to hear it mispronounced. But this in a great measure is to be attributed to the fact that a musical ear is very rarely found among Sussex people, a defect which is remarkably shown not only in the monotonous tunes to which their old songs are sung, but also in the songs themselves, which are almost entirely devoid of rhythm.

The Sussex pronunciation is, generally speaking, broad and rather drawling. It is difficult to say why certain long words are abbreviated, or why certain short words are expanded. In some names of places every syllable, and even every letter, is made the most of—as Eäst Hoädlye for East Hoathly—while others, like the name of my own village, are abruptly curtailed from three syllables to two by the most ruthless excision.

As far as I can reduce the pronunciation of the Sussex people to anything like a system it is this:—

a *before double* d *becomes* ar; *whereby ladder and adder are pronounced larder and arder.*

a *before double* l *is pronounced like* o; *fallow and tallow become foller and toller.*

a *before* t *is expanded into* ea; *rate, mate, plate, gate, are pronounced rèàt, mèàt, pèàlt, gèàt,* they become almost dissyllables and probably perpetuate the true Anglo-Saxon vowel sounds.

a *before* ct *becomes* e; *as satisfection for satisfaction.*

e *before* ct *becomes* a; *and affection, effect and neglect are pronounced affaction, effact and neglact.*

Double e *is pronounced as* i *in such words as sheep, week, called ship and wick; and the sound of double* e *follows the same rule in fild for field.*

Having pronounced ee *as* i, *the Sussex people in the most impartial manner pronounce* i *as* ee, *and thus mice, hive, dive become meece, heeve, and deeve.*

i *becomes* e *in pet for pit, spet for spit, and similar words.*

io *and* oi *change places respectively; and violet and violent become voilet and voilent, while boiled and spoiled are bioled and spioled.*

o *before* n *is expanded into* oa *in such words as pony, dont, bone; which are pronounced pöàny, döànt, and böàn.* That is the *long o* of bone. The *short o* of ton and Monday tends to become a *u* as in ordinary English.

o *before* r *is pronounced as* a; *as in carn and marning, for corn and morning.*

o *also becomes* a *in such words as rad, crass, and crap, for rod, cross, and crop.*

ou *is elongated into* aou *in words like hound, pound and mound; pronounced haound, paound and maound.*

The final ow, *as in many other counties, is pronounced* er, *as foller for fallow*

The final *ow* after *r* becomes *r*, but is almost elided; as bar'r for barrow, vur'r for furrow.

The peculiarities with regard to the pronunciation of consonants are not so numerous as those of the vowels, but they are very decided and seem to admit of less variation.

Double t *is always pronounced as* d; *as liddle for little, etc., and the* th *is invariably* d; *thus the becomes* de; *and these, them, theirs—dese, dem and deres.*

d *in its turn is occasionally changed into* th; *as in fother for fodder.*

The final ps *in such words as wasp, clasp, and hasp are reversed to wapse, clapse and hapse.* Or rather retain the Anglo-Saxon form.

Words ending in st *have the addition of a syllable in the possessive case and the plural, and instead of saying "that some little birds had built their nests near the posts of Mr. Wests's gate," a Sussex boy would say "the birds had built their nestes near the postes of Mr. Westes' gate."*

The Sussex half syllable is difficult to convey to one who has not heard it. The words bar'r and vur'r for barrow and furrow do not become actually monosyllabic, but the second syllable has no vowel sound and is barely distinguished from the first. Similarly the extended vowel as in gèàt for gate does not actually make the word a dissyllable, but very nearly does so.

f frequently becomes *v*, as in vur'r for furrow.

Thus I have tried as nearly as possible to define the rules of Sussex pronunciation —there are so many exceptions to all the rules that they can scarcely be called rules at all; but with regard to one letter a rule can be given which admits of no exception. The letter h *is never by any chance used in its right place; and any one who has ever attempted to teach a Sussex child to read, must be convinced that nothing short of a surgical operation could ever introduce a correct pronunciation of the aspirate into his system.*

This is unduly pessimistic. Many words are given in this dictionary both with and without the *h*. They are, in fact, usually very slightly aspirated. Over insistence on aspiration by teachers has such results as hood for wood.

I may here state that I have endeavoured to spell the words in this dictionary as nearly as possible as I have heard them pronounced; but in the examples of Sussex conversation, etc., I have not attempted to follow the exact pronunciation of the shorter words, because if I had done so, I should probably have rendered them incomprehensible to many of my readers and tiresome to all.

It now remains for me to state the principle upon which I have selected certain words for my dictionary, to the exclusion of others which have been given in the glossaries of Ray, Cooper, Halliwell and Holloway, as Sussex words.

I had to chose from,—

1. *Words found only in some parts of Sussex;*
2. *Words found in Sussex only; and*
3. *Words found in Sussex, and also in other Counties.*

With respect to the first two classes of words there was no question beyond that of identification, and as regards their identity as being actually in use in the county, I may say that I have by myself, or upon the authority of friends on whom I can rely, personally identified almost all of the eighteen hundred words which will be found in this collection. But the reader will easily understand that my chief difficulty has been in dealing with provincialisms unquestionably used in Sussex, but also in such common use elsewhere as apparently to deprive them of a distinctive character. The rule of my selection has been to include any provincial word not likely to have been adopted from a book, which I found in constant use among people who, as far as I could ascertain, had never been out of the county; and lest any of my readers should be inclined to complain of the admission of many words not distinctly belonging to Sussex, I have guarded myself in the title of the book I offer to their perusal, which is not only a dictionary of the Sussex dialect, but also a collection of provincialisms in use in the County of Sussex.

I have also endeavoured to illustrate the use of the words by specimens of conversation, most of which are taken from the life verbatim, and will serve to indicate some phases of character and thought which find frequent expression among our people. When the opportunity has occurred I have added examples of folk lore and proverbial philosophy which are rapidly becoming obsolete, and if not recorded may in another generation be entirely forgotten. Many of them point to superstitions, which are remarkable from the very fact they should exist at all in the presence of our advanced civilization, and many more are connected with old customs already passed away.

I hope that they may at least serve the purpose of inducing some persons to look through the pages of my book, who would otherwise have taken no interest in a mere collection of words; and perhaps when they see how many interesting points may be elicited from closer intercourse with their poorer neighbours, they may be persuaded to become in their turn collectors of old words and stories of the past.

I am convinced that there are many more words yet to be recorded, and I hope that some of my readers will send me materials for a larger dictionary of the Sussex dialect, which I hope some day to be able to complete. I have little doubt of finding many persons ready to help me in this respect, for I have already received much assistance from persons who were strangers to me till they saw my name in connection with this publication; and even up to the last moment, while my work has been in the hands of the printers, several words have been sent to me too late to find a place in the alphabetical list. I have, therefore, requested the publishers to add at the end of each volume a few blank pages, so perforated as to be easily detached without injury to the book, in the hope that such persons as are willing to help me, may write down and forward to me any words not hitherto published which may come under their notice; adding always the name of the locality in which they are used, their pronunciation if it seems necessary, and any proverb or anecdote which may add to their interest.

In making this announcement I acknowledge the imperfection of my own work. Such a work must of necessity be tentative and imperfect, but such as it is I offer it to the kind perusal of all who are interested in the old-world ideas and language of our kind-hearted old-fashioned Sussex folk, many of whom I number among my dearest friends.

A DICTIONARY

of the

Sussex Dialect

Note.—The letters e, m, or w, *after a word, indicate that it is used in East, Mid or West Sussex. By East is meant the extreme East of the County. The words marked with an asterisk are those which I have not myself been able to identify, but are given on the authority of the glossaries of Durrant Cooper, Halliwell, or Holloway.*

Other abbreviations are:—
Words from Kirkpatrick and Sharpe—†
Words from F. E. Sawyer, Brighton—§
Words from Jas. Fraser's book—‡
Sussex Archæological Collections—S.A.C.
Sussex County Magazine—S.C.M.
Sussex Sayings and Crafts, (an Appendix.)—S.S.&C.

A

A. The prefixed a-, as used in the Sussex dialect, generally adds some slight force or intensity, and is retained in such words as a-dry, a-lost, a-nigh, etc.
It is also almost invariably used with the participle; as, "I am a-going as soon as I can."

A-BEAR. [A-béran, *Ang. Sax.*] *An old form of bear, in the sense of endure or like. Used in the negative, "I never could a-bear that chap."*

A-BED. *In bed.*

ABIDE. [Abídan, *Ang. Sax.*] *To endure. Used with the negative in the same way as a-bear.* Can't abide 'em—don't like them.

ABILITY.† *A word occurring in old account books for an assessment rate, now probably obsolete.* As much as such an one ought, or is able, to pay.

ABOUTEN, e. [Abútan, *Ang. Sax.*] *Just on the point of having done anything. Always used with a past tense; as, "I was abouten going out, when Master Noakes he happened along, and he kep' me."*
The syllable en is more frequently omitted in Sussex; as, "My knife wants sharping."

ABROAD, m. *In all directions; all about.*
"When e'er I take my walks abroad." *I. Watts.*

ABUSEFUL, m. *Abusive.*

ABUSEFULLY, m. *In an abusive manner.*
"*As my missus was a-going home a Saddaday night, she met Master Chawbery a-coming out of the Red Lion, and he treated her most abusefully, and threw abroad all her shop-goods. He's a man as aint no account at all aint Master Chawbery.*"

ACCOUNT. Esteem; reputation.
"*The Princes both make high account of you.*"—Richard III., *Act iii. sc. 2.*

ACHE, e. *To tire* "*I am afraid you'll ache waiting so long.*"
To long for anything. "*Nancy just will be pleased, she has ached after a dole I don't know the time when.*'

ACROST. For across.

ADDER. This word generally qualified by 'deadly' and pronounced like 'harder' with or without the h, is very loosely applied not only to the Viper, but to the Grass-snake, Slow-worm (often distinguished as 'deaf-adder') and even the common lizard.

ADDER'S MEAT. The Greater Stitchwort. *Stellaria holostea.*

ADDER'S OIL. A specific for deafness. Dead adders were hung on a sunny wall and the fleed (inside fat) would melt and drop into small bottles.—A few drops were placed in the ear.

ADDER'S SPEAR. Large dragon-fly.

ADDLING. See Adling.

ADIN. [*Corruption of Within.*]
The initial w is mostly omitted in Sussex; and th is always pronounced as d; thus, the wood becomes de 'ood; and within idin or adin.

ADLE[1]. [*Ang. Sax.*, ádl.] *Pronounced ardle. Stupid.* "*He's an adle-headed fellow.*"
(*Cf.* addlepate, a fool; also Adle[(2)] and Eddel.

ADLE[2], *e.* (*Ádl*, Ang. Sax., ill, diseased. See note to Eddel.) *Slightly unwell.*
"*My little girl seemed rather adle this morning, so I kep' her at home from school.*"

ADLING, or ADDLING HIS SHOON. Earning his shoes; said of a horse when he rolls in pasture.

ADONE. [*Have done.*] *Leave off. I am told on good authority that when a Sussex damsel says* "*Oh! do adone,*" *she means you to go on; but when she says* "*Adone-do,*" *you must leave off immediately.*

ADRY. Thirsty. (*Cf.* Drythe, and dry-thirsky.)

AFEARD. [Afæred, *Ang. Sax.*] *Afraid.*
"*Hal, art thou not horribly affeared?*"—I Henry IV., *Act ii. sc. 4.*

AFFUT. A newt or eft. See Effet.

AGARVES, m. *May berries.* Haws. Also called Aigarces, Argarces Argaves, Eggas or Eggas-berries, (*q.v.*) Hogarves, (*q.v.*) Hogasses, Hog-gazels, (*q.v.*) and Hoghazels.

AGGY. Peevish; out of sorts; usually in reference to a child. The same meaning as Niggly.

AGIN. [Agen, *Ang. Sax.*] *Near to; against.*
"*He lived up agin the Church, and died about forty yeere agoo.*"

AGOO. Ago.

AGREEABLE. Acquiescent; consenting.
"*They asked me if I'd come in and have a cup o' tea, and I was quite agreeable;*" *meaning that he accepted the invitation.*

AGWAIN. Going.

AIG. Egg. "A' be agwain t'ave a biled aig for me brakfus dracly."

AIGARCES. Haws. Also Agarves and Hogarves, (*q.v.*) etc.

AÎNTES, *w.*‡ Mintes; cheese mites.

ALE HOOF or ALLIFF. Ground ivy. *Nepeta glechóma.* So called because formerly used in place of hops for clearing and preserving beer. Also known as Gill-ale and Lion's mouth.

ALLEY, or ALLEY-TAW. A Tolley, or shooting marble.

ALLMEES. Alms.

ALL-ON, m. *Incessantly.*
"*He kept all-on making a noise.*"

ALL-ONE. All the same; as,
"*Well, 'tis all-one whether ye do or whether ye döant.*"

ALLOW. To give as an opinion. To conclude.
"*As I was agwaine down the street, I ses to Master Nappet ses I, what d'ye think of this here job down*

at the blacksmith's? I ses, and Master Nappet he allowed that it was amost too bad!"

"I allowed you was over twenty" = thought you were.

"I allus allowed she were 'ees darter."

ALLTSINIT, m. [*All that's in it.*] *Merely.*

ALLUS¹. Always.

ALLUS². Alehouse.

ALONG-OF. On account of.

"*Along of her it was that we met here so strangely*"—Cymbeline, *Act v. sc. 5.*

This expression is often expanded into all-along-of, and even, all-through-along-on-account-of; as "Master Piper he lost his life all-through-along-on-account-of drink."

AMAKIN. Wild. Same meaning as Willocky.

"'E just drives me amakin with 'is goings-on."

AMENDMENT, m. *Manure.* Also called Manner.

'*You go down to the ten-acre field, and spread that amendment abroad, and peck up them ammut-castes.*"

AMMUT-CASTÈS. Emmet-castes; ant-hills. (*Cf.* Worm-casts.)

This form of plural is invariably retained in words ending with st, as postes, nestes. The reduplicated plural is also not unfrequently used; and a Sussex man would see nothing absurd in saying,—

"*I saw the ghostesses,*
Sitting on the postesses,
Eating of their toastesses,
And fighting with their fistesses."

AMMUTS, m. *Emmets; ants.*

AMOST. Almost.

AMPER. A flaw or fault in linen or woollen cloth.* A tumour or swelling.

*AMPERY*¹, m. [Ampre, *Ang. Sax.*, *a flaw.*] *Beginning to decay, especially applied to cheese.* [*Cf.* Hampery.]

*AMPERY*². *Weak; unhealthy.*

AMPRE-ANG. A decayed tooth.*

AN. Of. "*If you wants to be rid an him, you* lend *him a sixpence; I lay he'll never come anigh you no more.*"

ANCLEY, m., *ANCLIFF*, *e. Ankle.* Also Ankley.

ANCLIFF-BONE. In East Sussex, I have put out my ancliff-bone, is equivalent to I have sprained my ankle.

ANCONY. A 'bloom' of iron forged from the 'sow' with ends left square, wrought in the 'finery' to bar-shape in the middle, and when made, ready for further working in the 'chafery'. (See S.S.&C. under Iron-working.)

ANDIRONS. (Possibly from Brandirons). Fire dogs.

The ornamental irons on each side of the hearth in old fire-places, before grates were introduced. The andirons were sometimes made of superior metal, or gilt, and of very large dimensions.

"*Her andirons (I had forgot them) were two winking cupids of silver.*"—Cymbeline, *Act ii. sc. 4.*

The derivation of this word is obscure, see Brands, or Brandirons.

ANDREW MAC. Andromache. See S.S. & C.

ANDRING. A custom observed on St. Andrew's Day, November 30. (See S.S. & C. under Souling.)

*ANEWST.** [Neawest, *Ang. Sax.*] *Nigh; almost; near at hand.*

ANIGH. Nigh; near.

ANKLEY. Same as Ancley; ankle.

ANYWHEN. At any time. This word is very usual in Sussex.

ANYWHILE. During any period of time.

APPLE-PIE. Great Hairy Willowherb. *Epilóbium hirsútum.*

APPLE-STUCKLING. An apple turnover; a Flap Jack, (*q.v.*) or Crowdie.

*APPLETERRE.** [*Apple and* terre, *French.*] *An orchard.*

APPLETY, e. [*Apple and tye, an enclosure.*] *An apple-loft, where the fruit is kept. This word is used on the borders of Kent, in which county the word tye means an enclosure, whereas in Sussex it means an open common.*

APSE. [Æpse, *Ang. Sax.*] *An aspen tree.*

ARDER. *An adder. In Sussex the letters a and e are often pronounced as in French.*

The country people say that an adder can never die till sunset. If it be cut to pieces, the bits will retain their vitality till the sun goes down. They also say that on the adder's belly will be found the words,—

"*If I could hear as well as see,*
No man in life could master me."

"Them there deadly arders" is the usual phrase. See also Adder.

ARDLE. See Adle[1].

ARG, m. *To argue; to wrangle.*

"*These chapelfolks always wants to arg.*"

ARGARCES. See Agarves; Hogarves.

ARGIFY, m. *To signify; to import.*

"*I do'ant know as it argifies much whether I goos to-day or whether I goos to-morrow.*'

Also argue. My nurse used to say " Don't argify with me Miss Helena.'

ARK. A particular kind of chicken house, triangular in shape, is known as a " Sussex ark". It originated in the County.

ARN. Horn (Musical instrument.)

ARTCHITEX. Architects. See S.S.&C.

ARTER. [*Corruption of After.*]

ASCLE-TREE. Sussex pronunciation of axle-tree.

ASH. See Earsh.

ASH-CLOTH, m.† *Before the use of soda was understood, the washerwomen used to soften the water by straining it through a coarse cloth, which was fastened over the top of the wash tub and first covered with marshmallow leaves, and then with a layer of wood ashes.*

ASHEN. *Made of the wood of the ash.*

ASIDE. Become bankrupt.

" William Walder went aside this evening."—*S.A.C. LXXI.* p. 23.

ASK, or ASKED. Had banns published. (*Cf.* Church-bawled.)

" They were asked in Church last Sunday."

ASLEW, m. *Aslant.*

ASSART LANDS. [*Essarter*, French, to clear of wood for cultivation.] An old form of Manorial tenure of land cleared from woodland for cultivation, and for which Assart rents were paid. Specially called Forrep-land and Sookland. (*Cf.* Bondland, and see S.S.&C. under Borough English.)

ASTICALL MULLER. The ring next the touch hole. See Gun rings.

AT. See Been at.

ATHER DAVED. [Affidavit.] A certificate which had to be made by the officiating cleric at a funeral. See Goodman.

In the 18th century, the powerful staple trade had secured enactments protecting their interests; one of the provisions was that at every burial the corpse had to be shrouded in wool, *not* linen. The statutory declaration was made to protect the priest against action for failure to comply with the law.

ATWEEN. *Between. Also used in the Eastern Counties.*

ATWIXT. *Betwixt.*

AUMRY, e. [Aumoire, *Old French, a cupboard.*]

or

AWMRY, e. *A large chest.*

"*And when they had eaten, King Arthur made great clerks to come before him that they should chronicle the high adventures of the good knights; and all was made great books and put in almeries at Salisbury.*"—Sir Thomas Malory's Morte D'Arthur.

AVICK. Havoc. A " tidy avick " =a shocking mess. See S.S.&C. under Tidy.

AVILLER, or JACK AVILLER. Crabs; so called at Shoreham. Other forms of this word are Haviler and Heaver.

AVISED, e. [Aviser, *French*]. *Aware of. To know for a certainty.*

"*I'm well avised that John spent all his wages at the Barley-mow.*"

AWHILE. For a time.

"*We shan't have no gurt frostes yet awhile—not atwixt now and Christmas, very like.*"

AWMRY. See Aumry.

AX or AXE. Ask.

AXEY, e. *The ague. A complaint which is very prevalent in many parts of Sussex. There is a different name for it in almost every district. In some places it is believed that it may be cured by the following charm, which, to be efficacious, must be written on a three-cornered piece of paper and worn round the neck till it drops off,—*

"*Ague, ague, I thee defy,*
Three days shiver,
Three days shake,
Make me well for Jesus' sake!"

Some other names are Johnny, Old Johnny and Lord John.

B

BACKSTAYS, or BACKSTERS. Wide flat pieces of board, made like snow shoes, which are strapped on the feet and used by the fishermen in walking over the loose beach or soft mud on the seashore. Also called Mudpattens, flappers, cleat-boards, clip-boards, or spatter-boards. Similar boards are used on the vast expanse of shingle at Dungeness and the Norfolk Broads. I saw men using backsters at Lancing, but never women.

BACKTURNED, m, and *BACKWENT*, m. *These words, which are evidently of Saxon construction, can only be explained by giving instances of their use. "He was backturned when I saw him," means "he was standing with his back to me." "I only saw him backwent," means "I only saw him as he was going away from me."*

BACON PUDDING. See S.S.&C.

BAD HOUSE. A house in which there is much illness.

"We've got a very bad house."

BADSKIN. Condition of ill temper. (*Cf.* Skin.)

BAFFLING MATCH. The game blindman's buff. Sometimes called Jingling match.

BAGGING-BILL, or BAGGING HOOK. A deformation of Fagging-hook, (*q.v.*). Or a swap-hook, the word is used variously.

BAG-UP. A bagged-up cow is one marketed with her udder full, so as to appear a larger milker than she is.

BAIL, w.† *The handle of a bucket, pail or kettle.* That is the loop handle.

BAIT, m. *Afternoon refreshment, with which strong beer is given, in the hay and harvest field.*

BAKEN. Bacon.—*Lindfield Inventory*, 1804.

BAKING KIVER.‡ A kneading trough.

*BALDERDASH.** [*Probably derived from Ang. Sax.* Baldwyrda, *a saucy jester.*] *Obscene conversation.* More usually nonsense.

BALE. Of tobacco. Smuggler's term. Weight from 1 to 50 lb.

BALLET[1] m. *A ballad.*

BALLET[2]. Gossiping from house to house. "You may depend on't I shan't make no ballet of what we've been a'talkin' about."

BALLY, or oftener BALLIES. Belly.

"Lor Lizzie wot a tarble noise your ballies do make, 'tis like the roarin' of the sea." A father's comment on his daughter at table at Cooksbridge.

BALSAM. Uncomplimentary back-chat.

"I've had enough of her balsam."

BANDANNA. The gay coloured cotton kerchief, usually red-spotted, worn around the neck with the smocked frock or with the banyan[1].

BANNICK, m. *To beat.*

"*I'll give him a good bannicking if I catch him.*"

BANYAN[1]. A short jumper, close at the hips.

BANYAN[2]. Scraps of food; using up left-overs; no cooking.

" This is banyan day."

BARCA. Tobacco.

BARGEBOAT. The green woodpecker. Also called Galleybird and Yaffle, (*q.v.*).

BARK. To cough.

" I can't abear for my master to goo to church; for he keeps up such a barking, that nobody can't hear naun for him."

BARKING-IRON. A Tan-spud or Flawing-spud. An iron tool of various lengths, with a heart-shaped blade on a wooden handle used for Stripping, Flawing or Rining bark from oak trees directly they are felled. (*Cf.* Tan, and see S.S. & C. under Devil.)

Barking Iron

BARKING TARTAR. See Cruiser.

BARLEY-CHAMPER, w., BARLEY-HUMMELER, BARLEY NIBBLER, or BARLEY-NOLLER. A barley-awner. *An instrument for cutting off the beards of the barley.*

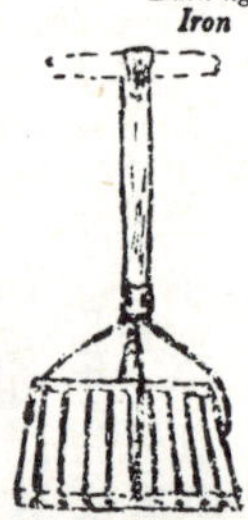

Barley-Champer

BARLEYEAR. The Furze chat or Whinchat.

BARN SHOVEL. A broad wooden shovel with a short handle, used variously for handling corn and other crops in the barn, malt house and oast.

Barn Shovel

BAR'R. A barrow. This word, and others like it, is pronounced almost as two syllables, the second having no vowel sound and being slurred into the first.

A boy was bidden " You go and ask Mr. Banfield for his iron bar," meaning his pitch. He came back reporting " Mus' Banfiel' sez 'e aint got but one bar'r 'n that's a 'ooden un and 'e be broke."

BARREL. The round part of the hook of a shepherd's crook. (See S.S.&C. under Bilbo.)

BARTON, m. [Bere-tún, *Ang. Sax., a court-yard.*] *The demesne lands of a manor. The manor house itself. More frequently the outhouses and yards.*

BARWAY, m. & *e. A field-gate, made of bars or rails so fitted as to draw out from the posts.* (*Cf.* Pair-of-bars.)

BASE RING. The first ring behind the touch hole. See Gun rings.

BAT. [Bâton, *French, a stick.*] Or much more likely from *bat*, Ang. Sax., a bat, club, staff. *A rough walking-stick.* Any kind of stick. The word ' stick ' is never used in real Sussex speech. *E.g.*, see S.S.&C. under Optics. To walk on two bats, or to cuddle, is to use a bat in each hand walking. " You mus' 'ave seen the old codger wot goos cuddling about on two bats."

BAT and TRAP. A game played chiefly on Good Friday, usually known as Trap Ball.

BATCH. A quantity of bread baked at once without heating the oven afresh. This was important in the old faggot heated brick oven.

> *" How now, thou core of envy?*
> *Thou crusty batch of nature,*
> *what's the news?"*
>
> —Troilus and Cressida, *Act v. sc. 1.*

BATED. When a fish is plump and with plenty of roe, it is said to be well bated.

BATFOWLER. One who takes birds at night with a large folding-net on long poles, called a batfowling net.

> Gon: *" You are gentlemen of brave metal; you would lift the moon out of her sphere, if she would continue in it five weeks without changing."*
>
> Steb: *" We would so, and then go a batfowling."*
>
> —Tempest, *Act ii. sc. 1.*

BATS.† *Logs of wood for burning*, or any odd pieces of wood.

BATTER. [Abattre, *French, to beat down.*] *A wall which diminishes upwards is said to batter.*

BAVINER. A bavin maker. He chopped twigs, bunching them into little bundles of firewood tied with twigs.

BAVINS. Pronounced Bah'vn. *Brushwood faggots.*

> "*The skipping king, he ambled up and down,*
> *With shallow justers and rash bavin wits,*
> *Soon kindled, and soon burnt.*"
> —I Henry IV, *Act iii. sc. 2.*

BAWDEKYN. A blue and white hanging for a tester bed.

BAWL, e. *To read aloud.*

A mother said of a child who did not go to school on account of illness, "I keeps him to his book all the same, and his father likes to hear him bawl a bit in the evening."

BAY[1]. *A pond-head* (or dam) *made up to a sufficient height to keep in store water.*

A tumble bay is a dam or small weir which the surplus water runs over to a floush-hole or spill-way.

BAY[2]. *A compartment of a barn. The space between the main beams of the roof: so that a barn crossed twice with beams is a barn of three bays.* Also called a Mow or Toss. (The width of a bay was always the same in ancient barns . . . the space necessary for the stabling of a yoke of oxen. The same width was kept between the beams in a house.)

> "*If this law hold in Vienna ten years, I'll rent the fairest house in it, after three-pence a bay.*"
> —Measure for Measure, *Act iii. sc. 2.*

BAY[3]. Of a waggon: where it bows out.

BAYLISS. A kind of rough plaster with small beach (*q.v.*) in it, used for surfacing walls, houses, etc. Rough cast.

BE. A common prefix to verbs, generally conveying a reflective and intensitive power, as be-smeared, be-muddled, be-spangled. (*Cf.* beloved, benighted, besotted.)

BEACH, m. *Shingle brought from the sea-coast is always called beach, as opposed to the inland gravel.*

Beadle

BEADLE or BITTLE. A form of Beetle, a large wooden hammer or mall.

BEAM. The top "bar" of a field gate to which the brace is attached and which passes through both harrow and head. The bars themselves are also called spleats.

BEAN-EATER. Long tailed field-mouse. See Meece.

BEAR. "If 't'd bin a bear 't'd o' bit yer." Said to one looking for something that is quite close but overlooked.

BEAT THE DEVIL ROUND THE GOOSEBERRY-BUSH, e. *To tell a long rigmarole story without much point.*

An old man at Rye said he did not think the new curate was much of a hand in the pulpit, he did beat the devil round the gooseberry-bush so.

BEAZLED, m. *Completely tired out.*

"*He comes home tired of an evening, but not beazled like boys who go to plough.*" "I be fair beazled."

BECK[1]. [Becc, *Ang. Sax., a brook.*] *A rivulet.*

BECK[2], w. [Becca, *Ang. Sax., a pickaxe.*] *A mattock.*

TO BECK[3], *is to use the beck or mattock.*

BEDHEAD STONE. Stone or wood on graves resembling the head of the old bedstead.

BEDSTEDDLE. A bedstead.

BEDWAGGON. A frame (containing a pan of charcoal) for warming or airing a bed, sometimes made of ashwood and otherwhiles of wrought iron.

BEEF-STONES. Flints found near Selsey subjected to prehistoric forest fires. The fracture has a streaky red appearance resembling a round of beef.

BEEN AT. Attended to. See S.S.&C.

BEEPOT. A beehive.

BEESKEP, e. [Scep, *Ang. Sax*, *a basket.*] *A beehive, or the straw hackle placed over the hive to protect it.* More recently a straw hive as distinct from a wooden one (*Cf.* Hackle[1]).

There is a superstition in the county, that if a piece of black crape is not put round the hive after a death in the family, the bees will die. See S.S.&C.

BEEVER, w. *Eleven o'clock luncheon.* (*Cf.* Coager and Elevener.)

BEEVES, m. *A corruption of Beehives; The i in the word hives being pronounced as in French.*

" *Well, John, how are you going to make out this winter?*"

" *Well, I reckon I shall have to make brooms and beeves.*'

BEGGAR'S KNEES. Fossil shell fish.

BEGRIDGE, m. *To grudge.*

BEHITHER, e. *On this side. It answers to beyond.*

" *The fifty-first milestone stands behither the village, and the fifty-second beyond.*"

BEHOPES. Let us hope.

" Well'm, behopes I'll be able to come earlier next time."

" I rackon this aig be a bad 'un."

" Behopes it wun't breàak then.'

BEHOWTEL, *w.* or BE'OWDIL. Letbehow'twill, (*q.v.*).

BEING. An abode; a lodging.

" *Return he cannot, nor*
Continue where he is; to shift his being,
Is to exchange one misery for another."
—Cymbeline, *Act i. sc. 6.*

BELEFT, m. *Perfect of believe.*

" *I never should have beleft that he'd have gone on belvering and swearing about it as he did.*" (See S.S.&C. under Hedge Carpenter).

BELIKES. Likely; very likely. " 'Tis vurry like." is an assent.

BELLARMINE. See Greybeards.

BELLEY. Felley or Felloe. One of the curved pieces of wood, which together make the circular rim of a wheel.

BELLICK. Bellow.

"Anything wrong 'e do bellick about the 'ouse."

BELL STAPLES. Fittings to sheep bell tops for holding the straps by which they are hung on the yokes.

Bell Staple

BELLUS. Bellows.

" I'll soon get the fire up with yer bellus."

BELVER, m. *To make an angry disturbance.*

BEMBLANDS. Shingle-covered foreshore with coarse vegetation.

BENCH. A widow's bench is the share of the husband's estate which a woman enjoys besides her jointure. That is to say, where the husband had been a copyholder of the manor, the widow's bench (*q.v.*) *was* her customary jointure. (See S.S.&C. under Borough English.)

BENDING-IN DAY. Opening of the mackerel season at Brighton. See S.S.&C.

BENNETS. Long grass that bends in the wind.

BE'OWDIL or BEHOWTEL. (Be how it will.) However it be. Whatever happens. Letbehow'twill, (*q.v.*)

BEST, m. *To get the better of anyone; to beat at any game.*

"*I bested him every time.*"

BETHANKS. Thank Goodness, etc.

BETHERED, e. *Bed-ridden.*

" *Poor creature! She was bethered three years before she died.*"

BETHWINE. The wild clematis. C. vitalba. Tom-bacca. Also called Pethwine.

BETTERMOST. Superior; above average. Generally qualified by the word rather.

" *The new people whe have come to live down at the cottage seem rather bettermost sort of folks.*"

BIBBER. To shake and rattle, as a window.

BIBLER-CATCH, w. [Bilboquet, *French.*] *The game of cup and ball.* Bilber-catch, usually.

BIDANCE. Abode=place where one bides.

BIDE[1]. [Bídan, *Ang. Sax.*, *to remain.*] *To wait*; *remain*; stay.

> "*If ye've got one you can run;*
> *If ye've got two you may goo;*
> *But if ye've got three*
> *You must bide where you be.*"
> —Sussex Proverbial Advice to a Young Mother.

BIDE[2]. Let bide, let alone; or Let that bide—Don't interfere with it. (See S.S.&C. under Hedge Carpenter.)

BIER. A billow-slip.

BIGORING. A marbles game where the players contribute equally to the pool of marbles placed in the middle of a ring 3 feet or so in diameter, and shoot in turns from the circumference. If the player knock out one or more marbles they are his spoil, and he can go on so long as he remains in the ring and gets one or more marbles out at each shot. If he remain in and fail to get a marble out he becomes dead and can be shot at by the others.

Also called Shoot-through-the-ring.

BILBER- or BILBO-CATCH. Cup-and-ball; Bibler-catch, (*q.v.*).

BILBO. A sheep bow; A V-shaped wooden frame to hold a sheep's head in shearing, clipping or trimming for the fair or show. See S.S.&C.

Bilbo

BILE. To boil.

BILL-HOOK. A sharp cutting tool, hooked at the end, used for pruning and for tapering off the points of spiles. Valued by hurdle makers. Not local but sometimes confused with a hand-bill (*q.v.*).

Bill-hook

BILLUS, w.† *To beat; to flog.*

BILLY-PINAFORE. A holland pinafore, clean every Monday morning, worn by the boys of the Brighton Proprietary Grammar School, founded 1835 and closed 1895.—*S.C.M. IX.* p. 108.

BIND-DAYS, w. *Days on which the tenants of certain manors were bound to work for their lord.*

BINDERS. See Heathers and S.S.&C. under Hedge and fence.

BINDING or BONDCORD. Manilla yarn slightly laid used to tie up sacks of corn, etc. Also for thatching in lieu of tar cord. (*Cf.* Peg[1] and Sparrer.)

BINE, m. *The hop stalk which binds round the pole.*

BIRCHET. A birch tree.

BIRDS WEDDING-DAY. St. Valentine's Day: February 14.

BISCUIT. In Sussex the words biscuit and cake interchange their usual meaning. A plum biscuit, or a seed biscuit, means a plain cake made of either of these ingredients.

BISHOP-BARNABY, e. *The lady-bird. In some parts of Sussex the lady-bird is called the lady-bug*; (lady-cow, *q.v.*); *in others, fly-golding, or God Almighty's cow, by which singular name it is also known in Spanish (Vaca de Dios). The children set the insect on their finger and sing,—*

> "*Bishop Bishop-Barnabee,*
> *Tell me when my wedding shall be*
> *If it be to-morrow day,*
> *Ope your wings and fly away.*"

BITTEN, m. [Bítende, *Ang. Sax.*, *biting.*] *Inclined to bite.*

"*Mind that dog, he's terrible bitten.*"

BITTLE[1], w. *A wooden milk bowl.*

BITTLE[2]. See Beadle.

BITTLE-BATTLE. The game of stoolball.

There is a tradition that this game was originally played by the milk-maids with their milking-stools, which they used for bats; but this word makes it more probable that the stool was the wicket, and that it was defended with the bittle, which would be called the bittle-bat; hence the word bittle-battle.

BLACKDOWN. (Bleak down.) The *highest point in Sussex* is on Blackdown in the parish of Lurgashall; 918 feet above Ordnance datum.

BLACKEYED SUSAN, m., or POND PUDDING. *A well pudding, with plums or raisins in it.* Made in a bowl, see S.S.&.C.

BLACK-GRASS, e.† Alopecurus agrestis. Fox-tail grass.

BLACK RAM NIGHT. A sheep-shearers' celebration. (See S.S.& C. under Ship.)

BLACK-SANDING. Looking for lost coins, rings, etc. on the beach when it has been moved by the sea, especially after a storm.

BLADE. A steelyard.

BLAME. A common substitute for a worse word.

"*Blame ye! ye be always at something; be blamed if I dòant give it yer one of these days.*"

BLANKET-PUDDING, m. *A long, round pudding, made of flour and jam; sometimes called a bolster-pudding.* Or Sore-leg pudding.

BLEAT, m. *Cold; cutting; applied to the wind.*

BLINDWORM. Slow-worm. See Adder.

BLINE. Blind.

BLIV. Believe; Bluv, (*q.v.*).

BLOBTIT, m. [*Blabbe*, Mid. Eng., to blab.] *A tell-tale.*

BLOBTONGUE, w.† [Blabbre, *Danish, to gabble.*] *A tell-tale.* (*See Blobtit.*)

BLOOM. [*Bloma*, Ang. Sax.] A mass of wrought iron. (See S.S.&C. under Iron working.)

BLOOMERY. A place where wrought iron was made by the old direct reduction process. (See S.S.&C. under Iron working.)

BLUE-BOTTLE, m.† *The wild hyacinth.* Hyacinthus non scriptus.

BLUE-BOWLERS. Bluish seaworn black flints collected and used for glass-making.

BLUE-GO. An out of the way occurrence.

A Withdean man's wife threw herself down the well and was drowned. Shortly after, the man being at the Brewery, the Brewer commiserated him "I was sorry to hear about your wife, Norton." The widower replied "Ah, that war a blue-go warn't ut."

BLUNDER[1], m. *A noise as of something heavy falling.*

"*I heard a terrible blunder overhead.*"

BLUNDER[2]. *To make a noise.*

BLUV, or BLIV. [*Corruption of Believe.*] "*I bluv*" *is often used at the end of an assertion in the sense of* "*you may take my word for it,*" *as* "*'Taint agoing to rain to-day, I bluv.*"

BLY, e. [Bleo, *Ang. Sax., hue.*] *A resemblance; a general likeness.*

"*I can see a bly of your father about you.*"

BOARDLAND, *w.* [*Board*, a table; for the table.] A Bosham name for demesne land, a part of the Bondland. (See S.S.&C. under Borough English.)

BOB. "On the bob solly"—a bell-ringer's phrase for a swinging bell which is not actually swung enough to strike. To be, or to be kept, on the bob solly is used as a figure of speech of a state of continuing uncertainty. (*Cf.* Solly.)

BOBBINGNEEDLE, m. *A bodkin.*

BOBS. Beetles, etc. (*Cf.* Pincher-bobs.)

BOCK. To nausiate; to vomit. (*Cf.* Boke.)

BOCO, e. [Beaucoup, *French, much.*] *A large quantity.*

This word is principally used by the fishermen.

BODGE,† w. *A water cask on wheels.* (*See* Bouge and *Budge*[1].) Any cask on wheels, as a Flour Bodge, etc.

BODGEN or BODGIN. Getting off; going away.
"I'll soon be bodgen home."

BODGER[1]. [*Corruption of Badger.*]

BODGER[2]. A botcher; a bungler. (*Cf.* Bunger [2].)

BODY-HORSE. The second horse from the waggon in a four or five horse team. See Team.

BOFFLE. A confusion or mistake.
"*If you sends him of a errand he's purty sure to make a boffle of it.*" (*Cf.* Of.)

BOFFLED. Browbeaten.

BOIL, *w.*‡ Bile. A counter-inversion, see Bile for boil.
"I feel very ill today. I believe Sir, it's the boil."

BOKE. [Bealcian, *Ang. Sax.*] *To nauseate.* (*Cf.* Bock.)

BOLSTER-PUDDING. See Blanket-pudding.

BOLT. To run to seed, as a lettuce does.

BOLTER. A kind of trot-line for shore fishing. (*Cf.* Trot.)

BOND.† [Bond, *Ang. Sax.*] *A band, as a hay-bond, bonds for fastening up the sheaves of corn, etc.*

BONDCORD. A Binding used as a runner in thatching. See Peg[1], and Sparrer.

BOND-KNIFE. A knife used for cutting the bond on sheaves of corn for threshing, and on trusses of hay or straw.

Bond-Knife

BONDLAND, w. (*Bonda*, Ang. Sax.; *Bondi*, Icelandic, a cultivator.) Cultivated land. [Bonde-land, *is defined in Bosworth's Anglo-Saxon Dictionary as land held under restrictions*, copyhold.] *Used in Framfield and Mayfield for old cultivated or yard-lands, as distinguished from assart-lands, which were parts of forests cleared of wood and put into a state of cultivation, for which rents were paid under the name of assart-rents.* (See S.S.&C. under Borough English.)

BONE-SETTER. A rough-gaited saddle-horse.
"Git up! you old bone-setter."

BOOK[1]. *The Bible is almost always spoken of by old people as the Book. Not many years ago the family Bible was the only book to be found in the cottages of the poor; now the frequent visits of the book-hawker have introduced a taste for reading into the remotest districts of the county, but still the Bible retains its title of the Book; and I was glad to hear a rough-looking carter boy say the other day,* "*I always read a bit of my Book before I goos to bed.*" Parish was writing in about 1870.

BOOK[2].† *A word used in old parochial accounts for a rate, as* "*a 2s. 6d. book produces £500 in Horsted Keynes.*"

BOOTED. Injured by frost; said of corn.

BOOT-LEGS, m. *Short gaiters, not reaching to the knee.*

BOOTLIGS. Long gaiters. See S.S.&C.

BOOTS ON. To die with one's boots on: a violent accident resulting in death. My old nurse used to tell me "Ah me lass, you'll die wi' yer boots on I warrant."

BORNS. All my borns: days of one's life. (*Cf.* Out-de-way.)

BOROUGH ENGLISH. A former system of tenure. See S.S.&C.

BORSTAL. See Bostal.

BOSS. To throw.

BOSSER. The shooting alley or 'tolly' of a marble player used at marble games played at Battle.

BOSTAL or BORSTAL. A pathway up a hill, generally a very steep one, and on the northern escarpment of the Downs; as the White Bostal near Alciston, the Ditchling Bostal, etc.

With respect to the derivation of this much-disputed word, Professor Bosworth has kindly given me the following:—Burg-stal, -stol, es; m. [*burg, beorg, beorh, a hill, stal a place, seat, dwelling*]. *A hill-seat, dwelling on a hill; sedes super collem vel clivum, Cot. 209. The names of places built on a hill, as Burstall in Suffolk, Borstall in Kent and Oxfordshire, etc.* Whence the Borstal system of reformatory school.

Mr. Kemble (Sussex Archæological Collection, vol. II, p. 292) takes " the first word of the compound to be the Saxon word beorh, *a hill or mountain, the passing of which into bor, is neither unusual nor surprising. The second word is not so easily determined. Were the word ever written borstill, Mr. K. should suggest the Saxon* stigel, *a stile or rising path; and beorh-stigel would be the hill-path or mountain path. He does not know whether, in that branch of the West Saxon which prevailed in Sussex, 'steal' did signify a road or way; but it is not without probability that some of the Anglo-Saxon dialects might have justified that use of the term; for 'stealian' or 'stellan' does sometimes seem to be applied in the sense of 'going or leaping'."*

BOTCH. To do a job badly, clumsily or inefficiently.

BOTCHER. One who botches.

BOTTLETIT. Longtailed tit, from the shape of its nest. (*Cf.* Muffle-tit.)

BOTTOM[1], m. *A valley in the Downs.* Also in the Weald any flat land near water.

BOTTOM[2], w. *A reel of cotton.*

BOTTOM[3]. Most inferior iron mine. See Mine.

BOUGE, m. [Bouge, *French.*] *A water cask.* (*Cf.* Bodge and Budge). *The round swelling part of a cask.* Sometimes called Bunt (*q.v.*); *cf.* the bunt of a sail, that is the swell of it. Bilge and Bulge are variants of the same word. *Cf.* in heraldry Bouget or Water Bouget used by Crusaders for carrying water.

BOUGH-HOUSE, m. *A private house allowed to be open at fairs for the sale of liquor.*

An old person describing the glories of Selmeston fair, which has now been discontinued many years, said " There was all manner of booths and bough-houses."

In former times putting up boughs upon anything was an indication that it was to be sold, and a bush at the end of a pole was the badge of a country ale house; which gave rise to the proverb, " Good wine needs no bush," i.e., *nothing to point out where it is sold.*

BOUGH-SPUD. A kind of heavy bill-hook used for trimming branches; also called a slasher.

Bough-Spud

BOULDER-BOAT. A stout lugger made to knock up the beach with the tide, used for collecting from the beach black flint seaworn boulders for the manufacture of glass.

My brother said:—" When I was a boy about 1870 there used to be a race at Shoreham Regatta of boulder boats which were sometimes called Bowler boats."

BOULDER-HEAD. A work against the sea, made up of small wooden stakes.

BOUT. A day's work.

" *I shan't do it this bout,*" *means, I shall not finish to-day.*

BOWLER BOATS. See Boulder boats.

BOX. A coffin—by old folk called a 'cawfin' (corefin).

Two boys were hanging about a churchyard. When one of them was leaving the other boy said, "Arn't yer goin' ter wait and see the old gent come out in a box?" *i.e.*, the funeral.

BOZZLER, m. *A parish constable; a sheriff's officer.*

BRABAGIOUS, e. *An adjective of reproach, the exact meaning of which is difficult to define; but it is generally considered available for use in a quarrelsome discussion between females.* "*You nasty brabagious creature.*" *It seems to combine the advantages of Mrs. Gamp's two principal epithets, bragian and bage.*

BRABBLE. The noise a rippling stream makes.

BRACE. The diagonal stay or strut of a five-barred or other field gate.

BRADES. Money. In Essex called 'Brads.'

BRAKE[1]. *The common fern.* Pteris aquilina. Plural, bracken.

"*I'll run from thee and hide me in the brakes.*"—Mid. Night's Dream, *Act ii. sc. 2.*

BRAKE[2]. *A kneading trough.*

BRANDS, BRAND DOGS, *or BRANDIRONS. Irons used for supporting the brands for burning wood in a wood fire.*

It frequently occurs that the Sussex form of a word preserves the Anglo-Saxon origin; and it is possible that "Brandiron" [from *Brandísen*, Ang. Sax., a branding iron or rod, a tripod] is the primitive form, and that the French and late Latin forms are derived from *it.* (*Cf.* Andirons.)

BRANDTONGS. Small smoker's tongs for holding an ember or taking small pieces of glowing wood from the fire for tobacco pipe lighting.

BRANDY LEAVES. Petals of the Madonna lily or of St. Joseph's lily soaked or pickled in brandy and used as a dressing for a cut or for a scrazed wound.

BRAVE[1], m. [Brave, *French.*] *Well in health.*

"*How are you, John?*" "*I'm bravely, thank you.*"

BRAVE[2], m. *Prosperous.*

"*I have been making out bravely since you were last here.*"

BRAYDS. Small charcoal, used to Mollify (*q.v.*) iron mine.

BREACHY[1]. *Brackish, applied to water.*

BREACHY[2]. [Brèche, *French, a breach.*] *A word applied to cattle which are wild and liable to break through the fences.*

BREAD-AND-BUTTERS, m. [*Compare*, Butter-brod, *German.*] *Pronounced brenbutters; Slices of bread buttered; used in the same way as the French word* tartine.

BREAD AND CHEESE. The tender green leaf-buddings of the Hawthorn.

BREAD-AND-CHEESE-FRIEND, e. *A true friend as distinguished from a cupboard-lover.*

"*He's a regular brencheese friend he is, not like a good many, always after what they can get.*"

BREAK.† *A cultivator used among potatoes and hops. (See Idget.)*

BREATHE. for Breath.

'There was'n a breathe of wind."

BREN. A contraction of 'Bread an', as Brencheese', 'Brenbutter.' (*Cf.* Jambreads.)

BRICKS, m. *The paved walk in front of a cottage, or paved path in a garden.*

"*I'm always pleased to see him a'coming up my bricks.*"

BRIFFENS.‡ Chaff; Cavings, (*q.v.*).

BRILE. Broil.

"Mind you put up yer brolly gaffer in this briling sun."

BRISH[1]. Quick as possible.

"I went along so fast as I could brish."

BRISH[2]. To trim a hedge.

BRISH[3], or BRISHINGS. Hedge clippings or cuttings; often called "Hedge brishings."

BRISHER. A hedger. See Brusher.

BRISTLE-BAT. Stone for sharpening a scythe and carried in a loop behind the mower's belt. Also called a rubber.

BRITT, m. [Brytan, *Ang. Sax., to break*]. *To shatter like hops from being over-ripe.*

BROACH, w. [Broche, *French.*] *A spit.*

"*Broached with the steely point of Clifford's lance.*"—III Henry VI, *Act ii. sc. 3.*

BROAD[1]. A Common.
BROAD[2]. A large flooded meadow.
BROAD[3]. A small place is said to be a little broad of another place; but not so big or important, such as "Walsted is a little broad of Lindfield," or "Small Dole is a little broad of Henfield." (*Cf.* Wide-of.)
BROADWHEEL WAGGON. The old waggon with wheels whose tread was multiserial and near 18 inches wide tapering outwards; the wheels were set out wider at the top.

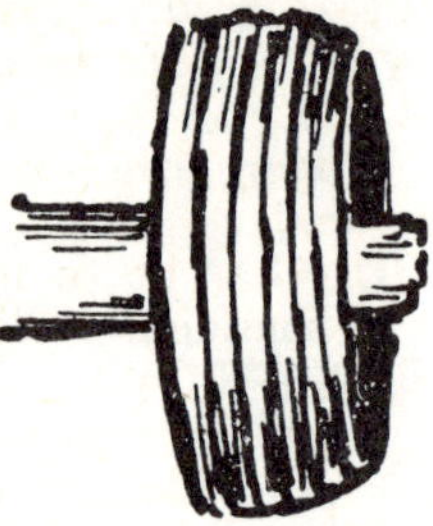
Broadwheel Waggon

The waggons went 2 miles an hour on a good road: their lanthorns were enormous affairs, two feet high with a socket for the whip so that the carter with his "Sussex-moon" had one hand free.
BROCKS. Cuckoo-spit bugs, (froghoppers), also badgers.
BROCKYLOE. Brocoli.
BROKE, w.† *A large quantity of timber.* Also a lot or group of felled trees in one place.
BRONK, m. *A disdainful toss of the head.*
"*She didn't choose to see me, so she just gave a bronk and passed on.*"
BRONTICLE. Bronchitis or Bronchial.
"I've bin 'avin' a touch of the bronticle lately."
BROODY. Ill-tempered. Sullen.
"She be fair broody to-day."
BROOK, m. *A water meadow.* (*E.g.* The Amberley Wild Brooks.)
BROOM-CLISHER, m. [*Clish, a bond.*] *A broom maker.* (*Cf.* Clish.)
BROOM-DASHER, m. *BROOM-SQUIRE*, w. *A dealer in faggots, brooms, etc. The word dasher is also combined in haberdasher.*
BROOM-KNIFE. A knife with curved 5-inch blade used by women to cut broom for making besoms.

Broom-knife

BROWN-BIRD, m. *Thrush.* Also called Grey-bird; but grey-bird is really the missel-thrush.
BRUFF, e. *Rough; short in manners and speech.*
BRUNG. Brought; did bring.
BRUSHER. A hedger. Brushing—trimming hedges.
(*Cf.* Brisher and Brish[2].)
BRUSHING. Training a hedge to obtain a wedge-shaped effect by the use of a bill-hook and giving all strokes an upward direction.
BRUSS, m. [*Compare French* Brusque, *blunt.*] *Proud; upstart.* One who spoke bluntly and briskly was "bruss".
"'E were crass too, 'e spoke monstrus bruss to me."
BRUSTLES. [*Variations of Bristles.*]
BRUTTE, e. [Brouter, *French, to nibble.*] *To browse or feed upon.*
BRUTTLE[1]. *Always in Sussex used for brittle.*
BRUTTLE[2]. A beast which is habitually a hedge-breaker.
BUCKING, m. [Buc, *Ang. Sax., a tub.*] *A washing of clothes.*
BUD, w. *A calf of the first year, so called because the horns then begin to appear or bud.*
BUDDY, w. *Stupid, in the same sense as the word calf is often used for a stupid fellow.*
BUDGE[1], w. [Bouge, *French.*] *A cask placed on wheels for carrying water.* (*See* Bodge and *Bouge*).
BUDGE[2], m. [Bouder, *French, to pout.*] *Grave; solemn.*
"*He looked very budge when I asked him who stole the apples.*"
BUDS. A spring complaint of children. Also Brimstone and Treacle given for a remedy.
"It's good for the buds."
BUG. Any hard-winged insect.

BULL-DOG. An iron implement for leading bulls in the same manner as a nose ring, but with the advantage of being easily removed.

Bull-dog

BULLOCK, m. *A fat beast of either sex.*

I was very much astonished when I first heard a farmer say, " Yes, she's a purty cow, a very purty cow indeed, and one of these days she'll make a nice bullock."

BULLOCK-LEAZE.† *The right of turning one bullock out on a common to graze. (Used at Berwick and other places.)* (*Cf.* Leaze.)

BULPIT GRASS.‡ A coarse, tufted grass.

BUMBLE. To talk wordily. (*Cf.* Oration.)

A country boy swapping long grass exposed a humble bee's nest: he was seen to be grinning over it, and was asked what amused him. He replied, " Why Miss they do so mind me o' Mark Antony's or-ation; you can see what they're driving at but they do keep all on bumbling about it."

BUMBLESOME, m. *Hunched up; misfitting.* Also, ineffectively fussy.

BUMBOO, m. *A mysterious compound of spirituous liquors, under the influence of which, Mr. Turner, draper, of Easthoathly, made the following entry in his diary:—" 1756* (Sunday), *April 28th. I went down to Jones', where we drank one bowl of punch and two muggs of bumboo, and I came home again in liquor. Oh! with what horrors does it fill my heart to think I should be guilty of doing so, and on a Sunday too! Let me once more endeavour, never, no never, to be guilty of the same again."*

Bumboo is composed of beer and brandy.

BUMPKIN. A standing spar used sometimes as a bowsprit. (*Cf.* Split[1].)

Bassett, the Brighton sailmaker, says that the bumpkin is properly the iron hook rigged on such a spar to take the foresail—not the spar itself.

BUMSTICK, *w.*‡ A kind of small mead, very heady.

" The washing of the bee-combs, a sweet drink."

BUNCH, m. *A swelling.*

" *It came out in bunches all over me.*"

" Her arm were all bunched up."

BUNG. A lie; a deliberate untruth; a considerable lie.

BUNGALOWS. Breeding colonies of slipper limpets.

So called by oyster fishermen, who dislike them intensely, because they interfere with the oyster beds.

BUNGER[1], m. (Pronounced ' bunjer.') *To do anything awkwardly.* (*Cf.* Bodger[2].)

BUNGER[2]. One who does anything awkwardly; a bungler.

BUNGER[3]. (Hard g.) A liar.

" Coo! what a bunger." *Our younger brother's comment on Jacob's answer to "Art thou my very son Esau?"*

BUNKER. To jump a hedge etc.; to escape by flight.

" Can you bunker over that ditch?"

BUNNY, w. *A wooden or brick drain laid under a road or gateway to carry off the water; also called a cocker.* Or a Coker or Craker.

BUNT[1], e. *To rock a cradle with the foot; to push or butt. A bunt is described to me as a push with a knock in it, or a knock with a push in it.*

" *I'll give you a middlin' bunt prensley if you döant keep still.*"

BUNT[2]‡. A small faggot, but larger than a bavin. Poor people were given " a fagot and a bunt."

BUNTER, m. *An old-fashioned machine for cleaning corn.*

BUNTING HUTCH. A bin into which flour is sifted.

BURGH, m. [Burg, *Ang. Sax.*] *A rising ground; a hillock. The term is frequently applied to the barrows or tumuli on the Downs.*

BURIES. (Pronounced 'berries.') Plural of bury; rabbit holes.

BURNERS. Charcoal workers under the master man called a collier. Later all charcoal workers were called colliers. (See S.S.&C. under Cording and Charcoal burning.)

BURNISH, e. *To grow fat. The expression, "You burnish nicely," meaning, "You look well," is frequently used in East Sussex, and is meant as a compliment.*

BURN-THE-MINE. See Mollify; & S.S.&C. under Iron-working.

BURY.† (Pronounced 'berry.') *A rabbit hole; a hole made by any animal.*

"Never did see surmany robbut buries in me life."

BUSH. A thorn.

"He's got a bush in his foot."

BUSHELER. A Tallyman, (*q.v.*); one who measures hops from the bin. (See S.S.&C. under Hop drying.)

BUSH OFFICER. A name for an irregular assistant preventive officer.

BUSSES. Short, heavy, tubby and very strong fishing boats characteristic of Hastings and used in the off season as traders.

BUSSICK, *w.*‡ A hassock. (*Cf.* Tussick.)

BUSTER.‡ Fleed-cake.

BUSTLING PART. See S.S.&C.

BUTTER-AND-EGGS. Birds'-foot trefoil. *Lotus corniculatus.* Also called:—God Almighty's thumbs and fingers; Ladies' fingers; Milk-maids; Pattens and clogs; Pigs'-pettitoes; and Shoes and stockings.

BUTTERFISH. A marine mollisc. *Tapes decussatus.*

BUTTER-MY-WIG, m. *A strong asseveration.* (*sic*).

"*No I wunt; butter my wig if I will!*"

BUTTER SPATTERS. Butter hands.

BUTTS AND BOUNDS. Metes and Bounds; the limits of an estate.

BUZZ. Throw away.

"If you don't want it, just buzz it."

BUZZING CLOCK. The cockchafer. Called also, May-bug and June-bug.

BUZZLE-HEAD.‡ A gooseberry or currant branch distorted by aphis.

BYSTE[1], m. *A couch made up of two chairs for a child to sleep upon in the day-time.*

BYSTE[2], m. *To lie down in the day-time.*

"*I was quite took to (ashamed) to think you should have come in the other day and found me bysted, but I was quite entirely eat up with the rheumatics, and couldn't get about no hows.*"

BY-THE-BYE, e. *By chance.*

"*He come along one day by-the-bye, or else he hasn't been a-nigh me for the last ten years.*"

BYTHEN. By the time that.

"*Bythen you've come back 'twill be coager-time.*"

C

*CAB.** [Cabaler, *French, to plot.*] *A small number of persons secretly united in the performance of some undertaking.* (*Cf.* Cabal.)

CABBAGE. To copy—crib. With school-boys to look over and copy a neighbour's work—plagiarise.

CACKHANDED. Awkward; left-handed, wrongly arranged for convenience. "It comes all cack-handed to me like this."

CADGER. Not only a travelling beggar, but anyone given to begging is called by this name in Sussex.

CAFFINCH, or

CAFFINCHER, w.† *The Chaffinch.*

CAGE[1], or SHEEP-CAGE. A frame or "feeder" of wattled hazel—like hurdle—to hold hay for sheep feed.

CAGE[2]. A squirrel's nest; a dray or draw.

CAGE[3]. The Town Cage. A cage or den for the detention of vagabonds and other malefactors. There is a stone one at Lingfield, Surrey. Sometimes they were of iron.

CAGE[4]. A Fire Cage is an iron basket for a fire beacon.

CALIMANCO. A mixed woollen cloth. In the will of Lady Shirley of Wiston, she leaves to her sister-in-law, her "calimanco gowne, kertle, cloke and doublet."

CALL. Cause. I overheard across the common, "'Ullo, 'ow be you?" "Oh, you ain't got no call ter worry I be auright."

CALLED OVER. Scolded.

"You'll get called over for that"—*i.e.* scolded. A threat often impressed by my nurse meaning my parents would do the calling over, she herself feeling inadequate to the task.

CALL OUT OF NAME, m. *To call a person out of his name is not to give him his proper title.* Or to revile him.

"*And then, what d'ye think he says? Why, he says ''ooman' and I aint a-going to be called out of my name by such a fellow as him, I can promise him.*"

CALL-OVER, m. *To abuse.*

"*He come along here a cadging, and fancy he just did call me over, because I told him as I hadn't got naun to give him.*"

CALLOW, m. [Calo, *Ang. Sax.*, *bald.*] *Smooth; bare. The woods are said to be getting callow when they are just beginning to bud out.* Also said of young chicks. Our gardener at Lancing said of a new brood, "Baint they lovely callow?"

CAMBER[1], e. *A harbour.*

Winchelsea Castle, built to protect Rye Harbour, is called Camber Castle.

CAMBER[2]. Also a creek or little bay or dock part of a harbour, as at Portsmouth, where fishing boats lie at anchor or moored.

CAMPHERING. The chamfer on a gun muzzle was so called.

CAMSTEERY, e. *A horse is said to be very camsteery when it does not go steadily. In Northumberland the word means crazy.* Camsteery is a Scots word.

CAN, CANISTER. Sheep bell (*q.v.*)

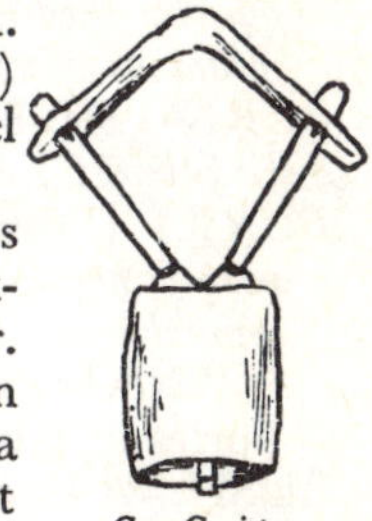
Can, Canister

CANDLES.‡ Hazel catkins.

CANKER. Robin's cushion. The excrescence on a briar. Sometimes worn round the neck as a protection against whooping-cough.

CANT[1]. *To upset or let fall.*

"*The cart canted over and he was canted out into the road.*"

CANT[2]. *A corner of a field.* A division of land or of work.

A haystack is said to be cut across in cants, and a field of wheat is divided into cants when it is partitioned out in slips for the reapers, each of whom takes one or more cants as his share of work. See S.S. &C., and under Copse—coppicing. (*Cf.* also Land-warps.)

CANTANKEROUS. A source of ill-feeling.

"The price of thet ole pig lay cantankerous atween 'em."

CANTERBURY or CANTERBURY HOE. A special hoe; see S.S. & C.

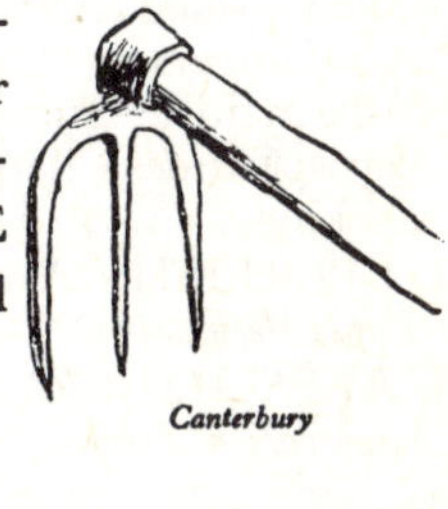
Canterbury

CAPTAIN. The head of a sheep shearing gang of about 20 men, a title retained for life. He wore a broad gold lace band round his hat and his "Lieutenant" a silver one. (See S.S.&C. under Ship.)

CARDIOUS†. *A mixed cloth made of wool and linen thread. A word which frequently occurred in old account books when spinning-wheels were in use.*

CARD'NLY. Accordingly.

CARFAX. [Carrefourgs, *Old French, crossways.*] A Partways; *A place where four* (or more) *roads meet*, but do not form a cross, *as the Carfax at Horsham.* (*Cf.* Cross-ways, Fourthrows and Went.)

CARN. Corn.

CARP-PIE. To eat carp-pie is to submit to another person's carping at your actions.*

CARRIERS.† *Part of a spinning-wheel fitted with wire hooks through which the thread passed to the reel.*

CARROTY. —of wood: having that character of the carrot that in transverse it is brittle and breaks 'short'. (*Cf.* Spalt, Sprow.)

CART. Lurch. Left in the cart means left in the lurch. See S.S.&C.

CARTBROAD. Of a way wide enough to take the trades (or treads) of a cart.

CAST[1].† *The second swarm from a hive of bees.*

CAST[2]. To warp or twist.

CAST[3]. *w.*‡ Four strides, setting out land-warps for ploughing.

CASTLE. An earthwork 'castrum,' as Edburton Castle, Hollingbury Castle, etc. Also used very widely of neolithic earthworks.

CAT or KIT. A stand for a dish made on the principle of three rods spreading from their middles. It could be used either way up, the three lower rods forming the feet and the three upper ones supporting the dish, or plate. Made either of iron or of wood.

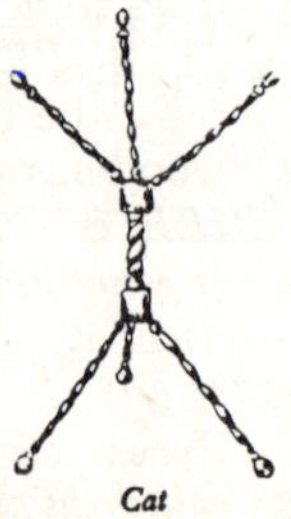
Cat

CATCH HOT, e. *To take fever.*

CATCH HURT, m. *To meet with an accident. An old man once told me that he catched hurt at Chiddingly Church, meaning that he got married there.*

CATERCROSS, w. *Slanting.*

CATERING, m. *From corner to corner.*

CATERWISE, m. *Diagonally.*

'If you goos caterwise across the field you'll find the stile."

CATERWOMTIOUS. A wide term used for things out of the straight or ordered way, such as the sagging roof of a shed, or a crooked, crumpled table cloth.

CATS TAILS. The male blossom of hazel or willow.

CATTERNING. To go catterning is to go round begging for apples and beer for a festival on St. Catherine's Day, and singing,—

"Cattern' and Clemen' be here, here, here,
Give us your apples and give us your beer,
One for Peter,
Two for Paul,
Three for him who made us all;
Clemen' was a good man,
Cattern' was his mother;
Give us your best,
And not your worst,
And God will give your soul good rest."

(See S.S.&C. under Souling.)

CAUL. A large oval wicker basket used by charcoal burners for the reception of the charcoal.

Caul

CAULKER-BRIDGE, w.† *A rough bridge made of logs and fagots.*

CAUSEY. A causeway. This is the Middle English word which became first causey-way, and was later shortened to causeway.

CAVING-RIDDLE, w., or CAVINGS-RUDDER.‡ *A seive for cavings.*

CAVINGS, w. [Ceaf, *Ang. Sax., chaff.*] *The short straws or ears which are raked off the corn when it is thrashed.* Also called Briffens.

CERTAIN SURE, e. *The superlative of certainly.* (Often 'Sartin-Shore'.)

"*I hope you are pretty well to-day. Certain sure, indeed!*"

CHAARK. Chalk.

CHACKET, m. *To cough.*

CHAFERY. The fire of an Iron Hammer or Forge, used for the second process of the Finery. (See S.S.&C. under Iron-working.)

CHAMP, w. *Firm; hard.*

"*The river has a champ bottom.*"

CHANCE-BORN, e. *An illegitimate child.* Or a Come-by-chance or love-child.

CHANGES. Shirts and shifts.

If you ask what a girl or boy stands most in need of on first going to service, you are sure to be told "changes." "I have not got a change means, I have no linen."

The following inventory of the outfit of a girl going to service is taken from the account book of Selmeston parish, 1745:—"An account of Grace Barber's cloaths,—14 caps and moobs, 2 changes, one gown, 2 white hancerchifs, 3 coats, 2 spackol hancerchifs, one white apron, 2 other aprons."

CHAPEL-MASTER, m. *A dissenting preacher.*

CHARGER, e. *A large platter or meat dish.*

"And his head was brought in a charger."—*St. Matthew.* xiv. 11.

See S.S.&C.

CHARLES, CHARLESES, or CHURLS. Local name for pinnacles of chalk on Beachy Head.

CHARLEY FROG, *w.*‡ The toad. "A frog! No, he jumps."

CHARM-STUFF, e. *Ague medicine.* (Not British Pharmacopoeia.)

In Sussex, medicine is generally spoken of as physical medicine, *but it is carefully distinguished from doctor's stuff, by which a tonic is meant.* See S.S.&C. under Doctor's medicine.

The use of charms, especially in cases of ague or wounds, is still prevalent in the country; and the following charm is not unfrequently used for the cure of a burn. It must be repeated three times,—

"*Two Angels from the North,*
One brought fire, one brought frost:
Out fire, in frost,
In the name of the Father, the Son, and the Holy Ghost."

CHASTISE, m. *To accuse.* To upbraid.

"*They've been chastising my boy of setting the faggot-stack a-fire.*"

On a question of an item in an account I was told, "Yes Sir, you're right, I'm sorry I chastised you Sir!" *i.e.* corrected or contradicted you.

CHAT[1]. Very small potatoes like marbles.

"Yes, they taters look purty good; but you come to lift 'em they be all runners and chats."

CHAT[2]. Talk.

I heard a bozzler at Findon sheep fair who had asked a booth man to pay the toll for his booth which he had refused to pay. The booth man began to argue aggressively when the bozzler said, "Look 'ere. I doänt want none o' your chat."

CHATTERNAG. Chatterbox.

CHAVEE. A small boy.

CHAVISH, e., and *w. A chattering or prattling noise of many persons speaking together.*

A noisee made by a flock of birds.

CHECK, m. *To reproach or taunt.*

"*He checked him of his cousin Tom (who had been sent to prison).*"

CHECK-PIN. The same as mumble-pin: the part to be dislodged in a wooden mole trap.

CHEE, e. *A hen-roost. Going to chee is going to roost.*

CHEESE. See S.S.&C.

CHEQUER, w. *The service tree.* Pyrus torminalis. *The fruit is called chequers*, serbs, or sorbs.

CHESS, e. *A plaid.*

"*I bought a chess shawl for mother.*"

CHIBBOL or CHIPPOLE. [*Ciboule*, French.] Small onions.

CHICHESTER SLOE FAIR. See S.S.&C.

CHICHESTERS. The Chichesters was an affection of depression got by first living at Chichester—a low fever.

CHICK. In East Sussex used as the plural of chicken.

"*I reckon you have got a good sight of chick here.*"

CHICKEN. In Mid-Sussex used as the plural of chick.

CHICKEN PED or PEDD. A box or crate made of willow for sending fatted, killed and plucked fowls to market.

Chicken ped

CHIDDESTER. Common form of Chichester—both City and Title.

CHILL. To take off the extreme coldness from any beverage by placing it before the fire.

"*I often gets my mistus to chill a drop of beer for me, when I comes home winter evenings.*"

CHIMPS.‡ Young bulls.

CHIN-BOARD. A piece of strong wood, usually oak about 6 by 3 inches, used to support a cow-bell, horse or other bell, when worn by a sheep. The bell being fixed to the centre of the board and the neck straps to each end of it because the bell has not two lugs (bell staples) like a sheep bell. One variety had two slits cut through it, one at each end; another four slits (two at each end).

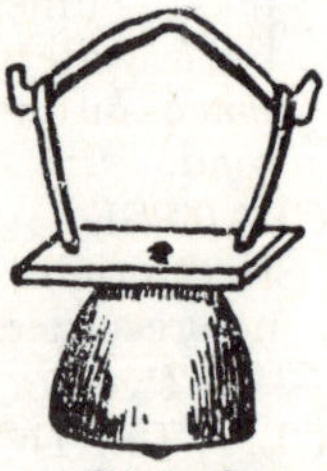
Chin-board

CHIN-COUGH. Whooping cough, the remedy for which complaint was a roasted powdered field mouse added to the milk drunk by the child patient.

CHINKERBERRY RINGS. Small escallops; so called by the fishermen of Brighton because they are taken from a place marked by the bearing on Chanctonbury Ring.

CHIP, w.† *The wooden part of a plough to which the share is fastened.*

CHIPPER, w.† *Lively; cheerful.*

CHIPPOLE. See Chibbol.

CHIZZLE. w. *Bran.*

CHIZZLY, e. [Ceosel, *Ang. Sax., sand.*] *Gritty; harsh and dry under the teeth.* Incapable of being brought to a fine face.

CHOCK. To choke.

CHOCKLY, m. *Choky; dry.*

CHOG. Choked up.

"It wouldn't work as the pipe were all chogged up."

CHOGS, m. *The refuse cuttings of the hop plants when dressed in the spring before being polled.* Also called Shrogs.

CHOICE, m. *Careful.*

"*He ain't got but two brockyloes, but he's middlin' choice over them I can tell ye.*"

"She's very choice over her hand-made wine." meaning rather stingy.

CHOP, *m*. To snap at . . . of a dog at bees, etc., from the sound made.

"They bees swarmed on her and she kep' on choppin' 'em. We took three pints o' bees out on 'er when she died." (She was tied up.)—*Said by a farmer at Woodmancote.*

CHOP BACKS. Hastings fishermen are so called. See Fishermen.

CHOPPER, w. *A dried pig's face. I.e.* chap.

CHOUSE or CHOWSE. A fraud; one who cheats in money matters.

"He choused me out of five shilluns."

CHOW, e. *To chew.*

"*The old cow's better this morning, she's up and chowing her quid.*"

CHUCKER, m. *Cosily; to chucker oneself is to chuckle over anything.*

" They chatted along quite friendly and chucker."

CHUCKLE- HEADED. Stupid. Wooden-headed.

CHUCKS, m. *Large chips of wood.* Smaller ones are called spalls.

CHUCLE. A triangular frame used to support the bilge-keep of a beached boat. Also called a Squat[3].

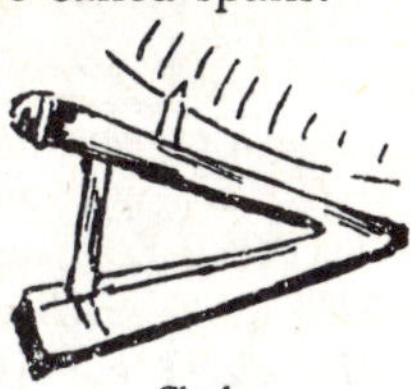
Chucle

CHUFF, m. *Churlish; surly.*

" *The old gentleman he went out to get a few chucks, and there they was, a sitting in the wood-house together jes' as chucker; and he was middlin' chuff about it, I bluv!*"

CHUMMY. A felt hat; a wide-awake; also known as parson's hat. Formerly the usual hat of a farm labourer, etc.

CHUMP.‡ A pain; a shooting pain.

CHURCH-BAWLED, *or* *CHURCH-CRIED*, m. *Having the banns published in church.* Also said ' asked in church '.

The tradition in Sussex is that if a person goes to church to hear himself cried, his children will be born deaf and dumb.

CHURCH-LITTEN, m. [Líctùn, *Ang. Sax., a burying-place.*] *A church-yard.* (*Cf.* Lightning.)

CHURCHMAN. A preacher of fine presence, and good voice.

CHURCH-STEEPLE, w.† *The common agrimony.* Agrimonia rupatoria.

CHURLS. Beachy Head pinnacles. See Charles.

CHURN-OWL. The nightjar; Eve-jar; Puck or Puckridge, (*q.v.*).

CLAM[1]. [Clam, *Ang. Sax., anything that holds or retains.*] *A rat-trap.* Such traps are also called Clombs, (*q.v.*).

This is most interesting as the Ang. Sax. words *clam* and *clom* are synonymous. Clambs and Clamp below are derived from the same root.

CLAM[2].‡ A cold sweat.

" I come over all of a cold clam."

CLAMBS. Harness-makers knee vice.

CLAMP. A stack of mixed fuel and material to be fired bound together. As:—Charcoal Clamp; see S.S.&C. under Cording and charcoal burning.

Bricks, tiles and pottery were also clamp (not kiln) fired; and mine to mollify it. (See S.S.&C. under Iron working.)

CLAP. To squat; as a hunted hare does to hide and let the hounds pass.

CLAPPER. The tongue.

" *He hath a heart as sound as a bell, and his tongue is the clapper; for what his heart thinks his tongue speaks.*"—Much Ado About Nothing, *Act iii, sc. 2.*

Also: The tongue of a bell. (*Cf.* Clipper and Knocker.)

CLAPPER. A raised platform or stones for passage in flood times by a watery place in the road.

Clapper

CLARPSE. [Obviously of Ang. Sax. origin, though the word is not recorded in literature.] Clasp.

" I've got a clarpse knife."

CLATTERDOWN GATE. A Stile gate or Tumbledown gate, (*q.v.*).

CLAVELS, w. *The separate corns in an ear of wheat.*

CLAWNEY. Ancestors; family relations.

" Tom (Cladpole) 'ent ashamed ov he's clawney."

CLEAT, e. *A piece of wood placed to prevent a door or gate from swinging backwards and forwards.*

CLEAT-BOARDS, w. *Mud pattens; broad flat pieces of board fastened on the shoes to enable a person to walk on the mud without sinking into it; much used by the eel-spearers at Chichester harbour and elsewhere.*
Also called Backstays or Backsters, (*q.v.*), etc.

CLEAVER. Another name for Frammard or Frow, (*q.v.*).

CLEDGY. Sticky. Earth sticking to the spade when digging is "cledgy." The same word as Clodgy. (*Cf.* Stuggy.)

CLEMMED. With hunger or cold. Also sometimes Shrammed, (*q.v.*).
"I be fair clemmed with the cold."

CLEMMENING. Going round from house to house asking for apples and beer for St. Clement's Day.
In spite of a proclamation made at London, July 22, 1540, that "neither children should be decked ne go about upon St. Nicholas.' St. Catherine, St. Clement, the Holy Innocents' and such-like days," the children in some parts of East Sussex still keep up the custom of catterning and clemmening, and the Sussex blacksmiths are particularly active in commemorating their patron saint; the anvils are fired with a loud explosion, and at least a half-holiday is kept. At Burwash, a few years ago, it was the custom to dress up a figure with a wig and beard and a pipe in his mouth, and set it up over the door of the inn where the blacksmiths feasted on St. Clement's day. Nov. 23. (See S.S.&C. under Souling.)

CLIM. To climb.

CLINKERS. Small bricks burnt very hard and used for paving. The hard refuse cinders from a forge fire.

CLIP-BOARDS. Cleat-boards or Backstays (*q.v.*).

CLIPPER. Clapper or knocker. The tongue of a sheep bell of various shapes.

CLISH, m. *The bond or band by which heath or birch brooms are fastened.* (*Cf.* Broom-clisher.)

CLISHING-GOAD. A besom stick; so called because when the pointed end is forced into the besom it tightens the clish.

CLITCH, w. *A cluster.*

CLITTERHEADED. Clutterheaded (*q.v.*).

CLOBBER. Rough working clothes.

CLOCKSMITH, m. *A watchmaker.*
"*I be quite lost about time, I be; for I've been forced to send my watch in to the clocksmith. I couldn't make no sense of mending it myself; for I'd iled it and I'd biled it, and then I couldn't do more with it.*"
(See S.S.&C. under Ile, for the original version of this story of the skipper of the smack *Caroline.*)

CLODBIRD. Corn Bunting; so called from its habit of sitting and singing on top of a clod.

CLODGY. (A variation of Cledgy.) Muddy and wet, like a field path after heavy rain. (*Cf.* Stuggy.)

CLOGUE[1], m. *To flatter.* Also to flirt.

CLOGUE[2]. Flattery, flirting talk.

CLOMBS. [*Clom*, Ang Sax., a clasp; prison.] Iron traps for vermin. Same as clam, (*q.v.*).

CLOPPERS, or CLOG-BOOTS. Boots with wooden soles, worn by the fishermen on some parts of the coast.

CLOSE, w. *A farmyard.* Walled or any *walled* inclosure.

CLOVERLAY. [Clæfer *and* leag, *Ang. Sax.*] *A field of clover which has been lately mown.* (Or rather, sown.)

CLUCK[1], m. *Out of spirits; slightly unwell. A hen is said to be cluck when she wants to sit.*

CLUCK[2], or CLUCKET. A sheep bell that is long and narrow, usually having an oak clapper secured by a leathern thong. It gives a high note. See Sheep-bells.

Clucket

CLUNG, m. *Cold and damp.* Musty; rotten.

The mown grass is spoken of as very clung after having been exposed to wet chilly weather, so that it has not hayed satisfactorily.

Faggots are clung when partly decayed; rotten through damp. Also wood when it is in that state of rottenness that it crushes underfoot when stepped on.

"Ash when it's green you may
burn before the Queen,
Ash when it's clung is as
rotten as dung."

CLUNG-HEADED. Stupid.

CLUTCH[1], e. *Close; tightly.*

"*If you takes up a handful of the hay and holds it pretty clutch, you'll soon see 'taint fit to carry, for 'tis terr'ble clung.*"

CLUTCH[2], w. *A brood of chickens or a covey of partridges.*

CLUTTERHEADED, or CLITTERHEADED. Clumsy; thick-headed; feather-brained.

CLUTTER-UP, m. *To throw into confusion; to crowd.* To litter a room or a place.

"Can't do naun in here till us has got the rubbidge out, 'tis all cluttered-up."

COAGER, m. *Luncheon.* Pronounced 'cojer'. *Called in some parts of the county an elevener,* (usually said 'levener',) *from the time at which it is generally taken by the labourers.* (*Cf.* Beever.)

COAGER-CAKE. A plain cake is often baked as the couger cake, for the week's consumption. See S.S.&C.

COARSE[1], e. *Rough; stormy; applied to weather.*

COARSE[2], e. *Childish.*

"*She is twelve years old, but she is so coarse for her years that you would not take her to be but ten.*"

*COAST.** [Coste, *Old French, a rib.*] *The ribs of cooked meat, particularly lamb.*

COBBLE-STONES. Pebbles on the sea shore. Also called Pitchers, (*q.v.*).

COBBLING. Simmering.

"Are those prunes cobbling nicely?"

COCKER, w. *A culvert; a drain under a road or gate.* (*Cf.* Bunny, Coker and Craker.)

COCKER-UP. To spoil; to gloss over with an air of truth.

"*You see this here chap of hers he's cockered-up some story about having to goo away somewheres up into the sheeres; and I tell her she's no call to be so cluck over it; and for my part I dunno but what I be very glad an't, for he was a chap as was always a cokeing about the cupboards, and cogging her out of a Sunday.*"

COCK FARE, or COKFARE. Brighton herring fishery carried out in Cocks in waters near their home port from the beginning of October to the middle of December. Cockheaks, (*q.v.*) or flews of three ranns were used, "three netts one with another" earning one share, (*q.v.*). (*Cf.* Fare.)

COCK HEAK. [A small, or half heak.] A fishing net used in Cock fare, 24 to 30 fathoms long (specified minimum 28 yards) and 2 Ranns deep. (*Cf.* Heak and Rann.)

COCKLE.‡ See coddle.

COCKS.§ [Kog. Kogge. *Danish.*] *Small boats, from two to six tons burden, used in the herring fishery. Their period of fishing was called cock-fare, and their nets cock-heaks.*

Carrying six or more men, with mast and sail they earned 1½ shares, without sail one share. (*Cf.* Shares.)

COCKSTEDDLE. Capsize; overturn.

"Now Master Selby you be careful or you'll cocksteddle back-'ards."—*A gardener to a boy on a wall at Cocking.*

CODDLE, e. or COCKLE, *w. To parboil.*

Apples so cooked are called coddled-apples.

To coddle eggs you put them into boiling water, take off the fire and let them stand 8 or 10 minutes.

CODGER. *A miser; a stingy old fellow.*

COG[1]. The forged up lug on the tang of a scythe blade which is secured to the Snethe by the Cray-ring.

COG[2], m. [Cogger, *Old English, a trickster.*] *To entice.*

"*I cannot flatter, and speak fair, Smile in men's faces, smooth, deceive, and cog.*" —Richard III, *Act i. sc. 3.*

COILERS. (*See Quilers.*)

COKE, m. [Kijken, *Dutch, to peep about*]. *To pry about.*

"There 'e be! 'ow 'e do coke around 'ere."

COKER. A culvert. (*Cf.* Cocker.)

COKFARE. See Cock fare.

COLE[1].* *Seakale.*

COLE[2]. Charcoal.

COLE[3]. To burn charcoal. (See S.S.&C. under Cording and Charcoal burning.)

COLLAPSE. Eclipse. See S.S.&C.

COLLIER. A charcoal burner; a maker of charcoal.

In the 16th and 17th centuries a collier, or collyer, was the master man—the workers were simply burners. (See S.S.&C. under Cording and Charcoal burning.)

COLLOUR. Inferior iron mine or ore. See Mine.

COLLYER. See Collier.

COLT. A young sheep-shearer learning the work was so called. (See S.S.&C. under Ship.)

COMB[1], m. *An instrument used by thatchers.* Also called a Rake-comb, (*q.v.*); it is used to comb out the straw when being laid on, for trimming up ricks and stacks and to measure up the work.

COMB[2]. The ridge of a thatch, pinned by Spars and Sparrers to the Dolly.

COMB[3].‡ Verdigris from church bells. Said to be a cure for shingles.

COMBE. See Coombe.

COME. *When such a time arrives.*

"*I shall be eighty-two come Lady-tide.*

COME-BY-CHANCE, or CHANCE-BORN. An illegitimate, or Love-child.

COMMENCE, m. *An affair; a job.*

"*Here's a pretty commence.*"

COMMON. Well in health; Sussex people never admit that they are quite well.

"How are you to-day, Mr. Grover?" "About as common thank ye Miss." (*Cf.* Middling and Tightish.)

COMP, m. [Comp, *Ang. Sax.*] *A valley.*

Some cottages in the parish of Beddington are called by this name, from which also the name of the village of Compton is derived.

COMPANY. To keep company; to associate.

"If I was to 'ave some of they Dorset yowes with the flock they would n' company with tethers—they wouldn' like each other."

A Sussex Shepherd.

CONCERNED IN LIQUOR, e. *Drunk.*

This is one of the many expressions used in Sussex to avoid the word drunk. To have had a little beer, means to have had a great deal too much; to have half-a-pint otherwhile, means to be an habitual drunkard; to be none the better for what he had took, means to be much the worse; to be noways tossicated, implies abject helplessness. A Sussex man may be tight, or concerned in liquor, but drunk never!

In the village of Selmeston the blacksmith's shop is next door to the public-house. I have met numbers of people going up to the forge, but never one going to the Barley-mow.

CONCHIFIED.‡ Cankered. Of fruit trees.

CONEY, m. *A rabbit.*

"*There is no remedy: I must coney-catch, I must shift.*"—Merry Wives of Windsor, *Act i. sc. 3.*

CONGERBOB. A confusion; disorder; as of ropes disorderly on a boat.

" They be all of a congerbob."

CONKERS or CONQUERS. (Deformation of conquerors.) Horse-chestnuts; also a game played with horse-chestnuts.

CONTRAIRY. [Contraire, *French*.] *Disagreeable; obstinately self-willed.*

A man describing his deceased wife, to whom he was really very much attached, said, " She was a very nice, pleasant 'ooman as long as no one didn't interrupt her, but if you had ever so few words with her, she'd be just as contrairy as ever was a hog."

CONTRAPTION, m. *Contrivance; management.*

A pedlar's pack is spoken of sometimes as his contraption.

COOCH-GRASS. [Cwic, *Ang. Sax.*] *A course, bad species of grass, which grows very rapidly on arable land, and does much mischief by the long stringy roots which it throws out in great quantities.*

Barnes says, with reference to this —Cooch, couch grass, quitch grass, creeping wheat grass, Triticum repens. *Mr. Vernon suggests that it was originally quick grass, from its lively growth.* More likely creeping grass because it grows creeping low under the ground. (*Cf.*, in heraldry, *couchant*, lying.)

COOLTHE, e. *Coolness.*

" *I set the window open for coolthe.*"

COOMBE, or COMBE, m. [Cwm, *Welsh, a valley.*] *A hollow in the Downs;* especially one in an escarpment.

This word is to be traced in the names of many Southdown villages and farms, such as Telscombe, Ashcombe, etc.

COOP. A tau (or T) shaped cutting in the turf to trap wheatears: also a pyramidal pheasant trap.

COP[1]. A heap.

COP[2], e. *To throw; to heap anything up.* Especially with regard to corn. (*Cf.* Shove.)

COPSE, COPPICING. Not dialect words but decidedly a Sussex industry. (See S.S.&C.)

COPSON, w. *A fence placed on the top of a small dam laid across a ditch for the purpose of keeping sheep from going over it.*

CORD. A cord of wood is a pile of wood cut up for burning, 8 ft. by 4 ft. and 4 ft. thick. (See S.S.&C. under Cording and Charcoal burning.)

CORDBATS, or *CORDWOOD*, m. *Large pieces of wood, roots, etc., set up in stacks.* Cut to the cord length of 4 ft. or 3 ft. See S.S. &C. under:—

CORDING AND CHARCOAL BURNING. See S.S.&C.

CORE, w. [Cœur, *French, heart.*] *The middle of a stack of hay which has been cut away all round.* (*Cf.* Stump.)

COSTREL A leather or wooden harvest bottle used by labourers, known also as a harves bottle.

Costrel

COSTS. See S.S.&C.

COTLAND, *w.* or COTMAN LAND, *e.* [*Coterie*, Old French, servile tenure.] Bosham and Rotherfield names for Bondland (*q.v.*). (See also S.S. & C. under Borough English.)

COTTED or COTTY. Matted; tangles in sheep's wool.

COTTERIL, w. *A pot-hook; or a hook to hang spits on.* (*Cf.* Pot-hanger.)

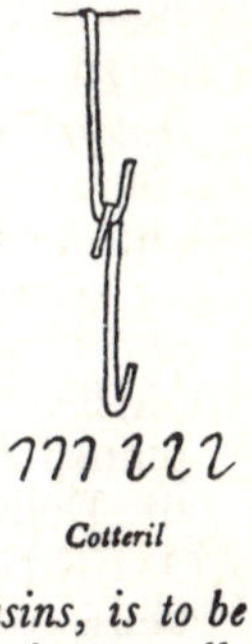

Cotteril

COUNTABLE. A contraction of unaccountable.

" *My missus is countable ornary agin to-day.*" (*Cf.* Ornary for extraordinary.)

COUSINS, e. *To call cousins, is to be on intimate terms; but it is generally used in the negative, as, " She and I doànt call cousins at all."*

COVE.† *A lean-to, or low building with a shelving roof. Pigeon-cotes are frequently called pigeon coves in East Sussex.*

COW-CLATTING. Spreading cow-manure, or other manure, on fields.

COWELL. A large tub or butt; sometimes water-cowel.

COWPAT. A cow or bullock dropping.

COWSTALL. A cowhouse arranged in stalls for milck kine.

CRAB TREE. A crab apple is more often called a crab tree.

CRACKLINGS, w. *Crisp cakes.*

CRACKPATE, or CRACKPOT. One with a bee in his bonnet.

CRADLE-SCYTHE. A scythe with a frame variously made to lay the corn neatly together for convenience in making the sheaf.

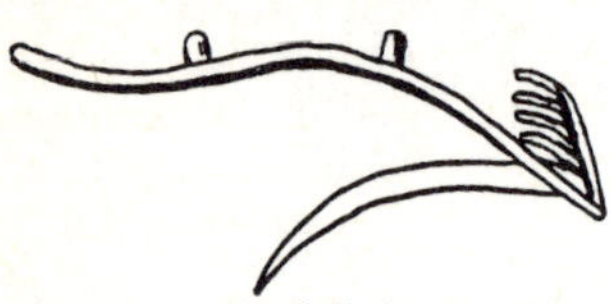

Cradle-Scythe

CRAKER. A culvert; a cocker, (*q.v.*).

CRANK, *CRANKY*, e. *Merry; cheerful; also drunk.*

CRAP, *or CRAPGRASS. Ray-grass.* Lolium perenne.

CRASS. Cross; bad tempered.

" 'E made me mighty crass."

CRATCH. A clothes pole. (*Cf.* Crutche.)

CRAY-RING, m. *The ring on the top of the long handle of a scythe into which the blade is fixed.* A Poll-ring.

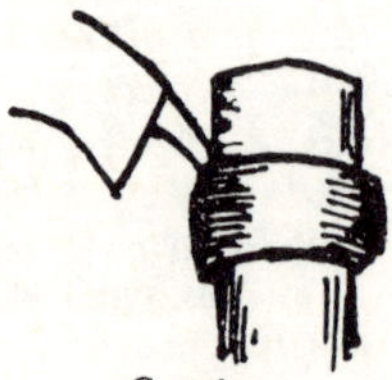

Cray ring

CRAZY. Out of order; dilapidated. An old decayed building is said to be crazy. A crazy craft is one unseaworthy.

CRAZY-HOUSE. A lunatic asylum.

CREATE. Object to; make a fuss about it.

On hanging flags across the street at Lindfield in 1935, one of the helpers said of the police,

" Everything was orright until they started to create."

CREEP, or CREEP UP. A method of getting up, with a special apparatus, tubs of spirits sunken or moored by smugglers.

CREEPERS, m. *Low pattens mounted on short iron stumps instead of rings.*

CRINGLE. A twisted withe used to secure a gate.

CRIP, *or CRUP. Crisp.* Short. Paths are ' crupping up ' when frost makes them feel crisp and crunchy under-foot.

" It's going to freeze hard tonight because the grass is crup already."

CRISSCROSS [*CHRIST'S CROSS*], m. *The alphabet; so called because in the old horn books it was preceded by a cross.*

In the north of England a crisscross is the mark of a person who cannot write his name.

CROCK[1], e. *A smut or smudge.*

" *You have got a crock on your nose.*"

CROCK[2]. [Crocca, *Ang. Sax., a pitcher.*] *An earthen vessel.*

" *Go to the end of the rainbow and you'll find a crock of gold.*"—Sussex Proverb.

The Bavarians have a similar proverb; but they say that the crock can only be found by one who was born on a Sunday, and that if such a person can find it and retain it in his possession, it will always contain three ducats.

CROCK BUTTER, m. *Salt butter, which in Sussex is usually potted down in brown earthenware crocks.*

CROFT, m. [Croft, *Ang. Sax., a small enclosed field.*] *A small piece of pasture-land near to a house.*

CROOK. Wooden yoke made usually of furze or yew branch to support sheep bells.

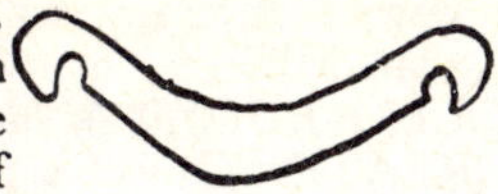
Crook

CROP. A Smuggler's cargo on any one " run," often of a sunken set of kegs.
CROPE. Crept; did creep.
CROP-EARED, or CROPPED. A roof or the thatching of a haystack of which *only the upper part* of the gable end—usually a third to half way down—is hipped. (*Cf.* Prick-eared.)

Crop-eared

CROSS-WAYS. A place where four roads meet. That is; where two roads cross one another directly. (*Cf.* Fourthrows.)
CROUCHMASS.‡ (Cross mass.) St. Helena's Day, August 18.
CROW. An unsympathetic person.
" They think I'm a crow 'cos I wunt drink with 'em."
" Because I dòan' go to their (Union's) meetings they thinks I'm a crow."—*Said by a Brighton porter.*
CROWBOROUGH. (Crow hill.) The beacon is the highest point on the *Ashdown Forest ridge.* 792 feet above Ordnance datum.
CROWDIE. An Apple-stuckling (*q.v.*), etc.
CROWNATION. Coronation.
" *I was married the day the Crownation was, when there was a bullock roasted whole up at Furrel (Firle) Park. I dòant know as ever I eat anything so purty in all my life; but I never got no further than Furrel cross-ways all night, no more didn't a good many.*"
(That was Queen Victoria's Coronation.)
CROWNER. Coroner; an officer representing the Crown.
"Ay, marry, is't; crowner's quest law."—*Hamlet,* Act v. sc. 1.
Coroners were very important, see S.S.&C. under Geldable.
CROWS. Used indiscriminately.
A Lindfield boy said to me, " I don't know any birds 'cept crows." He was referring to rooks on the common. (*Cf.* Scarecrow.)
CROWSFOOT. The butter-cup. Ranunculus bulbosus *and allied species.* Also called Gold cup.
CRUISER. Term used especially by smugglers, for Revenue Cutter, or Schooner: also called by them a Tartar or Barking Tarter.
CRUMBS. An interjection, as crikey, golly, lawks, etc.
CRUMMY. Fat; fleshy.
" *He aint near so crummy as what he was afore he went to Lewes jail.*"
CRUNDEL. A strip of thicket in open country always in a hollow and usually with running water in the middle.
CRUP. Crisp; short or surly; Crip, (*q.v.*).
CRUST-HUNGRY. Ravenous.
" The children aren't crust-hungry, they can wait for their dinner."
CRUSTLE. The bony part of a pig's nostril.
CRUTCH. (*Cruche,* French, a pitcher.) A cup; a pot.
" Come and have a crutch of tea with me."
CRUTCHE. A stick or pole with a fork; a clothes prop; also a rowlock pin. Cratch, (*q.v.*).
*CRUTCHES,*e. [Cruche, *French, a pitcher.*] *Broken pieces of crockery.*
CRY[1], e. *Several dogs of all kinds.*
" *I knew it was Miss Jane, by reason she'd got the cry with her.*"

Crutche

CRY[2], *w.* Demand.
CUCKOLD. A method of drying hops in a pan, either in the bread

oven or over the fire, where only a small quantity was grown for home consumption as distinct from the oast dried hops for the market.

CUCKOO[1]. If a tree fall not clear of other trees when it is felled it is said to be cuckoo.

CUCKOO[2]. A fool. (*Cf.* Gowk.)

CUCKOO-FAIR. Heathfield fair, held on April 14th. The tradition in East Sussex is that an old woman goes to Heathfield fair, and there lets the cuckoo out of a bag.

They call it Heffle fair or Huffle fair.

In Worcestershire the saying is that the cuckoo is never heard before Tenbury fair (April 21st), or after Pershore fair (June 26th).

With this may be compared the following German legend, given by Grimm in his "Deutsche Mythologie," p. 691:—"Our Lord was one day passing a baker's shop, when, feeling hungry, He sent in one of His disciples to ask for a loaf; the baker refused it, but his wife, who with his six daughters was standing at a little distance, gave him the loaf secretly, for which good deed they were placed in heaven as seven stars—the Pleiades; but the baker was changed into a cuckoo, which sings from St. Tiburtius' Day (April 14) to St. John the Baptist's Day (June 24), that is, as long as the seven stars are visible."

We in England see the Pleiades all the autumn and winter.

CUCKOO GATE, m. *A gate which shuts upon two posts which are connected with curved bars, so constructed that only one person can conveniently pass through at a time, and for this reason called in Hampshire a kissing-gate.*

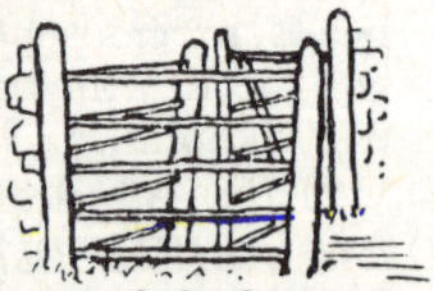

Cuckoo Gate

And so called in Sussex because you face back to your fellow companion, or because you can corner her in the gate. Also called "To-she-and-fro-she-gate."

CUCKOO PENNY. A spring custom. See S.S.&C.

CUCKOO'S BREAD AND CHEESE TREE, m. *The whitethorn* (or hawthorn).

> "*When the cuckoo comes to the bare thorn, Sell your cow and buy your corn.*"—Old Proverb.

It is very remarkable that this name should be given to the whitethorn, as among all Aryan nations this tree is associated with the lightning, while the cuckoo is intimately connected with the lightning gods, Zeus and Thor.

Children eat the young leaf buds and call them bread and cheese or brencheese.

CUDDLE. Said of an old man walking with two bats (sticks). This used to be a common sight when rheumatism was not so well treated. (*Cf.* Bat.)

"'Ere 'e be, cuddlin' along."

CUE. See Queue.

CULLS, or CULLERS. m. *The inferior sheep of a flock, culled from the rest and offered for sale in a lot by themselves.*

CULVER. A pigeon or dove. This name is retained in the name of a field at Selmeston, which is called the culver ake (the pigeon's oak). And at Culver House, Lancing.

CURIOUS, e. *Unsteady; drunk.*

"*Dòànt sit so curious when you're swinging, or you'll fall out.*"

CURMUDGEON, w.† *To mend up old clothes. A curmudgeon originally meant a hard-bargainer, a miserly fellow, and probably this meaning of the word is connected with mending up rags in a miserly manner.*

CUSHTI. Nice.

"This *is* a cushti pie, ain't it?"

CUSS. Surly; shrewish.

CUTCH. A gum used for tanning nets, sails, etc. Used at Brighton by fishermen as a remedy against diarrhoea.

CUTS, w.† *The cross-beams on the floor of a wagon.* (*Cf.* Dwairs.)

CUTTY, m. *A wren; also called a kitty*, juggy and scutty.
These words are sometimes used with the word 'wren' and sometimes alone.

CUT YOUR STICK. Be off.
This expression is either simply equivalent to a recommendation to prepare a staff in readiness for a journey; or it may be connected with the old way of reckoning by notches or tallies on a stick, and so imply a settlement of accounts before departure.

D

DAB. The sea-flounder.

DABSTER. One who is quick and able, as at a game, or at his calling.

DACKLES. Globules of water on walls etc., caused by damp.

DAGS. Schoolboy slang for daring.
"That's your dags," meaning you do not dare do it—an incitement to try it.

DALLOP[1], m. *A parcel of tea packed for smuggling, weighing from six to sixteen pounds*, or Dollop which generally weighed 2-3 lb, but a Bag (of tea) weighed 5 lb.

DALLOP[2]. *A clumsy, shapeless lump of anything tumbled about in the hands.*

DANES. Used to frighten children.
"I'll set the Danes on to yer if yer dòant do as I tells yer."

DANG or DANNEL. Substitutions for damn.

DAPPEN, m. *By the time; or perhaps an abbreviation of " should it happen."*
"*Dappen I've done this job I'll come and lend yer a hand.*"

DARE and DURSN'T DARE . . . for may and may not.
At Uckfield our brother's stable-boy reported to him;
"Them people wot lives in the lane they dare throw their pots in the pit, but other folks dursn't dare throw theirn."

DARK. "Dark as the inside of a cow" . . . comment on a small bedroom in the attic.

DARK CELLAR SOP. Bread soaked in strong beer, given to men in harvest time if they worked well.

DARKS, m. *A word used by sailors, but more particularly by smugglers, to signify those nights when the moon does not appear.*
In former times, everyone in the agricultural districts of Sussex within reach of the coast was more or less connected with smuggling. The labourer was always ready to help whenever the darks favoured " a run"; the farmer allowed his horses to be borrowed from his stable; the parson (certainly at Selmeston) expressed no surprise at finding tea and tubs buried in the churchyard vaults; the squire asked no questions; the excisemen compounded with the smugglers, and when a difficulty arose as to price, and hard blows were struck, the doctor bound up the wounds for nothing, and made no enquiry as to the dallops of tea or kegs of French brandy, which from time to time were found mysteriously deposited on his doorstep at daybreak.

DARLING, or DAWLIN, m. *The smallest pig of a litter; an unhealthy child.*

DARTER. Daughter.

DASENT. Decent.

DAWFIN. Black fly.
"My house beans (*i.e.*, broad beans or household beans) have got the dawfin bad this year."
(*Cf.* Dolphin.)

DAWLIN. A little one. See Darling.

DEAD ALIVE. Dull; heavy; stupid.

DEAD HORSE, e. *To work for a dead horse is to labour for wages already received, or to work out an old debt.*

DEAD MEN'S FINGERS. *Orchis máscula.* Early purple orchis. See Long-purples.

DEAF ADDER, *m.* The slow worm or blind worm.

DEAL. m, *The nipple of a sow.*

DEAN. A valley; used as part of a place-name, as Withdean, Rottingdean, Balsdean, etc.

DEARED. Deafened.

"*I was amost deared, they made such a noise.*"

DEARLY. Extremely. (See S.S. &C. under Sheep.)

DEATH, m. *Deaf. It is rather startling to be told that a person is afflicted with deathness.*

DEE[1]*, and TO-DEE. Day, and to-day.*

DEE[2]. See Deese.

DEEDILY, e. *Earnestly.*

"*You was talking so deedily that I didn't like to interrupt you.*"

DEEDY. Clever; industrious. Efficient . . . as a 'deedy stroke' or a 'deedy shot.' Notable.

DEESE, e., *or* Dee. *A place where herrings are dried, now more generally called a herring-hang, from the fish being hung on sticks to dry.* It is also called a smoke-hole and used for bacon as well as herrings. When the herring-hang or smoke hole is in use the odour therefrom is so strong that one can easily tell whether pork or fish is being treated. At the base of the hole is a small furnace where sawdust smoulders giving off a dense aromatic smoke, which after many days dries or cures what is hung therein.

DEEVE. Dive. The pronunciation of the i like that of the French i is very common in Sussex.

DENIAL, m. *A hindrance.*

"*His deathness is a great denial to him.*"

DENSHER[1]. See Swale.

DENSHER[2] *PLOUGH,* m. [*Devonshire Plough?*] *An instrument used for turf-cutting.*

DENTICAL, m. *Dainty.* Picksome.

"*My master says that this here Prooshian* (*query, Persian?*) *cat what you gave me is a deal too dentical for a poor man's cat; he wants one as will catch the meece and keep herself.*"

DEREAWAY. Thereabouts.

DEVIL[1]. *This word scarcely ought to have a place in a dictionary of the Sussex dialect, for the country people are very careful indeed to avoid using it. The devil is always spoken of as* he, *with a special emphasis.*

"*In the Downs there's a golden calf buried; people know very well where it is—I could show you the place any day. Then why doánt they dig it up? Oh, it is not allowed;* he *would not let them. Has anyone ever tried? Oh, yes, but it's never there when you look,* he *moves it away.*"

DEVIL[2]. But see S.S.&C.

DEVIL DODGERS. Those who go to church in the morning and to chapel in the evening or vice versa.

DEVILING. Swift, or screech, sometimes screecher, (*q.v.*).

DEVIL'S BOX. Harmonium. So called by some old Dissenters when it was a novelty.

DEVIL WEED. Field convolvulus. *C. arvensis.* So called from its being difficult to eradicate—a piece of root less than one inch will sprout. Also called 'lily.'

DEVOUROUS, *m.* Voracious.

"They ol' jays be very devourous birds."

DEZZICK, m. *A day's work.*

"*I aint done a dezzick for the last six months.*"

DIBBER. A primitive wooden pointed tool for making holes for seed sowing, sometimes called dibbler, or setter.

Dibber

DIBBLING-IRON. A pointed tool used for making holes for the sowing of beans, peas, potatoes, etc. Sometimes also called a dibbler. See S.S.&C.

DIBS. A game played by children with huckle-bones, (*q.v.*).

DICK. [Díc. *Ang. Sax., a trench*]. *A ditch.* (See S.S.&C. under Frouden or Frought-'n'd.)

Dibbling-Iron

DICKER FLINT. An illicit, fiery spirit that early in the 19th century was manufactured and flourished for a time in Ashdown Forest and on Dicker Common near Hailsham.

DIDDLER. A trickster; a swindler a Niggleygowger.

DIDICAIS. Gypsies; true gypsies of the better class; not Mumpers, (*q.v.*), nor Pikers (*q.v.*).

DIGHT. [Dihtan, *Ang. Sax.*, *to prepare.*] *To adorn; to dress.*

"*She is gone upstairs to dight up.*"

DIMSEL, e. *A piece of stagnant water, larger than a pond and smaller than a lake.* (*Cf.* Pell.)

DIPPING-HOOK. Used when dipping sheep, for prevention of scab. It was of iron with two curved ends and mounted on a stout pole about eight feet long.

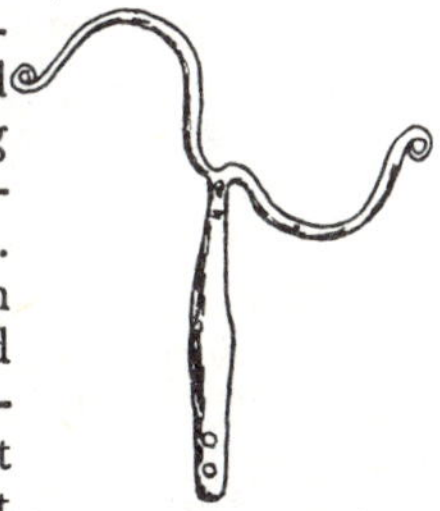

Dipping-Hook

DIRT-KNOCKER. A wooden mallet about ten inches in length used for breaking up dirt on the fleece of sheep, a flat piece of iron or wood being held under the wool.

Dirt-Knocker

DISEASED. Rendering of deceased through likeness of the words and association of cause and effect. See S.S.&C.

DISH. To make hollow. Term used by wheelwrights—the dish itself is the concavity of a wheel.

DISHABILL. [Déshabillé, *French*, *an undress.*] *Disorder.*

"*My house is not fit for you to come in, for we're all of a dishabill.*"

DISH OF TONGUES. *A scolding.*

"*He'll get a middlin' dish of tongues when his mistus comes to hear an't.*"

DISHWASHER. *The water-wagtail.* Also called Molly Dishwasher in West Sussex.

DISREMEMBER, m. *To forget.*

"*I can't think of his name; I do disremember things so.*"

DISSIGHT, m. *An unsightly object.*

DITCH-HOOK. A special kind of rake used for weeds. See S.S.&C. under Ditch-Hook and Ditch-Knife.

DITCH-KNIFE. Used for cutting weeds. See S.&S.C. under Ditch-Hook and Ditch-Knife.

Ditch-Hook

Ditch-Knife

DITCHLING BEACON. This is the highest point in *East Sussex*. 813 feet above Ordnance datum.

DOATY. Dry rotting. Decayed wood with its virtue gone. Chiefly applied to old trees.

DOBBIN. *Sea-gravel mixed with sand.* A primitive concrete.

DOBBS, *or* *MASTER DOBBS*, e. *A kind of brownie or house-fairy who does all sorts of work for members of the family.* "*Master Dobbs has been helping you,*" *is a common expression to use to a person who has done more work than was expected.*

DOCTOR BUDDINGTON. See S.S.&C.

DOCTOR'S MEDICINE. See Charm-stuff and S.S.&C.

DODDLE. *To wag; tremble; walk infirmly.*

DODDLEGRASS. Briza media, *or quaking grass, called in the north "doddering dick."* And more often called Totter-grass or Quaker grass.

Doddlegrass

DODDLISH. Infirm.
"*Old Master Packlebury begins to get very doddlish.*"

DOG[1], m. *An instrument used by thatchers*, to carry straw up to the stack. It was a natural forked branch, about four feet long.

Dog

DOG[2]. A male ferret, fox, or polecat.

DOGGER[1], w.‡ *A support for the shafts of a cart.*

DOGGER[2]. A tall hat. The nap of dog's hair.

DOG-JAMB. An implement for moving timber over.

DOGS. Small rests for logs in the old open hearths, the top or ornamental part of which very often had the head of a dog on it. Andiron or Brandiron (*q.v.*)

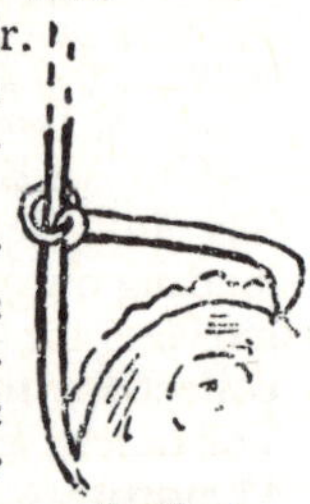
Dog-Jamb

DOG-SKIN or DOG'S-HAIR HAT A particular kind of tall hat, stoutly made by village hatters, said to be everlasting, quite impossible to wear out. It could be stood upon without a sign of yielding. Worn by shepherds and outdoor labourers.

DOG-STICK. A road-bat (*q.v.*)

DOG-TIRED. Completely wearied out.
"*Oh, master, master, I have watched so long That I am dog-weary.*"—Taming of the Shrew, *Act iv. sc. 2.*

DOLE[1], [Dæl, *Ang. Sax., a portion.*] *Gifts; alms distributed on St. Thomas' day.* December 21.

DOLE[2]. A division of a communal pasture-boundary baulk. Also called Doole.

DOLEAXE. (*Dæl æx*, Ang. Sax., a large cleaving axe.) A cleaving tool used for opening and levering the cleft in making spiles (stakes), and cleft oak paling.

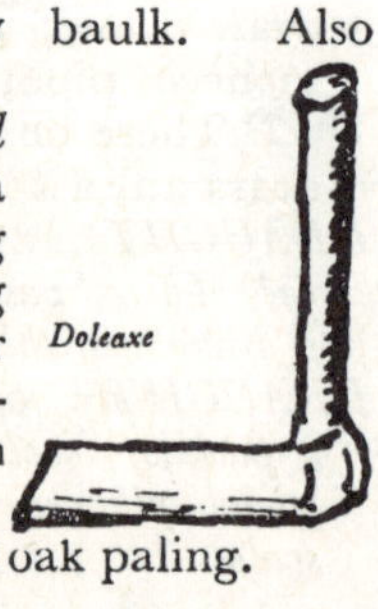
Doleaxe

DOLES, m. *The short handles on the snethe of a scythe.* Also called Dowlwoods; Hand-pins; Nebs or Nibs. The snethe or snead is the long handle.

DOLING, e. *A fishing boat with two masts, each carrying a sprit-sail. Described in Boy's History of Sandwich as "Ships for the King's use furnished by the Cinque Ports."*

DOLLERS. The people who go round gathering doles. I.e., the alms. Usually said 'dōlers'.

DOLLOP. See Dallop.

DOLLY. A low bolster of straw at the top of a stack or roof to pin the 'comb' to.

DOLPHIN. A fly which attacks beans. Same as Dawfin (*q.v.*).

DONE-OVER. Tired out; a transposition of overdone, in the same way as go-under is always used for under-go.

Dolly

DONE UP FOR THE WINTER. See S.S.&C.

DONKEY TEA. A cool drink made from charred bread. See S.S.&C.

DOOLE. A conical lump of earth, about three feet in diameter at the base, and about two feet in height, raised to show the bounds of parishes or farms on the Downs. A Dole[2] (*q.v.*). Also a real tumulus.

DOOR. Came to the door—a man or woman meaning a gypsy or 'traveller'.

"A woman that came to the door (gyspy) told me what to do. She says 'You get a quart of shellsnegs an' pum them up on a flat stone, and make a poultice of 'em with brandy, and put that to his neck . . . that'll do 'im good'." The advice was for the treatment of a boy supposed to be incurable so that the Doctor told his mother to let him have whatever he fancied to eat, "for he can't live nor get better." The remedy was tried and the boy lived to 50 or thereabouts, and though abnormal was a good worker in the garden, and pleasant to talk to. He died in 1930.

DOORMAN. A hand—not the Fireman—at a Blacksmith's and Farrier's.

DORNYX. A coarse damask cloth, called in the North " Darnex."

DOSS. A sleep—a nap. To " doss down for the night," settle for sleep.

DOSSES or DORSELS, e. *Panniers in which fish are carried on horse-back.*

DOTED. Rotten—decayed. Said of timber. (*Cf.* Pucksie.)

DOUST. To get along.

" I met her unexpectedly, we had a chat and then she dousted on." *Heard at Lancing.*

DOUT, e. [*Do out*]. *To extinguish the light of a candle.*

DOUTERS. Instruments like snuffers, used for extinguishing a candle without cutting the wick.

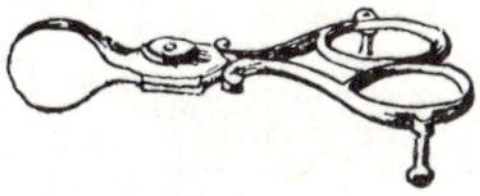

Douters

DOWELS, e. *Levels; low marshes in which the water lies in winter and wet seasons.*

DOWL-WOODS. See Doles.

DOWN. Laid up by illness.

" *He's down with a bad attack of brown crisis on the chest, leastways that's what the doctor calls it.*"

DOWN-BED. A bed on the floor. Or a shake-down, a temporary bed.

DOWNHEARTH. A large open chimney.

DOWNRIGHTS. The vertical slats usually three, that strengthen a field gate.

DOWNSITTING. Downright. See Upstanding.

DOWZE. Douse.

DOZZLE. A small quantity.

" *He came in so down-hearted that I couldn't be off from giving him a dozzle of victuals, and I told him if he could put up with a down-bed, he might stop all night.*"

A man invited to have another glass will politely decline; but when pressed will accept.

" Well, just a footy dozzle." (*Cf.* Footy.)

DRÄÄT. Draught; wind.

DRACLY-MINUTE. (From dracly, directly, and this minute.) *Immediately.*

" *Ye be to goo dracly-minute.*"

DRAGGLE-TAIL. A slut.

" *Dame Durden kept five serving maids*
To carry the milking pail,
'Twas Doll and Bet and Sall and Kate,
And Dorothy-draggle-tail."

DRAG-RAKE. Used for gathering hay into leeks or windrows for loading onto waggons, and in corn harvest for dragging behind to collect any that was left or dropped. For description see S.S.&C. under Windrow.

Drag-rake

DRAINING-SPOON, w. *An iron tool used by drainers to take out the earth which crumbles down to the bottom of the cutting.*

Draining-spoon

DRAR. Draw. As draw below; a fire; a tobacco pipe; etc.

" There be just time for 'Three drars an' a spit '."

DRAUGHT[1]. *A drawing.*

" *There was a gentleman making a draught of the church this morning.*"

DRAUGHT[2]. *61 lbs., or a quarter of a pack of wool (240 lbs.), with one pound allowed for the turn of the scale.*

DRAW[1]. A stratagem or device whereby a person is caught or drawn as it were into a trap.

DRAW[2]. See Dray.

DRAWED. To draw or paint a portrait.

"The vicar's darter she drawed me out oncet, but there I wunt no longer'n that (marking one forefinger with the other) when she drawed me out."

DRAWNETT. A mackerel fishing net. The Brighton Custumal does not specify size or value if lost. It was probably very large and expensive to make, but not liable to loss because of its method of fishery, which see below.

DRAWNETT FARE. Mackerel fishery in May and June along the shore, at which small Cocks, up to 3 tons, were used to set the draw net. At this fishery half the catch went to the boat and net, the other half was shared; one share to the vicar, churchwardens and master and one each to the ten or more men engaged. (*Cf.* Shares and Fare.)

DRAW-SHAVE. A draw-knife.

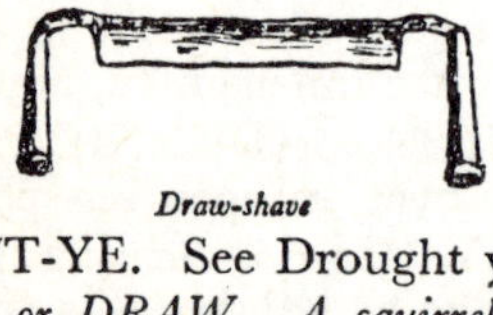

Draw-shave

DRAWT-YE. See Drought ye.

DRAY, or DRAW. A squirrel's nest. A drey.

On St. Andrew's day, November 30, there was in former times an annual diversion called squirrel hunting, when crowds of people went out into the woods with sticks and guns, with which they not only destroyed squirrels, but anything that came in their way. This custom was kept up in Sussex till within the last fifty years, but now, in consequence of the inclosure of coppices and more strict preservation of game, it is wholly discontinued. (Parish was writing about 1870.) (*Cf.* Cage[2].)

DRAZEL. A dirty slut; an untidy girl.

DREAN, m. *A drain.*

DREDGE[1]. A mixture of oats and barley, now very little sown.

DREDGE[2], m. [Dræge, *Ang. Sax., a drag.*] *A quantity of bushes, chiefly of thorn, bound together and drawn over meadows for the purpose of pulverizing dung or mould, called also a bush harrow.* (*Cf.* Drudge.)

DREE. Unpleasant, as of weather, place, etc.

DRIB. [Dripan, *Ang. Sax., to drop.*] *A very small quantity of anything.* (*Cf.* Drip and Dribble.)

DRIFTWAY, m. [Drífan, *Ang. Sax., to drive.*] *A cattle-path to water; a way by which sheep or cattle are driven, generally a greenway from high ground to low.* (*Cf.* Fordrough.)

DRILLATY, m. [*Corruption of dilatory.*]

DRINK, m. *Medicine for cattle.*

"I gave the old cow a drink last night, and she's up again and looking eversmuch better this morning."

DRINKER ACRE, e. *The land set apart on dividing brook-land (which was depastured in common) for mowing, to provide drink and provisions for the tenants and labourers.*

DRINTED.‡ Said of colours that have run in the wash.

DRIPLY. Weather, elsewhere described as Scotch Mist. When not actually raining the trees etc. are dripping.

DROPHANDKERCHIEF. The game of kiss-in-the-ring.

DROPPER. The assistant sower who followed the Dibbler.

(See S.S.&C. under Dibbling-iron.)

DROUGHT, or DRWAT YE. An imprecation. From God rot ye. Now generally reduced to "drat."

DROVE-ROAD. An unenclosed road through a farm leading to different fields. Especially, to the tenantry down in the manor.

DROVEWAY. A green road for droving cattle.

DRUDGE[1]. To harrow with bushes.

DRUDGE[2]. A bush harrow. (*Cf.* Dredge[2].)

DRUGGED, e. *Half dried; said of linen, etc.*

DRUV. Driven. "*I wunt be druv*" *is a favourite maxim with Sussex people.* In the shortened form, "Wunt be druv" has now become the motto of the County.

DRY FLOCK. A flock of wethers.

DRYTHE. [Drugath, *Ang. Sax.*] *Drought.* Thirst.

"*Drythe never yet bred dëarth.*"—Sussex Proverb.

"Take this 'ere ter squence yer drythe"—quench your thirst.

DRY-THRISKY. Another word for thirst.

DUBBY, e. *Short; blunt.*

"*I be dubersome whether she'll ever make a needlewoman, her fingers be so dubby.*"

DUBERSOME, m. *Doubtful. This Anglo-Saxon form of termination is not uncommon in Sussex; we find it in timersome for timid, wearisome, and other words. E.g.* Tempersome.

DUBS. Lead counters, used by boys in marbles games.

DUD. Did.

DUFF. This word, which is evidently only a variation of dough, is used for a pudding made with no other ingredients but flour and water; sometimes called hard dick.

Plum duff is the same with currants.

DUFFER, e. *A pedlar. This word is applied only to a hawker of women's clothes.*

DUMBLEDORE, w. *The humble bee.* Or bumble bee.

DUMPLINGS. See S.S.&C.

DUNCH, w. *Deaf; slow of comprehension.* Dunny.

DUNG-CART RAVES, w. *A framework fitted on to a cart to accommodate an extra load.* (*Cf.* Raves.)

On reading an announcement of chariot racing at Olympia, "Wot be these 'ere charts then Jesse?" "Oo, they be pretty much like a lil' dung-cart."

DUNGY.‡ Of a horse; same as Lapsy (*q.v.*).

DUNNAMANY, m. *I do not know how many.*

"*There was a dunnamany people come to see that gurt hog of mine when she was took bad, and they all guv it in as she was took with the information. We did all as ever we could for her. There was a bottle of stuff what I had from the doctor, time my leg was so bad, and we took and mixed it in some warm milk and give it her lew warm, but naun as we could give her didn't seem to do her any good.*"

DUNNAMUCH, m. *I do not know how much.*

"*She cost me a dunnamuch for sharps and pollard and one thing and t'other.*"

DUNNER. A facer. In the sense 'done in the eye.'

When the district nurse came into the room of a sick farm labourer supposed to be in extremis, he raised himself and said, "I'm going to get out o' bed, that's a dunner on ye, aint it?"

DUNNICK, or DUNNICKIN. A privy over an open cess pool.

DUNNY. Hard of hearing; Dunch.

"She had all her wits, but were a bit dunny at the last."

DUP[1], e. *To walk quickly.*

"*You was dupping along so, I knew you was late.*"

DUP[2]. To open.

My nurse said, to please me because I was only just tall enough to manage it; "Dup the door for me please."

DURMUT. Same as Turmut for turnip.

DURSN'T. Dare not. (*Cf.* Dare.)

DUTCH COUSINS, e. *Great friends. This expression is only used along the coast.*

"*Yes, he and I were reg'lar Dutch cousins; I feels quite lost without him.*"

DWAIRS, m. *Strong cross-bars in the floor of a waggon. The one in the centre is called the fore-dwair, the one at the back, the hind dwair. They are also called the cuts.* Sometimes Dwairs is said of the "horns of a waggon."

DYKE. A built up bank or earth wall; as a Hammer-pond dam, the Devil's Dyke or Poor Man's Wall, *i.e.*, the *vallum* of the Camp. It is only by confusion of terms that this name has become attached to the adjacent coombe. which if it were attributed to His Satanic Majesty would be the Devil's Dick.

E

'E. He; him; it. (*Cf.* 'Ee.)

EACH OTHER. Every other; alternate. (*Cf.* T'other-day.)

"The baker comes each other day."

EARL. See Harold.

EARN, EARNE, or ERNE. The heron, or herne (*q.v.*). See S.S. &C. under Herne.

EAROLES. Ear holes.

A countryman of 35, induced to bathe for the first time, was persuaded to put his head right under the water.

Afterwards he said: "Coo, with all that water arunnin' outer me earoles I misdoubted whether I was ever goin' ter come up agin."

EARS.† *The irons to which the bail of a bucket is fastened.*

Also handle-pieces of jars, pitchers, etc.

Hence the common proverb "Little pitchers have long ears," when talk is not meant for children.

EARSH, w. *A stubble field; as a wheat earsh, a barley earsh—frequently pronounced ash.* (*Cf.* Gratten)

EARTH. To turn up the ground as a mole does. Or to lodge as a badger does.

EDDEL. [*Ang. Sax.*, ádl, *corrupted.*] *Rotten.*

The Anglo-Saxon word conveyed all the various meanings expressed by the Sussex uses of this and the words Adle[1] and Adle[2] (*q.v.*)

EDDENBITE. A scattered and looped mass of cirrus cloud; a term used chiefly by fishermen.

EDDER. Ether (*q.v.*). (See S.S.&C. under Hedge and fence.)

EDDISH. The grass of a meadow after haying.

EDGET. See Idget.

'EE. Thee; thou; Ye; you; Them; they. (*Cf.* 'E.)

EEL-MICKET. A line with several hooked offshoots with lead or stone at the further end.

EELSHEAR, e, or EEL-SPEAR. *An iron instrument with three or four points, fastened to the end of a long pole*, 8 to 10 feet, *by means of which it is thrust into muddy ponds and ditches for the purpose of catching eels.*

Eelshear

EEL-WINDING. A method of catching eels in a weedy water by poking a long sapling, cut with a number of longish snubs at the small end, into the weeds in the water, rotating the sapling several times and then drawing out the whole onto the land, when the eels are found entangled in the weed. Frequently done at Burpham shuttles (low meadows).

E'EN-A'MOST. [*Corruption of even almost.*] *Nearly.*

"*'Tis e'en-a'most time you gave over eelshearing for this year.*"

EFFET, m. [Efete, *Ang. Sax.*] *A newt or eft.* Often pronounced Affut. *Dry efts are those found in the earth under hedge banks, and are said by the country people to be poisonous.*

E-GĖÀT. Same as Heave gate. (*q.v.*)

EGG. [Eggian, *Ang. Sax.*, *to excite.*] *To urge on; to incite.*

"They egged him on to fight."

EGGAS BERRIES. Haws. At Ditchling I heard them called Eggers. Also called Agarves and Hogarves (*q.v.*), etc.

EGGER-NOGGER. The fisherman's name for sleet.

EGGLER. See Higgler.

EGG ORCHID. White helleborine. *Epipactis grandiflora.*

ELDERN. *Made of elder.* (*See Ether.*)

ELDERN WINE. Elderberry wine.

ELEVENER, w. (Generally said Levener or Leveneses.) *A luncheon.* (*Cf.* Coager and Beever.) *In Durham the haymakers and reapers call their afternoon meal in the field their "four o'clock."*

ELEVEN FOOT PITTY. Very inferior iron mine. See Mine.

ELLAR and ELLET, e. [Elarn, *Ang. Sax.*] *The elder tree.*

ELLEM and ELVEN, m. [Ellm, *Sax.*] *The elm.* (Elven=made of elm wood.)

ELLER. *The alder tree.*

ELLET. Elder tree. Ellet wine another name for eldern or elderberry wine.

ELLUM. Elm. (*Cf.* Ellem.)

ELYNGE, m. [Ellende, *Ang. Sax.*, *foreign.*] *Solitary; far from neighbours; uncanny;* eerie. (*Cf.* Unked[1].) "*'Tis a terrible ellynge lonesome old house, and they do say as how there's a man walks under them gurt elven trees o'nights, but I've never seen him myself.*"

Cooper suggests a derivation from *ælenge*, Ang. Sax., long; and Ray, from *elend*, German, miserable, wretched, or from *elongatus*, Latin.

"The tense hush before a storm" has been described as ellynge or elenge.—S.C.M. xvi. p. 87.

ELVEN. Elm; made of elm.

END-ON, e. *In a great hurry.*

"*He went at it end on, as though he meant to finish afore he begun.*"

ENEW. *Enough.*

ENTHRALLED. Heavily in debt; bankrupt. See S.S.&C.

ERNE. This word does not mean eagle in Sussex; but Herne or Heron, usually Jack'erne. (*Cf.* Herne.)

ERNFUL. *Sad; lamentable.*

ETHER, or EDDER. [*Ang. Sax.*, éther, édor.] *A hedge. A piece of pliant underwood, wound between the stakes of a new-made hedge.*

"*An eldern stake and blackthorn ether*
Will make a hedge to last for ever."

(*Cf.* Raddles and Rossel-fence, and S.S.&C. under Hedge and fence.)

ETT. Eat; eaten.

"I be properly ett up wi' the Roomatics."

EVE-JAR. The night-jar; Puck or Puckeridge (*q.v.*); or Churn-owl.

EX-AXLE. EX-BED, or EX-BLOCKS. Woods to raise the cart clear of the axle.

EYED-AND-LIMBED, m. "*He eyed and limbed me*" *means, he anathematized my eyes and limbs.*

EYEPROOF. Evident; plain to see.

F

FACE-PIECES. Horse brasses.

FAD. *A whim.*

FADDY. *Fanciful.*

FAG[1], w. *To cut corn or stubble close to the ground.*

FAG[2], or FOG. The old last season's grass before the newly grown grass. (*Cf.* Fog and Toregrass.)

FAGGING-HOOK, or FAG-HOOK[1] *w.* A hook used for hedge or bush trimming, on a short handle offset from the blade to let the knuckles clear the ground. Similar to the swap-hook and generally heavier, but sometimes so called.

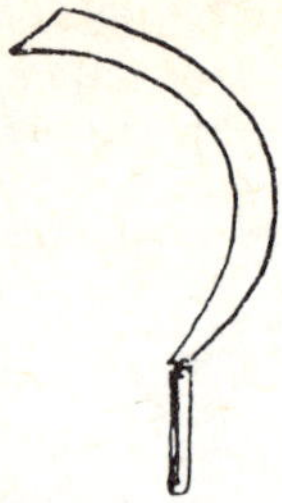

Fagging-hoook

FAGGOT, or FAGGOT OF HERBS. Bundles of dried herbs hung from the kitchen ceiling; also any dish seasoned with them.

"A delectable compound of strong seasoning."‡

FAG-HOOK[2], m. *A hook or bill fastened on a long stick for trimming hedges, or for fagging corn.*

Fag-Hook

FAGOT, m. *A good-for-nothing girl.* A baggage.

"I know I'm a saucy little fagot."—*A patient to her doctor.*

FAGOT-ABOVE-A-LOAD, e. *Rather too much of a good thing.*

"*Well, I do call it a fagot-above-a-load, to have to go down to Mr. Barham's twice a day.*" See also under Personable.

FAIL. To fall ill; generally used of catching complaints.

"*He looks to me very much as though he was going to fail with the measles.*"

FAIN, FAINITS. These words were always used by boys and girls at school in games. Fain was the principal player in the game, and Fainits was called if some suspension of the game were needed such as for tying up a boot-lace, but was not available for bettering of the game. Even as late as 1935 I heard Fainits used by boys playing on Lindfield Common.

FAIRIESES. (Plural of *Fairy*.) See Farisees.

FAIR TO MIDDLING. Tightish. See under Middling.

FAIRY-RINGS. Circles of grass which are higher, and of a deeper green than the grass which grows round them; attributed to the dancing of the fairies.

"*Ye elves—you demi-puppets, that by moonshine do the green sour ringlets make, whereof the ewe not bites.*"—Tempest, *Act v. sc. 1.*

Also called Hagrings and Hag-tracks (*q.v.*).

FAIRY-SPARKS, e. *Phosphoric light seen on various substances in the night-time.* Called also Shell-fire.

FALCONETTE. A one-pounder gun.

FALL[1], m. *The autumn.*

"*I have the ague every spring and fall.*"

FALL[2]. [Feallan, *Ang. Sax.*] *To cut down timber.*

"*These trees are getting too thick, I shall fall a few of them next year.*"

And used to mean the direction, as "I should take an' fall un this way"—so as to clear a young tree. (*Cf.* Throw.)

FALSE TONGUES. Large pieces of thick leather tied over the front of boots to keep out rain.

FAMBLY. Family.

FAN, e. *To banter; to tease.* Also to beat or thrash one.

"*Be not angry, most mighty princess, that I have adventured to try your taking of a false report.*
. . . The love I bear him
Made me to fan you thus; but the Gods made you
Unlike all others, chaffless. Pray you pardon."
—Cymbeline, *Act i. sc. 7.*

FANNER, w., or FANNER-HAWK. *A hawk.* The kestrel. He is also called Wind-fanner and Wind-hover because he hovers or fans the wind.

FANTIGUE. FANTEAGUE. Fuss; worry; bustle.

"Well, don't get into a fantigue about it."

FARDER or FARVER. Father.

FARE. § [*An old English word, probably connected with the German* fahren, *and Dutch* vaer.] The English word coming directly from *fare*, Ang. Sax., of a journey or voyage, from *fær*, a journey, that in which a journey is made. *A period during which certain kinds of fishing took place; as shotnet-fare, tucknet-fare, cock-fare, etc.* The above contributed by F. S. Sawyer from the *Brighton Custumal*, 1580.

The word also includes all the ancient fishing customs, the voyages, catches, sharing of catches, tonage of boats, nets and other gear used. Other Sussex ports had similar customs, but we are not so fortunate in their cases as to have them all set out. (*Cf.* Cock fare, Drawnett fare, Flew fare, Harbour fare, Shotnett fare, Skarborow fare, Tucknett fare, Yarmouth fare and Shares.)

FARES. (*Faire*, French, to make.) It will be; it is likely to be.

"It fares as if to be a hard winter."

FARISEES. [Fairieses.] *Fairies.*

By an unfortunate use of the reduplicated plural, the Sussex country people confuse the ideas of fairies and Pharisees in a most hopeless manner. A belief in fairies is by no means extinct in the South Downs districts, and among other stories the following was most seriously told me,—

"*I've heard my fèäther say, that when he lived over the hill, there was a carter that worked on the farm along wid him, and no one couldn't think how t'was that this here man's horses looked so much better than what any one else's did. I've heard my fèäther say that they was that fat that they couldn't scarcely get about; and this here carter he was just as much puzzled as what the rest was, so cardinley he laid hisself up in the stäable one night, to see if he could find the meaning an't.*

"*And he hadn't been there very long, before these here liddle farisees they crep in at the sink hole; in they crep; one after another; liddle tiny bits of chaps they was, and each an 'em had a liddle sack of corn on his back as much as ever he could carry. Well! in they crep, on they gets, up they clims, and there they was, just as busy feeding these here horses; and prensley one says to t'other, he says, 'Puck.' says he, 'I twets, do you twet?' And thereupon, this here carter he jumps up and says, 'Dannel ye,' he says, 'I'll make ye twet afore I've done wud ye!' But afore he could get anigh 'em they was all gone, every one an 'em.*

"*And I've heard my fèäther say, that from that day forard this here carter's horses fell away, till they got that thin and poor that he couldn't bear to be seen along wid 'em, so he took and went away, for he couldn't abear to see hisself no longer; and nobody aint seen him since.*"

FARTHING LAND, *m.* Rotherfield name for a part of the Bondland. (*q.v.*) (See also S.S.&C. under Borough English.)

FAT-HEN. The plant chenopodium album; *called also goosefoot.* (*i.e.* White goose-foot.)

FAT NOR WOOL. "That döänt make nuther fat nor wool." *i.e.*, does no good. Said of getting rafty or swarly, angry or getting anxious and worritted.

FAVOUR, m. *To resemble; a resemblance.*

Duke Sen: "*I do remember in this shepherd boy some lively touches of my daughter's favour.*"

Orla: "*My Lord, the first time that I ever saw him methought he was a brother of your daughter.*"—As You Like It, *Act v. sc. 4.*

"'e favours his mother" . . . has a likeness to her—a bly of her.

FAWTAGAWNSLE. Fore-top-gallant-sail. So usually pronounced on the Sussex coast.

FAY. To prosper; to go on favourably. "*It fays well,*" *sounds as if it was closely connected with* il fait bien. (*Cf.* Fares.)

FEGS. An exclamation.

"*Why! you are smart, fegs!*" (Fegs and ifegs are probably derived from Faith and Infaith.)

FELELOU. Fuss; hullabaloo.

FELL. A skin or hide; particularly skin with the hair on. In Sussex, a sheepskin with the fleece on.

FELLMONGER. One who deals in such; one who makes or sells articles made of untanned sheepskin.

FERRUCKING. Scratching.

FESTICAL, e. [*Corruption of Festival.*] *A feast.*

"*There ain't agoing to be any school festical to-year.*"

FESTIVAL. (For Fistula.) A flute; a recorder.

"There ain't goin' to be no festival in 'is band."—*Overheard complaint by Shoreham fisherman.*

FETCH. A trick; a stratagem; a false appearance.

"*Mere fetches; The images of revolt and flying off.*" King Lear, *Act ii. sc. 4.*

FETEL, or VETEL. Fettle; form or order.

FET'N ANON. Fetch him quickly; at once.

"You fet'n anon, 'e be bad."—*Command to boy to go for the doctor.*

FEWER.‡ The tenants of the Bishop of Chichester who attended the Courts of Ferring, from Billingshurst and thereabouts, were called Fewers (? foreigners). They might claim a dinner of pigeon pudding (with a bottle of port or a bottle of home wine), also hay for their horses but no "feed-corn."—Mr. Henty.

FID[1]. *To work too hard at anything. In Yorkshire the word foy has the same meaning.*

FID[2]. A kind of wooden marling spike, generally made of *Lignum Vitæ* (wood of life), or any peg to stop a spar from moving.

Fid

FIGHT. To flog. A standing complaint of parents against a school-teacher is, "*I wants more learning and less fighting.*" Also to stare offensively.

FIGURE. Oblique or longtitudinal section of medullary rays in oak and other woods. (*Cf.* Flower.)

FILE. A cunning, deceitful person.

In the same sense the word is used in speaking of a hare running her file.

FILL-DICK, m. *The month of February.*

"*February fill the dick,*
Every day white or black."
—*Sussex proverb.*

FINERY. A part of the forge; the fire and heavy water-driven hammer at which the first process of making the sow into wrought iron was carried out. (See S.S. &C. under Iron-working.)

FINGER-COLD. Frosty with a keen wind.

"It's wot I calls a finger-cold morning."

FINGER POST. A signpost. (See S.S.&C. under Floush hole.)

FIRE-CAGE. A beacon; an iron fire basket on a post.

FIRE-FORK, w. *An iron prong for raking ashes out of the oven.* And for manipulating logs of wood. The handle is about six times as long as the prong; some have in addition a spike at the side.

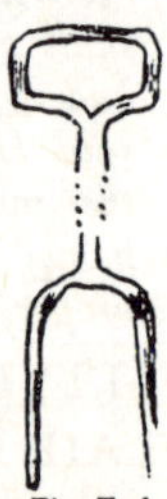

Fire-Fork

FIRE-SPANNEL, m. *A lazy person, who is always sitting by the fireside.*

FIRM, m. *A form; a bench without a back.*

FISH. See S.S.&C.

FISHERMEN. Along the South Coast fishermen have nicknames.

Hastings ... Chop backs. (From an ancient affray.)
Eastbourne Willicks, willickers. (Guillemots.)
Seaford ... Shags. (Cormorants).
Brighton ... Jugs.
Worthing... Pork bolters.

FITCH. (Variant of fitchew, *Fisse*, M. Du.) A pole cat.

FITCHES. Vetches.

FITTING, m. *Proper; right.*

"*I didn't think it was at all fitting that he should call me over, and bellick about house same as he did, just because his supper wasn't ready dracly minute.*"

FITTY[1]. *Subject to fits.*

The following extract from the Selmeston parochial account-book shows how afflicted persons were dealt with in former times,—

"*Ladiday, 1790. This is an agreement which is between the Churchwardens and Overseers and Parishioners of the Parish of Selmeston, in the County of Sussex.*

"*The said parishioners do agree that R. Hillman should take Jas. Norman at two shillings and sixpence per week so long as he continues in the fitty state, but when Mr. Hillman shall give it in that he can work well, and equal with other boys, he, the said Hillman, will do and keep him, the said boy, for as little and little money as any parishioner shall think proper.*"

FITTY[2]. Fitting; appropriate.

FLAIL HINGE. The hinge, thong, shuckle or swingel cap connecting the haft with the swiple and made of hide. The haft or hand-staff is usually of hazel wood and the swiple which strikes the corn is usually made of maple. See Striker.

FLAKE, e. *Cleft wood.* Flaking is making the flakes into hurdles very close and longer than folding hurdles and used for garden shelter, etc. (*Cf.* Talwood.)

FLAM, w. *A small net used in ferretting to cover the rabbit-holes.* The net is made into a bag shape.

FLANNEL. Hot spiced beer.

FLAP, w. *A large broad mushroom.*

*FLAP JACK. A sort of tart made of apples baked without a pan, in a thin piece of paste; also called **apple** turnover.* And Stuckling or Crowdie.

FLAPPERS[1], e. *Pieces of wood which the fishermen strap over their boots when they walk on the shingle. (See Backsters.)*

FLAPPERS[2]. *Young wild ducks which have just taken to the wing but are unable to fly.*

FLARKSY. Smart; showy; ostentatious.

"Wearing a flarksy tie."—*Lancing College opprobrium.*

FLASH. A very small pond or a pool.

"Now you take yer puppy down an' wash en in the flash."

FLASH BOX, or FLASHPAN. Apparatus for making signal flashes, used by smugglers, hovellers, etc.

FLASKET, w. [Fflasget, *Welsh, a shallow basket.*] *A clothes basket; a shallow washing tub.*

FLAT, m. *A hollow in a field.* Also low-lying water meadows.

"*The water lays so in these flats.*"

FLAW, m. *To strip bark; to flay.* Called also Rining.

"*He's got a job of tan-flawing.*" (*Cf.* Slipe.)

FLAWING SPUD. See Barking-iron.

FLECK, m. *FLICK, or FLOX.* [Flys, *Ang. Sax., fleece; down.*] *The fur of hares or rabbits.*

"*A pillowbedde stuffed with fflox.*" —**Inventory**, *1549.*

"*Old Mus Crackshott left two robbuts down at our house when he come to fetch his rent o' Saddaday. Purty much knocked about they was—so my mistus she put 'em into a pudden for Sunday, but when we come to set down to dinner they'd biled theirselves all away, and all the robbut as we could find was fower ounces of duck shot and some liddle bits of fleck for flavouring! and I says to my mistus, I says, 'If these be Mus Crackshott's robbuts I'd as lief have brencheese.'*"

FLEED. [Fléche, *French.*] *The inside fat of a hog before it is melted into lard.*

FLEED-CAKES. *Cakes made with fresh fleed: an indespensable adjunct to the family festival of pig-killing.* Also called Buster.

FLEET[1], e. *To be set afloat.*

A vessel is said to fleet when the tide flows sufficiently to enable her to move.

FLEET[2]. Flit (*q.v.*); shallow; thin.

FLEW.† [Flouw, Vlouw, *Dutch.*] *A kind of fishing net.*

The "flew als heak" was of various sizes for different fisheries, 2 to 4 ranns deep and usually 24 to 30 fathoms long. The specified minimum being 28 yards. (*Cf.* Cock heak, Heak, and Rann.) (*A flew-net, on land, is a net hung on poles for catching woodcocks.*)

FLEWARS, or *FLEWERS*.† *Boats of eight to twenty tons burden, used in herring fishery.* (*Probably* -certainly-*boats used with the flew nets.*) The larger boats earned three, and the smaller, two shares. (*Cf.* Flew fare and shares.)

FLEW FARE. Herring fishery carried on during November and December in the Thames estuary and down the Channel. The boats were Flewars carrying 8 men (more or less) and flew nets of three ranns; a man with above three nets took a half share for himself and a share for each three nets, other men took one share. This fishery was distinct from Yarmouth fare with larger boats carrying Norwards and going further afield. (*Cf.* Fare, Rann and Shares.)

FLICK. See Fleck.

FLIGHT. *To go to flight* (or to go flitting) *is to shoot wild ducks,* woodcocks *or plover at twilight.*

"*There was three of our chaps went out t'otherday evening purty nigh up as fur as Laughton to flight; but all as ever they brought home along wid 'em was Master Pelts, the shoemaker, as had gone up on the quiet two hours afore, and laid hisself up along wid a gurt bottle of whiskey; and when they got up to the brooks there he was a layin' on his back and a hollerin' of hisself hoarse, and shootin' up in the air at the rooks a-going over to Furrel, till they was forced to take his gun away from him and carry him home.*"

FLINDERMOUSE, e; *FLITTERMOUSE*, m.; FLIT, *or FLUTTERMOUSE*, w. *A bat.*

FLINT. See S.S.&C.

FLINT KNAPPER. See Knapper. (Also S.S.&C. under Flint).

FLINT SPUD. A stone fork; a large fork of 8, 9 or 10 speens used by road and quarry workers.

FLIT[1], m. or FLEET[2]. *Shallow; thin.*

When water is low it is said to be flit; and land is flit when there is only a slight layer of good earth upon it. A road was described as very fleet when the water and gas pipes were unusually near the surface.

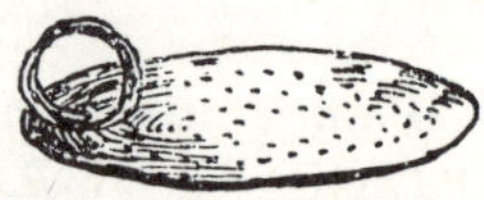

Flit

FLIT[2], e. [Flet, *Ang. Sax., cream.*] *A milk skimmer.*

FLIT[3], e. *A bat.* Also called flindermouse (*q.v.*), etc.

A bat coming indoors is considered an evil omen.

FLIT-MILK. Skim milk.

FLITTERMOUSE, *m.* A bat. See Flindermouse.

FLITTING. See Flight.

FLIT WELL. A shallow well; a surface well.

At places on the upper greensand, the beds both of sand and of the gault below, are very thin; the sand is full of water from the chalk kept there by the impervious gault. If a well is dug too deep here it will go right through the gault, and all the water be lost in the lower greensand.

FLOATERS. The small nimbus clouds moving rapidly below the stratus. They are a sure foreteller of rain.

FLOG, m. *To tire; to be wearied out.*

"*I was fairly flogged by the time I got home.*"

FLOOK. (*Flóc, flooc.*, Ang. Sax., a plaice, a flat fish.) See Flounders.

FLOUNDERS. Animals found in the livers of rotten sheep; also called flooks.

A sea flounder is also called a fluke or flook, and plaice is so in Scotland.

FLOUSH-GATE. A small gate on the top of a weir gate used to lower the surface of the water when the mill is not in stint.

FLOUSH-HOLE. [Fluissen, *Dutch, to flow fast.*] *A hole which receives the waste water from a mill pond* See S.S.&C.

FLOW¹. A length of straw in thatching; a handful or bunch of thatching straw.

" 'Twill take three flows yet to reach the comb."

FLOW². To flood with water.

" You'll flow the place."—make it all wet.

*FLOWER*¹. [*Corruption of Floor.*] (Pronounced flōwer.)

FLOWER². (Pronounced flōwer.) The figure (*q.v.*), in ornamental woods such as walnut and the like.

FLOWERING. To go a-flowering is to go gathering flowers or nosegays.

FLOWN-IN, e. *To be overtaken by the tide.*

"*You're too oudacious daring on they sands; if you dȯant mind you'll be flown in, one of these days.*"

FLOX. See Fleck.

FLUE. [Flaauw, *Dutch, weak, feeble.*] *Delicate; a flue horse is one which always looks thin, and will not carry flesh.*

FLUMMUX. Bewilder; put out.

" No use getting flummuxed about it."

FLUSHY, e. *Swampy; as ground after a continuance of wet weather.*

FLUTTERGRUB, m. *A man who takes a delight in working about in the dirt, and getting into every possible mess.*

FLUTTERMOUSE, *w.* A bat. See Flindermouse.

FLUX, e. *To snatch at anything; to blush.*

FLY GOLDING, e. *The ladybird.* (*See Bishop Barnaby.*)

Also God Almighty's cow, Lady Anne and Ladycow.

*FOB*¹, e. *To froth as beer does.*

*FOB*², e. *The froth of beer; the foam on a horse's mouth.* Sea froth.

FOG, w. *Long grass growing in pastures in late summer or autumn, not fed down, but allowed to stand through the winter.* Same meaning as Fag² (*q.v.*).

FOISTED.‡ (Fusty.) Musty.

FOISTS. Light, easy going, flat-bottomed boats used for merchandise. They carried goods from large ships to the shore.

FOLDING-BAR, w. *An iron bar used for making the holes in which the wattles are fixed for folding the sheep.* (*Cf.* Pitch¹.)

FOLD-TARE, or *FOLD-TAIL*, m. *The improvement of land caused by sheep having been folded on it.*

FOLLOWER. A bramble. See Lawyer.

FOOTMAN. Walker.

"Blackberries? Yus, thur be some, but they be all maggoty. Might be some on the hill, but I be a poor footman 'n I dintabin up thur."

FOOTY. Silly; foolish; worthless. Little.

"Just a footy dozzle"=just a small drink. (*Cf.* Dozzle.)

FORCED. Obliged.

"I was forced to putt on my spartacles."

FORDROUGH, e. *A cattle-path to water; a grass ride.* A drove or drift-way (*q.v.*).

FORE, m. *Front. In Yorkshire the spring is called "the fore-end of the year."*

FORECAST, m. *Forethought.*

FORE-DOOR, m. *The front door.*

FORE-DOWN, FOREHILL or FRONT HILL. A place lying near the foot of the north escarpment of the South Downs is described as being "Under the forehill,"—fore-down or front hill. The forehill being the Down that faces the Weald nearest to the place of speaking.

FORE GARTER. The ring before the trunnions. See Gun rings.

FORE-HORSE, m. *"He has got the fore-horse by the head" is a Sussex expression for "he has got matters well in hand."* "Taken time by the forelock." See Team.

FOREIGNER. A stranger; a person who comes from any other county but Sussex.

At Rye, in East Sussex, that part of the parish which lies out of the boundary of the corporation, is called the Foreign of Rye.

I have often heard it said of a woman in this village, who comes from Lincolnshire, that "she has got such a good notion of work that you'd never find out but what she was an Englishwoman, without you was to hear her talk."

Cornishmen and Welshmen are called "furriners." (Welsch—Welsh, Welch—means foreign. (*Cf.* walnut=the foreign nut.)

FORELONG. As soon as possible.

"I slipt inter the barn forelong, out o' sight."

FORERIGHT. Plain spoken; rude; obstinate.

"I döant know whatever I shall do with that boy, he's so foreright, and he döant seem to have no forecast of nothing."

FORE-SUMMER, w. *The top rail in front of a waggon. The corresponding rail at the back is called the hawk.*

FORGE. The iron mill. In old Sussex usage, the forge was the place where wrought iron was manufactured. It usually comprised the finery and chafery. (See S.S.&C. under Iron working.)

FORGOTTED. Forgotten.

FORNICATE, m. *To dawdle; to waste time.* To procrastinate. Also to trifle in speech. (Probably by confusion with prevaricating or fabricating.)

A girl said, "Oh sir! Now you're fornicating."

FORREP-LAND, w. (*Forest*, Old French, a forest.) *Used in the manor of Bosham for assart land, or land from which the wood or forest has been cut down, to bring it into cultivation.* (See S.S.&C. under Borough English.)

FORSTALL, or FOSTEL, m. [*Ang. Sax.*, fore, *before; and* steal, *a stall, place or stead.*] *The house and home buildings of a farm with waste land attached.*

FOTHER. To feed cattle.

FOUNDAY. The day on which the Iron was drawn from the blast furnace, usually at six day intervals. (See S.S.&C. under Ironworking.)

FOUNDER. Face of cliff that subsides; also the landslip it makes, and the debris when fallen.

FOUNDING. Making cast iron and articles of cast iron. The process originated in the weald and was largely practised there when iron working elsewhere was very primitive. (See S.S.&C. under Iron-working.)

FOUNDLE, m. *Anything found.*

"*I picked up a foundle yesterday, as I was coming home off the hill.*"

FOURTHROWS, *or* *FOURWENTS*, e. *A place where four roads meet.* Usually a Crossways, sometimes a Partways or Carfax. (*See* Throw and *Went.*)

FOWT, *m.* Fought.

FRAID-CAT. A child's term of reproach to one timorous; an insulting double accusation of both cowardice and spitefulness.

FRAIL, m. *Flail.*

"*Dame Durden kept five serving men*
To use the spade and frail."

FRAME. Used when speaking of a sick person becoming emaciated. "She's nothing but a frame."

FRAMMARD. Another word for Frow (*q.v.*), or cleaver.

FRANCY. Deformation of Francois.

FRAP. To strike; to beat. This meaning is the correct use of the word. The Concise Oxford Dictionary gives "(naut.) Bind tightly." This, so far as it goes is correct, but a binding is only frapped if the turns of rope are beaten, or frapped, to make the tightening. "You frap that carpet hard." "Then she frapped my knuckles, just 'cos I played a wrong note."

FRAY. To fray rooks, etc.—to frighten them from crops.

FRAYEL, m. (or frail). *A flexible basket made of bulrushes, commonly used for packing game.*

FREER. The muzzle ring of a gun. See Gun rings.

FRENCHY, e. *A foreigner of any country who cannot speak English, the nationality being added or not, as the case seems to require; thus an old fisherman, giving an account of a Swedish vessel which was wrecked on the coast a year or two ago, finished by saying that he thought the French Frenchys, take 'em all in all, were better than the Swedish Frenchys, for he could make out what they were driving at, but he was all at sea with the others.*

FRESH[1], m. *Home-brewed small beer, which must be drunk while new or fresh.*

FRESH[2], e. *To decorate; to renew.*

"*I freshed up my bonnet with those ribbons you gave me.*"

FRESH[3], e. *Fresh air.*

"*It feels very close to you coming in out of the fresh, but Jane she's had her fevers all day, and I dursn't set the window open to let in any fresh, for I was afraid 'twould give her cold.*"

FRESH[4]. *Not quite drunk, but rather noisy.*

FRET. Sea Fret. Fine rain, mist, or drifting spray blown up from the sea.

"'Tis beginning to rain."
"No, 'tis only fret off the sea."

FRIED STRAWS. Greased rushes (rush lights) ready for lighting. Miss Maud Robinson of Saddlescombe, says they were so called.
Wedded in Prison, p. 61.

Fried Straws

FRIT, e. *Frightened.* Frouden (*q.v.*)., etc.

"*I was quite frit to see him so near the water.*"

FRITH, e. *Young underwood; brushwood growing by the side of hedges.* The word is used for copse wood too young for coppicing. (See S.S.&C. under Copse—coppicing.)

FRONT HILL. See Fore-down.

FRORE, w. *Frozen. Spencer uses frorne in the same sense.*

FROSTBECK, w. *A strong handbill for cutting up turnips when they are frozen.*

Frostbeck

FROUDEN, m; *or FROUGHT*, w; or FROUGHT'N'D, *m. Frightened.* Frit and Frowten also express the same meaning.

I met an elderly man one evening going through the churchyard; it was too dark to see who he was, and I passed without speaking. To my surprise he stopped and began shouting as loud as he could; and recognising his voice, I went back to ask him what was the matter. "Oh dear me, sir!" he said, "is that you? I didn't know it was you, sir, I'm sure I beg your pardon." It was in vain that I enquired why he was making such a dreadful noise; no answer could I get, beyond that he didn't know who it was. So I wished him good night and went on, under the impression that he was drunk; but the matter was explained by his turning back to say, "I beg your pardon, sir, but I hope you doànt think I was frouden! Bless me, no! I was noways frouden, not at all! I'm a man as aint easily frouden at meeting anyone in the churchyard after dark."

FROUZY. Red in the face from exertion and heat.

FROW. An implement for splitting wood with the grain. It was held by the handle while the iron blade was struck by a wooden mallet. Also called a Cleaver, or Frammard.

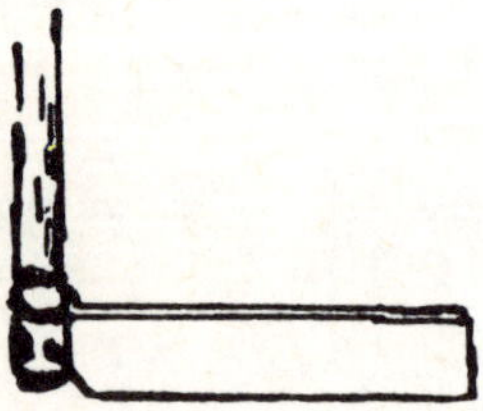

Frow

FROWST. Fugg. Air exhausted of oxygen. Frowst hole: a ventilator in Lancing College study.

FROWTEN. Frightened. See Frouden.

FUDGE. To fullock, *i.e.* increase the force of one's shooting with a marble, by jerking the hand forward at the same time which is illegal, not optional to the alert as "inching" is, or "knuckling up" is, when one has not been forestalled by the opponent's crying "knuckledown tight."

FULFERS. Fieldfares.

FULSOME. Filling; satisfying to one's hunger.

"Eggs be very fulsome."

FURET or FURT. Pronunciation of Ferret which is nearer the borrowed French word than Ferret.

FURLONG. A division of tenantry land. Not the normal furlong (furrow-long) of 220 yards, but a term applied to a parcel of land of any size. (*Cf.* Tenantry-acre.)

FURNACE. In Sussex "furnace" means invariably a blast-furnace with water driven bellows, where cast iron was made. It is quite distinct from the Iron mill (*q.v.*). (See also S.S.&C. under Iron working, and Tread the wheel.)

FURNAGE, w. *A sum formerly paid by the tenants of the lord of the manor for right to bake in his oven.*

FURRAGE. (about) move things in search.

"I've bin furraging about in the box-room." etc.

FURRIN. Places only a few miles off are termed foreign. Cornish cabbages are called "furriners."

FURROW. See Voor or Vur.

FURT. See Furet.

FUST. First. See S.S.&C.

"Fust of all you wash your hands."—*A constant injunction from my nurse.*

FUTTICE, e. *A weazel.* Also called Kime or Kine (*q.v.*).

FUTY. See Footy.

FUZZES. Hurdles covered with, or faggots made of, hawth; used for lambing folds. See Hoth.

G

GABERDINE, m. *A loose frock still worn in Sussex by farm labourers.*

"*My best way is to creep under his gaberdine.*"—Tempest, *Act ii. sc. 2.*

GAFFER[1], m. *Abbreviation of grandfather.*

GAFFER[2], m. *A master.*

"*Gaffer has given me a holiday.*"

GAGGED or GAG WIRE. Barbed wire.

GAGY, e. *Showery.*

GALLEYBIRD, or GALLOWSBIRD. The Woodpecker. The great green woodpecker, or yaffle (*q.v.*). Yaffle, from its cry; gallowsbird for frequenting old gallows or gibbets for maggots, etc. Also called Bargeboat.

GALLOWS. (Pronounced gallus.) *To die under the gallows is said to be the fate of a person who dies of overwork.*

GALORE. In abundance. This old Celtic word is still in common use in Scotland and Ireland.* It has lately become common generally.

GAMELING, e. [Gamen, *Ang. Sax., a game.*] *Romping about.*

GAMMER, m. *Abbreviation of grandmother.*

GANSE, e. *Merriment; hilarity.*

GANSING-GAY, e. *Cheerful; lively.*

"*Some people said the children would always be interrupting of us if we went to live so near the school, but for my part I likes to hear them, their voices is so gansing gay its quite company to me.*"

GANT.‡ Gaunt.

GANTSEY, or GANTY. Lively; frolicsome. A gantsey horse.

GAP, m. [Geapu, *Ang. Sax., a space.*] *An opening through the chalk cliffs on the Southdowns leading to the sea*, or to a river, *as Birling Gap, Copperas Gap, etc.; also called a gut.*

GAPE SEED. Something to stare at. A person staring out of window is said to be sowing gape seed.*

GARATWIST,* or GARTWISTED. *Altogether on one side.* Also said when seams pucker in sewing patchwork, etc.

GARDEN. See Hop garden.

GARIBALDI. A garment similar to a slop (*q.v.*), but made of red woollen material or of red flannel, and usually ornamented with narrow black braid.

GARM, GAUM, or GAWM. To be foul; especially to be sticky. (*Cf.* Stuggy.)

"It's all gawmed up with it."

GARNYSON. A garnishing. Usually a service of pewter, which, being kept polished on the dresser, made a brave show.

GARRETING, w. *Small pieces of flint stuck in the mortar courses in building.* Also, of ironstone in flintwork. (See S.S.&C. under Flint.)

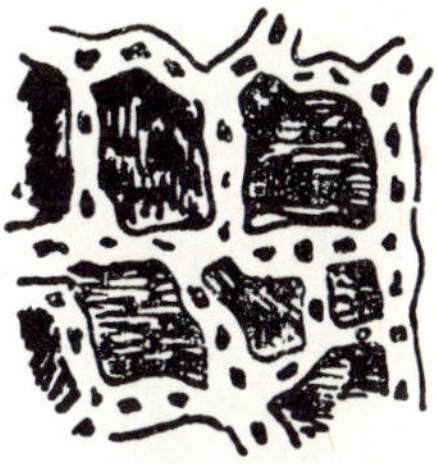

Garretting

GARTER. A marked line; a score in the ground to mark where a jump or a race starts from. If one go over the garter one is disqualified. Also a gun ring, see Fore garter and gun rings.

GASKIN, e. [*Gascony.*] *A kind of cherry largely grown in the neighbourhood of Rye, which is called indifferently "geen" or "gaskin," having been brought from France by Joan of Kent when her husband, the Black Prince, was commanding in Guienne and Gascony.*

In olden days a Lord of Berkeley finding housekeeping too costly, agreed with the widow of a Kentish nobleman for lodging and maintenance of himself, his wife, her two waiting women, six serving men, and horses for the whole party at £200 a year, but he died before the year was out of eating too many gaskins.

GATE, w. *A farmyard.*

"Go through the gate," *i.e.*, the farmyard gate.

GATE HOOKS. The hooks on the gatepost that receive the thimbles of the hinges on a gate. See Thimble.

GATE-PROUD. Said of a crop flourishing near the gateway, when manure has been unevenly distributed.

GAUGING. A popular term with needlewomen for honeycombing.

GAUNT, e. [Geanian, *Ang. Sax.*] *To yawn.*

GAWM. See Garm and Stuggy.

GAY. "All gay," is a common reply to "How are you?" or "How goes it?" etc.

GAY-GROUND, e. *A flower garden.*

"I likes to have a bit of gay-ground under the window for a look out."

GAYWHILK. A gay person.

"What, going away again! You are a gaywhilk, arn't you!"

GAZELS, e. [Groseiller, *a currant tree.*] *All kinds of berries, but especially black currants.*

Gazel tea is a favourite remedy for a cold.

GEAT. [Geat, *Ang. Sax., a gate.*] *The Anglo-Saxon form of the word is always used in Sussex.*

In a case of assault, Prosecuting Counsel to witness, "And where were you?"

W. "By the gèat."

P.C. "And where was the gate, at the side of the field? At the end of the field? In the middle of the field?"

W. "Wy you silly ole vule! 'Ooever seed a gèat in the middle of a veild!"

Laughter in Court.

GEE, m. *To get on well with a person.*

"*We've lived up agin one another for a good many years, and we've always geed together very nicely.*"

GEEMANY, m. [*Corruption of O Gemini!*]

"*Geemeny! you do mean to be spicy.*"

GEEN, e. [Guienne, *French.*] (*See Gaskin.*)

GEE-UP. Go on. To a horse, Gee =go, Up=on or forward.

GEE-WOOT. An expression used by waggoners to make the leading horse go to the off side; to the shaft horse the word for the same purpose is hoot. To woot is the contrary command . . . to ease off to the left or near side, or towards the teamster.

GELDABLE. (*Gældan*, Ang. Sax., to pay.) Taxable.

Residents of Pevensey not free-men of the liberty were so described in the Custumal. See S.S.&C.

GENERALLY-ALWAYS and MOST GENERALLY ALWAYS, m. *A superlative form of generally.*

"*My master generally-always comes home none the better for what he's had of a Saddaday night.*"

GENTLEMAN, m. *A person who does not earn his own living. Anyone who is disabled from work. The term is sometimes applied to a sick woman, or even to a horse.* "*I'm sure I've done all I could for mother; if she isn't a gentleman I should like to know who is!*"

Also used as an euphemism for Smugglers and Runners.

GERT. Great.

"She be grown a gert girl now, no mistake." (*Cf.* gurt.)

GET-ON-THE-LAND. Work on the soil.

" So wet yer can't get on the land." *I.e.* to plough, roll or even spread manure for its surface moisture.

GIBBLETS.‡ Pieces; rags; tatters.
" My apron's all in gibblets."

GIFTS. White specks which appear on the finger nails, supposed to indicate the arrival of a present.
"A gift on the thumb, is sure to come;
A gift on the finger is sure to linger."

GIFTY, w. [Giftig, *Dutch.*] *Unwholesome; poisonous.*
" The house smelt quite gifty-like."

GIGGLESOME. Given to giggle.

GILL TEA. A drink made by tramps and others from leaves of Alehoof or Ground Ivy, which is called 'Gill-creep-by-the-ground' in Somerset. The plant is also called Gill-ale. (Halliwell.) All pronounced with a soft g, and Lion's Mouth.

GILT CUP. Lesser celandine or pilewort. *Ranunculus Ficaria.*

GILTED. Gilded . . . of a frame.

GIMSY, e. *Smartly dressed.*

GIT. Go on. A ploughman speaking to his horse. Also " Now you can git."

GIVE-IN. To state an opinion.
" *Master Cockleshaw he gives it in that we shall have a change of weather before many days.*"

GIVE-OVER. Leave off.
" *You just give over messing-about among my cabbages.*"

GIVE-UP. Given leave to get up by a Doctor.
" How is your Mother?"
" Oh, the Doctor give her up last week."

GLADDEN.‡ Of a fire, to blaze up, or burn Rash.

GLADDING. A moment of pleasure; a celebration. Such as the sight of early spring flowers; a birthday party or other celebration.

GLANDS.‡ Snowflakes.

GLINCY. [Glincer, *Old French, to slide.*] *Smooth; slippery; applied to ice.*

GLUM. [Glóm, *Ang. Sax., gloom.*] *Gloomy.*
" *The weather looks very glum this morning.*"

GNANG, e. [Gnagan, *Ang. Sax., to gnaw.*] *To gnash the teeth.*

GOAD, e. *Any long stick. Pronounced gȯȧd.*

GOAD FLY. Gad fly. (*Cf.* Stout.)

GȮȦST. [*Guast*, Ang. Sax., a spirit.] A ghost; a spirit.

GOB. A lump. In cooking a gob of butter is about an ounce, a 'good gob' is about 1¼ oz.

GOBBET. [Gobet, *French, a hasty meal.*] *A large mouthful of anything; a lump.* A small gob.
" *Meet I an infant of the house of York,*
Into as many gobbets will I cut it,
As wild Medea young Absyrtus did."
—II HENRY VI, *Act v. sc. 2.*

GOD ALMIGHTY'S COW. Ladybird. Also Bishop Barnaby (*q.v.*), etc.

GOD ALMIGHTY'S THUMBS AND FINGERS. Bird's foot trefoil. *Lotus corniculatus.* Also called Butter-and-eggs (*q.v.*), etc.

GOE. A supper and punch meeting held in a public house at election times before the secrecy of the ballot was instituted in 1872.

GOLD CUP. The meadow ranunculus. The Butter cup. (*R. acris, R. bulbosus* and *R. repens* without discrimination.)

GOLE. [Gole, *Old French, the gullet.*] *A wooden drain pipe. In the north of England the word is used for a small stream.*

GOLLOP. To gobble.
" Don't gollop your bread and milk like that."

GONG or GONGE. Similar to Jakes—see below.

GONG-FARMER. A cleaner out of gongs, gonges, jakes, privies etc. Called also Jakes-farmer and Gonges-farmer: who clean out any kind of dirt or litter besides jakes (privies).

GONNOWES. Amberley gonnowes: a corruption of Amberley God knows; an inhabitant's description of his dwelling place in winter, and of his fellow inhabitants.

GOODEN, *or GOODENING*, or Gooders. *The custom of going from house to house for doles on St. Thomas's day (21st December). This was done by women only, and a widow had a right to a double dole; the presumed object being to obtain money or provisions for the enjoyment of the approaching festival of Christmas.* At Lewes, just inside a draper's shop on the north side of the Cliffe there was placed a large box full of old hats etc., labelled " For the Gooders."

GOOD FAULTS. Virtues; generally rather grudgingly admitted. See S.S.&C.

GOODMAN. An old title of address to the master of the house.

I find the following entries in a book of accounts of the parish of Selmeston,—

1745, December ye 22
" Goodman Gasson
payd fower men for Carring John Gasson to the ground 00–04–00
payd Tho. Jurden for buring John Gasson 00–02–06
payd for laying John Gasson foarth and one shilling for ather Daved " (affidavit) 00–03–00

GOODY. The title of an elderly widow.

Expences for the yeare 1743:
Payd Goody Gorge for washing and mending her suns cloath and Goody Pumphrey 6 pence 01–00–06

GOOSE-NECKED.‡ Said of ill-grown barley.

GORM or GAWM. Frequently ' gormed up.' See Garm and Stuggy.

GOSLINGS. Palm (*q.v.*)

GOSSIP, e. [Godsibb, *Ang. Sax., a sponsor.*] *This word is still used, though very rarely, by old people.*

" *They've brought a child to be christened, but they haven't got no gossips.*"

GOTERWEX. (Gutter-wax.) Candle gutterings. In churches the sacrist collected it, and was paid accordingly.

GOTHAM. (Pronounced goatham.) A Sussex origin. See S.S.&C.

GO-UNDER. Undergo.

" *The doctor says he must go to the hospital and go under an operation.*"

GOWK. A fool; a cuckoo.

GOYSTER, or YOYSTER. To frolic and laugh; to act tumultuously.

GRABBY, e. *Grimy; filthy; dirty.*

GRAFF, or GRAFFING-TOOL, m., GRAFT. or GRAFTER. [Grafan, *Ang. Sax., to dig.*] *A curved spade, generally made of wood shod with iron. Used by drainers.* It is narrow and long in shape.

A graff or graft was also used by woodmen to clear away soil, stones or any vegetation getting in the way of the axe when falling a tree. Made nowadays of steel, it is still used for the same purposes.

Graff

GRAFT[1]. A patch.

GRAFT[2]. To patch a garment.

GRAIN-SCOOP. For pouring out grain. Usually made of lime wood with handle slightly curved.

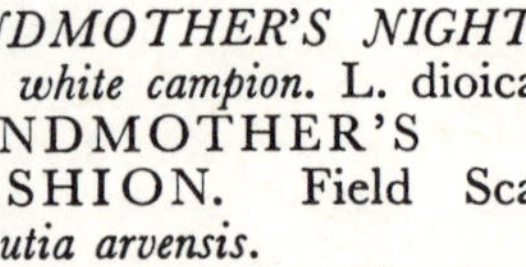

Grain-scoop

GRANDFATHER, m. *A daddy-long-legs.*

GRANDMOTHER'S NIGHTCAP.† *The white campion.* L. dioica.

GRANDMOTHER'S PINCUSHION. Field Scabious. *Knautia arvensis.*

GRAPE. A fork with three tines used for working rough dung. Used also in the north.

GRASPING. Some internal feeling kin to gripes. " This 'ere grasping gets me down."

GRASS COCKS. Heaps of undried grass.

GRASS-NAIL. A thin iron rod or stout wire which connects the blade and snethe of a scythe and prevents the angle between them from being choked with mowings.

GRATTEN[1], m. *A stubble field.* Or a rough fallow field which was at first an earsh (*q.v.*).

GRATTEN[2]. [Gratter, *French, to scratch.*] *To scratch for the grain that may be left on the grattens.*

" *By the time the pigs have been grattening for a week they'll look eversmuch better.*"

GRAVEL RASH. The wound sustained by scrazing. See Scraze.

GRAVES. Refuse meat in Tallow-making used for dog food.

GREEN-BREECHES. To wear green-breeches is to pretend ignorance: as when caught trespassing, etc.

GREEN ONIONS. Spring onions.

GREEN TRICK. (Green=Young.) Childish behaviour.

GREW, e. *A greyhound.* A Long dog.

" T'old grew guv Mus' Reynolds a tidy grib."

GREYBEARDS, m. *Earthen jugs formerly used in public-houses for beer, and so called from having on them the face of a man with a large beard.* Also called Bellarmines because they are effigies in ridicule of Cardinal Bellarmine the persecutor.

GREYBIRD, m. *The Thrush.* Properly the Missel Thrush. The Song Thrush is the Brown bird (*q.v.*)

GRIB, e. *Variation of grip. A sharp bite.*

GRIDGEN, m. *Grudging; stingy.*

" *If he has anything given him, he's that gridgen that he'll never give away naun an't.*"

GRIG[1], e. *Merry; happy.*

" *Master Harry he's always so grig.*"

GRIG[2]. A wag.

(A corruption of *greek*, a good fellow, a mad companion.—Halliwell.)

"As merry as a grig."

GRIG[3]. A young eel. Sometimes called a snig (*q.v.*)

GRIP. [Groep, *Ang. Sax.*] *A small ditch or drain.*

GRISSET, or GRISETTE. (From grease.) An oval iron dish for melting the fat into which rushes are dipped to make Grisset rush lights; or for making candles.

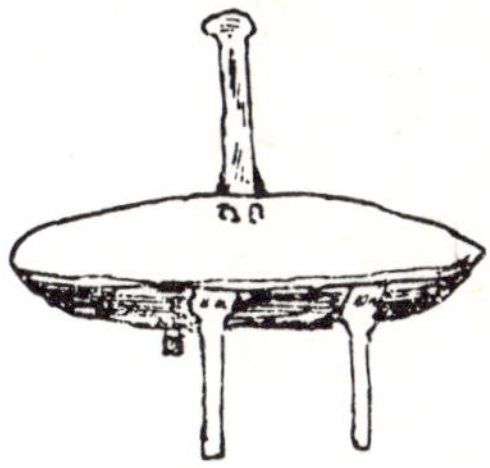

Grisset

GRIST. See gryst.

GRIZZLE, m. *To fret; to grieve.*

" *I know the child aint well, because she's been grizzling about so all day, and she's never one to grizzle when she's well.*"

GROM, e. [Grommeler, *Dutch, to wallow.*] *Dirty; to soil or make dirty.*

GROMMET. Nautically a ring of rope for fastening the upper edge of a sail to its stay; or to attach *two* spars etc., as a yard or a sprit to a mast. In the latter case it is drawn to a waist and called a snotter.

On steamships a grommet is a rope or other textile washer used for a joint packing. See S.S.&C.

Grommet

GROOM, m. *An instrument used by thatchers for carrying bundles of straw.* (*Cf.* Dog[1].)

GROUT-HEADED. Stupidly noisy.

GROUTS. Grounds.

"The pipe's all stopped up with coffee grouts."—*A Lindfield plumber.*

GRUBBER. A tool used for getting out the roots of weeds.

Grubber

GRUBBY, e. *To make in a mess.*

"*You've grubbied our pinney,*" *means* "*you have dirtied your pinafore.*"

GRUMMUT. An awkward boy.

Mr. M. A. Lower states that this word is a corruption of the old French gromet, *a diminutive of groom; the cabin-boy of the Cinque Ports navy was so called. The condition of the distinguished immunities of those ancient corporations was, that they should provide for the King's use a certain number of ships, and in each ship twenty-one men, with one boy, called a gromet*—" et in qualibit nave XXI homines, cum uno garcione qui dicitur gromet."—Suss. Arch. Coll. vol. xiii. p. 217.

GRYST. [Grist, *Ang. Sax., a grinding.*] Or grist. *A week's allowance of flour for a family.* Pronounced with a long y or i. Said now of inferior corn ground for fodder and poultry feed, a common complaint of latter day wind and water millers is " We are only grysting now," meaning only grinding cattle food, not flour.

GUBBER, e. *Black mud.* (*Cf.* Stug.)

GUDGE, m. *To probe.*

"*The doctor came and vaccinated our baby yesterday; nasty man! he just did gudge his poor little arm about.*"

GUESS-SHEEP, m. *Young ewes that have been with the ram and had no lambs; so called because it is doubtful or a matter of guess whether they will ever have lambs.*

GUIDE. The long thin end of a shepherd's crook continuing the barrel and set at an angle to the stock. It ends in a curl. (See S.S.&C. under Bilbo.)

GULL[1], w. *To sweep away by force of running water; a breach made by a torrent.* (*Cf.* Gullywash and Gully, a channel made by running water across a road.)

GULL[2]. *A gosling.* Young geese in Sussex are seldom called goslings.

GULL[3], *m. The blossom of the willow; called in Cambridgeshire goslins.*

GULLYWASH. A deep narrow ravine, generally dry but torrential in rainy weather. (*Cf.* Gull[1].)

GUMMUT. A lout; a stupid fellow. (See Grummut.)

GUMPTIOUS, e. *Smart; tawdry.*

GUN, m. *To examine carefully; to con over.*

"*When I gunned her over a little closer, I soon saw that she was too gumptious by half to be a lady.*"

GUN RINGS.

"The names of the several rings on the outside of Guns, as our people call them are:—The first behind the Touch-hole—The Base ring. The ring next the Touch Hole—The Asticall Muller. The ring before the trunnions —The Fore Garter. The next—The Muller before the Fore-garter. The next—The Freer with an Ogee behind it where it is cut off the square."

John Fuller, ironmaster, of Rosehill, Brightling, and the Heathfield and Waldron furnaces, writing in 1737.—S.A.C. LXVII, p. 41

GURGISE, w. *A fish-pool; lake, or pond.*

GURT. [*Corruption of great.*] Gert (*q.v.*).

GUT[1], m. [Gjota, *Icel.;* Gota, *Ang. Sax., a pourer.*] *An underground drain for water.*

GUT[2], *e.* In the Pevensey and other marshes, a main drain.

GUTTERDICK, m. *A small drain.*

"*'Taint no use at all for you to make that 'ere gutterdick, what you wants is a gurt gut.*"

GUTTER-MUD.

A simile for intimacy, "They two be just so thick as gutter-mud."

GUZZLE. A narrow ditch for running water.

GWAIN. Going.

"Well I aint gwain, so that's that."

GYLE. A brewing of beer.

H

HAAL. A broadened form of Heal (*q.v.*), to cover.

HABERN, w. *The back of the grate* Also the sides or hobs.

"*Why, whatever have you been a-doing with yourself? Your face is as black as a habern!*"

HACK[1]. *To cough faintly and frequently.*

HACK[2], w. *To rake up hay into thin rows.* (*Cf.* Windrow[2].)

HACK[3]. In brick-fields to set newly made bricks for first drying off. (*Cf.* Rindle and Skintle).

HACKER, m. *To stutter and stammer.*

HACK-HOOK, m. [Haccan, *Ang. Sax., to cut.*] *A curved hook with a long handle, used for cutting peas and tares, or trimming hedges.*

Hack-Hook

HACKLE[1], m. (*Hæcele, Ang. Sax., a garment.*] *A straw covering placed over beehives.* A protection in rough weather for the hive beneath. The Beeskep itself.

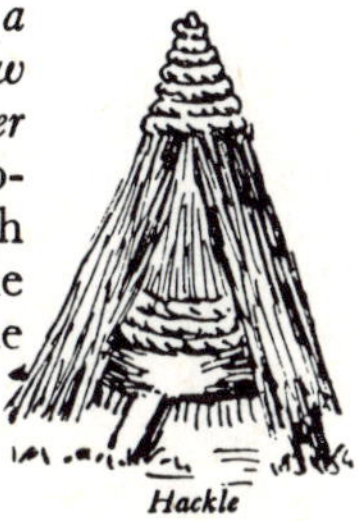

Hackle

HACKLE[2]. See Hansel.

HAFFER or HARFER. A heifer.

"*I leave to Jane, my wife's daughter, an haffer of 2 yerys age.*" —Will of Thos. Donet, of Burwash, 1542.

HAGRIDDEN, m. *To be hagridden is to have the nightmare.*

HAGRING or

HAGTRACK, m. *Circles of coarse green grass seen on the meadows and downs, supposed to be tracks of hags or witches who have danced there at night.* They are caused by a fungus. (*Cf.* Fairy-rings.)

HAITCH, e. *A slight passing shower.*

HAITCHY, e. *Misty.*

HALF-BAPTIZED[1]. *Privately baptized.*

"*If you please, Sir, will you be so good as to half-baptize the baby?*" "*Oh! certainly; but which half of him am I to baptize?*"

HALF-BAPTIZED[2], e. *Silly, foolish.*

"*You must have been half-baptized to water those flowers when the sun was full on them.*"

HALF-HAMMER, w. *The game of hop-step-and-jump.*

HALF-HIGH HATS. Hard felt hats with flat crowns which when painted were shiny and kept out rain. Shepherds usually painted theirs grey.

Half-High Hat

HALF-SWING PLOUGH, w. *A plough in which the mould-board is a fixture.*

HAM. [*Ang. Sax.*, hám; *German*, heim; *English*, home.] *A level pasture field; a plot of ground near a river.* A three-sided grass plot is also called a Ham.

"*In the country of the Angles as well as here (in North Friesland) every enclosed place is called a hamm.*" —Outzen's Glossary of the Frisian Language, *p. 113.*

HAMEL. [*Hamel.* Old French; *ham,* Ang. Sax.] A hamlet.

HAMMER. To chatter; hence Yellow Hammer, which is not from the German *ammer.* The bird's name means the yellow chatterer.

HAMMER-POND. A pond like a mill dam made by damming a stream to work the Iron Hammers in the Ironworks.

HAMMER-POST. Post of a whole oak tree 10 feet high in which an Iron Hammer was rigged or guided.

Hammer-Post

HAMPERY, m. [*Possibly from* empiré, *French, decayed.*] *Out of repair.* See Ampery, and the derivation of ampery.

HAMSHARE. See Hempshare.

HAMWOOD, w., or HAMOOD. [Hame-wood.] *Pieces of wood on the collar of a horse to which the traces are fixed.* Hames.

HAND, m. *To be a hand, is to cause a great deal of trouble.*

"*I was a terrible hand to mother all the time I was down with the titus-fever.*"

HANDBILL. A sharp tool with a short handle used in cutting underwood, etc. (*Cf.* Bill-hook.)

Handbill

HAND-IRONS. Brandirons.

HANDLE-DISH. m. *A bowl with a handle.*

HAND-PINS. The short handles on the snethe or snead of a scythe. Also called Doles, Nebs or Nibs, (*q.v.*).

HANDS DOWN. Opponent's order at marbles: then one has to shoot with one's hand on the ground, or on the other hand.

HAND-STAFF. The handle of a flail. Also called helve or haft. Usually made of hazel.

HAND-WRIST. Right hand wrist.

HANDWRITING. Work or style; characteristic; *e.g.* when some mischief has been done and an evidence discovered.

"Ah! I reckoned it were his handwriting;" or on a suggestion that such an one will do so and so—"That's just about his handwriting."

HANG or HUNG. A ferret does, and is, when stopped at the quarry in the earth.

HANGER, m. *A hanging wood on a hill side.*

HANSEL[1], m*; or HACKLE*[2], e. *To use anything for the first time.* A first handling; the same as Hansel below.

HANSEL[2], m. [Handsylen, *Ang. Sax., a giving into the hands.*] *The first money received in the morning for the sale of goods. The market women have a custom of kissing the first coin, spitting on it, and putting it in a pocket by itself for luck.* This word is common in Scotland.

HAP, m. *Perhaps.*

HAPPEN-ALONG, m. *To come by chance; to arrive unexpectedly.*

"*Master Tumptops, he's a man as you'll notice mostly happens-along about anyone's dinner-time.*"

HAPS[1], m. [Hæps, *Ang. Sax.*] *Hasp of a door or box.*

HAPS[2]. (*Hæpsian*, Ang. Sax., to shut to; to lock.) To catch or fasten a door or a window. Pronounced 'harps.'

HARBOUR FARE. Conger fishery with hooked lines from boats of 8 tons, carried on during the summer. The lines were 50 fathoms long, but the number of hooks is not specified. One man with 4 lines earned one share, the boat two shares (*q.v.*), and 12 lines (without a man) one share. (*Cf.* Fare.)

HARD[1]. Of ale—acidulous.

HARD[2]. The shore where there is a firm bottom, clear of mud or loose sand; a way to tide-water, such as the Dolphin Hard at Shoreham and Portsmouth Hard.

HARD-DICK. Sussex pudding, made of flour and water only. Also called Duff.

HARD OF. Near; nearly.

HARFER. A heifer. (*Cf.* Haffer.)

HARLING. Putting one leg of a rabbit through the other after it is dead. (*Cf.* Hox.)

HARME-HOOK. A hook used for pulling out wheat stubble which was the men's perquisite after the sporting season. The farmer lent his cart for carrying it, and the stubble was made into stacks for heating the baking oven. (*Cf.* Haulm.)

Harme-Hook

HARNESS, m. *Temper; humour.*

"*Master's in purty good harness this morning.*"

HAROLD. A common Christian name in East Sussex, which is always pronounced the same as the word earl. A woman we knew at Lancing chose it for her son, " because I allus liked the 'im (hymn), ' Hark the herald angels sing '."

HARR, HARRE, HARROW or HUR. The post that takes the hinges of a gate. (*Cf.* Head, Beam, Brace, Downright and Spleats.)

HARTH MONEY. Beer money. Given gratuitously to harvesters, charcoal burners, etc.

HARTOGS. Clothes; not new nor one's best, but of good quality in which one can rough it without care.

HARVES BOTTLE. See Costrel.

HASSOCK, e. [*Possibly from* Haso, *Ang. Sax., dry; rugged.*] *Anything growing in a thick matted state. A thick wooded shaw or little wood.* Hassock is also a dense root stock tuft of grass, much the same as a tussick, (*q.v.*)

HATCH[1], m. *To sicken for any complaint.*

"*I think she's hatching the measles.*" *This expression seems to correspond very closely with that used by physicians when they speak of the period of incubation.*

HATCH[2], m. (*Haccan*, Ang Sax., to hack.) *To dress the bark of trees.*

HATCH[3]. (*Hæc*, Ang. Sax., a gate.) *In names of places probably means a gate.*

It is usually found on the borders of forests, as Coleman's Hatch, Plawhatch and Claw-hatch, in Ashdown forest.

HATCH[4], w. *A gate; a half-door.*

HATCHEL, w. *To rake cut grass into small rows.*

HATCHELL[1], HITCHELL, or ITCHELL. To comb flax.

HATCHELL[2], HITCHELL, or ITCHELL. A flax comb; a hackle.

HATCHET-PIECES.† *Paul-pieces of land of irregular shape.* (*See Tenantry-acre.*)

HAULM. [Healm, *Ang. Sax.*] *The straw of beans, peas, tares, etc.*

HAUST, m. *A place for drying hops.* (*See Oast-house.*)

HAVE, m. *To lead or take.* To forcibly conduct.

"*I shall have him down to his grandmother while I go haying.*"

" . . . he . . . shall be had to the Town Bridge . . ." (See S.S.&C. under Geldable.)

To have him up; meaning to prosecute.

" I have him on the hip."

HAVILER, or HEAVER, e. [Heafer, *Ang. Sax.*] *A crab.* The green or mud crab. Also called Aviller and Jack-aviller.

HAWK, w. (*See Fore-summer.*)

HAWTH. See Hoth.

HAY-KNIFE. A knife with a cross handle and a sub-triangular blade, used for cutting hay in the rick to make trusses. See S.S. & C.

Hay-Knife

HAYWARD, w. [*Haw-ward; hedge-ward.*] *An officer of the lord of the manor, whose business it was to look after the hedges and see that the boundaries were kept right.* Also that the cattle of tenants on the common pasture did not exceed their allotment. In extreme cases he was authorised to impound (put into the Pound) any such cattle.

HAWORTH was the old form of the word, and Haworth's Hoth or as it is generally said Orword-sorth (now Haywards Heath) was a wild place at the extremity of the manor where the haworth and the tenants were perpetually at loggerheads as to grazing rights.

HAZEL-OIL. A thrashing (with a hazel rod.)

" Th' young varmunt wants a good dose o' 'azel oil, 'ee do!"

HE[1]. Him; it. (*Cf.* 'E.)

HE[2]. 'Tis a saying in Sussex that " Everything is 'he' excepting a Tom Cat."

HE[3]. A euphemism for the devil (*Cf.* Devil[1].)

HE[4]. One character in a game opposed to the other players.

" Who'll be he?"

HEAD[1], m. " *To your head* " *is the same as* " *to your face.*"

" *I told him to his head that I wouldn't have such goings on in my house any more.*"

" *To the head of Angelo accuse him home and home.*"—Measure for Measure, *Act iv. sc. 2.*

HEAD[2]. The post that holds the latch of a five-barred or other field gate.

HEAD-ACHE, e. *The corn poppy.* Papaver rhæas.

HEADLANDS[1], m. *The part of the field close against the hedges.* In Sussex when ploughing with four-yoke oxen the headlands were wider than today because more room was needed to turn the team. (*Cf.* Sidelands.)

HEADLANDS[2]. The tops of the Downs as distinguished from the bottoms or valleys.

HEADPIECE, m. (Not only local.) *The head considered with regard to the intellect.*

" *He's got a very good headpiece, and if he could have had a little more schooling he'd have made something better than a ploughboy.*"

HEAK.§ *Another name for the flew.*

Erredge (*History of Brighton*) *says that in Yorkshire the nets used for fishing in the river Ouse are still called heaks.*

Heak and Flew are somewhat confused, but it is probable that properly a heak was a net of four ranns depth, and the flew three ranns. Both are of specified minimum 28 yards long and in practice 24 to 30 fathoms (48 to 60 yds.), and the rann was always specified as 50 moxes. The heak, if lost at sea, was valued at ten shillings, or at least the owner could claim that compensation from the common fund, but no such valuation would appear to be set on the flew. (*Cf.* Flew Mox and Rann.)

HEAL, m. [Hélan, *Ang. Sax.*, *to cover or conceal.*] *To cover.* Sometimes said as broadly as ' hȧȧl.'

" *I healed up the roots with some straw.*" Somteimes expressed as " Heling up."

In Sussex houses are described as slate healed, tile healed, shingle healed, stone healed, etc. Also the first large pieces of bark removed from the oak trees were called healers because they were used to heal or roof the stacks of bark while drying.

"*In the ancient English dialect the word* 'hell' *was taken in a large sense for the general receptacle of all souls whatsoever, and it is so used in the old translation of the Psalms in our Common Prayer Book* (*Ps. lxxxix,47*), *which sense may be confirmed from the primary and original signification of the word; according to which it imports no more than an invisible and hidden place, being derived from the old Saxon word* 'hil' *which signifies to hide, or from the participle thereof,* helled, *that is to say, hidden or covered; as in the western parts of England, at this very day, to* 'hele' *over anything, signifies, amongst the common people, to cover it, and he that covereth an house with tile or slate is called an* 'hellier'*; whence it appears that the word* 'hell,' *according to its primitive notion, exactly answers to the Greek* 'hades' *which signifies the common mansion of departed souls, and was so called because it is an unseen place.*"—Lord Chancellor King on the Apostle's Creed, *pp. 233, 193, 194.* Ed. Lond. *1702.*

HEALED. [Hyldan, *Ang. Sax., to incline.*] *When a ship goes over to one side she is said to have healed over.*

The right spelling is heel; the ship heeled over; but the term is not only local.

HEALERS. Large pieces of tan bark. See Heal.

HEALING, m. *A coverlet; a counterpane.*

In the will of Rev. H. Marshall, he leaves "*2 pillowberes and a healing.*" (. . . ij pylowbers, a hillyng, . . .) The will was dated 9th August, 1550.—*S.A.C. XIII.* p. 53.)

"My missus she wants all the healing."

HEARN, HEARNE, HERNE, EARN, EARNE, or ERNE. Heron. None of these spellings is exactly phonetic, pronunciation varies, it is generally very slightly aspirated but almost impossible to reproduce in print; usually prefixed by jack-. See Jack-hearn and S.S.&C. under Herne.

HEART, m. *Condition; said of ground.*

"*I've got my garden into pretty good heart at last, and if so be as there warnt quite so many sparrs and greybirds and roberts and one thing and t'other, I dunno but what I might get a tidy lot of sass. But there! taint no use what ye do as long as there's so much varmint about.*"

Heart is used locally in deeds: tenant of a farm covenants to keep the land "in good heart and condition."

HEART-STRAND. The strand in some cordage around which the other strands are laid.

"Sound as the heart-strand of the mainbrace." See Strand.

HEARTH. The bottom, prepared, of an Iron furnace; made of sandstone.

HEATHERS or BINDERS. Used to weave in and out of stakes supporting a laid hedge. Often spoken of as Heathers and binders. (See S.S.&C. under Hedge and fence.)

HEATS. Irons to work.

"Dunnow what to be at we got so many heats in the fire."

HEAVE-GATE, m. [Hefan *and* geat, *Ang. Sax.*] *A low gate, so constructed as to lift out from the posts, instead of opening with hinges.* Often pronounced "E-gëat." especially in East Sussex.

Heave-Gate

HEAVER. A crab; see Haviler.

HEDGE AND FENCE. See S.S. &C.

HEDGE-CARPENTER. One who does carpentering but has not been apprenticed to a carpenter and properly learnt his trade. See S.S.&C.

HEDGE-HOG. Venus' comb. Scandix pecten-veneris. Or Shepherd's needle.

HEDGE-PICK, or HEDGE-MIKE, m. *The hedge sparrow;* or Dunnock.

HEDGE-PIGS or HEDGEHOGS. Used to be sold for 3d. each for meat.

HEDGING-HOOK. For cutting standing crops close up to hedge or wall. Handle 3 to 4 times the length of blade.

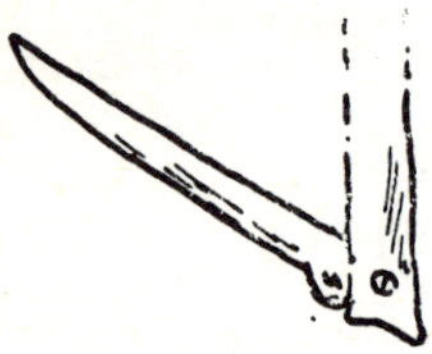

Hedging-Hook

HEEN, m. [Hæn, *Ang. Sax.*] *A hen.*

"*I throwed a stone at a liddle hedge-pick a settin' on the heave-geat, and killed Mrs. Pankurstes' gurt old packled heen.*" (Packled meaning "Speckled.")

HEFFLE. Heathfield. See Cuckoo-fair.

HEGGLING. Vexatious; trying; wearisome.

HEIGHTS in SUSSEX. See Black-down, 918 ft; Teglease, 837 ft.; Ditchling, 813 ft.; and Crow-borough, 792 ft.

HEIRS. Young timber trees.*

HELING UP. Same as heal (*q.v.*).

HELON. To cover; to hide.

HELP, m. *To give anything into a person's hands.*

"*I will help the letter to him if you'll write a few lines.*"

A letter by hand is marked "Obliged by" so and so. See S.S.&C.

HELVE[1], e. *To gossip.* (*Cf.* Nabble and Yape.)

HELVE[2], e. *A long gossip.*

HEM, m. *Very.*

"*Hem crusty old chap our shepherd is surelye! I says to him yesterday, I says, ''Tis hem bad weather, shepherd,' I says. 'Ah,' says he,' tis better than no weather at all;' and hem-a-bit would he say any more.*"

"What a hem of a noise they folks do make."

HEM-A-BIT, m. *Not a bit; certainly not.*

HEMMEL, e. *A fold. Connected with the Icelandic word* hemja, *to restrain.* To hem in.

HEMPSHARE, or HEMSHARE.†

Certain lands in the centre of Brighton, so named from having been used by persons engaged in the fishing trade for growing hemp for rope-making. The word is found in the court rolls, 1660.

In my house deeds (69 Ship Street) it is described as being "in the Hamshares of Brighton."

HENRIP, w. *A hen-coop.*

HERE-AND-THERE-ONE. An expression used to signify an average, or on an average, as "He aint much of a boy I know, but he's quite as good a boy as you'll find here-and-there-one."

HERN. Hers; belonging to her. As hisn, his (*q.v.*).

HERNE. Hearne, (*q.v.*); a heron; or more often Jack-hearn (*q.v.*). In Essex they talk of Frank Heron.

There is a proverb: "He can't tell a hawk from a herne-shaw." Herne or Hernshaw=heron. See S.S.&C.

HERRING. "As handsome as a herring." A Littlehampton timber merchant describing a cargo used fishy terms throughout. "Its as sound as a roach, as clean as a smelt and damme George as handsome as a herring."

HERRING-HANG, e.† *A place where herrings are hung up to dry; also called a dee*, or a deese.

HIDE. [Hyd, *Ang. Sax.*] *A hide of land is about 120 acres. In Saxon times it meant as much land as could be tilled with one plough; a family possession.*

HIGGLER, m. *A huckster; so called from higgling over his bargains.*

Especially an itenerant merchant of eggs and chicken. The

derivation is more likely from Eggler " one who goes about the country collecting eggs for sale." (North. Halliwell.), which exactly describes the main function of the Higgler up to the time of the Egg Marketing Board. The derivation of Higgle to Chaffer is probably an inversion, higgle being a snatching at haggle and higgler. (*Cf.* Higgledy-piggledy the mixing up of pigs, hens and eggs in the higgler's cart.)

A Horsham Market Deed of 1756 mentions restrictions on the activities of " Hawkers Higlers " etc.—*S.A.C. XLVI.* p. 183.

HIGH HURSTWOOD. See S.S. &C.

HIGH-LOWS. Children's footware, between boots and shoes.

HIKE[1], m. *To call roughly.* To pull out, as root-grubbing, etc.

" *He hiked me out of the pew.*"

HIKE[2]. A mess. (*Cf.* Ike and Stuggy.)

HILL, m. *The Southdown country is always spoken of as " The hill " by the people in the Weald.*

" *He's gone to the hill, harvesting.*" " Ower the Hill " is a phrase of folk living south of the Downs to express Lewes Prison.

" On the hill " means on the Downs generally, or on the near Down in particular.

HILL-UP, m. [Hélan, *Ang. Sax., to cover.*] *To hill-up hops is to raise small hills or heaps over the roots for the purpose of keeping them dry in the winter.*

HIME. See Hyme.

HINDERTAIN. (A blending of hinder and detain.) A word in general use.

" Well, I wunt hindertain you no more 's morning, Miss."

HISN, m. *His own.* His (Not now localised.)

The possessive noun is thus conjugated in Sussex—Mine, thine, hisn or hern. Ourn, yourn, theirn.

And an adage often drummed into us by our nurse,

" He as takes what isn't hisn,
When he's cotched 'll go to pris'n."

HITCHELL[1], ITCHELL, or HATCHELL. To hackle, or comb out flax before spinning. (*Cf.* Hatchell[1].)

HITCHELL[2], ITCHELL, or HATCHELL. A hackle or flax comb. (*Cf.* Hatchell[2], and see S.S.&C. under Tainter.)

HITHER, m. *Near.* Nearer to some definite position.

" *He's in the hither croft.*"

E.g., Hither and Further Blacklands, Lindfield.

HOAK. Singular for hoax; a false excuse or pretence.

" Some people make an 'oak of the war 'n say they can't get labour, 'n when a man goos for work they doänt want 'n."—*A farmer at Woodmancote.*

HOARDERS. Wardens, or keeping pears; winter pears.

HOATH. See Hoth.

HOB. The iron pin forming the mark for Quoits; often with a cleft in the upper end to take a white feather or a piece of paper.

HOBBLE, m. *A doubt; an uncertainty.*

HOB-LAMB, m. *A pet lamb, brought up by hand.* Also called a Sock-lamb (*q.v.*)

HOB-UP. *To bring up anything by hand.*

A parishioner of mine once came to complain to me that her husband had threatened to ill-use her on account of two little pigs which she was hobbing-up; but as I found that his objection rested on the fact that she was hobbing-up the pigs so carefully that she insisted on taking them to bed with her, I declined to interfere.

HOCKLANDS, HOOKLANDS, or OCKLANDS. [Hóh, *Ang. Sax., a heel.*] *Hock-shaped pieces of meadow land.*—Leo's Ang. Sax. Names.

(*Cf.* Hockses.)

HOCKSES. (*Hóh*, Ang. Sax., a heel; a hock.) The Sussex plural for a horse's hocks.

"Thou shalt hough their horses."—*Joshua*, xi. 6.

I.e. Hamstring them, or cut their hough (hoch) tendons to disable them.

HOCK-MONDAY, w. *The second Monday after Easter, kept as a festival in remembrance of the defeat of the Danes in King Etheldred's time.*

HODMANDOD. A snail, or an empty snail-shell. Other names are; snag, sneg and shell-sneg (*q.v.*)

HOE, w. *Fuss; anxiety.*

"*I dòant see as you've any call to putt yourself in no such terrible gurt hoe over it.*"

HOG. A yoke for carrying pails, etc.

HOGARVES, m. HOGASSES or or HOGHAZELS. *Hog-gazels; hawthorn berries.* Haws. Also called; Agarves (*q.v.*), Aigarces, Argarces, Argaves, Eggas, and Eggas berries.

HOGBOAT or HOGGIE. A big tubby fishing boat peculiar to Brighton, where it is no longer to be seen. The last hoggie, the '*Nil Desperandum*,' was burnt early this century in a Fifth of November bonfire on the beach. There is a fine model of one in the Brighton Museum.

Hogboat

HOG-FORM, w. *A bench on which pigs are laid to be killed and dressed.*

On the knuckle of a pig's fore-leg there are always six marks, about the size of a pea, which are believed to have been caused by the devil's fingers when he entered the herd of swine.

HOG-GAZELS. See Hogarves.

HOGGET, w. *A young sheep, just more than a year old.*

HOGGIE. A Brighton Hog-boat (*q.v.*)

HOGHAZELS. See Hogarves.

HOG-JET, w. *A small bucket, fastened into a long handle, by which the food is taken out of the hog-tub.*

HOGNEL MONEY, or HOGNEL-SILVER. A kind of rate, formerly collected for the churchwardens.

*HOGO.** [Haut gout, *French.*] *A strong foul smell.* Or any strong flavour accompanied with a powerful smell.

HOG POCK.‡ A disease, affecting the hands.

"It comes up in bunches like, but 'taint 'zackly like the chickun-pock of measles."

HOGPOUND, m. *The pigstye; a favourite rendezvous on Sundays.*

"*Ah! many's the time as we've stood over the hog-pound together, and looked 'em over, and rackoned 'em up, whiles people was in church; little did he think as he'd be putt in before that hog was killed! and he always allowed she'd weigh sixty stun.*"

(" Putt in " means buried.)

HOLE. The hole of a charcoal pet (stack of billets) is the central opening. (See S.S.&C. under Cording and Charcoal burning.)

HOLL, e. *To hurl; to throw.* Also said Hull.

*HOLLARDS.** *Dead branches of trees.*

HOLLERING POT. Hallooing. See S.S.&C.

HOLMESDALE. "The welds of Kent, Sussex and Surrey which were all anciently comprehended under the name Holmesdale."—*John Norden: Surveyor's Dialogue.* London 1607. p. 213.

HOLP, m. [Healp, *Ang. Sax.*] *The perfect of help.*

"*She had me round to the pound, to see a little hogget what she'd hobbed-up; and then she had me indoors and holp me to a cup of tea and some honey-bread.*"

HOLT[1], m. [Holt, *Ang. Sax., a grove.*] *A small plantation.* Also a wood gap, small and on the side of a hill, or a small plantation, usually alongside a hill, like Clayton Holt.

HOLT[2]. *A hold.*

"'*Tis just like a lawyer, if once it takes a holt 'an ye, ye dòant very easy get free agin.*"

HOLT[3], m. [*Corruption of Halt.*] *A call always used to stop a person.*

HOLT[4]. An otter's nest, den or nursery; or a badger's burrow.

HOLY-SUNDAY, e. *Easter-day.*

There is a tradition that the sun always dances on the morning of Holy-Sunday, but nobody has ever seen it because the devil is so cunning that he always puts a hill in the way to hide it.

HOME-DWELLERS, m. *People accustomed to live in houses, as opposed to tramps.*

"*A good many of these people who've come harvesting this year, look like home-dwellers.*"

HONEY-BREAD. *Bread and honey.* (*Cf.* Jambreads.)

HOOD. Wood; Ood, (*q.v.*)

" Now you jus' wait! Any one 'ud think you'd been brought up in the middle of a hood!" A frequent admonition to very youthful delinquents guilty of unseemly behaviour.

HOOK, *m.* To tear as on a hook. "I've bin an' 'ooked my finger."

HOOKE, *or Hook.* [Hóc, *Ang. Sax., a hook.*] *A name given to several places in Sussex.* Often to farms.

HOOKLANDS. Hocklands (*q.v.*)

HOOP-HIDE. Hide and seek game: the hiders call out "Hoop" when hidden.

HOB-BIN. A canvas trough on a pole frame into which hops are picked. (See S.S.&C. under Hop drying.)

HOP-DOG[1], m. *A caterpiller peculiar to the hop gardens.*

HOP-DOG[2], m. *An instrument used to draw the hop-poles out of the ground, for the purpose of carryiing them to the bin to be picked.* It was attached to a long wooden handle.

Hop-Dog

HOP DRYING. See S.S. & C.

HOP DRYING. See S.S.&C.

HOP GARDEN. The place where hops are grown is in the Kent-Sussex district invariably called the hop garden. In the Worcestershire hop country the name is hop yard. The derivations of garden and yard are connected.

HOP-HORSE, e. *A short ladder used by the hop-pickers.*

HOP-KNIFE. Used for cutting down the bines for picking.

Hop-Knife

HOP-MAND, w. [Mond, *Ang. Sax., a basket.*] *A vessel used in brew-houses.*

HOPPING JOHN. For breakfast. Skim milk with a little savoury broth poured hot upon bread.

HOP-PITCHER. See Pitch[1].

HOP-POCKET. A large sack used for the conveyance of dried hops. (See S.S.&C. under Hop drying.)

HOP-STRINGER. Used for tying hops to the poles and wires.

Hop-Stringer

HORN-FAIR, m. *Rough music with frying pans, horns, etc., generally reserved for persons whose matrimonial difficulties have attracted the attention of their neighbours. The fair annually held in Charlton, Kent (now abolished), was always known as Horn fair.* Originally a fair for the marketing of horns and horn products.

There is held annually a Horn Fair at Ebernoe on July 25, St. James's Day, whereon they roast whole a horned sheep and whose horns are awarded as an honour to the cricketer who makes the highest score at the match played that day. The Revd. E. T. Shealey of Lurgashall tells me that in rationing days the Fair was carried on, but the horned sheep was not roasted: that for two years after the War, Lord Leconfield gave a deer's horns to the man who made the highest cricket score. Many horns found in the pavilion, won by men now dead, were cleaned up and given to the winner. In 1954, after a lapse of fifteen years, the old custom was restored and a horned sheep roasted whole as before. The opposing teams are Ebernoe and Lurgashall.

HORNICLE, w. *A hornet.* The sound of this word is more nearly represented by "Aarnicle", it is very slightly aspirated.

HORSEBEACH or HUSBEECH, w. *The hornbeam.* (Usually spelt horsebeech.)

HORSE-BELLS. The globular bells were called Rumblers or Rumble Bells.

HORSE BLOCK. A Jossing-block (*q.v.*), etc.

HORSE-DAISY, w. *The ox-eye daisy.* (Chrysthemum leucanthemum.)

HORSE-LEG. A Bassoon.

HORSE-STOPPLES. Holes in wet muddy ground made by the feet of horses.

HOSTE, e. *Described by Durrant Cooper as "A vendor of articles out of shops or houses," so used at Hastings. From the old French word Hoste, which meant both a host and a guest.*

This word is used in the second sense,— a guest, a person allowed to come, a stranger.

" *Every person not lotting or shotting to the common charge of the Corporation, who should be a common* hoste *in the fishmarket.*"—Hastings Corporation Records, *1604*.

HOT, m. *To warm up.*

" *I was that cold when I got indoors that gaffer hotted up some beer for me.*"

*HOTAGOE.** *To move nimbly; spoken of the tongue.*

HOT-CHILLS, m. *The fever that accompanies the ague.*

HOTH, m. *Hawth. The name of Hoathly seems connected with this word.*

" *'Tis very poor ground, it wont grow naun but heath and hoth.*"

Pronounced hoàth, hōwth or ōth, it is the local name for gorse, whin or furze. When cut, faggots of it are used for making the walls of a lambing yard and then called fuzzes.

HOT-POT, m. *Hot ale and spirits.*

HOUGH (or HUFF). To breathe heavily upon; as on an object for polishing.

" I've houghed the silver, Mum, *and* Master's brown shoes."

HOUNDS, w. *The part of a wagon to which the fore-wheels and shafts are attached.*

HOUND'S TOOTH. A simile for, or gauge of whiteness,

" Why it's as white as a 'ound's tooth." (*Cf.* " black as a sloe.")

HOUSE BEANS or HOUSEHOLD BEANS. Broad beans.

HOUSED, e. *When hops have a great deal of bine, and the poles are thickly covered over the top, so as almost to shut out the light and sun, they are said to be " housed.*"

HOUSE IN. To cover in: a cabin is housed in, and a tent when fixed is housed down.

HOUSEL, m. *Household goods.* Hustlement.

" *Whose housel is that up on the wagon?*"

HOVEL. Open-sided shed or shelter for cattle.

HOVELER, e. *A pilot.* Latterly, an unlicensed pilot.

HOVELERS, e. *Men who go out to sea in boats for the purpose of meeting homeward-bound vessels, and engaging with the captain to unload them when they enter the harbour.* (*Cf.* Huffler at Shoreham.) Also for many other purposes.

HOVELLING. An ancient long-shore-seafaring occupation, which formerly included anything from near-piracy and wrecking to life-boat work. *I.e.* any pickings which might be had from any ship in any kind of distress.

Latterly, in more sheltered times, it comprised salvage of jettisoned cargo, creeping up contraband which smugglers had had to sink, supply, after very hard bargaining, of any maritime requisite from an extra hand to work a shorthanded ship up Channel to an anchor, slops or twists of tabacco to an ill found outward-bounder, and pilotage.

In this latter sense it was still practised at the beginning of the present century.

HOVER[1], m. *Light; spoken of the ground or soil.* Friable, not clayey.

HOVER[2], m. *Looking cold and shivery.* "*Some of the children looked middlin' hover as they went along to school this morning through the snow.*"

HOVER[3], m. *To hover hops is to measure them lightly into the basket.*

HOVER FLIES. Sawflies.

HOVING. Sheep bursting with over-eating rich plants such as rape, clover, etc.

HOWK, e. *To dig. Possibly connected with the Dutch word houwen, to hew.*

HOWLERS, w. *Boys who in former times went round wassailing the orchards. A custom now nearly obsolete.*

The custom of wassailing used to be observed on the eve of the Epiphany, when the howlers went to the orchards, and there encircling one of the best bearing trees, drank the following toast,—

"Here's to thee, old apple tree,
May'st thou bud, may'st thou blow,
May'st thou bear apples enow!
Hats full! Caps full!
Bushel, bushel, sacks full!
And my pockets full, too! Huzza!"

The wassailers derived their name from the Anglo-Saxon salutation on pledging one to drink, which was wæs hæl, *be of health; to which the person pledged replied* drinc hæl, *I drink your health.*

HOWSUMDEVER, m. or HOWSUMEVER. *However.*

HŌWTH. Hawth; Hoth (*q.v.*)

HOX, w. *To cut the hamstrings; to cut the sinew of a rabbit's leg and put the other foot through, in order to hang it up.* Or rather between the sinew (without cutting) and the bone. (*Cf.* Harling.)

Hox

HUCK,[1] e. *The pod of a pea.*

Children get the pods and cry to each other,—

"Pea-pod hucks,
Twenty for a pin;
If you döant like 'em
I'll take 'em back agin."

(*Cf.* Kid[2].)

HUCK[2], e. *A hard blow or knock rudely given.*

HUCK[3], e. *To spread anything about, such as manure.*

HUCKLE-BONE, e. *The small bone found in the joint of the knee of a sheep, used by children for playing the game of dibs.*

Dr. Clarke, in his travels in Russia, 1810, vol. I., p. 177, says, "In all the villages and towns from Moscow to Woronetz, as in other parts of Russia, are seen boys, girls, and sometimes old men, playing with the joint bones of sheep. This game is called dibbs by the English. It is of very remote antiquity; for I have seen it very beautifully represented on

Grecian vases, particularly on a vase in the collection of the late Sir William Hamilton, where a female figure appeared most gracefully delineated kneeling upon one knee, with her right arm extended, the palm downwards, and the bones ranged along the back of her hand and arm; a second is in the act of throwing up the bones in order to catch them. In this manner the Russians play the game."

Huckle-bone

HUCKLE-MY-BUFF, e. *A beverage composed of beer, eggs and brandy.*

HUCKMUCK, w. *A wicker strainer used in brewing.* It was 3ft. 2 in. long.

Huck-muck

HUFF[1], e. *To scold or take to task.*

HUFF[2]. To breathe upon; Hough (*q.v.*).

HUFF-CAP. Extra strong ale.

HUFFLE. Heathfield. See Cukoo fair.

HUFFLER. One whose duty is to assist a vessel to tie up at a wharf and to help in any other way if the vessel go aground in the port. This word appears to be a variation of Hoveler peculiar to the port of Shoreham.

HUFFY, e. *Liable to take offence.*

HUGGER-MUGGER, m. *In disorder; without system.*

" *We have done but greenly in hugger-mugger to inter him.*"—Hamlet, *Act iv. sc. 5.*

HULL[1], e. *To throw.* (*See Holl.*)

HULL[2], m. [Hulze, *Dutch, a shell of a pea; a case.*] *The husk or chaff of corn; the shell of a nut; the pod of peas.*

HULL[3], w. *To shell peas; to strip off the outside covering of anything.*

HUMBLE-COW, e. *A cow without horns.* Sometimes called a Moiley cow, a muley cow or a not-cow.

HUMMELER. A barley-champer, (*q.v.*)

HUNCH, m. *A nudge.*

" *I thought they were sweethearts, because I see him give her a hunch in church with his elbow.*"

HUNG. See Hang.

HUNG-UP, m. *Hindered.*

" *I was so hung up for time all last week I couldn't come.*"

HUNKS. A miserable, stingy old fellow.

HUR. Another form of Harr, Harre of Harrow (*q.v.*)

HURLEY-BULLOO, m. *A disturbance.*

HURR, m. *Tart; rough-tasting.*

" *The doctor's ordered me to drink some of this here claret wine, but I shall never get to like it, it seems so hurr.*"

HURST, m. [Hurst, *Ang. Sax.*] *A wood.*

HURTER. A distemper in calves caused by worms.

HURTS, w. *Whortle berries*, blaeberries; bilberries; hurtleberries.

HUSBEECH. The hornbeam. The leaves of beech and hornbeam are similar and both trees keep their withered leaves all the winter. Also called Horsebeech.

HUSK. A calf that runs with its dam all the summer.

HUSS[1], m. *To hiss; to buzz; said of insects.*

" *The old owl I fancy did huss and spet when I went to take the eggs! and just did scratch a gurt plåäce in my harnd wud he's old to-a-nails, too.*"

HUSS[2], e. *To caress.*

The children play a game, which is accompanied by a song beginning,—

" *Hussing and bussing will not do,*
But go to the gate, knock and ring,—
Please, Mrs. Brown, is Nellie within?"

HUSSER-AND-SQUENCHER, e. *A pot of beer with a dram of gin in it. (See Squench.)*

HUSTLEMENT. Housel; Household goods.

HUT. See Rickle.

HUTCH[1]. A corn chest.—*Lindfield Inventory*, 1804.

HUTCH[2]. The penstock and sluice by which the flow of water to a mill wheel is controlled.

HUTCH[3]. A wooden trap for vermin.

HYME. Nest of wasp, wild bee, etc. (Possibly connected with home or hame.)

HYPOCRITE, e. *A lame person.*

This word may be possibly connected with, or a corruption of the old word hippand, *meaning limping or hopping.*

"*Yes, she's a poor afflicted creature; she's quite a hypocrite; she can't walk a step without her stilts.*"

I

ICE-BONE. The edge-bone of beef. The aitch bone.

ICHON'EM. Each one of them. Each of them. (*Cf.* On[1].)

IDGET, w. *A horse hoe; called also a nidget* (*q.v.*), a Nideot *or edget.* These names are variants of the same word. The tool is also known as a Break.

IDIN. Within; Adin (*q.v.*)

IDLE. Mischievous; rude. Also high spirited; playful.

" 'E be an idle boy 'e be."

IDLEBACK or IDLEHOOK. A lazyhook (*q.v.*); a kettle-tilter.

IFEGS. See Fegs.

IKE or HIKE. A mess. (*Cf.* Stuggy.)

" 'E come home in a fair hike, a mass o' mud."

'A fair ike'—a regular mess.

ILE. Oil. See S.S.&C.

ILL-CONDITIONED, m. *Ill-tempered.*

"*He's the most ill-conditioned impersome young chap I know; a proper out-and-outener.*"

ILL-CONVENIENT, m. *Inconvenient.*

ILL SPEAK . . . of a person—speak ill of him.

IMPERSOME, e. *Impertinent.*

IMPITCHER. See Pitcher.

IN[1], w. [Innian, *Ang. Sax.*, *to take in.*] *To inclose land.* Also spelt Inn.

"*I inned that piece of land from the common.*"

An Anglo-Saxon estate was usually divided into two parts; one of which, called the inland, *was occupied by the proprietor with his establishment; and the other, called the* útland, *was ceded to the servants in return for rent and service, as a reward for their assistance, or as the means of support to those who were not freed-men.*

IN[2], w. *To house corn.*

"*The corn was all inned before Michaelmas day.*"

INCHING. The practice of the privilege a shooter at marbles has of approaching with his hands the target so that the shot is less in length; sometimes only a span.

INFORMATION. Commonly used for inflammation.

"He's got information in his tonsers (tonsils)."

"I couldn't see her, she's in bed; she's got information in her lungs."

ING. [Ing, *Ang. Sax.*] *A common pasture or meadow.*

INGENURIOUS, e. *Ingenious.*

"*For my part I consider that King Solomom was a very ingenurious man.*"

INK-HORN, m. *Inkstand.*

"*Fetch me down de inkhorn, mistus; I be g'wine to putt my harnd to dis here partition to Parliament. 'Tis agin de Romans, mistus; for if so be as de Romans gets de upper harnd an us, we shall be burnded, and bloodshedded, and have our Bibies took away from us, and dere'll be a hem set out.*"

INN. To enclose. See In.

INNARDLY, m. *Inaudibly; inwardly.*

" *This new parson of ours says his words so innardly.*"

INNARDS. Entrails.

" Doctor 'e 'lows my innards be wore out."

" I sez as 'ow er innards is gone wrong." Inwards, (*q.v.*)

INNINGS, w. *Land that has been enclosed from the sea.* (*See In.*) Also used of Pevensey and other marshes in East Sussex.

INNOCENT, m. *Small and pretty. Generally applied to flowers.*

INPITCHER. See Pitcher.

INTERRUPT, m. *To attack.*

This word is used to express all kinds and degrees of assault.

INTES, or MINTES, *w.*‡ Cheese mites.

INWARD, m. *Silent; reserved.* Usually said " Innard."

" *I can't abear going to work along ud Master Meopham, he be so inward.*"

INWARDS, or INNARDS. *Intestines.* Also internal organs.

A story is told in the neighbourhood of Rye of an old man who informed the clergyman after he had been preaching about veracity, that he thought his a capital good sermon, but he did not know what he meant by saying so much about the innards of a hog. (*I.e.*, the viscera.)

IRON MILL. A forge, finery and chafery, as distinct from a furnace. See Furnace, also:—

IRON WORKING. See S.S.&C.

ITCHELLS. Often used as a figure for closeness, of the pins forming the teeth of the hackle used to comb flax. (See Hitchell and S.S.&C. under Tainter.)

" My little boy's got chicken pox; thick as itchells they poxes be."

ITEM[1].* *A hint.*

ITEM[2]. A dose.

" If I didn't take them little items I was sure to be bad."

IX. [Ex, *Ang. Sax., an axis.*] *An axle tree.*

J

JACK. A heron, even without the addition of heron or herne: generally it is " Old Jack," " Jackern," " Jackearne," or" Jack-hearn," (*q.v.*) See also Hearn, Herne and S.S.&C. under Herne.

JACK AVILLER. A crab; Haviler (*q.v.*) etc.

JACK-BY-THE-HEDGE. Garlic Mustard. *Alliaria officinalis.*

JACKET, m. *To flog*, or dust his jacket; *i.e.* beat the dust out of it with him inside.

" *I'll jacket him when he comes in.*"

JACKETTING[1], m. *A hard day's work.*

JACKETTING[2]. A scolding; a Nowling (*q.v.*)

JACK-HEARN, m. *A heron; always spoken of as " a gurt old jack-hëarn.*" Vowel and aspirate as Hornicle. (*q.v.*)

" *Parham Park, in West Sussex, can still boast of one of the most interesting heronries in the south of England.*"—Knox's Ornithological Rambles in Sussex.

See Hearn and S.S.&C. under Herne.

JACK-IN-PRISON, e. Nigella damas cena. Love-in-a-mist.

JACK-IN-THE-HEDGE, e. Lychnis diurna. Red Campion.

JACK-UP[1], m. *To give up anything in a bad temper.*

A man came to my house by himself one Christmas Eve to sing carols, and at the end of each line he stopped to explain why the other singers were absent. He began,—

" *While Shepherds watched their flocks by night.*" " *If you please, sir, my party's all jacked up*"—" *All seated on the ground*"—" *Yes, sir, there was young Harry down here, and my brother Jem, and Tom and George, we've all been a practising together, and now they're properly jacked up"* (*and so on to the end of the hymn.*)

JACK-UP[2]. To stop, as a game.
"We were having a good game till you came and jacked it up."

JACK-UP[3]. To give over one's work.
"I shall jack it up for tonight."

JACKUT. Coat. A Sussex countryman always spoke of his 'jackut' never of his coat. Probably from *Jaque*—jacket, which word has been superseded by 'coat'.

JACOB'S POST. A post of a gibbet dated 1734 on Ditchling Common.

Jacob's Post

JAKES. An earth-closet.

JAKES-FARMER. See Gong-farmer.

JAMB. See Dog-jamb.

JAMBREADS, m. *Slices of bread and jam.* Sussex folk say brencheese, brenbutter, but never brenjam; always jambread and always honey-bread.

JANUARY-BUTTER, e. *Mud. It is considered lucky to bring mud into the house in January.*

JATTY. A lead off from a surface water channel at Clayton. A drain layer used the word. Also a gully cut through the verge of a road to take off surface water.

JAUNCE, e. *A weary journey.*
"*I doànt justly know how far it is to Hellingly, but you'll have a middlin' jaunce before you get there.*" "'Tis a hem tidy step."

JAWBATION. A reprimand; Jobation (*q.v.*)

JAWLED-OUT, w. *Excessively fatigued.*

JET or JUT. A pail with a long handle.

JEST. Just.

JIB[1], e. *The under-lip. To hang the jib, is to look cross.*

JIB[2]. A likeness, especially the nose.
"I tho't I knew the cut of his jib"—recognised his face or his profession by his appearance.

JIDDER. Variant of skidder which means caterwise.
A direction given us at Albourne was—"You jidders round by the rick-yard"— go following the round of it.

JIGGER. A mild oath.
"O jigger the thing."

JIGGER-PUMP, e. *A pump used in breweries to force the beer into the vats.*

JINGLING MATCH. Blind man's buff game: also called Baffling Match.

JINNIPERS. Junipers.

JOBATION. Sometimes Jawbation. A reprimand; a severe lecture A Nowling (*q.v.*)

JOHN-A-DORY. The fish John Dory.

JOHN JACK. Little John Jack. See end of '*The Mummers' Play.*

JOHNNY, m. or LORD JOHN, *e.*
"*Old Johnny*" *is one of the numerous names given to the ague.* Another is Axey, (*q.v.*)
"*Old Johnny has been running his finger down my back.*"
A spider is considered a useful insect for the cure of the ague. If taken internally, it should be rolled up in a cobweb and swallowed like a pill. If applied externally, it should be placed in a nutshell and hung round the neck in a bag of black silk. The ague generally hangs about Sussex people a long time.

JOINT-STEDDLE, *or JOINT-STOOL*, w. *A stool framed by joinery work, so called in distinction from stools rudely formed of a single block.*

"*Away with the joint-stools, remove the court-cupboard.*"—Romeo and Juliet, *Act i. sc. 5.*

JOIST-BEAST. A just-beast (*q.v.*)

JONNICK[1]. Fortunate; pleasant. See S.S.&C.

JONNICK[2]. Staunch; straightforward. In 1825 the word is used in a smuggling report.—*S.C.M. IV.* p. 34.

JOOK. A dog, especially so called by gypsies.

JORAM, m. *A capacious bowl or goblet; called in Norfolk a Jeroboam.*

JOSSING-BLOCK, e. or JOSS BLOCK; also called upping stone, mounting stone or horse block. *A block by which a rider mounts his horse, often seen at the gate of a country churchyard in Sussex.*

Jossing block

JOSS-UP, e. *To mount a horse.*

"*Ah! she josses up like a feather, she doànt want no jossing-block nor chair either.*"

JOSTLE, m. *To cheat.*

JOUND, m. *Joined.*

"*I jound in with them up at Burwash Wheel, and they jostled me out of ninepence.*"

JOURNEY, m. [Journée, *French.*] *A day's work. This word is spelt in old parochial account-books jorney, but in such MSS. the spelling seems to have depended upon the taste or caprice of the writer.*

JOWER.‡ To scold.

JOWL. The slight ornament at the wider hinged end of the beam (top rail) of a gate, or of a wooden pump.

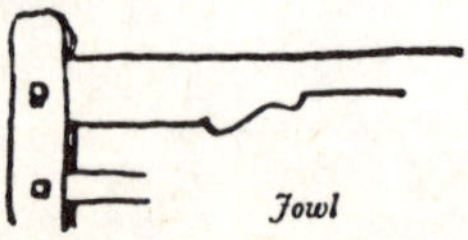

Jowl

JOY. *A jay.*

"*Poor old Master Crockham, he's in terrible order, surelye! The meece have taken his peas, and the joys have got at his beans, and the snags have spilt all his lettuce.*"

JUB[1], e. *To move slowly and heavily, like a sluggish horse.*

JUB[2], e. *A slow trot.*

JUG. *A nickname given to the men of Brighton.* More particularly to the fishermen. It was along Juggs borstal, the steep road down the north-east angle of Kingston Down that the Brighton fishwives entered Lewes to sell their loads of fish carried by donkeys.

JUGGY[1]. The Wren. Also called Cutty or Scutty (*q.v.*), and Kitty.

JUGGY[2]. The squirrel. Also called Scuggy, (*q.v.*)

JUMPING-BETTY, e. or JUMPING-JACK. *Impatiens balsamina.* Specifically *Noli-me-tangere*; Touch-me-not.

All these names as well as:—"The name signifying *impatient*, was given from the sudden curling of the valves of the capsule when touched . . . into a spiral form, and spring with considerable force many feet from the plant, dropping the seeds in the way."—*Johns, Flowers of the Field.*

JUMP-LITTLE-NAG-TAIL. Weak horses; A school-boys' game.

JUMP-ROUND-AND-HANG-BY NOTHING, e. *To make haste.*

She's a capital good girl to work, she can jump round and hang by nothing, I can tell you."

JUMP-UP-AND-KISS-ME, m. *The pansy.* Viola tricolor.

Also called Kiss-me; Kiss-me-at-the-garden-gate; and Three-faces-under-a-hood.

JUNE-BUG, m. *The green beetle*, or the Rose beetle. Also the cockchafer.

JUSTABOUT, m. *Certainly; extremely.*

"*I justabout did enjoy myself up at the Cristial Palace on the Foresters' day, but there was a terr'ble gurt crowd; I should think there must have been two or three hundred people a-scrouging about.*"

JUST-BEAST, or JOIST-BEAST, e. *A beast taken in to graze. This word is probably a corruption of agist-beast. Agistment was the feeding of cattle in a common pasture at a fixed price. In the year 1531 the agistment of a horse for the summer cost 3s. 4d.*

JUSTLY, m. *Exactly*. Rightly.

"*I dòant justly know how old I be, but I knows I be above sixty years of age; for ye see I went to work when I was somewhere's about nine years old (that was in old Mus Ridge's time) and I kep on till I was somewheres about fower-and-twenty; and then a young woman got me into trouble, and I was forced to goo away to sea; but I didn't hold to that above six or seven years, and then I come home and got drawed for the Militia and sarved ten year, and then volunteered for a sodger and sarved by time fifteen years; and then I comed back to the farm, and there I've worked for fower-and-farty year, till I got quite entirely eat up with the rheumattics, and now I aint done naun for these last ten years, and sometimes they be better than what they be othersome; so I knows I be* above *sixty year old, though I dòant justly know how old I be.*" The account works out he was 109.

JUST NOW.‡ Recently; presently (at this moment); or immediately following; according to intonation.

JUT. See Jet.

K

KATHEREN. A cauldron.

KEBLOCK, w. *The wild turnip.*

KECK. Cow-parsley.

KECKSIES or KECKS. See Kex.

KEDDLE-NETS. Stake nets.

KEELER, m. [Coélan, *Ang. Sax., to cool.*] *A shallow tub used for cooling beer.* When used for yeasting, it is called yeast- or yest-keeler.

KEG. Small cask; also called tub. Made in France to carry French brandy, holding about 14 quarts.

KELK. Charlock; see Kilk.

KELL, m. or KILL, *w.* [Cyl, *Welsh.*] *A kiln.*

"*I've been quite out of kelter ever sen I've lived up aside of the lime-kells; the reek's enough to choke one otherwhiles.*"

KELLICK, m. *A romp.*

KELTER, m, or KILTER,*w. Condition.*

"*This farm seems in very good kelter.*"

KEN, m. [*Corruption of Kin.*]

KERF, w. [*Ang. Sax.*, ceorfan, *to cut;* cyrf, *a cutting.*] *The cut made by a saw;* a *notch.* Also a long horizontal cut made partway through a board for the purpose of bending it.

KETTLE, w. *A swelling; a dark lump found in suet or pork.*

KETTLE BENDER. A quickly made dish with bread, etc. See S.S.&C.

KETTLEMAUL. The angler fish. *Lophius piscatorius.* An ugly fish with a large mouth.

"Your mouth's like a Kettle-maul."

KETTLE-TILTER. A lazyhook (*q.v.*) Also called Idleback or Idlehook.

KETTLY, w. *Full of kettles or kernels.*

KEVELING, m. *The name given at Brighton to the skate; at Hastings the fish is called "a maid", and at Dover "a damsel."*

KEW. See Queue.

KEX, e. *The dry hollow stalk of hogweed, cow parsley, and other unbelliferæ* (Welsh *cecys*, plural, hollow stalks. Of Celtic origin. *Skeat.*] Shakespeare uses the word in *Henry V* Act v, sc. 2. (52). Plural, Kecksies or Kecks.

KICKEL, e. [Cicel, *Ang. Sax.*] *A sort of flat cake, with sugar and currants strewn on the top.*

KID[1], e. *A small wooden tub.*

KID[2], w. *The pod of peas or beans.* (*Cf.* Huck.)

KID[3], *w.* To form pods; particularly, to form them near to the ground.

" Peas just do want a drop of water when they comes to Kidding."

KIDDLE[1], e. *To entice; to coax.*

KIDDLE[2], e., or KITTLE. [Citelian, *Ang. Sax.*, *to tickle.*] *To tickle.*

" *Those thunderbugs did kiddle me so that I couldn't keep still no hows.*"

KIDDLE[3], w. *Delicate.*

KILK, m., or KELK. *Charlock*, sinapis arvensis, *a weed with a yellow flower which grows among the corn.*

The employment of children at kilk-pulling is a serious obstacle to education in the agricultural districts.

KILL, *w.*‡ A kiln. (*Cf.* Kell.)

KILTER, *w.*‡ State; Condition, whether good or bad. (*Cf.* Kelter.)

KIME, m., or KINE. *A weazel.* Also called Futtice.

A lady who had been giving a lesson to a Sunday school class upon Pharoah's dreams, was startled to find that all the boys supposed that the fat and lean kine were weazels.

KIMMEL, m., or KYMELL. *A tub used for salting meat*, and in the brewhouse.

KIND[1], m. *Fat; doing well, said of beasts.*

KIND, *w.*[2] Said of land: Good; easily worked with good results.

" Nice kind land I ca's it."

KINE. A weazel; See Kime.

KING GEORGE. Labourers' name for the Red Admiral butterfly, possibly derived from the gorgeous cloaks of the 18th century kings.

KINK, m. [Kink, *Dutch, a twist in a rope.*] *To twist; entangle.*

KIPS. The common tern. So called by Rye and other fishermen.

KISSING-CRUST. Soft crust, formed when two hand made loaves touch while baking.

KISSING-GATE, w. *The same as a cuckoo-gate.* (*q.v.*) Also called To-she-and-fro-she-gate.

KISS-ME, e. *The wild haertsease.* Viola tricolor. Pansy.

Also called: Jump-up-and-kiss-me, Kiss-me-at-the-garden-gate and Three-faces-under-a-hood.

KIT. A tripod stand; see Cat.

KITE[1]. The belly.

" He loves to blow his kite out."

I.e., to have a feast.

KITE[2]. A person untidy either in the house, in dress or in habits.

" She come down the lane looking a proper kite."

KITTLE. See Kiddle.

KITTY. The wren. Also called Cutty, Juggy and Scutty.

KIVER, m. *A large shallow tub.*

Kiver

KNAB, NABB, KNAP (*q.v.*) or KNEPP. A small hill; the crest of a hill.

Brighton Place, as it is now styled officially, is still known to some old inhabitants as the Nabb. In a rental of 1665 it is the Knapp, and it has otherwise been written Knepp and Knap. (For derivation see Knap[1] below.)

" I wus comin' over Oreham Common an' jus' as I come to they two cottages on the Knab the mare started at sumthin'."

KNABBLER. See Nabbler.

KNAP[1]. [Cnæp, *Ang. Sax.*, *top.*] *The top of a hill, or any piece of rising ground.* (*Cf.* Knab.)

KNAP[2]. To break by striking. Particularly, to break flints to a predetermined shape.

KNAPPED FLINT. Flint so broken as for building, gun flint etc. (See S.S.&C. under Flint.)

KNAPPER. One skilled in the craft of Knapping. (See S.S.&C. under Flint.)

KNEB. Attachment on horse wagon to take ox harness.

KNEE-HOLM, *w.*‡ Butcher's Broom. *Rúscus aculeátus.*

KNELL. Variant of Knoll. The Knell at Wepham near Burpham, a copse on high ground; and the Knells at Beeding.

KNEPP. Same as Knab, Knap (*q.v.*)

KNETTAR, e.; *or KNITTLE*, w. [Cnittan, *Ang. Sax.*, *to knit.*] *A string fastened to the mouth of a sack to tie it with.*

KNITBANDS. See Nitbands.

KNOBBING-IRON. Implement for screwing knobs (usually of brass) on the tips of oxens' sharp horns. The ridges on the iron tool clipped into the slits cut in the knob which the iron turned round the thread inside, cutting its way into the horn.

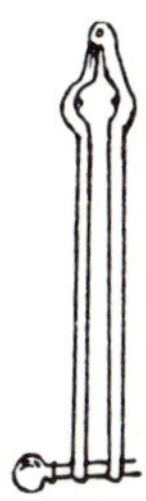

Knobbing-iron

KNOCKER. The tongue of a sheep bell. Also called clipper or clapper.

KNOT-LEGGERS. See Nollegers and Yorks. (*Cf.* Nims.)

KNOW, m. *Used as a substantive for knowledge.* (*Cf.* slang ' in the know.')

" *Poor fellow, he has got no know whatsumdever, but his sister's a nice knowledgeable girl.*"

KNOWLEDGEABLE, e. *Well-educated.*

KNOWLING. Occasional spelling of Nowling (*q.v.*)

KNUCKER. [Hnægan, *Ang. Sax.*] *To neigh or whinny.*

KNUCKERHOLES, or NUCKERHOLES. Springs which rise in the flat lands of the South Downs. They keep at one level, are often 20 feet or so across and are reputed to be bottomless. The water is cold in summer but never freezes, in a frost it gives off a vapour, being warmer than the air. Knuckerholes are found at Lyminster, Lancing, Shoreham, Worthing and in many other ' flats.'

KYMELL. A tub, a Kimmell (*q.v.*)

L

LADDER. A Lade (*q.v.*)

LADDER-TYING. Fastening the upper branches of the hop-plant to the pole, which is reached by women standing on ladders. Latterly it was done by men, the women doing the lower tying from the ground.

LADE. (*Lád*, Ang. Sax., a watercourse.) To ' lade the brook ' is to make temporary dams, above and below a hole or pool so that you can bail the water out and take the fish.

LADES. [Ladan, *Ang. Sax.*, *to load.*] *Rails which project round the top of a waggon to enable it to bear a greater load.* Sometimes called Ladders. (*Cf.* Raves.)

LADIES' FINGERS. *Lotus corniculatus.* Called also Butter-and-eggs, (*q.v.*), etc.

LADSLOVE. Southernwood. Artemesia abrotanum.

LADY ANNE, LADY BUG, or *LADYCOW. The ladybird.* Other names are:—Bishop Barnaby, Fly Golding and God Almighty's Cow.

It is held extremely unlucky to kill a cricket, a ladybird, a swallow, martin, robin redbreast, or wren. Or a spider or red spider. (*Cf.* Scutty.)

LADY'S-SMOCK. Convolvulus sepium. *The* (greater) *bindweed of the hedges.* Also called Milkmaids and Old-man's nightcap.

The name Ladysmock is more often given to *Cardamine pratensis*, which is also called Cuckoo-flower or Milk-maid.

LAG, or LEG, w. and *m. A long narrow marshy meadow, usually by the side of a stream.*

LAID OUT. Abed through illness, etc.

" Them two pore boys be laid out."—*Reply to enquiry after health of a family with 'flu.*

LAINES. Open tracts of arable land at the foot of the Downs. They have fixed names as other fields that are hedged or walled. In Brighton the several laines were five in number: West Laine, Little Laine, East Laine, Hilly Laine and North Laine. Other portions were White Hawk and Church Hill. These Laines were divided into furlongs, separated by narrow roads, called Leakway roads (*q.v.*) See Tenantry-acre.

LAIT. Thin almost colourless flame issuing from a charcoal-making pet. (See S.S.&C. under Cording and Charcoal-burning.)

LAMBSTONGUE. Plantago media. Hoary Plantain. See White man's footstep.

LAME.‡ Injured, in either hand or foot.

LAMENET. A contrivance like a very large butterfly net placed in a stream while the streams above were stirred about to drive the fish down into it.

LAMENTABLE, m. *Very.*

This word seems to admit of three degrees of comparison, which are indicated by the accentuation, thus,—

Positive—Lamentable, as usually pronounced.

Comparative—Larmentable.

Superlative—Larmentàable.

" *Master Chucks he says to me says he, ' 'tis larmentable purty weather, Master Crockham.' ' Larmentàable!' says I.*"

LAND, m. *Low ground, especially arable land, as distinguished from the hill, used in the Southdown country.*

LANDS, or

LAND-WARPS. The raised rows between the drains in ploughland. Also called cants. (See S.S.&C. under Cant.)

Land-warps

LANSCOT, or LANDSCOTE. The assessment of lands for the maintenance of the church. Now obsolete. (*Cf.* waterscot, a rate for keeping up levels and river banks.)

LAP-EARED. Said of a horse not carrying his ears well.

LAPSY. Lazy; slow; indifferent. Lurgy, (*q.v.*)

LARDER[1]. *A gamekeeper's larder is the place where he nails up the weazles, stoats and vermin which he kills.*

LARDER[2], m. (*Corruption of Ladder.*) Like arder for adder.

" *Master's got a lodge down on the land yonder, and as I was going across totherday-morning to fetch a larder we keeps there, a lawyer catched holt 'an me and scratched my face.*"

LARDY-JOHNS. Small flat cakes made of flour, lard, etc. See S.S.&C.

LARGY. Lurgy (*q.v.*)

LARN. Teach, to cause to learn; also to chastise. See Learn.

" That'll larn 'im!"

LARRUP. To thrash a person. Larruping. A hiding; a thrashing.

LASH, m. *To get into a passion.*

" *He makes me lash and swear otherwhile when he be so lapsy; soonasever I'm backturned he's off after the birds-nestes, or up to some game or another.*"

LASH-HORSE. The third from the wagon in a 4 or 5 horse team. See Team.

LASHINGS. Plenty; as lashings of beer; unstinted supplies.

LAST[1], e. *A last of herrings is ten thousand.*

LAST[2], e. *A court of twenty-four jurats who levy rates for keeping up the marshes.* That is for the Romney and Guldeford Marshes. For Pevensey they were twelve in number, called Shawers (*q.v.*)

LASUS. A water meadow.

LATCHELS. The water ways among the saltings: word used also in Poole Harbour.

LATCHETY. Not working properly.

"That ole chaff cutter be fair latchety." *I.e.* almost unusable.

LATHER. To thrash. Leather (*q.v.*)

"You young varmint, I'll lather ye if I ketch 'ee."

LATS. [Latta, *Ang. Sax.*] *Laths.*

LATTEN. (Old English). A kind of brass or bell metal of which cattle bells are made. Latten was also the material used for "brasses," and was composed of copper, zinc, lead and tin: modern brass being an alloy of copper and zinc.

LATTEN BELLS. Horse and sheep bells of latten which give a mellow note.

LARTIN, w., or LATTEN. *Plate-tin. Spelt lattyn in an inventory dated 1549, but in that year people spelt as they pleased.*

LAURENCE. A mysterious individual whose influence is supposed to produce indolence. "*Old Laurence has got hold of me*" *means* "*I have got a fit of idleness.*"

LAVANT, w. [Lafian, *Ang. Sax., to sprinkle with water; or*, Laver, *French, to wash.*] *A violent flow of water.* "*How it did rain! It ran down the street in a lavant.*"

In West Sussex the word is used of streams having subterranean reservoirs and thus liable to unpredictable flooding. That at Chichester, in Speed's map (1610) called the "Lavant Flude," is the most notable. It is now called the River Lavant and has two villages on its banks perpetuating the name.

LAWYER, e. *A long bramble full of thorns, so called because,* "*When once they gets a holt an ye, ye doànt easy get shut of 'em.* (*Cf.* Holt[2].)

Used by boys to extract rabbits from their buries, engaging their fur by twisting. Also called Follower.

LAY[1], m., *or LEY.* [Leag, *Ang. Sax.*] *Land laid down for pasture; not permanently, but to be broken up every three of four years.* (*Cf.* Ley.)

LAY[2], or LAYER. To partly sever a quick and raddle (or weave) it between stakes to make a hedge. (See S.S.&C. under Hedge and Fence.)

LAYERS. Quicks; growing plants, reared or set for a hedge, which have been so treated. (See S.S. &C. Fence.)

"I should lay them quicks and splash 'em down so's they'd grow all over."

LAYLOCK, m. *The lilac tree.*

LAY-OFF[1]. To be without work.

"I never 'ad to lay off." *I.e.* "I have always been in work."

LAY-OFF[2]. A meadow is laid off for hay when it has been drudged in the spring. No cattle—or persons—are then allowed in it until the hay has been cut.

LAY-UP, m. *To hide and lie in wait for any one.* Of a ferret, to catch a rabbit in the earth. (*Cf.* Liner.)

LAZY BELLOWS. Bellows with long handles to save stooping over the fire.

LAZY BOY. An iron tripod to take the weight of a horse's leg when shoeing him: properly called a Stanley.

LAZY-HOOK. A balanced hook with handle to support kettle over a down fire and save lifting the kettle: also called Idleback, Idle-hook or Kettle-tilter.

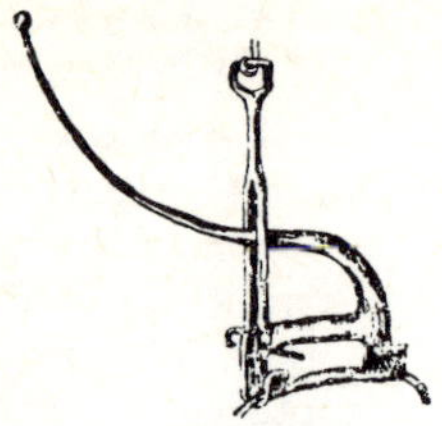

Lazy-hook

LEADERS. Cord-like tendons especially on the back of the hand.

LEAKWAY.† *A road dividing one furlong from another in the tenantry-acre.* (*See Tenantry-acre.*)

Leakway roads were long and narrow separating the furlongs (divisions) of laines; terms used at Brighton. Furlongs (*q.v.*) were sub-divided into long narrow strips called paul-pieces (*q.v.*) running at right angles to the leakway roads, which later became the main streets running east and west of the central valley and the paul-pieces which ran north and south the side streets.

LEAN, m. *Unprofitable.*

"*Ah, sir! stone-breaking's a lean job for those that aint used to it.*"

LEAN-TO, m. *A shed constructed against the side of another building.*

LEAP[1], e. [Leap, *Ang. Sax.*, a basket; also *a basket for catching fish.*] *A large deep basket.*

LEAP[2], e. *Half-a-bushel.* (*See Seed-leap.*)

LEAR. *Thin; hungry; faint.* Especially for want of food.

" I shall be glad when we gets home, I feel a bit leary."

LEARN. *To teach.* Usually said " Larn."

"*I'll lay-up for him one of these nights and leather him middlin' if I catches him; I'll learn him how to steal my apples, letbehow'twill.*"

Although the use of this word is now considered a provincialism, it was formerly good English. In the Psalms used in the Prayer Book from Coverdale's Great Bible, " learn " is so used; but in the Authorised Version the word " teach " is substituted.

LEARND. (For learned; the second syllable is not accented.) Well-read; well-informed.

LEASE, m. [*Lese*, Ang. Sax., gathering, from *lesan*, to gather.] *To glean.*

LEASE-WHEAT, m. *The ears of corn picked up by the gleaners.*

LEAST. [Læstan, *Ang. Sax.*] *To last.*

" *I've picked up a little leasewheat, but that wont least very long; leastways not above a week or two.*"

LEASTWAYS. [*Leastwise*]. *At least.*

LEATHER[1]. *To flog.* Usually said " Lather," (*q.v.*)

LEATHER[2]. To go on continuously with some task.

" I'll leather on with the job, you needn't worry."

LEAVEBE. Let be, (*q.v.*)

" Leavebe! leavebe I tell yer!" —Small girl to smaller brother stile mounting.

LEAZE, m. [Læse, Ang. Sax., of pasturage, of common; i.e. common right of pasturage.] *The right of feed for a bullock or sheep on a common.* That is, of the copy-holders of a manor on the waste land of that manor. Leaze also means land on which such rights existed.

(*Cf.* Bullock-leaze, Sheep-leaze and Tegleaze.)

LEDGER. The horizontal members of a boarded door.

LEEKS. Grass, or partly dried hay, raked into thin rows for fully drying. Also called wind-rows.

LEETLE. [*Diminutive of Little.*]

" *I never see one of these here gurt men there's s'much talk about in the peapers, only once, and that was up at Smiffle Show adunnamany years agoo. Prime minister, they told me he was, up at*

Lunnon; a leetle, lear, miserable, skinny-looking chap as ever I see. 'Why,' I says, 'we doànt count our minister to be much, but he's a deal primer-looking than what yourn be'."

LEG[1]. The last player or comer. "Leg-lapper" is a common term of reproach for a person who is habitually behind.

LEG[2]. See Lag.

LENT. A loan.

"*I thank you for the lent of your horse.*"

LEPE. Same as seed-cord, seed-lip or side-box. Leap (*q.v.*)

LET BE. Let bide. Leave it alone —imperative.

LETBEHOW'TWILL, m. *An expression always pronounced as one word, meaning, let the consequences be what they may; abbreviated in West Sussex into behowtel.*

LETTERING. Letter writing.

"I'm afraid I'm a bad hand at lettering"=the writing of letters.

LEVENES, LEVENER, or LEVENSES. (Elevenses, from the time at which it is taken.) Lunch. (*Cf.* Caoger and Beever.)

LEW. [Hleowth, *Ang. Sax., warmth.*] *Sheltered from the wind.*

"*My garden is nice and lew.*"

They say of a lanky tall lad or girl, "Ye can see he, or she, grew the lew side of the hedge." (*Cf.* Looes.)

LEWS. A coarse coir netting when used as a wind break for hop garden or for orchard is called "lews."

LEWTH. Shelter.

"*You wont find but very little lewth on the hill.*"

Also a concrete noun, a protection hedge. "It's a very good lewth"; not merely it makes or affords good lewth.

LEY. Ley farming, called locally Lay (*q.v.*), was introduced in Sussex towards the end of the 17th century.

LIBBET, e. *A stick used to knock down fruit from the trees. When throwing at cocks was a fashionable sport, the stick which was thrown had lead let in at the end, and was called a libbet.*

"*The old custom of throwing at cocks on Shrove Tuesday is said to date from the fact of the crowing of a cock having prevented our Saxon ancestors from massacreing their conquerors, another part of our ancestors, the Danes, on the morning of a Shrove Tuesday, when they were asleep in their beds.*" —Brand's Popular Antiquities.

LIDDLE. Little.

LIDDS, m. *Large open fields.*

LIFTING. A custom among shepherds. See S.S.&C.

LIGHTEN. To lift and let fall lightly, as haying grass to let the air through the swathe.

"I shall take an' lighten it up a bit now an' pick it up 'sarternoon."

LIGHTENING, *w.*‡ Chichester corruption of litten.

The Lightening schools in the Bishop's Lightening."

LIGHTING[1]. *For lightning.* (*Cf.* Lizend.)

"*There was a good deal of lighting last night.*"

LIGHTING[2]. For lightening. In cookery, baking powder or other lightening for pastry, etc.

LIGHTS. Rising of the lights: a disorder of Sussex women, which they seek to cure by swallowing quantities of small shot—"to keep them down."

LIGHT UP. Refreshment of small beer taken at specified intervals of work by itinerant gangs of sheepshearers who worked under a "Captain."

LIKE. This word added to adjectives somewhat qualifies the force of their meaning.

"*She seems so melancholy-like*" *means* "*she seems rather melancholy.*"

LILY, m†. *The field convolvulus.* Convolvulus arvensis. Also called Devil weed.

LIMMER. Trees grown up tall and spindly in a thick wood.

"These 'ere trees be growed up limmer."

LINE. Rope made of twisted hair: used for drying purposes.

LINER. A ferret with a line attached—generally or often a polecat dog. Used to locate a laid-up ferret.

LINK. [Hlinc, *Ang. Sax., a ridge of land.*] *A word used in the Southdowns for a green wooded bank, always on the side of a hill between two pieces of cultivated land.*

Also Lunch. This would appear to be the same word as linch or linchet generally used for downland terraced by cultivation.

LIONS MOUTH, m. *Ground Ivy.* Glecoma hederacea. Also (among other names) Alehoof and Gill-ale, because used in brewing ale. The leaves are often dried and made into tea, called Gill-tea (*q.v.*) A soft g.

LIP. [*See Leap.*] *A wooden box of a peculiar shape, which is carried by the seedsman when sowing.* Curved to fit the body: the same as seed-cord or seed-lip, (*q.v.*)

LIPPY, m. *Impertinent; apt to answer saucily.*

LIST, m. *To leak.*

"*That new lean-to of yourn is a poor temporary thing; I reckon it wont least long, for the water lists through the roof already.*"

LITHER[1], e. *Idle.*

LITHER[2]. (Lithe, from *lithe*, Ang. Sax., gentle; soft.) *Supple; lithy; pliable.*

LITTEN. [Líctún, *Sax.*] *A churchyard.*

LITTER[1], m. *Loose straw or anything thrown into a farmyard for cattle to lie upon and tread into manure.*

LITTER[2]. To make a bed for a horse, etc. in a stable.

LITTLE MAN. (Probably from *main*, French a hand.) A miniature wooden spade with a short straight handle, used to scrape gardening tools clean; usually kept in the top of the worker's boot.

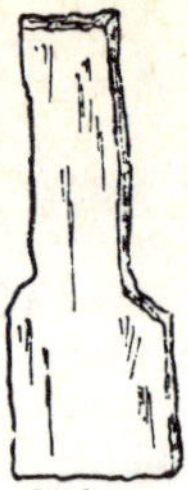
Little man

LIVE, e. *Real.*

"*She thinks she looks like a lady, but no one would take her for a live lady.*"

LIVERSICK. *A hangnail on the finger.*

"Let me cut off your liver-sicks."—*My nurse.*

LIVERY. Wet, heavy land which when ploughed has the appearance of sliced liver.

LIVE SAND. Brighton boys' name for quick sand.

When the grains of the sand are so rounded by the action of waves, and the interstices between them so filled with water that they do not pack or bind, the sands become live or quick.

LIZARD. See Arder.

LIZEND. Struck by lightning. (*Cf.* Lighting[1].)

LIZENED. *Lean; shrunk, as applied to corn.*

LOADER. The one who puts up sheaves to the wagon at harvest. (*Cf.* Pitcher.)

LOANST. *A loan.*

"*Will you lend mother the loanst of a litte tea.*"

LOAST, LOCES, or LOWSES. Cart ruts; Rowts or Trades.

LOCARAM, or LOKARAM. Linen.

"Fine sheete."—*Annys* (*Agnes*) *Pellet, will, 8 June 1597. S.A.C. XXXVIII, p. 112.*

(Lockram, a kind of cheap linen. N. Country.—*Halliwell.*)

LOCES. See Loast.

LOCH.* *The rut of a cart-wheel.—Halliwell.*

(*Cf.* Loast, Loces, or Lowses.)

LOCK FURROW. A drainage furrow ploughed across the lands.

LOCKS. Wool from sheep after tailing operation. Locks were thoroughly washed and sold separately.

LOCKYER. Wooden pegs, generally of yew, used to attach sheep-bell straps to yoke ; sometimes made of bone sawn out of sheep ribs and wasted to keep them from working loose.

Lockyer

*LODE**. [Lád, *Ang. Sax., a way; a canal.*] *A drift-way, or cut for water; a ford.*

LODGE[1], m. *An outhouse; a shed.* Particularly, a shed having one or more sides open. *E.g.*, Cart-Cow-lodge.

> "*I found him here as melancholy as a lodge in a warren.*"—Much Ado About Nothing, *Act ii. sc. 1.*

LODGE[2]. [Logian, *Ang. Sax.*] *To alight or fall on anything so as to remain there.*

"*My ball has lodged up on the window-sill.*"

LODGED. Corn or grass beaten down by wind and rain is said to be lodged.

> "*We'll make foul weather with despised tears;*
> *Our sighs, and they, shall lodge the summer corn,*
> *And make a dearth in this revolting land.*"
> —Richard II, *Act iii. sc. 3.*

LOGGERHEAD. The tadpole.

LONESOME. Lonely; far from neighbours.

LONG-DOG[1], m. *A greyhound.* A Grew (*q.v.*)

LONG-DOG[2]. To outrun easily; as a long-dog would outrun an ordinary dog.

"They tried to match me for a race against a villager with a reputation for running; but he declined, saying, 'Coo, he'd just about long-dog me'."

LONG-PURPLES. The flowers of orchis mascula. Early purple orchis: leaves stained with dark purple spots.

> *And long purples,*
> *That liberal shepherds give a grosser name.*"
> —Hamlet, *Act iv. sc. 7.*

The name being Dead men's fingers, on account of its finger-like root lobes. Also called Ramshorns.

LONG ROPE DAY. Good Friday. For a custom held on that day, see S.S.&C.

LOO.‡ A lottery; a raffle.

"Sarah's patchwork quilt is going to be looed for drackly."

LOOES. Thatched hurdles that charcoal burners keep for sheltering their fires from the wind. The looes can be moved round as the wind changes and are held upright by poles. Same word as Lew (*q.v.*)

LOOKER, e. [Lócian, *Ang. Sax., to look.*] *A shepherd or herdsman; a man employed to look after cattle in the marshes.*

LOOKERING. The occupation of a 'looker' in the marshes.

LOOK-OUT, e. *To open. Said of a window.*

"*It's no manner of use your trying; the window wont look out, for there was such a terr'ble big draught come in that father he took and made it fast.*"

LOOP. A mass of partially smelted iron ore, or reheated sow iron. (See S.S.&C. under Iron-working.)

LOOT or LUTE. The protecting splashboard counter of a beaching boat to prevent the surf waves coming aboard.

LOPE-OFF. To go away in a secret, sly manner (probably connected with the word elope). (The same root: *hleóp*, Ang. Sax., leapt, ran, fled.)

"*The old dog was round here just now, but he must have loped off somewhere, he's gone off along with the shepherd very like.*"

LORDINGS, e. *The best kind of faggots. The branches and tops taken off the wood which is being cut for hop-poles.*

LORD JOHN. The ague; Johnny, (*q.v.*), or Old Johnny, etc.

*LOURDY.** [Lourd, *French*, *dull.*] *Heavy; sluggish.*

LOVE CHILD. See Chance-born.

LŎW. Allow; conclude; reckon.

" 'E didn't low she were 'is darter, only 'is step-darter."

LOWANCE. Allowance; provisions for workmen. (*Cf.* Usage.)

LŌWSES. Deep cart ruts. Rowts, Trades, Loast (*q.v.*) or loces.

LUGGER. One who digs for lugworms, a craft of cunning for the worm disappears quickly.

LUGGING. Digging for the lugworm that buries itself in the sand, but leaves surface casts along the coast line.

LUNCH[1]. Another word for link (*q.v.*)

LUNCH[2].‡ Any meal not at table; as, harvest tea, etc.

LURGY, *w.*, or LARGY, *e.* Relaxed; inert.

" This muggy weather do make yer feel lurgy doànt it?"

A horse that seems disinclined to work is ' lurgy ' or ' lapsy and lurgy.'

LURRY[1], e. *A rapid, indistinct mode of reading.*

LURRY[2], e. *To hurry over work in a careless, slovenly manner.*

LUSTY, m. *Fat; in good order.*

" *You look as though what you've had sen' you was here last has done you good, you be got quite lusty!*"

LUTE. See Loot.

LUTON. A projection from a house, such as a bow window.

LYDE or LYDD. The lower slope of a hill.

LYNSEPIN. [*Lynis*, Ang. Sax., an axle tree.] Linchpin. Called also Prog or Sprog. It goes through the axle end to keep the wheel on.

M

MAD. Enraged.

"*Ah! he just will be mad if he comes to hear an't.*"

MADBRAINS. Equivalent to madcap, scatterbrains.

MAD JACKET. A straight waistcoat. So called in the Inventory of the goods in the Parish Workhouse at Lindfield in 1772.

MAGGOT, *e.*‡ A whimsical person. *W.D.P.*

MAGICO. A cat, usually black, used by witches in their magical art.

MAGNIFY. Matter.

" It dont magnify much whether I goos today or tomorrer."

MAGPIES. Sand-shoes; plimsoles.

MAID[1], e. *This word is still sometimes used for children of both sexes who are too young to work.*

" *Words not a few were once applied to both sexes alike which are now restricted to the female, it is so even with girl, which once meant a young person of either sex.*"—Archbishop Trench, " English Past and English Present."

MAID[2]. A Hastings Skate. That caught, or landed, at Brighton is a Keveling, (*q.v.*)

MAIN. Very; much.

" I be main glad to see yer."

MAKE or MEND, e. *To interfere.*

" *He must go his own way, I'm not a-going to make or mend any more.*"

Make amends: induce one antagonist to make amends.

MAKING BREAD. See Quilt.

MALLEFACTOR. Manufacturer.

MALT-STIRRER, w. *A stick with a sort of lattice-work at the end, used for stirring the malt in brewing.*

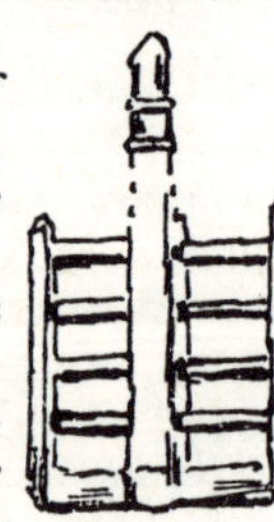

Malt-stirrer

MAMMICK. See Mommick.

MANNER. Manure. Also called Amendment.

MANNERED, m. *A meadow abounding in sweet grasses is said to be good mannered.*

" *You wunt have such a very out-de-way gurt swarth, but 'tis countable purty mannered stuff, I call it.*"

MARCHET, w. "*Every widow holding by her bench is bound by the custom of the manor to pay unto the lord of the said manor, at the time of her next marriage after she is first a widow, her best beast of any manner of quick cattle, for and in the name of a Marchant, otherwise called a Marchet.*"—Customs of the Manor of Bosham.

(Or heriot.) (See S.S.&C. under Borough English.)

MARDY, or MANDY, *w.*‡ A cross-patch.

MARE, w. *A shallow lake*. Broadmare Common: Maresfield.

Mere and mare are regular Sussex developments of Old English Meer.—*Mawer & Stenton, Place Names of Sussex.*

MARESTAILS. Streaky white clouds, said to indicate wind.

They are generally turned up at one end.

MARKING IRON. A tool used for marking sheep. It is dipped in a solution of dye, or more often in Stockholm tar. (*Cf.* Tiver.)

Marking Iron

MARMANT. A marmit, a small cooking pot.

MARMISH. The taste of a sleepy pear or a medlar.

MARN. Man.

"When I wur a young marn." etc.

MARROL. Marl. A marrol pit is a marl pit. Both marn and marrol are examples of the Sussex broad extension of the vowel.

MARS. A particular use of the word Master[1]. (*q.v.*)

MARTIN, e. *When a cow has two calves, one of which is a male and the other a female, the latter is called a free-martin, and it is supposed that she will always be barren.*

MARVEL. Hoarhound. (Should be horehound.) *Ballota nigra.*

MAS, MASS. A particular use of the word Master[1]. (*q.v.*)

MASK. Completely covered with anything, but generally mud or blood.

"*Why! you're one mask! Wherever have you been?*" "*The boys shoved me into the masoner's mortar mixen.*"

MASONER, m. *A bricklayer.*

MASS, MAS. A particular use of the word Master[1]. (*q.v.*)

MASSICREE. Massacre.

MASSYPANME. (A corruption of Mercy upon me.) A Common expression of surprise.

When we were naughty children our nurse would say "Massypanme, what next I wonder."

MASTER[1]. (*Pronounced* Mars, Mas or *Mass.*) (Marce is really nearer the sound round which the word said varies.) *The distinctive title of a married labourer.*

A single man will be called by his Christian name all his life long; but a married man, young or old, is "Master" even to his msot intimate friend and fellow workmen, as long as he can earn his own livelihood; but as soon as he becomes past work he turns into "the old gentleman," leaving the bread-winner to rank as master of the household.

"*Master*" *is quite a distinct title from* "*Mr.,*" *which is always pronounced Mus, thus,—*

Mus *Smith is the employer.*

Master *Smith is the man he employs.*

MASTER[2]. *The old custom of the wife speaking of her husband as her* "*master*" *still lingers among elderly people; but both the word and the reasonableness of its use are rapidly disappearing in the present generation.*

It may be mentioned here that they say in Sussex that the rosemary will never blossom except where "*the mistus*" *is master.* 'Tis said too that catmint will not grow in one's garden unless it be stolen.

MASTERFUL. Overbearing. Self-willed.

MAUN. Must not.

MAUND. [Mand, *Ang. Sax., a basket.*] *A hand basket with two handles.* Also described as a handbasket with two lids or opening covers. Used by market-women to carry butter and eggs.

Maund

MAUNDER[1], e. [Maudire, *French, to curse.*] *To mutter or grumble.* To speak with a beggar's whine; also a beggar who carries a maund.

MAUNDER[2]. *To wander about thoughtfully.*

MAUVEN.‡ See Morgan.

MAVIN.* *The margin.*

MAWK. A girl, usually of the teen-age.

MAWKIN, w. *A scarecrow.*

MAXON, m. [Meox, *Ang. Sax., dung.*] *A manure heap.* (*Cf.* Mixen.)

MAY-BE and MAYHAP. Perhaps.

"*May be you knows Mass Pilbeam? No! dònt ye? Well, he was a very sing'lar marn was Mass Pilbeam, a very sing'lar marn! He says to he's mistus one day, he says, 'tis a long time, says he, sence I've took a holiday—so cardenly, nex marnin' he laid abed till purty nigh seven o'clock, and then he brackfustes, and then he goos down to the shop and buys fower ounces of barca, and he sets hisself down on the maxon, and there he set, and there he smoked and smoked and smoked all the whole day long, for, says he, 'tis a long time sence I've had a holiday! Ah, he was a very sing'lar marn—a very sing'lar marn indeed.*"

MAY-BUG, m. *Cockchafer.* Also called June-bug.

MAY-WEED, m. Anthemis cotula. Morgan. Stinking Camomile.

MAZARIN. A deep metal plate.

MAZED. Amazed; bewildered; distracted; stupefied.

MEAD. [Mǽd, *Ang. Sax.*] *Still used for meadow.*

MEAL. [Mǽl, *Ang. Sax., a fixed portion.*] *The quantity of milk taken from the cow at one milking.*

MEAL TIME. Dinner time. Never any other meal.

MEECE, m. *Mice.*

"*The meece just have tarrified my peas.*"

Among other Sussex remedies it is said that a mouse roasted alive is good for the whooping-cough. Whether it is really good for the whooping cough or not I cannot say, but I am sure it must be bad for the mouse.

Local names for mice are:—Bean-eater, The Long-tailed Field Mouse, Picked-nose mouse, The Shrew, Sheep-dog mouse, The Field vole or Short-tailed field Mouse, Sheere-mouse, (constantly confused with the field-mouse). Sleep-mouse, the Dormouse.

MELANCHOLY. Much; like terrible.

"It's a melancholy fine crop this year."

MEMBER. A lively venturesome fellow; a broth of a boy; a strong man. See S.S.&C.

MEND[1], m. *To spread out manure (amendment) over a field.*

MEND[2]. See Make and mend.

MENDS. Amends; recompense; recovery.

MERE.‡ (*Meáre*, Ang. Sax.) A boundary.

MERESMAN, m. (Meáre, Ang. Sax., a boundary.) *A parish officer who attends to the roads, bridges and water-courses.* Sometimes called a Waywarden (*q.v.*), which strictly means a keeper of *Private* roads.

MERRY-TREE, w.‡ (*Merise*, French.) *The wild cherry tree. Cérasus sylvestris.*

MERSC. [Mersc., *Ang. Sax.*] *A marsh.* (*Cf.* Mesh and Mush.)

MESH, m. (Marsh). *The Southdown folk always speak of Pevensey level as The Mesh.*

"*I went down to Pemsey last week, and walked out on The Mesh. Beautiful place, surelye! No hills, no trees, nor nothing to interrupt the view.*"

MESS. Sufficient picking of greens, etc. for one meal; also the dish thereof.

MESSENGERS. Large white flying clouds, indicating rough weather.

MEUSE, w. *A hole through a hedge made by a rabbit or hare; an old French sporting term.*

MEW. [Méu, *Ang. Sax.*] *A seagull.* A seamew, or common gull.

MICKET. See Eel-micket.

MIDDLING. This word has many different meanings which are expressed by the tone of voice in which it is said.

It may mean very much, as "He lashed out middlin', I can tell ye!"

Or it may mean tolerably well, as "I dòant know but what she made out purty middlin'."

Or it may mean very bad, as, "How did the wedding go off?" "Middling, thank you, sir." "What, only middling! wasn't it all right?"

"*Why, no sir, not quite, for you see the parson he entirely forgot all about it, and he'd gone away, so we was forced to wait in church two hours.*"

Most old goodies will never admit that in health they are better than middling, or, more often, 'fair to middling.' (*Cf.* Tightish and Common.)

MIDDLINS. A quality of refuse siftings of flour—see Pollard.

MIDGE. [Mycg, *Ang. Sax.*, *a gnat.*] *All gnats are called midges in Sussex.*

MIDHURST BATHING PLACE. See S.S.&C.

MIDSTEY. The Mow or Mows of a double barn between the two threshing floors.

MIFF. To give slight offence; to displease.

MIGHT. Power; opportunity of exercising strength.

MILEMAS, m. [*Corruption of Michælmas.*]

MILE-STONES. The churches in the Downs are called Sussex mile-stones.

MILKMAIDS[1]. *Cardamine prætensis.* The Cuckoo-flowers or Lady-smocks.

MILKMAIDS[2], e. *The flowers of the* convolvulus sepium. The great bindweed. Also called Lady's-smocks and Old-man's-nightcap.

MILK-MAIDS[3], w.† *Birds-foot trefoil.* Lotus corniculatus. Also called Butter-and-eggs (*q.v.*), etc.

MILLER. The Revd. C. L. Dodgson (Lewis Carroll) says Canon Gray told him it was an old custom of millers to leave their mill sweeps St Andrews' wise, so ×, when work was entirely suspended for the day; but to leave them plain, so +, if about to resume work later on in that day.

MILLER'S GLORY or MILLER'S PRIDE. Sweeps set at the sign of St. George's Cross said to bring Good Luck to the milling and so placed whenever there was a wedding in the family. Among millers themselves the Glory or Pride position was a conventional sign of mourning.

In the days of the old common sail, it was of course necessary to bring each swift to this position every time sail was made or shortened.

MIND, m. [Mynan, *Ang. Sax.*] *To remember.*

"*I minds him well, he was along here last Milemas.*"

Also means reminds—"That minds me of so and so."

Also, of a mind; intended; inclined. As, "I was minded to do so and so."

An artist friend of ours wishing to sketch in a field where the farmer was, asked him, " Do you mind my painting here?"

" Noa," replied the owner, " I disremember ever seein' you afore, when was it?"

MINE. Iron ore itself—not the pit it comes from.

Mine was graded:—Best, Veins or fine; then, Collour; Pitty or coarse; Eleven foot pitty and Bottom. (See S.S.&C. under Iron-working.)

MINE PIT. The place whence the mine was obtained. The miner still refers to his place of work as " The Pit."

MINNIS, e. *A piece of rising ground. One of the rocks on the East Hill, at Hastings, is called The Minnis Rock. In Kent the word is used for a high common.*

MINTS. The mites in cheese, meal or flour.

MINTY. Full of mites.

MIS or MUS. A frequent shortening of Mister. A boy referred to the late Squire as 'Ole Mis Bridger.' See Miss and Master[1].

*MISAGIFT.** or MISAGAFT. *Misgiven; mistaken.*

MISAGREE, m. *To disagree.*

" *I dòant see how anyone can be off from misagreeing with these here people next door, for the old man's that miserable that he wont lend nothing to nobody, and the children be that mischieful that one dòant know where to be for 'em.*"

MISCHIEFUL, m. or MISCHEEVIOUS. *Full of mischief.*

MISERABLE, m. *Miserly; stingy.*

MISHEROON. [Mousseron, *French.*] *A mushroom.* Or Musheroon. I heard musheroons in London, when I asked a would-be swindler how much the gold chain he said he had picked up and tried to sell me, cost to make; he replied, " Wy we grow 'em like musheroons."

MISLIKE. [Mislícian, *Ang. Sax.*] *To dislike.*

" *My lord of Winchester, I know your mind;*
'Tis not my speeches that you do mislike,
But 'tis my presence that doth trouble you."
—11 Henry VI, *Act i. sc. 1.*

MISS. Abbreviation of mistress. The title of a married woman; single ladies being addressed as Mrs.

Mis is also used for short of Mister.

" Who lies in there?" I asked an Old Shoreham boy of a hugh tomb.

" Ole Mis Bridger, Ma'am," he answered—that was a former Squire. See Master[1].

MISTUS. Is the usual pronunciation of mistress.

It is very difficult to say at what age a Sussex man's wife ceases to be his mistus *and becomes* the old 'ooman, *and finally lapses* (*probably in her second childhood*) *into* the old gal.

MISWORD, m. *A cross, angry, or abusive word.*

" *I am sure my master's never given me a misword all the years we've been married.*"

MIXEN. [Mixen, *Ang. Sax.*, from *mix, meox,* dung.] *A heap of mixed manure.* A dunghill. (*Cf.* Maxon.)

MIZMAZE. Confusion.

" *He came upon me so quick, and axed me so suddent, I was all of a mizmaze.*"

MOAK[1]. [Max, masc, *Ang. Sax., a mesh, a noose.*] *The mesh of a net.*

" *Ordered, that no fisherman of the town should fish with any trawl net whereof the moak holdeth not five inches size throughout.*"—Hastings Corporation Records, 1604. (*Cf.* Mox.)

MOAK[2], or MOKE. An ass; a donkey.

A countryman says he used to drive a team of ten mokes and one horse in the thills drawing stones and flints on and from Streat Hill.

"Sometimes drove 'em to Lewes I did an' just about did make the folks stare."

MOB. To gather together as cattle or rooks do under apprehension of attack by hawk, etc.

MOCK-BEGGAR-HALL. A house which has an inviting external aspect, but within is poor and bare, dirty and disappointing. A farm near Rye bears this name.

MOIL. Trouble; vexation.

MOILY or MIOLEY or MULEY. Without horns; a moily cow or a humble-cow is a cow without horns. (*Cf.* Not.)

MOITHERED. Tried out. Also bothered; perplexed.

"I'm so moithered this marnin' I can't do nothin'." Or ". . . I don't know *which* to do."

MOK. An iron pot for coal.

MOKE. See Moak[2].

MOLE PLOUGH, w. *A draining plough.*

MOLE'S FEET. Mole's hands, a pair of which (price 2d.) worn around the neck is said to cure toothache. A countryman at Henfield has sold many a pair and still believes in their efficacy.—1920. See S.S.&C.

MOLLIFY. An Ironworking term. To burn the mine (ore) or heat it in a clamp of alternate layers of mine and small charcoal called Brayds to make it friable, and easily broken into small pieces before smelting. It can then be well mixed with charcoal and does not Tumble, or form half smelted lumps in the furnace. (See S.S. &C. under Iron working.)

MOLLY DISHWASHER. The Water Wagtail; Dishwasher (*q.v.*)

MOMMICK, m., *or MAMMICK. To cut or carve awkwardly or unevenly.*

"*Whether his fall enraged him, or how 'twas, he did so set his teeth and tear it; O, I warrant how he mammocked it!*"—Coriolanus, *Act i. sc. 3.*

MONEY-PURSE. A purse.

MONGER. [Mangere, *Ang. Sax., a dealer.*] *A man who has anything for sale.*

A field at Selmston is called The Monger's Plot. (*Cf.* Ironmonger; felmonger, etc.)

MOONSHINE. Smuggled spirits.

MOONSHINER. A beast that will not fat; a diseased beast that has to be driven off to the butcher's yard by night.

MORAL. Model; likeness.

"She's the very moral of her mother."

MORE. As big-more, or as long-more, means as big again, or as long again.

"*'Tis as fur more from here to Hellingly as what it is from here to Hailsham.*"

MORGAN. May-weed. Anthemis cotula. Stinking camomile. Also said Mauven.

MORGAN-TEA.‡ Camomile-tea.

MORT. [*Icel.*, Mart, *neuter of* margr, *many.*] *A great many.*

"*Yes, I've got a mort of children, but there's not one that's bringing in anything.*"

MORTACIOUS. Mortal; very.

"*My old sow's mortacious bad, surelye!*"

MORTAL[1]. Much; many; very. As, "'Tis mortal cold."

"I be mortal tired."

If something were not understood it was "mortal queer."

MORTAL[2]. A term of reproach.

"*What a young mortal that is; he's always at something!*"

MORTIFICATION.‡. Dying; sinking slowly.

MOSEY. Musty; soft; woolly.

MOSS. See Short.

MOST-IN-GINRAL, m. *Generally.*

"*I most-in-ginral goos to church, but I goos to chapel otherwhile when 'tis so slubby.*" See Slub[1].

Also 'I mos' genrally,' or 'mos' gennally allus does' so and so. Most used for almost. (*Cf.* Generally-always.)

MOTHER, e. *To take care of.*

"*I dòànt mind mothering the dog for you for a week or two.*"

MOTHERING. The service for the churching of women.

It is considered most unlucky for a woman after giving birth to a child to cross the high-road, or to pay a visit before she has been to church to return thanks.

Lupton, in his first book of notable things, ed. 1660, p. 49, says:—"If a man be the first that a woman meets after she comes out of the Church, when she is newly churched, it signifies that her next child will be a boy; if she meets a woman, then a wench is likely to be her next child. This is credibly reported to me to be true."

MOTHERING-PEW. The pew reserved for women who desire to be churched. It is on record that an elderly maiden-lady once found her way by accident into the mothering-pew in a strange church, and joined devoutly in the service, which included that appointed for the churching of women, but did not discover that she had herself been churched till the clerk handed her the alms-dish for her offering.

MOTHER-WO. A contraction of "come hither wilt thou."

A carter's call to his horse to come towards him.

MOTHERY. Mouldy; generally applied to liquor which has become thick and incrusted.

MOUCH, or SMOOCH. To prowl about fields and wood-sides, etc., on the look out for any spoils or profitable appropriation. Also to ramble about without such an aim.

"Go for a mouch round,"—go for a ramble.

MOUCHER. One who mouches.

MOULDER.‡ To decay; to waste.

MOUNTING STONE. Same as Jossing block or Upping stone.

MOUSE-EARED. A deprecatory term for small ill-grown leaf crops, as mustard, cabbage, rape, etc.

"Got plenty of ship-food this winter Shepherd?"

"No, ther' bent overmuch an' what ther' be be poor little mouse-eared stuff."

MOUTH-MEN. Harvesters.

MOUZLE.‡ To scrumple up.

MOVE. On the move; said of water near boiling.

MOW. A BAY[2] (*q.v.*) of a barn. Also called a Toss.

MOWBURNED, m. *Hay which has fermented in the stack.* Or in the mow.

MOX.† [*Ang. Sax.*, max; *Dutch*, masche.] *The mesh of a net* (*Called at Hastings a moak.*) This Brighton mesh is mentioned several times in the custumal. The number specified for a rann of netting is always 50, but the size is not specified as it is in the case of the Hastings Moak for trawl nets. It probably varied for the different kinds of fishery, but was so well known, or so little advantage was taken of using too small a mox, that it was not considered necessary to mention it.

(*Cf.* Cock heak, Flew, Heak, Moak[1], Rann and Shotnett.)

MUCH ONE. Much of a muchness.

MUCK, m. *To hurry; to overwork.*

"*She's mucking about from morning to night.*"

MUCKED-UP. All in confusion.

"*I dòànt know as you'll find a seat, for we be all so mucked-up this morning.*"

MUCK-GRUBBER. A sordid miser. The sort of man who would search in the dung-heap or any filthy place for the sake of money.

MUCKLE. Short straw. (*Cf.* Mudgelly.)

MUCK-OUT. To clean thoroughly. Especially to clean out a stall.

"*I dòànt think that old house has been properly mucked out for the last ten years.*"

MUDDLE-ABOUT. To do a little work.

"*I'm ever so much better, and I shouldn't wonder but what I shall be able to muddle about in a day or two.*"

*MUDGELLY.** *Broken, as straw is by being trodden by cattle.* (*Cf.* Muckle.)

MUDPATTENS. Backstays (*q.v.*); etc.

MUFFLE-TIT. The long-tailed titmouse. (*Cf.* Bottletit.)

MULEY COW. See Moiley. A muley church is one without tower or spire.

MULLER. A ring cast on the outside of a gun. See Gun rings.

MULLER BEFORE THE FORE GARTER. A particular gun ring.

MUMBLE PIN. The check pin of a woodenmole trap.

Mumble pin

MUM-CHANCE, m. *A stupid, silent fellow.*

MUMPERS. Tramps; travellers in carts, etc., not leading a gypsy life, and looked down upon by true gypsies or didicais (*q.v.*) (*Cf.* Pikers.)

"They mumpers be worse muckgrubbers not wot the didicais be."

MUN. Must.

"I mun goo now."

MURDER, or MURDER DOWN. To fell or fall a tree in a somewhat slovenly manner.

Speaking of a big ash tree which had to be thrown at Woodmancote in 1915, when they were shorthanded:—"Surelye us two can murder down this 'un."

MUS, or MIS. Mister. See Master[1], Mis and Miss.

MUSE. A gap or hole in a hedge or fence; a regular run in such places; sometimes enlarged for the passage of persons.

MUSH, e. *A marsh.* Also Mersc and Mesh.

"*He's a stupid mumchance chap; seems as though he'd lived all his time down in the mush and never spoken to no-one.*

MUSIC. Any musical instrument.

MUTT. Moth. "These clozemutts are a bother."

MUTTER. To crumble as the sides of a pit or stream bank.

MUVVER. Mother.

N

N or UN. One, for him or it. See One[3].

NABB. Kneb; Knap (*q.v.*)

NABBLE, m. *To chatter; to gossip; to idle about.* (*Cf.* Helve and Yape.)

NABBLER. A gossip. One who talks much to little purpose. Also spelt Knabbler.

NABBLE-TRAPS. Mouths when chattering; gossiping intently . . . not always kindly.

NAIL. A weight of eight pounds. A Stone.

"The hog weighed twelve nails."

NAPERY, w. [Nappe, *French, a table-cloth.*] *Linen, but especially table linen.*

NARRE, w. [Knorren, *Dutch, to growl.*] *To growl like a dog.*

NARS. Narrows. Channels in navigable waters.

NARY. Not any.

"I've looked through these stamps an' nary one o' Finlan '."

NATIVE. Birthplace; native place. Used as a substantive.

"*Heathfield is my native. I was borned at the cottage just beyond the pay-gate where there's postes beside the road.*"

NAUGHTY-MAN'S-PLAYTHING. Stinging nettle. Urtica dioica.

NAUN, m. *Nothing.*

NAUN-BUT. Only; answering to the northern expression nobbut.

"*I should have gone to Lewes market naunbut I hadn't got naun to take there.*"

NAYTHUR. Neither.

NEAR, m. *Stingy*. Close; closefisted. " I only ask 'im for a shillun' but he's that near he wouldn't give me naun."—*At a charity bazaar.*

NEAT. *Exact; full; said of measurements, as " 'Tis ten rod neat, no more nor no less."* (*Cf.* Net—net profit, and neat spirit.)

NEB[1], e. [*Neb, Ang. Sax., the bill or beak.*] *The pole of an ox-cart, or timber tug, so called from its shape.*

NEB[2], m. *The handle of a scythe*. The short handle, called also nib, dole, or handpin. The long handle is called a snethe or snead (*q.v.*)

NEEDLE. See Thatching needle.

NEIGHBOUR'S FARE, e. *The same bad luck.*

" *We've got neighbour's fare, for we've neither of us got an umbrella.*"

NEIGHBOUR-TOGETHER. To be good friends.

NEST-BROODED. Said of a baby scarcely awake.

" She's not nest-brooded yet!"

NESTLE. To be restless.

NESTLE-ABOUT, m. *To work about a little in and out of the house.*

" *I aint done naun but just nestle about house for the last three weeks, and I be quite nett-up this weather.*"

NETTLE BEER. A drink made in the spring from nettle leaves. See S.S.&C.

NETTLE-CREEPER. The white-throat.

NETTLE-SPRING, The nettle-rash.

NETT-UP. Exhausted with cold. Like field-fares in hard frost.

NEWS. To tell anything as news.

" *It was newsed about.*"

NEXDY. [*Contraction of next day.*] *The day after to-morrow.* (*Cf.* T'other-day.)

NEXT - TO - FORE. The horse fourth from the waggon in a five horse team; and third in a four horse team. See Team.

NI, w., NIDE, or NYE. [Nid, *French, a nest; spelt ni in old French.*] *A brood of pheasants.*

NIB. See Neb[2].

NIBBLER. A Barley-champer (*q.v.*)

NICK-STICK. A tally stick.

When counting sheep a nick or notch was cut or scored for each 20 sheep and repeated until the flock was numbered.

This is the origin of the number 20 being called a score. The cricket score, like that of the inn-keeper, where each run, or drink, was nicked, notched or scored separately was unconcerned with the number twenty. (See Notch and S.S.&C. under Tell.)

NIDE. See Ni.

NIDEOT. See Nidget[2].

NIDGET[1], e. *A little bug.*

NIDGET[2]. *A horse-hoe used for cleaning the ground between rows of hops, called in some parts of East Sussex an idget (q.v.)* Other variants are Edget and Nideot; it is also known as a Break.

NIFF. To quarrel; to be offended.

NIFFY. Dudgeon; quarrelsome.

" 'E be middlin' niffy 'smornin'."

NIGGLEYGOWGER. One who would act unfairly; cheat; take advantage; a Diddler, or trickster.

NIGGLY. Same meaning as Aggy (*q.v.*)

NIMS. Knee-cords; cords worn below the knees to keep the trouser legs up and to prevent dragging at the knees. To nimm is to take in, to gather with a cord.

Leather straps used for the same purpose are called Nollegers (*q.v.*), etc.

NIP, e. *A stingy fellow; a close and sharp bargainer; just honest and no more.*

NIPPER, m. *A common nickname for the youngest member of the family, or for one who is unusually small for his age.*

NITBANDS, or KNITBANDS. Rawhide bands to fix swingel-cap of flail.

NOBODY. Not one.

"I'm a nobody f'r ridin', never wuz."

NOD. The back of the neck.

"It catched me right across the nod of my neck."

NODDLE-BOX. Skull; brain-pan.

"'E ain't got no sense in 'is noddle-box."

NOGGING. Courses of bricks worked in between a frame of wood work in a building.

Nogging

NOHOWS, m. *In no way. Often expanded into "no-hows-de-wurreld," for no how in the world.*

NOLLEGERS. Labourer's leathern straps below the knee to prevent drag of trouser on the kneecap; sometimes called knot-leggers, and sometimes yorks. (*Cf.* Nims.)

NOLLER. A barley-champer (*q.v.*)

NONAGE.‡ Dotage.

NONCE, w. *Purpose; intent; design.*

"I have cases of buckram for the nonce, to immask our noted outward garments."—I Henry IV, *Act i. sc. 2.*

NON-PLUSH. [Non-plus.] Completely bewildered.

NO-ONE-WHERES. Superlative form of nowhere.

"I shouldn't have been no ways consarned about it, naunbut my mistus she took on so; she was quite non-plushed she was, for she couldn't find that young nipper no-one-wheres."

NO-OUGHT, m. *"You had no-ought" is the same as "you ought not."* Or rather "you had no right."

"*You* had no-ought to interfere with the nipper."

NORATE, m. [*Corruption of Orate; as nidget, from idget.*] With a snatching at 'Narrate.' *To talk officiously and fussily about other people's business.*

"Master Norman he got nabbling over it, so it very soon got norated about all down the street."

NORATION. An unnecessary publication of any piece of news or a secret.

"You have no-ought to have made such a noration about nothing, for you warn't no-ways consarned."

Or a fuss about a matter. (*Cf.* Bumble and Oration.)

NOWARD.§ (Possibly of Norwegian, or reputedly Norwegian pattern). *A peculiar kind of net.* Comparatively short and very deep; specified minimum 20 yards, in practice ten to fifteen fathoms long and five ranns deep. It was used on the largest boats on Skarborow and Yarmouth fares; if it were lost at sea the owner could claim ten shillings from the common fund. (*Cf.* Fares and Rann.)

NOSE-HOLES. Nostrils. Nostril really means nosehole (from Ang. Sax. *nósthyrl*: O.E. *nosethril* or *nosethirl. Thyrl* or *thyrel* meaning a hole.)

NO-SENSE. Not properly; in no conceivable manner.

NO-SURE. Certainly not. (*Cf.* Sure.)

NOT, w. [Hnot, *Ang. Sax., shorn, cut.*] *Polled; said of sheep or cows without horns.* (*Cf.* Moily.)

"Mus' Stapley he's been and bought some more of these here not-cows. I can't fancy them things no-hows-de-wurreld.'

NOTCH. A run at cricket; so called from the custom in the country districts of reckoning the runs by notches cut in a stick.

NOTIFIED. Noticed.

NOTTABLE, m. [Notable, *French, remarkable.*] *Thrifty; industrious;* and clever in housewifery.

Mr. Lower says that this word is never applied in Sussex to a man.

No, he says he never heard it so applied—*S.A.C. XIII* 217.

"*Mrs. Allbones she be a nottable 'ooman, surelye!*"

NOVER, e. *High land above a precipitous bank.* Hills or Ridges at Brighton (Dyke Road); Seaford towards Cuckmere Valley and Selmeston called now 'High an' Over' may be popular renderings of 'Highnover'.

NOW-AND-AGAIN. Sometimes.

"*I goos across the nover now-and-agin, but I mostly keeps to the road, for 'tis terrble nubbly for walking.*"

NO-WAYS. In no way.

NOWLING. A jacketting; a good talking to. (*Cf.* Trouching; Jawbation and Jobation.)

NUBBLY, e. *In lumps; full of small clods.*

NUCKER HOLE. See knucker-holes.

NUDDLE. To dawdle; to waste time in a stupid dazed way.

"She got nuddling about till she got behind for the train."

NUNTING, e. *Awkward looking.*

NUNTY[1], e. *Dressed in a shabby or old-fashioned way.*

NUNTY[2], m. *Sulky.*

"*Ye be middlin' nunty this marnin' seemingly; I dòànt know naun what's putt ye out.*"

NURSES. Wood or underwood of fairly tall growth left round the tellers to cause them to grow straight without low branches, thereby forming a good timber growth.

NURT[1], w. *To nurture; to train or bring up a child.*

NURT[2], m. *To entice; to allure.*

"*He got linked-in with some chaps as wasn't no good, and they nurted him away, and he never come back nuther.*"

NUTHER. [*Corruption of Neither.*]

NYE[1]. A slip or three-cornered wood or rough thicket.

At Ditchling and elsewhere.

NYE[2]. A brood of pheasants; see Ni.

O

OAK TREE. Sussex weed.

OAST-HAIR. A hair sieve used in oast-houses. (See S.S.&C. under Hop drying.)

OAST-HOUSE. A place for drying hops.

With respect to the origin of this word, Mr. Durrant Cooper gives the following explanation,—

"*As hops were introduced into England from Flanders, probably persons who understood the culture and cure of the article were brought with them; hence the word* heuse, *a house, was applied by these foreigners to the building where the hops were dried; subsequently* heuse *was corrupted into* haust *or* oast, *and the word* house *very improperly appended by those who did not know the import of the original*" Sussex Glossary, *pp. 63–64.*

I think, however, that Rev. J. C. Egerton, of Burwash, has got nearer to the true derivation of the word. He informs me that, in Dutch, August is called oogst-maand, the harvest month, and tracing a connection between oogst and oast, he is of opinion that oast-house is nothing more than oost-haus, the harvest-house, and that a close similitude may be found in the words August, août, oogst, and oast.

With respect to this suggestion, Rev. W. W. Skeat considers that oogst is more likely to be connected with the Latin, Augustus, amd that the meaning of harvest is quite secondary. He is of opinion that oost in oast-house is a mere corruption or dialectic variation of the Dutch eest, a drying kiln. But why not from *ast*, Ang. Sax., a kiln? (See S.S.&C. under Hop drying.)

OBEDIENCE. [*Obeisance.*] *A bow or curtsey.*

OCKERD. Awkward.

OCKLANDS, m. (*See Hocklands.*)

ODDGAITS. Extraordinary.

"It's an oddgaits sort of place."

OF. On. Just as On is used for Of, so is Of for On.

The example given by Parish for Boffle is interesting, as although both would usually be changed, there is no set rule.

OFF. Is frequently used with ' of' as " You come off of that gate." When I spoke of Lloyds Bank at a small newsagents the man said, " Oh! I deals off of them."

OFFER-UP. Try: see how a thing looks in proposed site, as a picture, etc. " Lets offer it up." And by craftsmen when making a part for a special purpose to put it in position to see how it fits or acts.

OILS, w. *The beards of barley.*

OLD CLEM. A figure dressed up with a wig and beard and pipe, and set up over the door of the inn where the blacksmiths held their feast in honour of their patron Saint on St. Clement's day (23rd November.)

OLD FASHIONED. Askance; dubious.

" He looked at it pretty old fashioned."

OLD-FATHER, m. *The person who gives away the bride at her wedding.*

Among the labouring classes in Sussex it is not the custom for the bride to be accompanied to church by her father. The bridal procession is very simple, and consists usually of four persons only—the bride and bridegroom, the bridesmaid, and the old father, who is usually the sweetheart of the bridesmaid if she is a single woman (which is not necessarily the case.)

I was once marrying a shepherd who had arrayed himself in a very tight pair of white kid gloves; and suggested before the service began that he had better remove the glove from his right hand. " What!" he exclaimed, " Must I have her off? Then if she takes as long to come off as she did to putt on, we shan't get this here job over to-day."

OLD JOHNNY. The ague; see Johnny; Lord John.

OLD LAND. Land that has lain untilled for a long time and is now recently ploughed up.

OLD-MAN'S-NIGHTCAP. Convolvulus sepium. The great bindweed. Also called Lady's-smock, and Milkmaids.

OLD MET. (Presumably an abbreviation of old well met.) Old fellow.

OLE'S BEAM.‡ Owl's beam (*q.v.*)

ON[1]. Of.

" If I could on'y ketch hold on 'em."

ON[2]. One.

" On' e' they," means " one of them."

ONCET or ONST. Once.

" Onst I used to goo there."

ONE[1], e. *To be at one, is to be consistent and determined.*

ONE[2]. *To be one, is to be good friends; to be at two is to quarrel.*

ONE[3]. (Pronounced un or 'n.) Him. See S.S.&C.

ONST. See Oncet.

OOD, m. [*Corruption of Wood.*] Like 'ooman for woman. (*Cf.* Hood.)

OPEN, m. *Not spayed; said of a sow.*

OPTICS. See S.S.&C.

ORATION. A fuss, not necessarily expressed by words. (*Cf.* Noration and Bumble.)

" *He makes such an oration about anything.*"

ORDER, m. *Bad temper.*

" *He's in middlin' order, I can tell ye.*"

ORE, e. *Seaweeds washed on shore by the tides.*

ORE BASKET. A basket used by the iron-workers to charge the furnace.

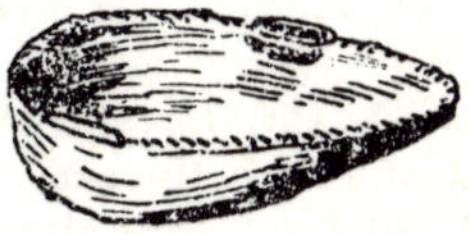

Ore basket

ORNARY. [*Corruption of Ordinary.*] (Or rather, an elision of extra-ordinary.) *Inferior; unwell.*

(*Cf.* Countable for unaccountable.)

ORRIGHT. (All right.) In comparatively good health.

ORTS, m. *Odds and ends; fragments of broken victuals.*

"*The fractions of her faith, orts of her love,*
The fragments, scraps, the bits, and greasy reliques,
Of her o'er eaten faith, are bound to Diomed."

—Troilus and Cressida, *Act v. sc.2.*

OTH. Hawth; Howth (*q.v.*)

OTHER. Second; alternate. See T'other-day.

OTHERSOME. Some other.

"*Sometimes my old gal's better than what she be othersome, but she be hem ornary again to-dee.*"

OTHERWHERES. Some other place.

"*The King hath sent me otherwhere.*"
—King Henry VIII, *Act ii. sc. 2.*

OTHERWHILE, or OTHERWHILES. *Sometimes; occasionally.* Now and then.

"*I has a horn of beer otherwhile, but never nothing to do me no hurt.*"

"I jest goos an' has a look roun' otherwhiles."

OUGHT, m. [*See No-ought.*]

OURN. Ours. (*Cf.* Hisn.)

OUT-ASKED, or OUT-OF-ASK. To have had the banns published three times. (*Cf.* Ask.)

OUT-BOUNDERS, w. *A word used in old parochial account books for ratepayers who pay rates in a parish where they do not reside.*

OUT-DE-WAY, m. [*Corruption of out of the way.*]

"*I never did see such tedious out-de-way larmentable poor ground in all my borns.*" (Or all my 'born days.')

OUTERMOST.‡ Utmost.

"I tells her she must do her outermost to please her Missus, and be a good girl."—(*W.D.P.*)

OUTRIGGER. A spar at the stern of a Hoggie or lugger to work the mizzen boom on, or mizzen sheet on.

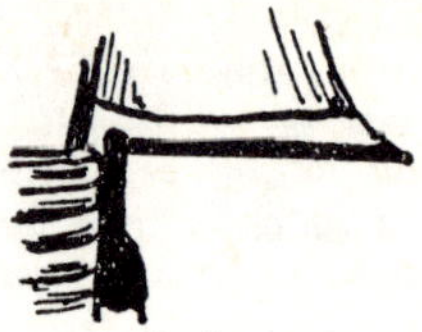

Outrigger

OUT-STAND. To stand out against; to oppose and overcome.

"*He wanted to have the calf for three pound ten, but I out-stood him upon that, for all that he was so set and contrairy.*"

OVEN-RAKE, e. [Ófenraca, *Ang. Sax.*] *A rake for clearing the ashes aside in a brick oven.*

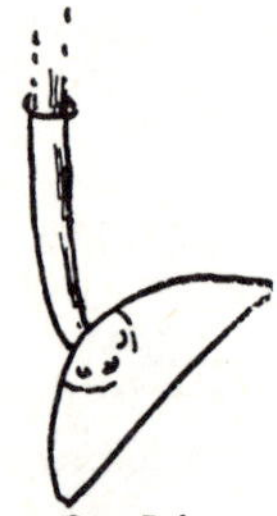

Oven Rake

OVEN-SLICE, w. *An iron shovel for taking the ashes out of the oven.*

OVER, e. *To cross over.*

"*You must over the bridge and keep straight on a-head.*"

OVERGET, e. *To overtake.*

OVERHANG. That part of the roof that projects beyond the long walls of a house, etc., as eaves do at the ends.

OVERLAY. To oversleep; to sleep after one's intended time for rising.

OVER-RIGHT. Opposite.

"His cottage is over-right the pond."

OWL. A moth; so called for it's night-flying habit.

OWLER. Export smuggler—dealer who evades export duty: first applied to the wool smugglers.

OWLET, m. *A moth.*

OWL'S BEAM. The large tie beam of a barn roof principal.

OXBEAM. The heavy wooden beam of the yoke.

OXBOW. The wooden hoop part of the yoke.

OX QUEUE. See Queue.

OX-STEDDLE m. *Stabling or stalls for oxen.*

Oxen are still used as draught-beasts; the Sussex breed being specially useful for the purpose. A team of eight oxen drawing a load is not an unusual sight in East Sussex, though it is not seen so frequently as it was twenty years ago.

Now the roads are better they frequently dont shoe the oxen with queues as they always used to do.

OX-TIGHTS, w. *Chains for use with oxen.* Attached to yoke for drawing the load. (See S.S.&C. under Yoke.)

OYSTER. The blade bone of veal prepared with the meat on.

P

PACKLED, m. *Speckled.*

PACKWAY. A packhorse road so deep and narrow that goods could be conveyed only on packhorses.

PACKY. Clouds packed closely together as before a thunderstorm.

"It do look packy doânt it?"

PADDLE, m. *To trample about in the wet and dirt.*

PADDLEQUACK. A duck.

PADDLE-STAFF. A long staff with an iron piece 3 inches by 2 inches at the end of it like a small spade, used by mole catchers.

Paddle-staff

PAD GIRTH. Leather strap about 4 inches wide to secure the pad to a horse's back.

PAD INN. See S.S. & C. under Pad.

PAG[1]. A peg.

PAG[2]. Verb—to peg. A Brighton bozzler told us, "Ye see she'd jus' come out and Muster Pärson's van pagged her up agin the wall; but she warn't much hurt."

Pag

PAG-WOOD, or PEG-WOOD. Wood from which mumpers make clothes pegs and steal for that purpose.

PAINFUL. Painstaking.

There is an inscription on a brass in Selmeston Church, dated 1639, which commences thus,—

The body of Henry Rogers,
A painfull preacher in this church
Two and thirty yeeres.

On the brass the spelling is "painefull."

PAIR-OF-BARS, w. *Rails made to lift out of the sockets, so as to admit of a cart passing through; called in East* and Mid *Sussex a bar-way.*

PALLANT. [Palent, *Palant, Ang. Sax., a palace.*] *The Pallant is a district of Chichester opening from the West-street.*

Murray says "It forms a miniature Chichester with its own four streets, and is the palatinate, *or Archbishop's peculiar."*

PALM. The bloom of the willow, which is worn on Palm Sunday. Also called from its colour and quality "Goslings."

In Kent yew-trees are always called palms.

PANCH or PARNCH. Paunch.

As a boy my brother was going one day to paunch a hare that had been shot. An old rustic beater said, "Eh! y' maun pänch 'ee." "Why not? I used to paunch a rabbit." "Elp's ee goo bad," was the answer.

A rustic will paunch a rabbit at once, but not a hare which must be kept a few days before paunching.

PANDLE, m. *A shrimp. Also used in Kent.*

PANIK. Pant; stertorous breathing.

PANNAGE, m. *The mast of the oak and beech on which swine feed in the woods.*

A copyhold right to these existed in one of the manors of Brighton.

PARGET. [*Old English* pariet, *a wall; derived from the Latin* paies.] *To plaster with cement; especially to plaster the inside of a chimney with cement made of cow-dung and lime.*

Parget has a soft 'g'. The word is not now local.

PARLY, or PARLEY FRANCY. [Parler, *French, to talk.*] *To talk French, or to talk unintelligibly.*

A fisherman said, "I can make shift to parly a bit myself, but deuce-a-bit can I make out when the Frenchies begins to parly me."

A maid servant being asked who was with her master, answered that she didn't rightly know, but she knew he was a Parly-German!

PARNCH. See Panch.

PARRELL. Cheese rind.

PARSON-ROOK or PASSON-ROOK. *A Royston-crow.* The hoodie- or grey-crow.

This species has obtained the specific name given by the Romans to some bird of the crow kind, deemed of unlucky omen—sinistra cornix. (Or *Corvus Cornix Cornix.*)

PARSON'S HAT. Same as a Chummy (*q.v.*)

PARTIAL. To be partial to anything, means, to like it, generally in the sense of relishing.

"*I be very partial to a few pandles.*"

PARTICULAR, m. *To look particular, is to look unwell.*

"*He's been looking very particular for some time past.*"

PARTWAYS. A place where several roads meet (or part); generally *not* strictly a cross ways (*q.v.*) Also called Carfax and Went (*q.v.*)

PASSEL, m. [*Corruption of Parcel.*] Used for flock: a passel of boys; a passel of nonsense.

PASSON-ROOK. See Parson-rook.

PASSTIME, m. *Time passed.*

"*He mustn't expect to get well all in a minute. I tell him there's no passtime for that yet.*"

PASTIME, m. [*Pass and time.*] *This word is used according to its original acceptation, not so much to express amusement, as occupation for the mind.*

"*I likes evening school, 'tis such a pastime; but there's a passel of chaps that comes and doànt want to learn naun themselves, and wunt let any one else.*"

PAT. A hog-trough. Also called Tro or Trow.

PATHERY. Silly; applied to sheep which have the water on the brain. Sometimes 'Patherish,' or 'Puthery.'

PATS.‡ See Spats.

PATTENS AND CLOGS, e. Lotus corniculatus. *Also called pigs'-pettitoes, and ladies' fingers.* Also God Almighty's thumbs and fingers, Butter-and-eggs. (*q.v.*), etc.

PAUL. [*Pal, Ang. Sax., a stake.*] *A division of tenantry land at Brighton, usually containing about the eighth part of a tenantry acre.* Set out by a stake or post called a pall or pale. See Tenantry acre.

PAUNCH. To disturb and break up.

"They cows do paunch about the mud so." Also poach, stoach or stug.

PAWLE. Pole or sapling used as a spring in a wood-turning lathe for making chair legs, etc.

PAWN or PORN. A lot.

"They mus' be making a pawn o' money."

PAT-GATE. A turnpike gate.

PEAKED, m. [Piqué, *French.*] *Fretful: unwell.*

"*Weary seven nights, nine times nine,*
Shall he dwindle, peak and pine."
—Macbeth, *Act i. sc. 3.*

Often said "Pekid."

PEAKED TEETH.‡ Eye teeth. *Canines.* (*Cf.* Picked.)

PEA-RISES or PEA-RICES. Pea-sticks. Rice (*q.v.*) A withe; a twig.

PEAS. A saying: "The peas are getting above the cask." meaning "too big for his boots."—above his station.

PEASHALM. [Healm, *Ang. Sax.*, *stubble.*] *Pea-straw.*

PECK[1]. *A pick-axe.*

PECK[2]. *To use a pick-axe.* To pick a hole.

These words illustrate the following evidence given by a witness in a case of manslaughter,—

"*You see he pecked he with a peck, and he pecked he with a peck, and if he'd pecked he with his peck as hard as he pecked he with his peck, he would have killed he, and not he he.*"

PEEK. To peep cautiously.

PEEL, m. [*Pelle, French, a shovel.*] *A wooden shovel with a long handle, used for putting the bread into the oven.* Also made of iron.

Peel

PEERT, m. *Lively.*

"*She just is a nice pleasant peert young lady.*"

"Baby do seem better—she'm more peert-like."

PEEWITS PINCH. A hard winter when peewits cannot get food.

PEEZE. *To ooze out; to leak.*

PEG[1]. A Sparrer (*q.v.*) A short twisted hazel used for keeping runners in place in thatch, the runner (usually twine) being threaded through it.

PEG[2]. To pin down or against something. (*Cf.* Pag[2].)

PEG-AWAY. *To eat or drink voraciously.*

In ancient times the liquor was handed round in a wooden vessel, marked at different distances from the bottom with pegs; each drinker in his turn drank as much as would reduce the liquor down to the next peg below; hence, to peg away, is to drink fast, so as to lower the liquor in the vessel very quickly. Also to work. "Keep pegging away at it."

PEG-WOOD or PAG-WOOD. Saplings, mostly hazel, used to make clothes pegs by the mumpers and a constant source of trouble with the gamekeepers. (*Cf.* Pag-wood.)

PEKID. Unwell.

"'E be very pekid these days 'e be."

Same word as Peaked (*q.v.*)

PELL[1]. *A hole of water, generally very deep beneath a waterfall.*

A broad shallow piece of water, larger than an ordinary pond. The Pells at Lewes; Pells at Buxshalls, Lindfield; and other places. (*Cf.* Dimsel.)

PELL[2], e. *To wash away the ground by the force of water.*

PELTS. See Spelts.

PEN, m. *A stall for a horse in a stable.*

PENNER. An elliptical perforated box for retaining live prawns, etc., as bait; generally boat-shaped, and painted white.

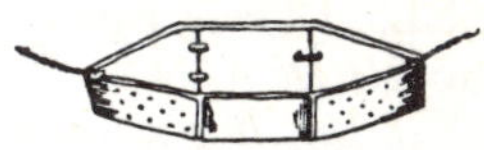

Penner

PENNOCK, PENNOLD or PINNOLD. *A little bridge over a water-course; a brick or wooden tunnel under a road to carry off the water.*

PENNY-RATTLE, w. *Yellow rattle.* R. crista Galli.

PEN POND. A subsidiary pond above a hammer pond, from which all the water could be drawn to maintain the working head of the hammer pond.

PENT. Penetrate.

"The sun don't pent in that room."

PEPPER, *e.* Paper. To pepper a room is to paper it.

PERCER, w. [*Perçer, French.*] *A piercer; a punch used by blacksmiths.*

Percer

PERCH[1]. A young tree set up to mark the banks of a tidal channel; also called a wand.

PERCH[2]. To set perches or wands.

"The channel is well perched."

PERK-UP. To toss the head disdainfully.

> " *Verily*
> *I swear, 'tis better to be lowly born,*
> *And range with humble livers in content,*
> *Than to be perked-up in a glittering grief,*
> *And wear a golden sorrow.*"

—King Henry VIII, *Act ii, sc. 3.*

PERRAMBLE. [*Corruption of Preamble.*]

" *He set to and punched into him without any perramble whatsumdever.*"

PERSONABLE. Comely.

" She's a personable young 'ooman, but jest a fagot above a load."

PERSOOM. Deformation of presume.

" I persoom you'm gooin' to Findon Fair."

PESKY. Plaguey; troublesome.

" She's a pesky nuisance everlastin' comin' in."

PEST. A common ejaculation.

" *What the pest has become of the watering pot?*"

PET, m. [Pett, *Ang. Sax.*] *A pit.* With charcoal makers, colliers, the pet (pit) is built up of the bats of wood set round a central hole to be made into coal, the whole stack being the clamp. (See S.S.&C. under Cording and Charcoal burning.)

PETER-GRIEVOUS, m. [Petitgrief, *French, little grief.*] *Fretful; whining.*

" *What a peter-grievous child you are! Whatever is the matter?*"

PETER-OUT. Come to an end gradually, as when the breeze dies away to nothing.

PETHWINE. Traveller's Joy. (*Clematis Vitalba.*) Bethwine (*q.v.*)

PETTIGUES, e. *Troubles; vexation.*

" *She's not one as would tell her pettigues to everyone, but she's had as many as most for all that.*"

PHARISEES. Great uncertainty exists in Sussex as to the definition of this word according to its acceptation in the minds of country people, who always connect it with fairieses (their plural of fairy).

A Sussex man was once asked, " *What is a pharisee?*" *and answered, with much deliberation and confidence,* "*A little creature rather bigger than a squirrel, and not quite so large as a fox,*" *and I believe he expressed a general opinion.*

Since writing the above, I find that polecats are called varies in Devonshire; so that possible the person who gave this answer had been brought in contact with some west-country folk and had heard the word from them. It is not Sussex.

Halliwell gives " Fairy: a weasel. Devon."

PICKÈD, or PIKED, w. *Pointed.* (*Cf.* Peaked teeth.)

PICKED-NOSE MICE.‡ Shrews. See Shrews.

PICKING MINE. A former Bognor industry. See S.S.&C.

PICKPOCKETS, w. *Shepherd's purse.* Capsella bursa pastoris.

PICKSOME[1]. *Dainty.* Fastidious; particular.

" She be that picksome and dentical."

PICKSOME[2]. Hungry; peckish. *—Halliwell.*

PICK-UP. To overtake.

" *I picked up the postmen between Selmston and Berwick.*"

PICK-UPON. To annoy. Choose for a but rather.

" *They always pick upon my boy coming home from school.*"

PIE. The hollow where sheep-washers stand to wash sheep; often it is a barrel waist high.

PIE-POWDER COURT. The Bishop's Court which, during the Sloe fair at Chichester, superseded the ordinary civic government. (See Chichester Sloe Fair, S.S.&C.)

PIG[1]. Pig-iron; a Sussex word which with other ironworking terms has passed into the language. The crude cast iron was run into a series of trenches in the sand like a gigantic comb or rake head with only 4 or 5 teeth. The teeth were the pigs and the back the sow. The simile is obvious to anyone with an agricultural background. It is probable that the smaller furnaces made only sows.

PIG[2]. A term used by smugglers for spirits, being a small keg of about two gallons.

PIGEON-COVE, w. *A dove cot.*

PIGGIN. A small wooden bucket like a half barrel with one stave longer than the rest for a handle.

PIG-MEAT. Fresh pork. By the word pork alone, salt pork is always meant.

PIGSCOT, w. *A pigstye.* A hog-pound.

PIGS'-PETTITOES. Bird's-foot Trefoil; *Lotus corniculatus;* Also called Butter-and-eggs (*q.v.*), etc.

PIKE[1]. A picker of horse-mushrooms, water-lily blooms, sedges, watercress, rushes for making toy-whips, etc. on Pemsey (Pevensey) marshes.

PIKE[2]. Strictly speaking this word means a bar. Turnpike means a gate openable on paying the necessary fee. In Sussex, as in some other places, Pike is misused to mean the Main road rather than the gate on the road and quite frequently for roads, now main, which never were turnpike roads.

PIKELET. A thin kind of tea-cake.

PIKER. (From pike[2], a highway.) *A gipsy or tramp.* Particularly, a foot-slogging tramp. (*Cf.* Didicai and Mumper.)

PILLAR. A large thick pile of white (cumulus) *clouds.* They indicate thunder.

PILLOWBERE, w; *and PILLOW-COAT*, e., or PILLOW-TIE. *A pillow case.*

PILRAG, e. *A field that has been ploughed up and neglected.*

PIM. Poor in quality—weak tea is pim.

PIMPS, m. *Small bundles of chopped wood for lighting fires.*

PIMPWOOD. Faggot and other wood cut about 15 or 18 inches, and tied in a bundle about 12 inches in diameter; contains kindling and sticks.

PINCHER-BOBS. Stag beetles.

PINNOLD, *e. A small bridge.* (*See Pennock.*)

PIPE-KILN, w. *A framework of iron, in which long dirty clay pipes are put, and placed over a hot fire or in an oven, till they burn white and clean again.*

The kiln our father always used was made of wrought iron.

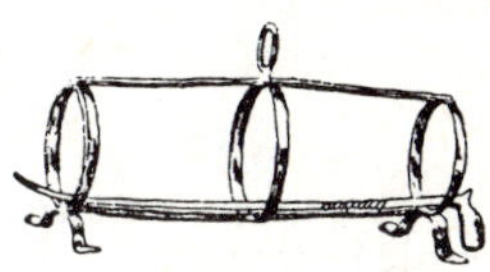

Pipe-Kiln

PITCH[1], e. *An iron stake for making holes in the ground for hurdles; called in West Sussex a folding bar.* Also when used in hop gardens called a hop-pitcher.

Pitch

PITCH[2]. To set hurdles for a sheep fold. Also to build regular walling or paving. See S.S. & C. (See also Shackle and S.S.&C. under Flint.)

PITCHER, m. *The man who lifts and pitches the corn or hay up on to the wagon. Those who unload the wagons on to the stack or rick are called impitchers, or inpitchers.*

A very large fork used for lifting hay onto ricks and waggons; A Rick-pitcher (*q.v.*) See also S.S.&C.

PITCHERS. Cobble-stones; round sea-worn boulder flints; suitable for use in pitched walling or paving. A man in Brighton told us he found a snake in a pitcher; it was an ammonite in a beach boulder. (See S.S.&C. under Flint and Pitch.)

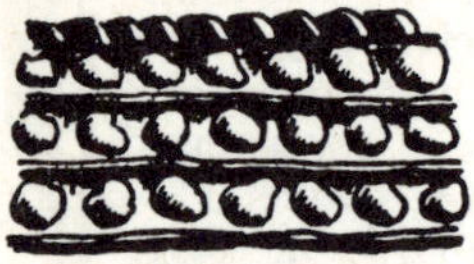

Pitchers

PITHERED, m. *Gummed-up.*

" *I've had such a terr'ble gurt cold, my eyes seem quite pithered-up o' mornings.*"

PITTAWAY. A slat-pick; a double-pointed pick, secured on a short ashwood handle by a wooden wedge; used for slatting roof stone.

Pittaway

PITTY. (Of the pit.) Inferior iron-mine procured from a considerable depth in the mine-pit. That got from great depths was called " eleven foot pitty," (*q.v.*), etc. (See also Mine and S.S.&C. under Iron-working.)

PIZE, e. *A strong expression; thought by some to be connected with swearing by the pyx.*

" *What the pize have you got to do with it?*"

PLAIN, m. *Any piece of ground that is level, no matter how small it may be.*

PLANETY. Dead calm weather with close moist air.

PLANT. Anything cultivated, *i.e.*, planted. *Not* a weed or any self-sewn vegetation

" Doctor says as I got my 'and poisoned on some plant. I aint touched a plant for weeks, only bin weedin'."

PLARIM. The fish room in a boat: term used at Brighton.

PLASH.‡ (Splash.) To layer a hedge. (*Cf.* Splash.)

PLAT. A small flat pasture.

PLATE-BONE. The blade-bone.

PLATFORM. The iron disc outside a smithy used in fitting iron tyres to wainwheels.

PLATTY, e., or PLETTY. *Uneven; usually said of a crop.*

To say that " apples are very platty this year " would mean that there is a quantity in some places and none at all in others.

PLAW, e. *A small wood; a plantation.* (*Cf*.. Plawhatch, Ashdown Forest.)

PLAYCARDS. Placards; precis of newspapers.

Speaking of a German reverse a country-man said to us: "That's what it sez on the playcards."

PLETTY. See Platty.

PLIM. To rise or swell. (*Cf.* Plum.)

" That toothache do make 'er face plim."

" The cake won't plim if you keep opening the oven door."

PLINKED. Splashed.

" The water dripped and plinked about all over the place."

PLOG.‡ To clog or hinder.

PLUCK, e. *The lungs, liver and heart of a sheep or lamb.*

PLUM. To get stiff as mud dries. Said of the ground.

" It's bin terrible slubby but 'tis plumming up with this wind." (*Cf.* Plim.)

PLUM-HEAVY. A small round cake made of pie-crust, with raisins or currants in it. The 'h' is always silent in this word in rustic use.

Dr. J. C. Sanger, of Seaford, when Government Surgeon at the Cape of Good Hope, was sent for to see an English settler. Reaching the house at tea-time, he joined the family at their meal, and on sitting down to the table he said, " You come from Sussex." " Yes," was the answer, " from Horsemouncies (Hurstmonceux), but how did you know that?" " Because you have got plum-heavies for tea," said the doctor, "which I never saw but when I have been visiting in Sussex." See S.S.&C.

POACH, m. [Pocher, *French, to thrust; poke.*] *To tread the ground into holes, as cattle do in wet weather.*

"*Mus' Martin's calves got into our garden last night; there was fowerteen 'an 'em, and they've poached the lawn about middlin' I can tell ye! Master will be mad!*"

Also Pauch, Stoach or Stug. (*Cf.* Pooch.)

The word poacher evidently has the same derivation; the sportsman regards his game as his own, but the poacher intrudes, or pokes into the property of another, as explained in Cotgrave. Or it might be derived from 'poke' (of the pig)—and mean one who "carries off game in a bag.'—*Johnson's Dictionary.* (*Cf.* Pōcuts.)

People frequently talk of poached eggs, as if they had been stolen, instead of delicately cooked (as they ought to be) in poches or bags of wire or muslin.

POAD-MILK, e. *The first milk given by cows after calving.* Also called Quail-milk.

PŌCUTS or PŌKUTS. Pockets.

"I'll putt 'e in my po-cut, Mighty 'andy things these 'ere po-cuts."—*A medicine fetcher at Hove in 1901.*

POD. The body of a cart.

PODDIES. Employers.

POINTING-STETHE, w. *A small anvil or stithy.* When in use it is set in the socket hole of the large anvil.

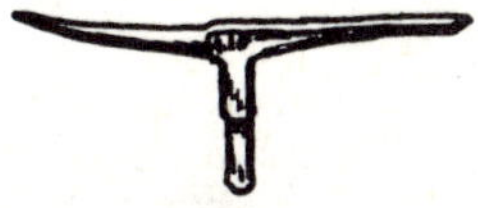

Pointing-Stethe

POISON-BERRY, w. *Black bryony.* Tamus communis.

POKE, w. [Pocca, *Ang. Sax., a pouch.*] *A long sack.*

"*To buy a pig in a poke*" *means to buy it in the sack and so to take a thing for granted without proper enquiry.*

POKER PLANT.‡ The Great Reed-Mace. *Typha latifolia.*

POLE (Poll.) Part of an axe through which the Poleshaft or helve goes, the opening which receives the axe handle.

Pole

POLE-PULLER. The man whose business it is to pull the hop-poles out of the ground and lay them down for the pickers.

In former times, at the commencement of the hop-picking season, the pickers purchased a neck-cloth for the pole-puller. The article was of some showy colour, to make him more conspicuous in the hop-garden, and its purchase seems to have been attended with some convivialities, if we may judge from the following extract from the diary of Mr. Turner,—

"*September 23, 1756.—Halland hop-pickers bought their pole-pullers nick-cloth and, poor wretches, many of them insensible.*"

POLLARD. Often said Pollards. *The refuse siftings of flour, finer than bran and coarser than sharps.* There is another quality called middlins, and also a coarser food of all sorts called Sweypings. When the Sussex man says "pollards" he is using the word correctly. Pollard =that from which the head has been cut. Pollards—the parts cut off.

POLL-RING. A Cray-ring (*q.v.*)

POLT, e. *A hard driving blow. The form* pult *occurs in early English.*

POND-BAY. The dam of a hammer pond or mill dam.

POND-PUDDING. Another name for the Black-eyed Susan (*q.v.*)

POOCH. (*See Poach.*) *To push or dig into anything.*

POOCHER, m. *An instrument used by thatchers.*

POOK. A nudge or gentle poke, accidental or otherwise.

"Don't pook me!"

POOKER. A tool to loosen earth, etc.

POOK-HALE. Puck's Hall: the fairy's cottage.

A cottage at Selmeston goes by this name, and one of our numerous ghosts is still said to frequent the spot.

There are many farms and closes in Sussex which owe their names to having been the reputed haunt of fairies.

POOKING-FORK. Made of wood with iron tips to the tynes, or of iron. The fork was pushed along a swath of corn and when full, released. Usually a woman followed up to tie up the sheaves.

Pooking-Fork

POOK-NEEDLE. The cockle in corn.

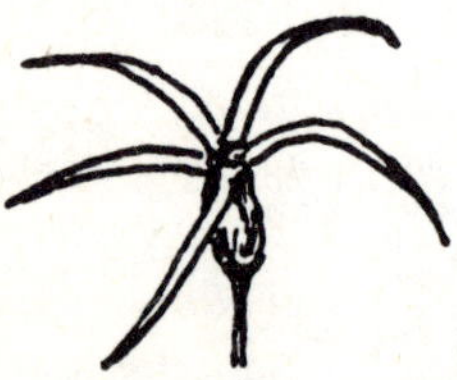

Pook-Needle

POOK-NOODLE. A muddler or one who fails to do a thing thoroughly.

POOR. Thin. The proverb "as poor as a church mouse" is connected with this meaning of the word. When the numerous candles which adorned the altar, or were placed before shrines of patron Saints, were removed at the Reformation, the mice which formerly frequented the churches were starved out.

This word is pronounced *pore* (like pore of the skin) as Spenser does in the Faerie Queen to rhyme with lore.

POOR-MAN. The Devil. Poor Man's Wall—The Devil's Dyke. See Dyke.

POPERY. Pot-pourri.

POP-HOLE.‡ A rat's escape hole, not the main entrance.

POPPERS. The small round or oval air bladders of Bladder-wrack and Whistle-weed seaweeds.

POPPLE, e. *To bubble. A poppling sea is when the waves rise and fall with a quick sudden motion.* (As they do off a pier at high water.)

PORK BOLTER. Worthing fisherman. See Fishermen.

PORN. See Pawn.

PORTBOYS. Small low clouds in a clear sky.

POSNET, w. *A skillet; a small saucepan.* A Stusnet.

Posnet

POST-BIRD. The spotted Flycatcher, so called from his habit of watching from, and returning to, a post.

Post-bird

POTATO RAKE. A thin scoop on a long handle, used for pulling baked potatoes out of the oven.

Potato Rake

POT-HANGER, w. *A hook shaped like the letter S on which the black pot was hung over the fire to boil.* Our first lessons in writing (with a quill) were the making of "pot-hooks and hangers." (*Cf.* Cotteril.)

POTTIPOLE. The right to cut one stout holly tree every year as a pot pole for use over the open fire.

But the right is doubtful.—S.C.M. XV. p. 101.

POUD. An ulcer; a boil.*

POULTS, w. *Beans and peas sown and harvested together.*

POUND, m. [*Ang. Sax.* púnd, *a fold;* pyndan, *to pen up.*] *A small enclosure. A pig-stye is called a hog-pound*, or pig-pound. A village pound was for enclosing any strayed animal. See Hayward.

POUNTLE, w. *Honest reliable.* [*Probably a corruption of Punctual.*]

POVERTY. Corn Spurrey. *Spergula arvensis.* Because it grows on the poorest soil.

POWDERING-TUB, m. *A tub for salting meat.* When ready the result was called powdered beef, etc.

> " *From the powdering tub of infamy,*
> *Fetch forth the lazar kite of Cressid's kind.*"
>
> —King Henry V, *Act ii, sc. 1.*

PRANKY. Mottled; as in skin complaints or freckles.

PRAPPER. Usual pronounciation of Proper (*q.v.*)

PRATT, w. *The bar of a plough to which the traces are fastened.*

PRAY[1]. A foot-bridge over a stream.

PRAY[2]. A covert; a thicket; a hidden place.

" I found 'im at last 'iding in the pray."

PRAYERS-GOING, e. *Service in church.* In these days it means chapel-going rather than church-going.

" *We only have prayers-going once on a Sunday at our church.*"

PRAYING-BOOK, e. *The Prayer Book.*

PRENSLEY, m. [*Corruption of Presently.*] It and ' presently ' are still used to mean ' at present ' or now.

" If I give you some apples I reckon you'll eat them prensley."—Our cousin, Kate Norton (aged 100).

PRICK-EARED. A roof, mainly hipped with only a small part at the top gabled. The opposite of Crop-eared (*q.v.*)

PICKERS. Iron spears used by the preventive men to pierce through suspected smugglers' nets in search for hidden goods. Intensely disliked by fishermen because they damaged their nets.

PRICKLES. Baskets, each holding a bushel; used by fishermen for herrings.

PRIDE OF SUSSEX. The wild flower Round-headed rampion. *Phyteuma orbiculáré.* Peculiar to the South Downs, but Spiked Rampion (*P. spicatum*) is found ONLY in Sussex.

Pride of Sussex

PRIGS. Nails used for attaching shingles to the roof.

PRIMED. Half tipsy; overcharged with drink and ready to explode into any kind of mischief.

PRINT-MOONLIGHT, e. *Very clear moon-light.*

" *He* must *have been primed to fall into the pond such a night as that was, for t'was print-moonlight.*

PRUSSY. Mincing; dainty; rather over refined.

" Oh, aint she prissy 'olding 'er cup o' tea." *I.e.* with the third and little fingers cocked.

PRITCHELL[1]. A small iron bar for use with a hammer in excavation, well-digging, etc.

(*Cf.* Pritch for prick; an instrument for making holes.)

PRITCHELL[2]. To excavate with the pritchell.

PROG. A linch-pin. Also Sprog and Lynsepin (*q.v.*)

PROMISCUOUSLY. Fortuitously.

" 'E come along promiscously like."

PRONG, m. *A hayfork with two speens.*

A garden fork is sometimes called a spud, sometimes a fork and sometimes a prong.

PROPER. Thorough. Unexpectedly good. Often said " Präper."

" *He's a proper old rogue !* "

That very fine day which sometimes comes in February is " A Präper day " but not usually a fine day in Summer.

PROUD OF, *m.* Fond of; interested in.

Speaking to an afflicted father about his little girl killed in an accident, I said, " I was always friends with the little maid, and very fond of her." He replied, " Yes, there's a many seem to a' got proud of her."

PUCK. The nightjar; also called Churn-owl; Eve-jar and Puckridge (*q.v.*)

PUCKER. A fuss. Over-anxiety, with a little touch of ill-temper.

PUCKERED-UP, m. *Shrivelled up with cold.*

PUCKETS. Nests of caterpillars.*

PUCKRIDGE. A disease in calves, supposed to result from attacks by nighjars.

Also the attacking bird itself. Called otherwise, Puck; Churn-owl and Eve-jar.

PUCKSIE. Rotten (of wood). (*Cf.* Doted.)

PUDDING-CAKE. A composition of flour and water boiled; differing from a hard dick in shape only, being flat instead of round.

PUDDING-LIFTER. An iron fork used for taking a pudding out of a pot. A spoon-shaped lifter studded with holes was used for the same purpose.

Pudding-lifter

PUDDOCK. A frog.

PUDING ABOUT.‡ Doing a little light work. (*Cf.* Spuddle.)

PUG. A kind of loam. Particularly the sticky yellow clay found in many places in the Weald.

" You are in a hike John !"

" Ay, good old Sussex pug, ain't it ? "

Also a term for a fox; especially a hunted fox.

PULL. To summon before the magistrates.

" 'E wer pulled up for poachin'."

PUM, or PUN. [*Punian*, Ang. Sax., to pound in a mortar.] To beat up; to pound.

PUMMEL-TREE. (Pommel-tree.) The larger bar of a whippance, (*q.v.*): sometimes confused with the splinter-bar as both are used with two horses abreast. In a four-in-hand both leaders draw on the pummel-tree, and both wheelers on the splinter-bar.

PUMPKIN PIE. A harvest time pie unlike any other. See S.S. & C.

PUMPLE-FOOTED. Club-footed.

PUN. See Pum.

PUNNER. [*Punere*, Ang. Sax., a pestle.] A pounder or punch for setting clay, earth, etc., as round a newly-set gate post, or over a land drain. (*Cf.* Pum.)

PURILL. Spiced sack.

PURTY. [Corruption of Pretty.]

PURVENSION. Responsibility.

" *It is none of my purvension* " *means* " *I am not answerable for it.*" *i.e.* not my duty to prevent, etc.

PUT BY.‡ Prevent.

Don't let anything put you by from coming."

PUTHERY. Same as Pathery (*q.v.*)

PUTT. Put. Often pronounced pat (long before golf was common in the South.)

" She come in an' putt 'er basket right on my lap." See S.S.&C.

PUTT-IN. To bury.

" *Master Hackleford is a man I always respacted, and if I knowed when he was a-going to be putt-in, I'd goo for sartin.*"

PUTT OVER. Pass.

" Putt over the butter. Milly, there's a good lass."

Q

QUAIL-MILK. Same as Poad-milk (*q.v.*)

QUAINT. [*For acquainted.*]

QUALITY[1], w. *This word occurs in old parochial account books for a kind of tape.*

QUALITY[1]. The gentlefolk and nobility.

When sympathising with some neighbours whose house caught fire a villager said to me, "You needn't worry Miss, they aint the quality."—Lindfield, 1924.

QUALIVER. (Caliver.) A hand gun.

"Ten qualivers with their flashes and touch boxes."—Brighton Custumal, 1580.

QUANT. See Quont.

QUARREL-PICKER. A glazier, particularly one dealing with leaded squares or lozenge-paned windows. Often used contemptuously.

QUARTERING, w. *The wooden framing of a house, the upper story of which is made of wood-work covered with tiles.*

Or rather the sawn timber of which the framing is made. Formerly smaller trees and large branches were pit sawn in quarters and one edge made roughly paralled with the adze for this purpose.

QUEASY. Nervous; squeamish.

QUEER, m. *To puzzle.*

"*It has queered me for a long time to find out who that man is; and my mistus she's been quite in a quirk over it. He do'ant seem to be quaint with nobody, and he do'aint seem to have no business, and for all that he's always to and thro', to and thro', for everlastin'.*"

QUERN, w. [Cwéorn, *Ang. Sax., a mill.*] *A hand-mill to grind malt.*

"*Are you not he*
That frights the maidens of the villag'ry,
Skim milk, and sometimes labour in the quern?"
—Midsummer Night's Dream, *Act ii. sc. 1.*

QUEST, e. *To give tongue like a hound.*

QUEUES. (So called because of their shape.) Ox-shoes. Spelt also Cue and Kew.

Queues

QUEUE NAILS. Nails for attaching the Queue. They are straight along the top, and look like miniature walking sticks $1\frac{3}{4}$ inches long.

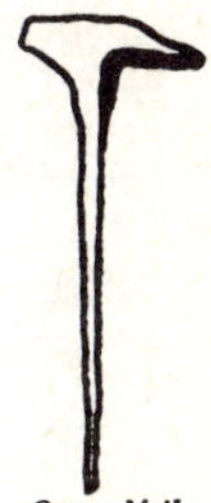

Queue Nail

QUICK[1], w. *Pregnant.*

"*Faith, unless you play the honest Trojan, the poor wench is cast away; she's quick.*"
—Love's Labour Lost, *Act v. sc. 2.*

QUICK[2]. [Cwic, *Ang. Sax., living.*] *Alive.* "*I thought that the sheep was dead when I first saw it, but I found it was quick still.*"

QUICK[3]. *To hurry; used actively and reflexively.* "*I'll quick him fast enough if he doesn't quick himself a little more.*"

QUICK[4]. *An expression applied to the sands when they are insecure from not being sufficiently firm and dry.*

Quick sand is live sand; active. The Brighton boys call it Live sand (*q.v.*)

"*You should not ride on the sands so soon after the tide has turned, for they are sure to be quick and shifting.*"

QUICKS. Growing plants reared or set for a hedge. See Layer, and S.S. & C. under Hedge and Fence.

QUID. *A cud.*

QUIDDY, e. [Que dis tu? *French.*] *What do you say?*

"*Quiddy? I didn't hear what you said.*"

QUID-WORM.‡ A centipede.

QUILER-HARNESS, w. *The trace-harness.*

This is a misapprehension. Quiler harness is worn by the Thill-horse or wheeler, Trace harness by the leaders.

QUILERS, OR QUOILERS, w. *Part of the harness of a cart horse; the breeching.* Its function is to hold back the cart or wagon when going downhill and for backing. The word means queller. (*Cwellere*, Ang. Sax., a killer, a queller.)

QUILL[1], w. *A spring of water* (*Variation of Well.*)

QUILL[2]. A pipe taking water from land, not otherwise drained under the head water of a mill to a counter drain discharging below the mill.

QUILLY, m. *The roughness of the skin produced by cold, sometimes described as goose-flesh;* or goose-skin.

QUILT. To claw and pound with the paws, as cats do upon a carpet; also called "making-bread." When the cat makes bread it is a sign of rain. Also to beat.

QUIRK, m. *A fuss; a whim; a fancy.*

"*I may chance have some odd quirks and remnants of wit broken on me, because I have railed so long at marriage . . . When I said I should die a batchelor, I did not think I should live till I were marry'd.*"

—Much Ado About Nothing, *Act ii, sc. 3.*

QUOILERS. See Quilers.

QUONT, or QUANT. [*Compare* contus, *Latin.*] *A barge-pole*, with a divided end; also a punt pole.

Quont

QUOTTED. Satiated; glutted.

QUYER. Enquire.—*On a journey—*

"I thought 'twas time to quyer."

R

R is very little sounded in Sussex, especially the final r. So roar is sounded like raw, pour like paw, and so forth. The indescribable word ARR, (AH !) frequently a sentence in itself and infinitely varied by intonation, is used to express almost any sentiment.

RABBITS, e. *An ejaculation.*

"*What the rabbits ! Why, it's never you out in such weather as this, surelye !*"

RABBIT'S-MEAT, m. *Wild parsley.* Anthriscus sylvestris.

Usually known as the wild beaked-parsley on account of its smooth, shortly-beaked fruit.

RABBIT-SPEAR. An iron rod for probing to locate hole or its direction.

Rabbit-Spear

RACKETTING-RIDDLE, w. [Hriddel, *Ang. Sax., a sieve.*] *A cane-bottomed sieve.*

RACKON, m. [*Corruption of Reckon.*] (*q.v.*)

"*The fire burns middlin' rash; I rackon 'tis because 'tis so frosty.*"

RACK-UP. To supply horses with their food for the night. I.e. to put the food or fodder up into the rack.

RAD [*Corruption of Rod.*] *The shaft of a cart; a measure of 16½ feet, by which distance is more frequently measured than by yards, as elsewhere.* Forty rods—1 furlong, 1/8th of a mile.

RADDLES. [*Diminutive of Rod.*] *Long supple sticks of green wood interwoven between upright stakes to make a hedge.* (See S.S. & C. under Hedge and fence.)

RADDLE or RATTLE *AND DAB. Frame-work of timber filled in with* wattle and *mortar*, or with wattle and mud.

RADDLE-FENCE, e. *A hedge made with raddles.* (See S.S. & C. under Hedge and fence.)

RADES, w. *The rails of a wagon.*

RADICAL, e. *Tiresome; Disobedient.* A radical is a bad, mischievous lad.

"*He's that radical that I dòànt know whatever'll become an him. I've told him adunnamany times not to ride on the rads, but 'tis no use what you says to him.*"

RAFTY[1], e. *Very.*

RAFTY[2], w. *Ill-tempered; difficult to manage.*

RAFTY[3]. Fusty; rancid. (*Cf.* Reesty.)

RAGGED-JACK[1], e. *Scotch kale.*

RAGGED-JACK[2], e. *Ragged robin.* Lychnis flos-cuculi.

RAINIFIED.‡ Likely to rain.

"It looks very rainified."

RAKE[1], e. *The sea is said to rake when it breaks on the shore with a long grating sound.* Or rather when the draw-back or under-tow makes a loud noise rolling the shingles generally; the sign of heavy weather at sea and more to come.

RAKE[2]. "*As lean as a rake*" *is a common proverb among Sussex people, who use the word in the same sense as in the following passage*—

"*Let us revenge this with our pikes, ere we become rakes; for the gods know, I speak this in hunger for bread, not in thirst for revenge.*"—Coriolanus, *Act i, sc. 1.*

"*As lene was his horse as is a rake.*"—Chaucer, *Prol. I. 287.*

RAKE[3]. See Oven-rake.

RAKE-COMB. A Comb used by thatchers to dress the sides of rick and thatching; used also as a measure for squaring up the work to ascertain the pay due. It is generally made with long wire nails and marked off in feet from the tined end.

Rake-Comb

RAMP, e. *To grow rapidly and luxuriantly.*

RAMSHACKLE, *m.* A petting term of endearment of mother to baby.

"You're a little ramshackle arn't yer ?"

RAMSHORNS. *Orchis mascula.* See Long-purples.

RANDY. Restive, especially of a horse.

RANDYPOLL. Rascal; boisterous person; frisking dog; etc.

"Down ! down ! you little randypoll !"—*To a barking, over-attentive dog.*

RANIER, or RANIOR. (*Ran,* Romany, a rod.) A gypsy-tent rod.

RANK. Smoke. (This is probably a printer's error for Rauk.)

RANN.† (Run, in the sense lenth.) *A division of a net. Nets are ordered to be* "*in deepness two ranns, every rann fifty moxes deep.*" Or rather a measure of netting. The large fishing nets are made up in lengths, and 2, 3, 4, 5 or more of these lengths are joined together, one above the other, to make up the net. In the *Brighton Custumal* the nets are specified as of such a length in the top rann and so many ranns deep for the various kinds of fishery. The ranns are always specified as of 50 moxes deep. If a net less than the specified dimensions (other than one damaged at sea and not yet landed) were found in a boat the owner of the net would be fined. This was because the fisherman taking nets to sea earned a share of the catch for a specified number of nets so taken. (*Cf.* Cock heak, Flew, Heak, Mox, Norward and Shares.)

*RAP-AND-RUN, or RAP-AND-REND.** [*Icel.* hrapa, *To rush head-long.*] *To seize and plunder ; to seize hold of everything one can.*

RAPE. [Hreppr, *Icelandic.*] *A division of a county comprising several hundreds.*

The Normans divided the county of Sussex into six rapes—Hastings, Pevensey and Lewes, in East Sussex;

Bramber, Arundel, and Chichester, in West Sussex. Each of these rapes had a castle near the coast, and an available harbour at its southern extremity, and formed what was called " a high road to Normandy."

RAPE GREENS. The tops of swede turnips, cooked like spinach.

RAPID. Violent; severe.

" 'Is pain was that rapid we 'ad the doctor at onst."

RARE[1], m. [Hrére, *Ang. Sax.*, *raw.*] *Underdone.*

RARE[2]. Notable; considerable.

" Putt on some holly, (to make the bonfire burn up) there's a rare body o' grease in holly."

RASH[1]. [Ræsc, *Ang. Sax.*, *a flash.*] *Fierce and clear; said of a fire in frosty weather.*

> " *His rash fierce blaze of riot cannot last,*
> *For violent fires soon burn out themselves*"
> —Richard II., *Act ii. sc. 1.*

RASH[2]. Quickly; as cooked too rash—burnt outside and raw within.

RATCH. To stretch. (*Cf.* Wratch.)

RATHE.‡ *Early; as rathe in the morning.* (*Ray.*)

RATHER-RIPE. [Hræth, *Ang. Sax.*, *early.*] *The name of an apple which ripens early.* Generally spelt "ratheripe", and pronounced " rath'ripe." (*Cf.* Rathe above.)

RAT'S RAMBLE. Deprecatory term for poor land. A rat would have to ramble about and hunt well before he could satisfy his hunger. Paythorne Farm, Fulking, was so called.

RATTLE AND DAB. Wattle and daub. (*Cf.* Raddle and dab.)

RATTLEBONE. Worn out; tumbling to pieces.

RAUK, or *RANK* ? [*Réc, reác, roec,* Ang. Sax., smoke, reek, vapour.] Smoke. (*Cf.* Reek, Roke.)

RAVE-CART. A common cart fitted with raves. I.e. so built that raves may be fitted, the raves being detachable. (*Cf.* Dung-cart raves and Raves.)

RAVEN. The cormorant. Called in West Sussex a Shag.

RAVES. Two frames of wood which are laid on the top of a wagon in such a way as to meet in the middle and project on all sides beyond the body of the vehicle, so as to enable it to carry a larger load. Or rather, are set at the front and rear projecting upwards and outwards, but not at the sides. (*Cf.* Lades, Ravecart and Sideboards.)

Raves

RAYTHER. Rather.

RAZZLE. A scolding.

" Missus 'ull fair razzle me if I'm late for dinner."

REACH. A long stretch of space.

" There's a reach of parkland there."

REAFE. [Reáfian, *Ang. Sax.*, *to seize; seize upon.*] *To anticipate pleasure; to long for the accomplishment of anything; to speak continually on the same subject.*

REAPHOOK, RIPHOOK, REAPINGHOOK. A sickle-shaped corncutter with a serrated edge. It is used in the reverse direction to that of a sickle and is put behind the stalks to be cut, then drawn towards one backwards from left to right.

Reaphook

REARING-FEAST. *A feast given to the workmen when the roof is reared or put on the house.* There is a similar custom known as "wetting the top brick." When the topmost brick was laid on the chimney of a house under construction it was the custom for the builder to stand drinks all round to the bricklayers.

REBEL. A long-handled hoe with a large square blade used by charcoal burners.

Rebel

REBELLIOUS. [*Corruption of bilious.*]

"*I should be very much obliged for a few of them rebellious pills.*"

RECEVYOUR. The Port-reeve or Bailiff of Pevensey.

RECKON, m. *To suppose. A Sussex man uses the expression, "I reckon" as often as an American uses "I guess."*

Usually pronounced "rackon", but sometimes said "riggin"; see Riggin[2].

> "*Did put the yoke upon us; which to shake off,*
> *Becomes a warlike people, whom we reckon*
> *Ourselves to be.*"
> —Cymbeline, *Act iii. sc. 1.*

RECOLLECTS, e. *Memory.*

"*I quite lost my recollects, and the doctor he redeemed it was through along of the fever.*"

REDDING. A glade in a wood; a clearing.

REDEEM, m. [*Corruption of Deem.*] *To consider; to give an opinion.*

REEDER. A leather wedge or washer used to secure and adjust sheep bells.

REEK, m. [Reác, *Ang. Sax.*, *smoke.*] *Fog or mist rising from the marsh.* (*Cf.* Rauk; Roke.)

> "*You common cry of curs! Whose breath I hate*
> *As reek of the rotten fens.*"
> —Coriolanus, *Act iii. sc. 3.*

REESTY, REISTY or RUSTY. Applied to bacon going rotten inside. (*Cf.* Rafty[3].)

REEVE. [Ge-réfa, *Ang. Sax.*] *A bailiff; an officer of the lord of the manor.*

REFUGE[1], e. *To separate the inferior sheep or lambs from the flock.*

REFUGE[2]. [*Corruption of Refuse.*] *Worthless; unsaleable.*

RELATIONS. A phrase indicating the loosened tongue.

An old farmer dispensing some old bottled cider, said to me, an appreciative youngster,

"Look 'ere young man, you be careful! if you drink much of that you prensley begin to talk about your Relations!"

RENDER[1]. *To give the finishing coat of plaster to a wall.*

RENDER[2]. The setting of a splice, grommet, bend or knot.

RERE. (Rare.) Unusual: excessive.

REVE, or *REVES*, m. *Rent or tithes. The fishermen at Brighton are liable to pay six mackerel as reves each time they return from mackerel fishing.*

REW. A rough hedge and ditch division between fields. The same meaning as shaw. Also spelt rue.

REYNOLDS. "*Mus Reynolds*" *is the name given to the fox. When I was first told that "Mus Reynolds come along last night" he was spoken of so intimately that I supposed he must be some old friend, and expressed a hope that he had been hospitably received. "He helped hisself," was the reply; and thereupon followed the explanation, illustrated by an exhibition of mutilated poultry.*

RHEUMATTICS. *A woman once said to me, "There's so many new complaints now-a-days to what there used to be; there's this here rheumatism there's so much talk about. When I was a gal 'twas the rheumattics, and I doänt know as there's much odds in it now—naun but if you wants to cure the rheumatism you wants a lot of doctor's stuff; but for my part, if ever I be troubled with the rheumattics (and I be quite eat-up otherwhile) I goos out and steals a tater, and carries it in my pocket till the rheumattics be gone.*"

Many carry a potato (better if stolen) for rheumatism even now (1920). A neighbour of ours at Lindfield always carried one in his trouser pocket.

RIB-LADE, w. *The bar on the side of a wagon parallel with the lade.*

RIB-SHOVEL. A kind of scoop rake used for picking up charcoal.

RIBSPARE. Spare rib.—*Lindfield Inventory, 1804.*

RICE, w; *RICE-HEADING*, e. [Hrís, *Ang. Sax., a twig.*] *Underwood cut sufficiently young to bear winding into hedges or hurdles ...* or the tops of trees; brushwood. See Pea-rises, and S.S. & C. under Hedge and fence.

RICKLE. From 12 to 16 stooks of corn form one rickle. Sometimes called hut.

RICK-PITCHER. A large pitchfork used for lifting hay from the ground to the rick. (See S.S. & C. under Pitch—Pitcher.)

Rick-pitcher

RICKSTEDDLE[1]. m. [Hreac *and* Stéde, *Ang. Sax., a rick place.*] *An enclosure for corn or hay ricks.* Rick steading or standing.

RICKSTEDDLE[2], w. *A wooden frame placed on stones on which to build the ricks,* in order to keep the ricks ventilated, the bottom hay dry and preventing rats and mice getting in. (See Steddle, treddle and S.S. & C. under Steddle.)

RIDDER, e. [Hridder, *Ang. Sax.*] *An oblong coarse wire sieve used with a blower for winnowing corn, the ridder being moved to and fro on a stake in front of the blower.*

RIDDLE, w. [Hriddel, *Ang. Sax.*] *A large sieve for sifting wheat in a barn ...* or for sifting ashes. Sieves generally are called riddles.

RIDE[1], m. *Any bridle-road, but generally a green way through furze or woodland.*

RIDE[2], e. *A rut, or wheel mark.* Also trades (*q.v.*) etc.

RIDE[3], m. *To be a burden.*

"*I didn't want to ride the club, so I declared off.*"

RIDE-HORSE, e. *A saddle-horse.*

RIDES, e. *The iron hinges on a gate by which it is hung to the post and so swings or rides.* Strictly, that part of a ride-hinge which differentiates it from other hinges; the ride or rides being the part or parts which stretch or ride to distribute the load. Gates commonly have one ride hinge at the top and one ear hinge at the bottom. On doors, and particularly on Church doors the rides may be very highly ornamented. Really a technical term and not provincial.

RIDGE-BAND, e; RIDGER; *RIDGE-STAY*, w., or RIDGE-TIE. Back-band. [Hryg, *Ang. Sax., the back.*] *That part of the harness which goes over the saddle* (pad) *on the horse's back, and being fastened on both sides, supports the shafts of the cart.* These terms are not exactly synonymous. Though sometimes indifferently used, generally Ridge-band is a strap for the light harness of a dog-cart or trap; Ridger or Ridge-stay is an iron yoke with a chain at each end for tip carts etc. where the unbalanced load may at times be considerable. Ridge-tie is most often used of a continuous chain, generally of double or triple interlinked curb type, used on wagon and chain trace harness where only a small load is supported.

RIDGE-BONE. The weather boarding on the outside of wooden houses, common in Sussex and Kent. Sometimes called Ridge-laves.

RIDGER. A chain or yoke that takes the weight of the thills or shafts. See Ridge-band above.

RIDGE-TY, *w.*‡ or RIDGETY HOOK. The hook on the thills to which the ridge-stay is secured.

RIFE, w. *A ditch on the moorland.* (*See Rythe.*) Also a level for draining. *E.g.* Pagham rife, from which the high tide is excluded by the sluice, and which drains at low tide.

RIFLE. Mower's tool made of steel for smoothing or setting edge of scythe. (*Cf.* Ripe-stick.)

RIGGIN[1]. Rig out. Clothes; attire generally.

RIGGIN[2]. Reckon (*q.v.*)

"You can riggin her out if you reads this 'ere letter of 'ers."

RIND. To bark trees as rabbits and goats do. See Rining.

RINDLE. To place undried bricks in a herring-bone pattern on the drying racks. (*Cf.* Hack[2] and Skintle.)

RINGER[1]. The iron rod used by furnace men.

RINGER[2]. A quoit that, when thrown, settles on the hob or pin.

RING-FLINTS or RINGING FLINTS. Long flints that will give bell-like notes.

RINGLE[1]. [*Diminutive of Ring.*] *A small ring, such as that put into the snout of a pig to prevent him from rooting up the floor of his sty.*

I find among the manorial customs the following regulation,—" It is also ordained that every one do yoke or ring his hogs before the feast of St. Michael the Archangel next, and the same keep so yoked or ringed until the feast of St. John the Baptist then next following, under pain of forfeiting to the lord, for every hog, for every week, 3s. 4d."

Ringles Cross, Uckfield, so called probably because a "little ring" once formed part of the cross.—*Mawer and Stenton, Place-names of Sussex*, p. 397.

RINGLE[2], m. *To put rings in hogs' snouts.* And when this is done the hogs are ringled. Ringled also means married.

RINING. (Rinding.) Stripping the bark from felled oak trees for tan bark. Also called tan-flawing, (*q.v.*) (*Cf.* Rind and Slipe.)

RINING BIRD. The wryneck; because it comes at the time oak bark is stripped.

RINING-SPUD, *w.*‡ A Flawing spud or Barking-iron, (*q.v.*)

RIP[1]. *To reap. The sickle is called the rip-hook.* See Reaphook and Sickle.

RIP[2]. A hen coop.

RIPE. [Ripa, *Latin.*] *A bank or sea-shore. A village in East Sussex is called by this name.* Ripe also means bank, shore, edge and Ripe is on a small ridge above marshy ground. It was probably coastal when it got its name. In Norman times Lewes was on the fore-shore.

RIPE-STICK. Made of oak and used instead of a stone to whet the blade of a scythe. It is fixed on the upper end of the snethe, smeared with grease and sanded, the grease and sand being carried in cows' horns. (*Cf.* Rifle and Strickles.)

Ripe-stick

RIP-HOOK or RIP'OOK. See Reaphook.

RIPIERS. [*Icel.*, hrip, *a basket.*] *Men from the coast who carry baskets of fish to inland towns and villages. The word rip is still used in Scotland for a basket.*

RIPPLEY. Rainy: pouring, continuous wet: heavy drizzle.

RISE. See Wrist and Turnryst or Turnwrist.

RISING, e. *Yeast.*

RIVETTY. Restless; said of man or of beast.

ROACH. Sound as a roach. (Corrupted from the French, *sain*

comme une roche, (sound as a rock.) (*Cf.* Herring.)

ROAD-BAT. A bat or sprag used to trail uphill behind a wagon axle to strut against the road when the horses stopped pulling. It had an iron fork at the end. Also called a dogstick.

Road-bat

ROADEN SCYTHE. A scythe with a straight pole and single neb used to clear ditches by the roadside.

ROADERS. Tramps; travellers on foot as distinct from gypsies or mumpers.

ROBBUT. [*Corruption of Rabbit.*] *Sometimes pronounced as broadly as robert.*

" *Robbuts ! Ah, I lay you never see such a plààce for robbuts as what ourn is ! I never should have beleft, without I'd seen 'em in my garden, that there was so many robbuts in the wurreld. Why they be ready to eat us up alive !* "

ROBINETTE. The smallest kind of gun formerly cast in Sussex, a half-pounder.

ROCHET. A very short surplice.

ROCKET. The double row of holes made by the dibbling-iron used by a sower to receive seeds. (See S.S. & C. under Dibbling iron.)

RODS. The shafts; Sharps, or Thills of a cart or waggon. Also the frame sticks of a hurdle in the making.

ROIL. To fidget about; vex; disturb. Same word as rile.

ROKE. [Roec, *or* Reác, *Ang. Sax.*, *smoke.*] *Steam; mist.* See Rauk and Reek.

ROLLER. The winding barrel of a well.

ROMAN. Anything beyond living memory is called " Roman."

ROMNEY MARSH. There is a saying in East Sussex that the world is divided into five parts—Europe, Asia, Africa, America, and Romney-marsh.

ROOKERY, m. *A disturbance; a fuss and chattering. " I never knew of a wedding but what the women-folks made a middlin' rookery over it."*

ROOSTER. The common cock. The Americans invariably call cocks by this name. (*Cf.* " Cock of the Roost.")

ROSSEL-FENCE, w. *The same as raddle-fence.* (See S.S. & C. under Hedge and fence.)

ROSSEL-WALL or ROSSEL-STILE. A wall usually of flint built with a part so low as to make it easy to step over. (See S.S. & C. under Hedge and fence.)

Rossel-Wall

ROTHER, w. [*Hryther*, Hruther, *Ang. Sax.*] *A horned beast.*

ROUGH[1]. *Passionate; angry.*

" *Mus Moppet he'll be middlin' rough if he sees you a throwing at he's rooster.*"

ROUGH[2]. A piece of land too poor to be worth cultivation. Sometimes poor pasture or wood, as Cobham Rough, Poynings.

ROUGHINGS. Rowens, (*q.v.*)

ROUGH MUSIC. Charivari. Expression of popular disfavour; especially in bad matrimonial cases. The " music " is made by a din of sticks, pots, pans, etc. by boys who parade the village and conclude with burning the effigy of the offender which has been carried in procession. (*Cf.* Hornfair and Rousting.)

ROUGH-RUNNERS, *w.*‡ Scarlet runners.

ROUGHSPUN. Rude; unpolished.

" They be roughspun the 'ole lot on 'em."

ROUNDEL. A circle; anything round. A ring. The firing place and flue of an oast house is called the roundel. So also was the circular building round the post windmill and a round flower bed would be the rose roundel or according to the flower it was planted with. When very small called a Rundlet (*q.v.*) See also S.S. & C.

ROUND-FROCK. A loose frock or upper garment of coarse material, generally worn by country-people over their other clothes. A white round frock is considered mourning, and when worn (as I have sometimes seen it) under a greatcoat, the effect is by no means good, particularly when viewed from behind. This garment when highly ornamented with smocking was properly called a smocked frock, but generally contracted to smock (*q.v.*) Neither Round frock nor Smock are strictly local to Sussex. (See also S.S. & C. under Smock.)

ROUNDHOUSE. An opensided roofed shelter for horses, oxen and gear: usually a conical thatched roof, supported by tree trunk pillars. Also for housing the roundabout horse gear by which early mechanisation was powered.

ROUPEY. [*Connected with the Ang. Sax.*, Hreop from hrépan*: or the Icelandic*, hrópja, *to scream out.*] *Hoarse.*

ROUSERS. Extra large squibs used at Lewes on bonfire night, November 5th.

ROUSTING, *w.*‡ Disapproval expressed by mobbing and violence.

ROWENS, m*: or ROUGHINGS*, e. *The latter grass which comes after mowing, and is frequently left for cattle to eat in the winter when it becomes coarse and rough.*

RŎWET. Old withered grass.

RŌWT. A rut—deep and made by wheels. See Trades.

RUBBER. The stone used for whetting the scythe. Also called a Bristle-bat. Putting the keen edge on to the scythe is called sharping, (*q.v.*)

RUBBIDGE. Rubbish; especially weeds in a garden.

RUDDLE. Oil and red ochre used for marking sheep. (*Cf.* Tiver.)

RUDY, m. *Rude.*

"*They boys! They boys! They be so rudy.*"

RUE, w. [Rue, *French*, *a street.*] *A row; a hedge-row;* rough land; a rough lane; a Shaw; usually spelt Rew.

RUMBLE BELL or RUMBLER. A globular horse bell or sheep bell (*q.v.*), which has no tongue or clapper; but carries a stone or iron ball, about the size of a cherry, which when moving gives a rumbling sound. The letters R and W are sometimes included in the design, which it is thought may possibly prove their origin at the bell foundry of Robert Wells of Aldbourne, Wiltshire.

Rumble bell

RUMMAGE. To go through things on search, especially on a suspected smuggling craft.

RUN[1]. The carrying and landing of a smuggler's cargo.

RUN[2]. Sheep run: the range of a flock over a farm arable as well as down turf.

RUNAGATE. A good-for-nothing fellow.

"*There let him sink, and be the seas on him!*
White-livered runagate, what doth he there?"
—Richard III, *Act iv. sc. 4.*

RUNDLET. A small circle. [*Diminutive of Roundel*] q.v.

RUNNER[1]. The French or Redleg partridge.

RUNNER[2]. A person who conveyed smuggled goods inland.

RUNNER[3]. A spar (*q.v.*) of quartered hazel or other sapling, or a bondcord for keeping thatch in place. (*Cf.* Peg[1] and Sparrer.)

RUNT[1], w. *To grub up the roots of trees by drawing them out of the ground in a way which does not much disturb the soil.*

RUNT[2]. A steer, as Black runts; Red runts (Sussex), Welsh runts (black), etc. (See S.S. & C. under Frouden or Frought'n'd.)

RUSHLIGHT. See Grisset.

RUSTY[1], w. *Unruly; ill-humoured.*

RUSTY[2]. Se Reesty.

RYTHE, w. [Ríthe, *Ang. Sax.*, *a fountain; well; rivulet.*] *A small stream; usually one occasioned by heavy showers of rain.* (*Cf.* Rife.)

S

S of the possessive case takes " e " before it after " st ", e.g. " The pig spent the night in Mrs. Westes (West's) garden. And in some plural words: " Those postes (posts) be crooked.

SABBED. Wet; saturated; sopped. (*See Sape.*)

SAD. Sodden; heavy; said of bread which has not risen well. And of beer that is flat.

SAD'DY. A common form of Saturday.

SAFE, w. *Sure; certain.*

" *He's safe to be hanged.*"

SAG. [*Connected with* Sǽgan, *Ang. Sax., to cause to descend.*] *To fit badly; to hang down on one side; to subside by its own weight or an overload.*

> " *The mind I sway by, and the heart I bear,*
> *Shall never sag with doubt, nor shake with fear.*"
> —Macbeth, *Act v. sc. 3.*

SAKER. A medium sized gun; a 12 pounder.

SALIMOTE, m. *The court of the lord of the old manor of Brightelmston in 1656 was described as the Salimote Court.*

SALLET. A salad. (*As ballet for ballad.*)

" *Sunday, May 13, 1764. Myself, Mr. Dodson and servant at church in the morn. We dined on a calf's heart pudding, a piece of beef, greens and green sallet. Mr. Hartley came to bring me a new wigg. Paid him in full for a new wigg £1 15s., and new-mounting an old one, 4s.*"—Diary of Mr. Turner, of East Hoathly.

Shakespeare uses the word,—

> Clown.—" *Indeed, sir, she was the sweet marjoram of the sallet; or, rather the herb of grace.*"
> Lafeu.—" *They are not sallet herbs you knave, they are nose herbs.*"
> —All's Well that Ends Well, *Act iv. sc. 5.*

SALLY[1], e. [Salig, *Ang. Sax.;* Salix, *Latin.*] *A willow.* Or a sallow.

" I planted a row of sallies to make it more private like."

SALLY[2]. The same as Solly (*q.v.*); a precarious condition; tottery.

SALTS, e. *Marshes near the sea, overflowed by the tides.* (*E.g.* Salts Farm, Lancing.)

SAPE. [Sæp. *Ang. Sax.*] *Sap.*

SARE. [Searian, *Ang. Sax., to dry.*] *Withered; dry; said of wood.* (*See Sear.*)

> " *Burn ash-wood green,*
> *'Tis fire for a Queen:*
> *Burn ash-wood sare,*
> *'Twool make a man swear.*"

SARMENT. A sermon.

" *I likes a good long sarment, I doos; so as when you wakes up it aint all over.*"

SARSEN. [Sar'cen stones, for Saracen, or foreign.] Detached boulders apparently foreign to the district being the only remains of a geological formation once over-lying the chalk. In the ancient " Romance of Merline " in the folio of Henry B. Wheatley, F.S.A. the Editor of Percy's

Reliques of Anc. Eng. Poetry the Saxons themselves that came over with Hengist because they were not Christians are constantly called Sarazens.

SARTERNOON. This afternoon.

SARTINTLY and SARTIN-SURE. Certainly, certain.

SASS. See Sauce.

SATTERED, m. *Thoroughly soaked.* (*Probably a corruption of Saturated.*)
"I was fair sattered."

SAUCE, m. (*Pronounced Sass.*) *Vegetables; but generally used of cabbages. The Americans speak of garden-sass.* "*I reckon I shàànt have no sass at all this year, all through along on account of the drythe.*"

SAVING-GO. Smuggler's term for an interrupted run wherein they saved enough to make the attempt worth while; losing a fifth or sixth part of their venture.

SAY, *w.*‡ (Pronunciation of sea.)

SAYE. *Serge or woollen cloth.*—Cheeseworth Inventory, *1549*.

SAYS, *m.* Indicates.
"It says Thunder, dont it, when the flies bite ?"

SCAD, m. *A small black plum which grows wild in the hedges.*

SCADDLE, m. [*Scæthig, Ang. Sax. hurtful.*] *Wild; mischievous; thievish. The Anglo-Saxon word* sceatha *has the same double meaning (1) a robber; thief; (2) an adversary. Applied to a truant boy, or a cow which breaks through hedges, or a cat which steals.*

SCADE. Harm; mischief.

SCALE, *m.* A scale ceiling-room; one wherein the roof slant cuts off part of the ceiling and a vertical section is not rectangular. See Skeel ceiling.

SCALLOP. Escallop.
"'N ther she stood a talkin' an' talkin' 'n 'er mouth a openin' and shutten like a great scallop."

SCALY, w. *Inclined to steal.*

SCAMBLE, w. *To make a confusion of anything.*

> "*The scambling and unquiet time*
> *Did push it out of further question.*"
> —King Henry V., *Act i. sc. 1.*

SCANDALISE. To use abusive language to a person.

SCAR, e. [*Possibly connected with Icel.,* skár, *open, exposed.*] *Exposed to.*
"*Our house lays quite scar to the sea.*"

SCARCEY, m. *Scarce. Also used in Kent.*

SCARRIFUNGE. A to-do with cleaning a dwelling.
"They're having a tremenjus scarrifunge next door, gettin' ready for the wedding I allows."
Especially used of spring-cleaning; "a regular scarrifunge."
When a room was turned out for painters a Lindfield woman said to me,
"We been having a rare old scarrifunge."

SCATTEL. Untrustworthy; troublesome.

SCAWP. Scrape.
"They went scawping up what was left on the wheat field."

SCHEECH, or SCHEECHER. Screech, Screecher, (*q.v.*). The Deviling or swift; also the Stormcock or missel thrush.

SCIVE. A scythe.

SCONCE. [Schans, *Dutch, a sconce.*] *A socket fixed in a wall for holding a candle.*

SCORIA. Slag from the bloomeries; prized by the later ironfounders who used it as a flux. Much used by the Roman, and by other road makers. A part of the Rye-Uckfield ridgeway, north of Framfield, is called Scoria Lane. (See S.S. & C. under Iron working.)

SCORING-AXE. An axe used to chip round the stem of a tree, previous to falling (*i.e. felling it*). The handle is about three times the length of the blade. This procedure was followed with oak trees only. The

Scoring-axe

object was to remove the best of the bark in large pieces which were called healers. After the tree was thrown the scoring axe was used to cut round the trunk at the ends of the pieces of bark to be flawed. (*Cf.* Heal and Set-in.)

SCORSE. To exchange. Like scrunch for crunch, this word is corruption of the Old English word corse, which means to barter, exchange, etc.

" *This catel he got with okering,*
And spent al his lif in corsing."

i.e., " *This cattle he acquired by usury, and led all his life in bargaining.*"—Old Metrical Homilies.

Spenser also used the word,—

" *And therein sat an old old man, half blind,*
And all decrepit in his feeble corse,
Yet lively vigour rested in his mind,
And recompenst them with a better scorse;
Weak body well is changed for minds redoubled forse."

—The Faerie Queene, *Book II, Cant. ix. 55.*

The following instance will illustrate the modern use of the word,—

A gipsy boy, with whom I was on friendly terms, used to travel about this part of the country selling trumpery brooches and ornaments. As he was one day exhibiting the contents of his basket, I was surprised to see half-a-dozen onions loose among the jewelry. " *What,*" *I said,* " *do you sell onions too ?* " " *No, sir,*" *he replied,* " *but I scorsed away a pair of diamond ear-rings for these few onions, with a lady down at the cottage yonder.*"

SCOT. A tax on acres at Pevensey and other levels, particularly a tax paid to a drainage authority on land liable to flood. A word recently resuscitated in this sense.

SCRAG. The tall green pole put in the middle of the 5th of November bonfire at Slaugham which, after the fire had burned down was carried on the men's shoulders to the Carpenter's Arms, the White Horse and the Sundial and sold for drinks. The pole was charred but not burnt.

SCRATCH-ALONG. To pull through hard times.

" *What with otherwhiles a day's turmut-hoeing, and otherwhiles a day's tan-flawin', and otherwhiles a job of gardenin', I've just managed to scratch along somehows.*"

SCRAZE. [*Connected with graze.*] *To scratch, or rather to scratch and bruise at the same time.* (*Cf.* Gravel Rash.)

" *She was climmin' up after some scads and fell down and scrazed her knees.*"

SCREECH or SCREECHER. The Swift. Also called Squeaker and Deviling.

SCREECH OF DAWN. Very early.

SCREECH-OWL. The barn owl.

SCREECH-THRUSH or SCREECHER. The Missel-thrush or Storm-cock. All these words are variously said SCHEECH, SCRITCH and SREECH.

SCRIER, or SCREER, e. *A high-standing sieve which is used for cleansing corn from dust and other rubbish; sometimes called a screen.* The implement is more commonly called Scry, possibly from Ang. Sax. *scrypan*, to scrape. Scrier is derived therefrom. Screer is a snatching between scry and screen. Screen is mostly used of the various mechanical sifting devices, and in that sense is not local.

SCRIG. To sift or riddle; to scry.

SCRIGGLE. To squeeze through as when in a close crowd.

SCRITCH. See Screech.

SCRITCH OWL. The barn owl. So called owing to its weird shriek. Its eyes are larger than those of any other bird. Screech-owl (*q.v.*)

SCROOP. A grating squeak, like the noise of a wooden chair being pushed over a stone floor.

SCROW, or SCROWSE, e. [*Connected with the Old English word crus, wrathful.*] *Angry; dark and scowling.*

SCROUNY. Short, scrappy, rather mean.

" I've only had time to write her a scrouny letter today."

SCROWGE. Crowd.

"A dozen people scrowged into a van."

SCRUFFLE. (A word between scrape and shuffle.) To drag one's feet on stone pavement. (*Cf.* Scuffle².)

SCRUMBLED. Crumpled; out of order.

"I've ironed your riband; it was all scrumbled up."

SCRUMP, e. [Scrimmian, *Ang. Sax., to wither up.*] *Anything undersized.*

In Hampshire a small shrivelled up apple is called a scrumpling.

SCRUTCHELL. See Scutchett.

*SCRY*¹, e. *To sift corn through a scrier.* (q.v.)

SCRY². The implement. It is more often called by this name, the word scrier being used for the operator.

SCUD. Driving rain; mist.

*SCUFFLE*¹, e. *An outer garment worn by children to keep their clothes clean; a coarse apron for dirty work.*

SCUFFLE². To walk without lifting feet; particularly of children in fallen leaves.

"Don't scuffle (or scuff) your feet." (*Cf.* Scruffle.)

SCUFFLE-PLOUGH, w., or SCUFFLER. *A skim;* a shim³, (*q.v.*); *a horse-hoe.* It had a share like an arrow-head, and was drawn by a horse between the ridges where turnips and other crops had been drilled to root out the weeds, thus acting like a Dutch hoe, but on a larger scale. (*Skim* is probably a printer's error for shim.)

SCUGGY. (From scut, a tail.) The squirrel. Also called Juggy.

SCUPPIT. A wooden shovel used by maltsters and hop-driers. Shaped like a large dustpan that is used in the house.

SCUTCHETT,* w., or SCRUTCHELL. *The refuse of wood.* (*Cf.* Spilwood.)

SCUTTY, m. *A wren; also called a cutty,* juggy and kitty.

The Sussex small boys have a Small Birds Act of their own, which is found sufficient for the protection of all birds which they consider entitled to protection, and commands much more respect and obedience than a recent Act of Parliament.

"Robins and wrens
Are God Almighty's friends;
Martins and swallers
Are God Almighty's scholars."

At Lancing we heard the rhyme:—

"Robins an' wrens
Be God's cocks and hens;
Martins and swallers
Be God's good scholers."

SCYTHE. A scythe is said to preserve it's temper and edge best if kept hanging in a Holly tree, or failing that a Blackthorn.

SEAFRET. Sea mist, or fog.

SEAM. [Seam, *Ang. Sax.*] *Eight bushels, or a horse load.*

SEAN, or SEINE. [Seine, *Old French, still used in France.*] *A very large net used for catching mackerel or herrings.*

SEAR. [Searian, *Ang. Sax., to dry up.*] *Dry; withered; burnt up by the sun. (See Sare.)*

"My May of life
Is fallen into the sear, the yellow leaf."
—Macbeth, *Act v. sc. 3.*

SEASON, m. *Ground in good condition.*

SEE. Used always as the perfect for saw . . . sometimes 'seed'.

"*I never see such larmentable poor ground as this here. I've been diggin' it over to get a season to plant a little onion seed, but I shan't make naun an't.*"

(See S.S. & C. under Hedge Carpenter.)

*SEED-CORD.** [*Connected with the Dutch word* korf, *a basket.*] *A wooden vessel in which the sower carries the seed,* shaped to the body and with shoulder strap. A seed-lip.

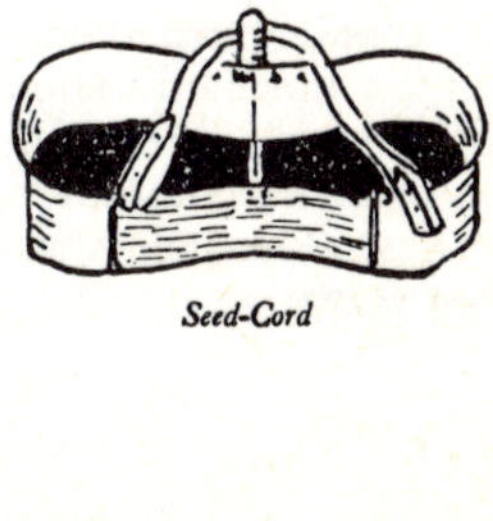

Seed-Cord

SEED-LEAP, SEED-LEPE, or *SEED-LIP*, m. [Sæd-leap, *Ang. Sax.*] *A basket for seed; a seed cord.* The same as lepe or side-box. (*Cf.* Leap.)

SEEDSMAN, m. *The foreman of the farm, whose business it is to sow.*

SEEM. Pretend . . . as mowers paid by time went through the motions of mowing without cutting all the time.

" They jess seem to mow."

An old carpenter who was being sketched was about to put away his smoked pipe. The artist told him not to stop smoking.

He compromised by " Well I'll seem to smoke."

SEEP. To ooze as water damping through a dam. (*Cf.* O. E. *Sipian to soak.*)

SEN. Since.

The Sussex word is the older form, and is traced to the Ang. Sax. siththan, *which became* sin, sen, *or* sithen, *from the last of which was formed* sithens, *whence since.*

" *I haven't been over to Selmeston not sen I was seedsman at Mus Allwork's. Ah! he was a set sort of a man, he was, and no mistake.*"

SENSE. Properly; effectively. Generally in the negative.

" I've broke my spartacles an' carn see to wroit no sense."

SERAPHIM. A church Barrel-organ.

SERB, SHERVE, (*q.v.*) or SORB. Generally plural, serbs. The fruit of the wild Service Tree. *Pyrus Torminalus.* Also called the Chequer.

Serb is often used for the Rowan (Mountain Ash), *P. aucuparia* (otherwise known as Twig-bean, *q.v.*); and occasionally for the White Beam, *P. aria.*

The true Service Tree, *P. sorbus*, is said to grow wild in Sussex.

SESSIONS. A great deal of business; a fuss.

" *There's always such sessions over lighting up the church in winter time.*"

SET. Obstinate; self-willed; determined.

SET-ABOUT-HOUSE.‡ To show a person the way to do anything, rather officiously.

" Mrs. Beach went to church along with Harry Potter when he was married, and she set him about house all the time."

(This is in Fraser's annotated Parish, in Parish's own handwriting. It is not signed, but the example is quite in Parish's Handwriting (*q.v.*)

SET-IN. When falling a tree, to clear round the trunk for the saw, and to make the set, towards which the saw will cut, the position of which governs the direction in which the tree will fall. The scoring axe is used for this operation.

SET-OUT. A disturbance.

" *There's been a pretty set-out up at the forge.*"

SETTER, *w.*‡ A dibber, (*q.v.*)

SETTLE. [Setl, *Ang. Sax., a seat.*] *A wooden seat with a back and arms.*

" *He fell down off the settle and scrazed his nose and made as much set-out as though he'd been killed.*"

SETTS. Willow saplings. Also hop plants and almost anything to be planted out.

SEVERALS, m. *Portions of common assigned for a term to a particular proprietor; the other commoners waiving for a time their right of common over them.*

> " *My lips are no common, though several they be.*"
>
> —Love's Labour Lost, *Act ii. sc. 1.*

Ayscough gives the following note on this passage. :—

" *This word (several), which is provincial, means those fields which are alternately sown with corn, and during that time are kept several or severed from the field which lies fallow and is appropriated to the grazing of cattle, not by a fence, but by the care of the cowherd or shepherd, and in which the town bull only is allowed to range unmolested.*

The name survives. *E.g.*, The Severals, Midhurst.

SEW[1], e., or SUE. [Sychu, *Welsh, to dry up; cognate with Latin* siccare.] *To drain land.* Or a pond.

SEW[2], e. *An underground drain.* Hence sewer. Also a main drainage channel.

SEW[3], w. *A cow is said to be gone to sew when her milk is dried off.*

SHACKLE[1], w. *To idle about; to waste time; to be very busy about nothing.*

SHACKLE[2]. A twisted pethwine bond securing thatch to the rafters. A similar smaller ring for connecting hurdles in pitching a fold. An iron ring for the same purpose.

SHACKY. Shabby; ragged.

SHADE. [Shard.] *A piece of broken tile or pottery.*

SHAG[1], w. *& m. A cormorant.* Also called a Raven.

"*As wet as a shag,*" *is a common expression, taken from the idea of a cormorant diving frequently under the water.*

SHAG[2]. (From the number of cormorants formerly nesting on Seaford Head.) A Seaford fisherman. See Fishermen.

SHAKEN OAK. See S.S. & C.

SHARD, e. *A gap in a hedge. This word, like shade, is derived from the Anglo-Saxon sceard, which means (1) a sherd; (2) a division.*

SHARES. The Brighton fisheries were carried out on a co-operative basis. The catch was divided into shares. One share was always subdivided, one half to the vicar, one quarter to the churchwardens for ecclesiastical and general civic expenses, including the defence of the town from French raiders and other pirates; the remaining quarter to the master of the ship. The ship itself took one to four shares according to its tonage and the kind of fishery engaged in. Each man without nets had " one share for his body," *i.e.*, for his personal service. A man taking nets to sea with him had half a share for his body and a share for each specified number (usually three) of nets; in some fisheries lines instead of nets, or both.

Thus the number of shares into which a particular catch had to be divided depended on the number of men, the nets or lines they took with them, the number due to the boat plus always the tithe share. (*Cf.*, Fare.)

SHARP[1].* *The shaft of a cart.* (*Cf.* Thills.)

SHARP[2].‡ Singing. Means of time, too soon; not of pitch.

SHARP[3]. Sharpen.

SHARPED. [*Scerped*, Ang. Sax.] Sharpened.

SHARPING. Sharpening. (The declension of the Anglo-Saxon verb can be deduced from the above three words.)

SHARPS. The finest refuse siftings of flour. (See Pollard.)

SHATTER, m. *A number or quantity.*

"*There's a tidy shatter of hops this year.*"

SHAUL, or SHAWLE. A wooden shovel without a handle, used for putting corn into a winnowing machine. This word is a variation of shool or shovel.

"*I, said the owl,*
With my spade and showl."

SHAW, e. *A small hanging wood.* Also called Rew, or Rue. *Ray defines it as* " *a wood that encompasses a close.*"

SHAWER. [*Sceawere*, Ang. Sax., a beholder, spectator, spy.] The twelve jurats appointed by the Receyvour or Bailiff of Pevensey immediately after his election, to assist him in his conduct of the town's business, and particularly as assessors of scot, collectors and overseers of works of Pevensey

Marshes and sea defences, were called shawers. They sat in a Court called Last. (*q.v.*)

SHAWLED. Warped. A board warped in drying is shawled.

SHAY. A faint ray of light. A flash of light; a halo.

In Kent the word means a general likeness, and seems to correspond to the Sussex bly.

A man who was trying to describe to me a fearful apparition which he had seen in Firle Park, said, after much cross-examination, that it passed quite close to him in the form of an enormous white horse, and there was a bluish shay. I should myself have supposed that a horse and shay was a sufficiently common object of the country not to have excited undue influence, but on this occasion the appearance was so overwhelming that the man was ill for several days.

Speaking of lighting . . . A farmer at Woodmancote said, " In the shay of it I could see the fork." Shay was the flare in general and the fork the streak of brighter light. " I though we should 'ave rain today, there was such a shay round the moon last night."

SHAYBANG. Char-a-banc.

On August 4th, 1919, Bank holiday a farmer at Woodmancote who was remembering the date in 1914, said, " They goes shay-banging about and dont think of anything."

SHEAR, e. *A spear, as an eel-shear.*

SHEAT, e. *A young hog of the first year.* (*See Shoot*[1].)

SHEEN. A machine.

SHEENING. Threshed wheat.

SHEEP. Usually pronounced Ship by the peasants. See S.S. & C., and under Ship.

SHEEP-BELLS or SHIP-BELLS. The names of the various bells are: Can, or canister; Cluck, or cluckets; Swift; and Rumble, or Rumbler.

SHEEP BOW. See Bilbo.

SHEEP-CAGE. A framework out of which sheep eat their hay, etc., in a strawyard. (*Cf.* Cage.)

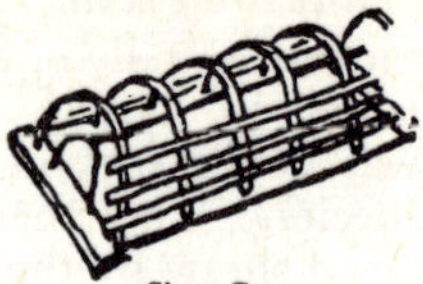

Sheep Cage

SHEEP-DOG MOUSE. Field vole, or short-tailed fieldmouse. See Meece.

SHEEP HOOK. Another name for sheep crook.

SHEEP-LEAZE,† or TEG-LEAZE. *The right of turning out one sheep to feed on a common.* See Leaze.

SHEER[1]. [Scir, *Ang. Sax.*, *clear, white.*] *Smooth and shiny, as flesh which is swollen.* (*Cf.* Smolt.)

SHEER[2]. Water from a pricked blister.

SHEERES. The true Sussex man divides the world into two parts. Kent and Sussex forms one division, and all the rest is " The Sheeres." I have heard China and Australia both described as in the sheeres; but I confess that I was somewhat startled at being told that I was myself " a man as was well acquaint with the sheeres, and had got friends in all parts *of this world and the world to come." This statement was meant as a compliment, but when I came to consider it afterwards, I was not sure that it was altogether complimentary to some of my friends.*

SHEERE-MAN. A man who comes from the shires (and not necessarily sure of a favourable reception in Sussex.) See S.S. & C.

SHEERE-MOUSE[1]. *A field mouse. A shrew-mouse.* Properly speaking a shrew is a vole, not a mouse. See Meece.

The country people have an idea that the harvest-mouse is unable to cross a path which has been trod by man. Whenever it attempts to do so it is said to be immediately struck dead.

This accounts (they say) for the numbers which on a summer's evening may be found lying dead on the edge of the field footpaths without any wound or apparent cause of death.

This idea is usually of the shrew not the harvest mouse; formerly there was no distinction between these species. The phenomenon of the dead shrew by the roadside has disappeared, the sight was common enough when we were children.

SHEERE-MOUSE[2]. *An epithet of derision applicable to a sheere-man. The phrase " the sheeres " is found in many other parts of England, and is generally expressive of a certain degree of depreciation. In Shropshire the manufacturing districts are spoken of as " down in the shires."*

SHEERE-WAY, e. (Shire-way). *A bridle-way.*

SHEETS . . . to go through—to have a night abed.

A woman at Holmbush going into a shed where a fox had harboured was overcome by the scent and fainted.

Later asked how she was she answered, " Better thank ye mum, but there ye never feel quite right till yer been through the sheets, do yer ? "

SHELL-FIRE. Phosphorescent light from decaying matter; called also fairy sparks. Possibly so called from its occurring in heaps of shell-fish shells.

SHELL-SNAGS or SHELL-SNEGS. Snails as distinguished from slugs. See S.S. & C. Snails are also called hodmandods, and snags or snegs without distinction from slugs.

SHELVE, e. *To throw manure out of a cart by raising the fore-part so that the bottom may shelve or slope.*

SHEPHERD'S ACRES. A piece of tenantry land which the shepherd inherited and let to his master. See Tenant-try-acre.

SHEPHERD'S CROWN. Local name for the fossil sea-urchin found in chalk.

SHERVE. Service tree and service fruit; Serb (*q.v.*); Sorb.

This name supports Johns' opinion (*The Forest Trees of Britain*, p. 127) that " service " is a deformation of *sorbus*.

SHET. Shut in the sense of joining or fitting together.

SHET O' HANDS. A complete gang ready for work.

SHIFT. To divide—parcel out. A division of land among co-heirs is called a shifting. Also to provide as in " shift for himself " and " Oh let it shift " take its chance.

SHIM[1]. [Schim, *Dutch, a shade or ghost.*] *A glimpse of anything.*

" I thought I saw a shim of the carpenter going by the gate just now, but I'm not sure."

SHIM[2], e. *A narrow strip or glimpse of white on a horse's face.*

SHIM[3]. *A horse hoe for cleaning the ground between rows of beans or hops.* A scuffle-plough (*q.v.*)

SHIMBOYS OR SHIMROYS. Gnats.

SHIMPER. [Scímian, *Ang. Sax., to shine or shimmer.*] *To shine brightly.*

SHINGLES. Small wooden tiles made of split oak used for roof, steeples, etc.

There are several church spires in Sussex covered with these shingles.

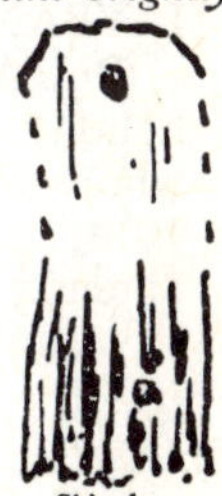

Shingle

SHINGLING TONGS. Tongs used by iron workers making a bloom by the process of shingling. See S.S.&C. under Iron working.)

SHIP[1], m. *Sheep.*

Seldom used in the singular. Some inland " Ship " Inns refer to sheep not to ships. See S.S. & C.

SHIP[2]. A Royal Naval Ship of any sort is called " A King's Ship," *e.g.*, A big smoke on the horizon: "Ah that be a King's Ship I warrant."

SHIPFEED. Green crops and natural grass to feed the flock upon during the winter time.

"We'n got a plenty o' shipfeed this winter."

SHIP-IN-THE-TWIST. See Shut-in-the-twist.

SHIPPOND. Sheep pond; dew-pond.

SHIP YARD. A fold or yard, as a lambing yard, for sheep.

SHIRE-WAY. Pronounced 'Sheere-way.' A bridle path.

SHIRTY. Easily offended. A man who has quickly lost his temper is said to have got his shirt out . . . i.e., he has taken off his coat as if to fight.

SHOCK. A sheaf of corn used only in the singular as distinct from stook which is a collection of shocks. The word sheaf is considered pedantic in Sussex.

SHOD. [*Perfect of Shed.*] *Spilt. This word is correct, the Anglo-Saxon past tense being sceód.*

"*I sent him up to fetch a little beer, but he shod half of it bringing of it home.*"

SHOES AND STOCKINGS, m. *Lotus corniculatus. A wild flower of the* cypripedium genus (*Holloway) called in East Sussex* "*pattens and clogs*" *or* "*butter and eggs.*" (*q.v.*)

Also God Almighty's thumbs and fingers."

SHOG. The core of an apple.

SHOKE, m. [*Scóc*, Ang. Sax., perfect of *scacan*, to shake.] *The original form of shook.*

"*He shoke his fistes in my face, he did !*"

SHOOKED, e. *Shook.*

"*I shooked in my shoes to hear what words he used.*"

SHOOLER, e. *An idle, lazy fellow; described as* "*a man who goes about with his boots undone.*"

SHOON. Shoes.

SHOOT[1], w., or SHUT. *A young growing pig.* (*See Sheat.*)

(This word is difficult to render phonetically, it has been spelt shoat and shote, but shöoert is nearer the mark.)

SHOOT[2]. *A gutter round a roof for shooting off the water.*

SHOOTING ALLEY. A large marble used by players when knocking marbles out of a circle chalked on the ground.

Named also Tolly, and at Battle a 'Bosser.'

SHOOT THROUGH THE RING. A game of marbles. See Bigoring.

SHORE[1], m. *To shelve off; to cut off evenly.*

"*If the road was better shored at the sides the water wouldn't lay so much as what it does.*"

SHORE[2]. [Schoren, *Dutch, to prop up.*] *A prop, a support.*

SHORN-BUG, m. [Scearn, *Ang. Sax., dung;* scearn-wibba, *a shorn-bug.*] *A beetle. To eat shorn-bugs for dinner is a proverbial expression for the extremity of poverty.*

SHORT[1], m. *Out of temper; unable to give a civil answer.*

"Guvnor were tidy short wi' me, short as moss 'e wur."

A shepherd at Hove station, 1898.

SHORT[2]. *Tender.*

A rat-catcher once told me that he knew many people who were in the habit of eating barn-fed rats, and he added, "*When they're in a pudding you could not tell them from a chick, they eat so short and purty.*"

SHOTNETT. A mackerel fishing net of the same specification as the Cock heak, but possibly of a different size mox, (*q.v.*), or used in a different manner, as trawling, etc. If lost at sea the owner could claim four shillings from the common fund. Each 4 nets took one share. (*Cf.* Shares.)

SHOTNETT FARE. Mackerel fishery from mid-April to June around the coast. Every man taking above four nets (? 4 nets or more) took half a share, every other man, one share. (*Cf.* Fare and Shares.)

SHOTTERS.† *Boats of six to twenty-six ton burden, used in the mackerel fishery.* They carried 8 to 12 men, from 6 to 10 tons 2 shares, 10 to 18 tons 2½ shares and over 18 tons 3 shares.

SHOTTY, w.‡ Corn which is ripe, hard and loose in the ear.

SHOVE, e. *To put the loose corn into cops or heaps, that it may be more conveniently taken up.* (*Cf.* Cop[2].)

SHOVEL. To put to bed with a shovel. To chastise.

"Them young reskels they tarrify me above a bit, they do, I'd like to put some on 'em to bed wi' a shovel otherwhiles."

SHRAMMED. Benumbed with cold; Clemmed.

(I never heard any present tense if it be a verb.)

SHRAPE, e. *To scold.*

*SHRAVEY.** *A loose sub-soil, something between clay and sand.*

"The ground is more shravey up here than it is down by the pond."

SHRIEVY, e. *Unravelled; having threads withdrawn.*

SHRIKE. Call of badger in the rutting season.

SHRITE. A name for the missel thrush. Also called Sheech- or Screech-thrush (*q.v.*) Storm cock and Greybird.

SHROGS, e. *The refuse trimmings of hop-plants; also called chogs.*

SHRUCK[1], e. *Shocked.*

SHRUCK[2], e. *Shrieked.*

An old woman who was accidentally locked up in a church where she was slumbering in a high pew, said, "I shruck till I could shruck no longer, but no one comed, so I up and tolled upon the bell."

SHUCK[1]. *Another form of the perfect tense of the verb to shake.*

SHUCK[2], e. *To undress; to shell peas, etc.*

One shucks off wet clothes.

SHUCK[3], m. *A husk or pod*, or chrysalis sheath; also the empty shell of a snail.

SHUCK ([4]). Drawing swords. See S.S. & C.

SHUKISH or SHUCKY. *Unsettled; applied to the weather.*

"Better take yer brolly, it be shuckish like." (*Cf.* Rainified.)

SHUCKLE, or SWINGEL CAP. The connecting part, variously made, of the hand-staff and swiple of a flail.

Shuckle

SHUN. *To push.*

"*He shunned me off the pavement.*"

SHUNNISH. To treat unkindly especially where children are concerned.

SHUT, w. *A young pig; also called a sheat or shoot.*

SHUT-IN-THE-TWIST, or SHIP-IN-THE-TWIST. Sheep that do not walk properly.

SHUT-OF, m. *To be rid of.*

"*Once he gets indoors, you'll be troubled to get shut an' him; I dunno but what you'd best shun him out of the fore-door at oncest.*" (*Pronounced Wunst.*)

SHUTTLES. Low meadows at Burpham with knucker-hole pools in them are called "The Shuttles."

SIBB. [*Sib*, *sibbe*, Ang. Sax., friendship, relationship, alliance.] Friendly; intimate; related.

"She be sibb to us," *i.e.*, she is my cousin.

SICKLE. A reaping hook with a plain cutting edge, used on the right-handed stroke as distinct from the Reaphook (*q.v.*)

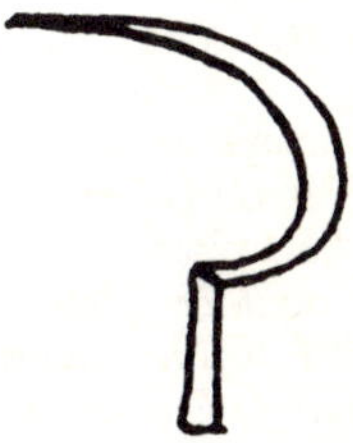

Sickle

SIDEBOARDS, w. *Rails fitted on the top of the sides of a wagon, so as to admit of the addition of an extra load.* (*Cf.* Raves.)

SIDE-BOX. Same as lepe, seed-cord or seed-lip (*q.v.*)

SIDELANDS, w. *The outside parts of a ploughed field, adjoining the hedges, where the plough has been turned, running parallel with the lands or warps.* (*Cf.* Headlands[1].)

*SIDY.** *Surly; moody.* Rather haughty; stand-offish.

This word is older than the expression "put on side."

SIEVER, e. *All the fish caught at one tide.*

SIGHT. A quantity; a great deal; very much.

"It's a long sight further on."

SILLY SUSSEX. Sælig Sussex. See S.S. & C.

SILT, e. *Sand or mud deposited and left by the tide or a flood.*

SILT-UP. *To become so choked-up, with mud or sediment of any kind, as to stop the passage of water in a ditch or the bed of a river.* (*Cf.* Swarve.)

SILVERTAIL. The *Lepisma;* the silverfish.

SIMARY. (St. Mary.) St. Mary's Hospital at Chichester is called "The Simary."

SIMPLE, e. *Unintelligible, or stupid.*

"*Will you be so good as to lend mother another book? for she says this one is so simple she can't make it out at all.*"

SISSEL[1], m. *The usual pronunciation of thistle.*

SISSEL[2], or SIZZLE[1], PUDDING. Warmed-up beef-steak pudding, usually fried.

SIZZING. *Yeast or barm. It is probable that this word may have its origin in the sound made by beer or ale in working.*

SIZZLE[1] PUDDING. See Sissel[2].

SIZZLE[2]. To burn oil paint; to remove it from the wood with hot irons or a blow-lamp.

SKADDLE. Tiresome; mischievous.

A rare old skaddle 'e be, an' she b'ent no better."

SKARBOROW FARE. (Scarborough.) A fishery from June to September off the Yorkshire coast, and possibly extending to the Dogger Bank, for "codd . . . beginning about 40 years agone" (circa 1540). From Brighton, only the largest boats, from 18 to 40 tons were employed; those from 18 to 28 tons took 4, and upwards of 28 tons, 5 shares; they carried 12 or more men, every man in the biggest bringing "a lyne a lead fower lines of hooks and two Norward netts conteyning twenty fower yeards length or thereabouts hath used to take for his bodye & the necessaries aforesaid one share." In the smaller boats a man with 2 lines, 2 leads and 1 heak of 28 yds. took $1\frac{1}{2}$ shares, with 2 lines, 2 leads and 2 heaks "as aforesaid", 2 shares.

When we remember that Drake's *Pelican* was 100 tons, and that two of the fleet of 5 with which he set out to conquer the Pacific were *Marygold* 30 and *Christopher* 15 tons, it will be seen that these were, for their time, quite large ships. This, the most recently organised, was the most particularised of the Brighton fisheries.

(*Cf.* Fare, Heak, Norward and Rann.)

SKEARED. Scared.

SKEEL CEILING. One with a slanting due to the roof shape.

"There's only one bedroom . . . one proper bedroom; the other room upstairs has only a skeel ceiling." (*Cf.* Scale.)

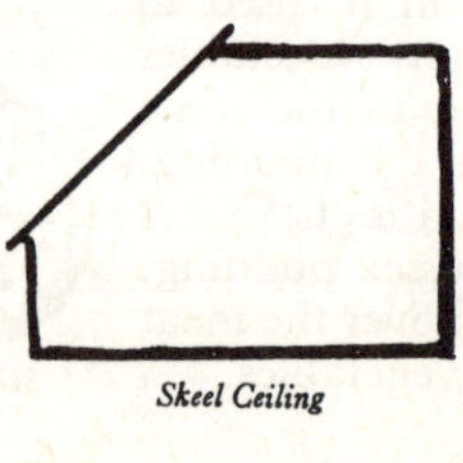

Skeel Ceiling

*SKEELING.** *The bay of a barn; the side of a garret or upper room, where the slope of the roof interferes with the upright.* (*Cf.* Skeel ceiling.)

SKEP[1], [Scep. *Ang. Sax., a basket.*] *A beehive, or the straw hackle placed over it for protection.*

SKEP[2], e. *A hat; a broad flat basket,* made of rushes or straw.

SKEW-WHIFFETY. Slanting or sideways.

"If you stand skew-whiffety to the church you can see the old house much better." (*Cf.* Caterwise and skitterwaisen.)

SKICE. To run quickly and slily, so as to avoid detection.

"*I just saw the top of his skep as he skiced along under the hedge.*"

SKID[1]. *To check a wheel going down hill.*

SKID[2]. At Hastings a boat skid is called a trough, (*q.v.*)

SKIDDER, *m.* To go caterwise; to Jidder (*q.v.*)

SKID-PAN. The iron used for skidding. (*Cf.* Skid[1].)

SKILLET. A saucepan with legs. Varieties of it are the posnet and Stusnet (*q.v.*)

Skillet

SKILLON. A shed or outhouse.

SKIM-COULTER. That part of a plough which goes in front to take off the turf.

SKIM-DICK. Home-made cheese of a rather poor quality because it is made of skim milk.

SKIMMER. A large wooden spoon with holes in it, used to lift out vegetables cooked in the same pot as the pudding.

SKIMMER CAKE,‡ *w.* Sussex pudding, boiled over the meat and vegetables.

Skimmer

SKIN. Bad skin; ill temper.

"He's in a bad skin s'morning, 'e's got out o' bed the wrong side."

SKINNY, w. *Mean; inhospitable.* (*Cf.* Skinflint.)

SKINTLE. In brick-making to move the bricks edgewise when on a drying rack. (*Cf.* Hack[2] and Rindle.)

SKIP, e. *A small wooden or metal vessel for taking up yeast.*

SKIRMISH, m. *To run about in a mischievous manner.*

"*It's no use to try and keep a garden tidy as long as the children are a skirmishing about over the flower borders.*"

SKITS. Plenty, a great number.

"There's skits of ripe blackberries now."

SKITTERWAISEN, w. *From corner to corner.* (*Probably a corruption of Caterwise.*) (*Cf.* Skew-whiffety.)

SKIVEL, w., or SKIVER. *A skewer. In the west, dogwood, of which skewers are made, is called skiver-wood.*

SKREEK, *w.* or

SKREEL, e. *To scream.*

SKROW. Surly; ill-tempered.

SLAB[1], m. *A rough board; the outside cut of a tree which has been sawn up in planks.*

SLAB[2], SLOB, or SLUB. Thick mud. (*Cf.* Stug.)

SLABBY, m. *Dirty; wet and slippery; greasy; sticky.*

Also said Slobby and Slubby. (*Cf.* Stuggy.)

"*Make the gruel thick and slab.*"
—Macbeth, *Act iv. sc. 1.*

SLACK, m. *Loose conversation.*

SLACKS. Pea-pods. (*Cf.* Slates and Huck[1].)

SLAM. To do any work in a slovenly manner.

SLANK, w.‡ Sagging; Hollow surfaced.

SLAP, m. *In good condition; hearty.*

"*I don't feel very slap this morning.*"

*SLAPPEL.** *A portion; a large rough piece of anything.* (*Cf.* Slavven.)

SLAP UP. Smart; thoroughly well done.

A slap up affair or turnout.

SLASHER. A heavy bill-hook. Called also a Bough-spud.

SLAT[1], m. *A slate.*

SLAT[2]. To make the holes in slates or roofing stones to take the nails or pegs with which they are fastened.

SLATER. The *Ligia;* woodlouse. Called also Sow-bug.

SLATES, m. *The pods of peas, etc.* (*Cf.* Huck[1] and Slacks.)

"*The peas seem to be out in bloom a long time before they hang in slates this year.*"

SLAT PICK. See Pittaway.

SLATS. The vertical bars of a gate; sometimes called downrights (*q.v.*)

SLAVVEN. A large piece. (*See Slappel.*)

"I give 'im a slavven o' puddin'."

SLAY, or SLEIGH. A slope.

SLEECH, e. *Mud or sea-sand used as manure. The sediment deposited by the river Rother is called sleech.* (*Cf.* Stug.)

SLEEP MOUSE. A dormouse. See Meece.

SLEY. Slats of hurdles.

SLICE. An iron spade-like implement, used for lifting pies from ovens; and for withdrawing the hot embers. The handle is two and a half times as long as the blade.

Slice

SLICK. [Slíkr, *Icel., smooth.*] *To comb the hair; to make it sleek.*

This word is used frequently in America in this sense.

SLIDE. An iron for trolling an iron hoop, shaped like a long-handled button hook.

Slide

SLIM. [Slim, *Dutch.* Schlimm. *German, bad; sly.*] *To do work in a cunning deceitful manner.*

SLING. A cow or ewe which brings forth her young prematurely is said to sling her calf or lamb.

SLIP[1]. A narrow passage between two buildings; one by the Tiger at Lindfield is so called.

SLIP[2]. A small narrow field.

SLIPE[1]. *To take off the outside cover from anything; especially used of removing the bark from trees.* (*Cf.* Flaw and Rind.)

SLIPE[2], or SLYPE. A mud flat on a river bank, but not on the sea coast. So named on the Courtwick Manor map of 1759 anent the banks of the Arun at Clymping Reach.

SLIPPID. Slender.

SLIRRUP. To lap up any liquid noisily. Or to draw into the mouth liquid and air simultaneously—as hot soup, tea, etc.

*SLIT.** [*Connected with the Dutch word* Sluiten, *to shut or lock.*] *To thrust back the lock of a door without the key.*

SLIVER, w. [Slífan, *Ang. Sax., to cleave.*] *A slice.*

Sliver'd in the moon's eclipse."
—Macbeth, *Act iv. sc. 1.*

SLOB. Thick mud. (*Cf.* Slab, Slub and Stug.)

SLOBBY. A state of muddiness where it is difficult to extricate the boot at each step. (*Cf.* Slabby and Stuggy.)

"The way also here was very wearisome through dirt and slobbiness."
—Pilgrims Progress.

SLOCK, e. [*Corruption of Slack.*] Loose; ill fitting.

SLOCKSEY, e. *Slovenly.* (*Probably connected with the word slack.*)

SLOE. Simile or guage for blackness, especially for black eyes.

"So black as a sloe."

SLOGH. The same meaning as slough; a muddy hole.

SLOMMACK. A slut; a sloven; very untidy person.

SLOMMAKY, m. *Untidy; dirty.* Sometimes spelt slummocky.

SLOP, m. [Slóp, *Ang. Sax.*] *A short, full-made frock, of coarse material, worn by men over their other clothes;*

it reaches to the waist, where it is fastened by a band.
A garibaldi, (*q.v.*), was a similar garment but it was made of woollen material.

SLOPE, or SLOPE OFF. Go away. (*Cf.* Cut your stick.)
" Now young man, you slope off please."

SLOW-WORM. See Adder.

SLUB[1], SLAB, or SLOB. *Thick mud; used as slush is elsewhere.* Particularly very thick mud. (*Cf.* Stug.) " Like slub." Cledgy.

SLUB[2], or SLUB-UP. To make muddy or soil with very stiff mud. (*Cf.* Stuggy.)
" He come 'ome all of a slub."

SLUBBER. To slip; to slip over.
" I slubbered over the stile tidy smart for 'e (the bull) was arter me and 'e wur a bit o' a dabster too."

SLUBBY. Dirty with stiff and extremely tenacious mud. (*Cf.* Slabby, Slobby and Stuggy.)

SLURRY. Diluted mud as distinct from Slub; saturated with so much water that it cannot drain itself; mud churned up into a cream or paste with water. (*Cf.* Stug.)

SLUT'S FARTHINGS, e.‡ Little hard particles found in loaves when the dough has not been properly kneaded.

SLYPE. See Slipe[2].

SMEECH, m*; or SMUTCH*, e. [Sméc, *Ang. Sax.*, *smoke*, *vapour.*] *A dirty black sort of smoke or mist.* Any *bad* smell made by *burning*, but not otherwise.
In the west of England the word means a stench, and is applied to the smell of the snuff of a candle.

SMEERY. Wet and sticky; slippery on the surface, as a lane is after rain; but not so bad as clodgy or slobby, (*q.v.*) (*Cf.* Stuggy.)

SMOCK. A Sunday-best round frock, so highly ornamented with smocking as to be distinct from the working frock. See S.S. & C.

SMOCK-WINDMILL. A windmill boarded down to the ground, as opposed to a post-mill. So called from its similarity in appearance to a smocked round frock or smock. The post mill was a timber structure in which the whole of the working part of the mill was balanced on a vertical post and was capable of being rotated to wind the sweeps, *i.e.* to turn them to face the wind. The smock mill, like the Tower mill which differs from the smock mill in being constructed of masonry, has a fixed main structure of timber weather-boarded over and only the cap is winded, invariably by a fantail. The terms are not local.

SMOKE-HOLE. See Deese, Dee.

SMOKEY. Foggy misty weather, because it looks like smoke.

SMOKING CANE. Stem of Wild Clematis used for cigars, also called Tom-bacca.

SMOLT, e. [Smolt, *Ang. Sax.*, *smooth.*] *Smooth and shining.* (*Cf.* Sheer.)

SMOOCH, or MOUCH. To saunter; walk aimlessly. Also to prowl felonously.

SMOORN, e. *To smear.*

SMORTHER, *w.*‡ (Smother.) Suffocating smoke.

SMUGS, *m.* At Slaugham, if marbles were played in public after Good Friday, they could be snatched away, and kept by the snatcher, after the word " Smugs " had been said.

SMUTCH, e. *To smudge.* Also same as Smeech (*q.v.*), a dirty smoke.
" *What, hast smutched thy nose!*"
—Winter's Tale, *Act i. sc. 2.*

SNAG, or SNEG. *The common snail.* Or more usually the slug, for when snail is particularly meant shell-sneg (*q.v.*) is generally used.
With respect to this word, which I had been inclined to derive from the Anglo-Saxon snæg-el, *Mr. Skeat informs me that it is the old original*

word of which snæg-el *is the diminutive; hence snag is not derived from* snæg-el, *but* vice versa.

The children say,—

"*Snag, snag, put out your horn,*
And I will give you a barley corn."

The snail is also called Hodmandod (*q.v.*)

SNAIL-CREEP. The joints running at random, in flint work of which only the face is struck off. (See S.S. & C. under Flint.)

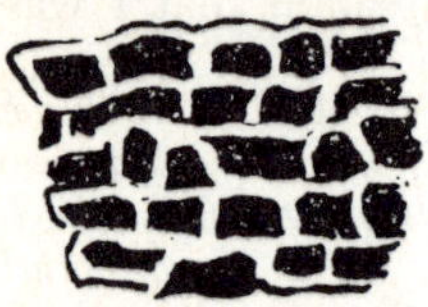

Snail-creep

SNAPE, SNAPEY. Poor boggy land where nothing will grow well.

"It's a snapey bit o' land I tell yer."—*Our gardener, talking to the under-gardener.* Lancing, 1880.

SNAP-PLOUGH, w. *A plough with two wings, so fixed as to snap or move from one side to the other, though only one projects at a time.*

SNASTE or SNEST[1]. The snuff or wick of a candle.

SNASTE or SNEST[2]. To snuff or to to snest a candle.

SNEG. A slug or snail. (*Cf.* Snag and Shell-snag.)

SNELL. A good lump.

"I only asked for a *little* putty and 'e sends me this 'ere snell."

SNETHE, m; *or SNEAD*, w. [Snæd, *Ang. Sax.*] *The long handle of a scythe.* The short handle is called a neb[2], (*q.v.*)

SNICKER, m. [Snikken, *Dutch, to gasp.*] *To sneer; to laugh inwardly.*

SNIG[1]. A small eel. Also called Grig.

SNIG[2]. To catch eels.

"We go snigging today."

SNIGGLER, m. *A slight frost.*

SNOB, m. [*Connected with Icel.*, snápr, *a fool and knave.*] *A travelling shoemaker; a cobbler.*

In the neighbourhood of Burwash it is considered a most unfavourable description of a stranger to say that he is "a broken down snob from Kent."

SNOTTER. A loop of rope into which the foot of the sprit of a hog boat was fitted, and which was pushed up the mast of the boat to set the sail properly.

SNOTTY-GOG. A yew berry or fruit.

As children we used to eat them, expelling the pips.

SNOULE, e. *A small quantity of anything. Used in Norfolk for a short thick cut from the crusty part of a loaf or a cheese.*

SNOWBALL ROSE.‡ (Snowball *tree* + *Guelder* rose.) *Viburnum Opulus.*

SNUB. A short peg left on a stick or pole.

Snub

SNUDGE, m. *To hold down the head; to walk with a stoop looking on the ground as if in deep thought.*

"There they goos, acrost the Common, snudging along." — *Heard at Lindfield.*

SNUFFY, m. *Angry. A common nickname for a testy person.*

"*Old snuffy came snudging along here just now, and wanted to borrow a few Brussels sprouts, but I lent him a brockylo once and never got it back again, so I warn't agoing to be took in a second time.*"

SO . . . AS. Comparitive.

"An' there lay 'is bones, so white as a hound's tooth."—*Speaking of a skeleton.*

SOCK, m. *A blow.*

"*I'll give that old sow-cat o' yourn a sock aside the head if I catches her in my house agin !*"

SOCKHEAD. A stupid person; usually applied to a male.

SOCKISH, m. (*Probably a variation of Suckish.*) *Requiring to be petted and nursed; said of a child.*

SOCK-LAMB, m. *A lamb brought up by hand.* Also called a hob-lamb.

SOCKLE, m. *To suckle.*

SODGER, m. *A red herring; literally a soldier.*

The sirloin of a jackass, stuffed with sodgers, is a Sussex man's definition of coarse, univiting food.

SO-EY. So; like that; thereabouts. About so-ey: somewhere near. (See S.S. & C. under Hedge-carpenter.)

SOKELAND. See Sookland.

SOLE. The bottom or tread of the felloe of a wheel.

When a wagon wheel is shod with plates and not a full tyre, the plates are called sole plates.

SOLID. Grave; serious; Responsible.

SOLLY, e. *A tottering or unstable condition.*

"*That cart-lodge of Mus' Dicksey's is all of a solly; t'wunt least but a very little while longer afore it comes down.*"

Solly is a deformation of Sally, to move or run from side to side, to pitch forward, or up and down as the sallies on bell ropes. (*Cf.* Bob-solly.)

SOME-AND-SOME. Here and there; not all from one place.

"May I pick some of your lent liles, please?"

"Surelye, Miss, pick 'em some and some."

SOME-ONE-TIME, m. *Now and then; occasionally.*

"*Some-one-time I goos across to the Chequers, but döant make no rule of it.*"

SOME SORT.‡ When said of weather it means bad.

SOMEWHEN. At some time.

So usual that a fairly well educated Sussex man does not recognise that it is provincial. Anywhen is just as usual.

SOOKLAND or SOKELAND, e. [*Soc.* Ang. Sax., a right or privilege of court, or of taking action at court.] (*Cf.* Soke of Peterborough.) *A name in the manor of Wadhurst for assartland.* (See Bondland, and S.S. & C. under Borough English.)

SOOR[1], m. *An exclamation expressive of surprise.*

SOOR[2]. [*Corruption of Swore.*]

"When I told him that the calves was got into the greenhouse, he jumped up and soor that dreadful that I was all of a shake."

SOPS-AND-ALE. A curious custom formerly prevalent at Eastbourne, which has fallen into disuse in the present century. The senior bachelor of the parish was elected by the inhabitants to the office of steward, and had committed to his charge a damask napkin, a great wooden bowl, twelve wooden trenchers, a dozen wooden knives and forks, two wooden candlesticks and two wooden sugar basins.

Whenever a matron within the parish increased her family, it was the duty of this official to go to the church door on the Sunday fortnight after the interesting event, and there publicly proclaim that sops and ale would be provided that evening at a certain house agreed upon, where the following arrangements were made. Three tables were placed in some convenient room, one of which was covered with the damask table cover and furnished with a china bowl, plates, and silver-handled knives and forks; the bowl was filled with biscuits steeped in wine and sweetened with fine sugar. The second table was also covered with a cloth and decently provided with knives, forks and china, and a bowl containing beer-sops sweetened with fine sugar. The third table had no cloth, was furnished with the wooden trenchers, candlesticks, etc., and had its wooden bowl filled with beer-sops sweetened with the coarsest sugar. After evening prayers the company assembled at the house of their entertainer, and were placed in the following order:—The persons whose wives had presented them with twins sat at the first table, and were addressed as "benchers"; those whose partners had blessed them in a less degree were ranged round the second table; while those who were married but childless, were placed with the old bachelors at the third table. Various toasts were given, and the company always broke up at the temperate hour of eight, "generally very cheerful and good tempered."—Sussex Archæological Collections, *vol. xiii. p. 228.*

SORB. See Serb.

SORE-LEG PUDDING, *w.*‡ Blanket pudding (*q.v.*), etc.

SOSS-ABOUT, e. *To mix different things together; generally applied to liquids.*

"*To soss*" *in the North means to go about in the dirt.*

SOSSEL[1]. *To make a slop.*

SOSSEL[2]. To have a good drink.

"We had a fine game sure 'nuff, and when the match was over we all went to the White Hart and had a grand sossel."

SOUL CAKES. Hot spiced buns, given to children who went souling.

SOULING. Going from house to house on All Souls Day (Nov. 2) with a collecting box. See S.S. & C.

SOUTER. A shoemaker. A term still used. A shoemaker in Sussex so described himself when claiming exemption before a Military Tribunal during World War I.

SOW[1]. *A word used among the old Sussex iron-workers for a weight of 2,000 lb.* (See S.S. & C. under Iron-working.)

Strictly a sow was a large piece of crude cast iron from the first smelting, only nominally of any particular weight. See Pig[1].

SOW[2]. A female rat.

SOW-BADGER. Female badger.

SOW-BUG. Woodlouse; Slater (*q.v.*) *Ligia.*

SOW-CAT, m. *A female cat.*

SOW TRACK. The old ridge way across Rushton Park by Mountfield to Netherfield was known in Tudor times by this name. It was used for hauling sows and guns to Winchelsea and Rye.

SOW-WAPS. The queen wasp.

In some parts of the county a reward of sixpence is offered for each sow-waps killed in the spring.

SPACE[1]. *A measurement of three feet. Spaces and rods are almost the only terms of measurement I have ever heard used by country people.*

SPACE[2]. *To measure ground.* One spaces it out by taking yard long paces.

SPACKLE or SPACKOLD. Speckled.

SPADGE. A plough paddle or plough staff (for clearing the plough).

SPADGERS. Sparrows.

SPALE. Another name for spile[2] (*q.v.*)

SPALLS, *m.* Small chips that fly off from the axe when felling timber: larger ones are called Chucks.

SPALT, e, or SPOLT. [*Connected with the Dutch* spalten, *to split.*] *Split; brittle; decayed. Applied to timber* . . . that breaks carroty (*q.v.*) as horse-chestnut does. (*Cf.* Sprow.)

SPALTER, w. *To split or chip off.*

SPANNEL, m. *To make dirty footmarks about a floor, as a spaniel dog does.* Like Stabble, (*q.v.*)

"*I goos into the kitchen and I says to my mistus, I says ('was of a Saddaday), the old sow's hem ornary, I says. Well, says she, there aint no call for you to come spanneling about my clean kitchen any more for that, she says; so I goos out and didn't say naun, for you can't never make no sense of women-folks of a Saddaday.*"

Shakespeare uses the word in the sense of dogging the steps,—

"*The hearts that spaniel'd me at heels.*"
—Antony and Cleopatra, *Act iv. sc 10.*

SPANNER, w. *A wrencher; a nut-screw.*

SPAN-NEW. *Quite new.* Very new and smart.

SPAR, or SPARRER. [Spére, *Ang. Sax., a spear.*] Called also Spick, Speek and Spelk. *A stick pointed at each end, and doubled and twisted in the middle; used by thatchers to secure the straw on the roof of stack or building.*

This is more often called the sparrer; spar alone usually refers to the running spar or runner which is laid along the roof and pinned to the thatch with the sparrer.

SPARGAD. A rod of hazel quartered, from which spars and sparrers are made.

SPARR. [*Corruption of Sparrow, as Barr for Barrow*] (q.v.)

SPARRER, or SPARROW. A spar, two feet long and pointed at each end, twisted in the middle and bent like a large staple; used to pin the running spars, runners or bond-cord to the thatch. Also called a peg.

Sparrer

SPARROW. A sparrer, (*q.v.*)

Because a twisted spar with which a running spar is sparred to the thatch is called a sparrer, contracted to sparr'r; and because a sparrow (the bird) is called a sparr'r, for sparrer, for sparrow; the peg sparrer is also by typical Sussex transposition, called a sparrow. (*Cf.* Farisees and Pharisees.)

SPARTACLES. [*An invariable corruption of Spectacles.*]

SPAT. *A slap or blow.*

SPATS, m. *Leather gaiters reaching above the knee.* Sometimes said 'Pats.'

SPATTER BOARDS. Backstays, (*q.v.*) etc.

SPATTLEDASHES, m. *Short leather gaiters not reaching much above the ankle.* The real word is 'Spatterdashes' and is contracted to 'spats.'

SPEAK AFTER, *w.*‡ To repeat gossip.

SPEAR[1], m. *The sting of a bee.* Also the tongue of a snake or lizard which are said to 'sting.'

A bee is always said to bite *in Sussex.*

SPEAR[2]. *To sprout up out of the ground.*

"*Soonsever the peas begins to spear, the meece and the sparrs gets holt an' em.*"

SPEAR-POLE. A wooden spear used for catching flat fish in rivers.

SPEECHMENT. Talk. Rare speechment—*i.e.* cultured manner of speech.

SPEEK or SPELK. Spar (*q.v.*), (for thatching.)

SPELTS. *Iron toes and heels for boots.* More often called Pelts.

SPENE, or SPEEN. *The prong of a pitchfork*, or other forked implement. (*i.e.* Tine or spine.)

SPENES. [Spana, *Ang. Sax.*] *The teats of a cow.*

SPET. *Spit.*

"*The old cat set there, and there she set, and spet and soor and went on all the whole time.*"

SPICE. [Espéce, *French.*] *A slight attack of illness.*

"*I had a spice of the ague last week, and I doànt want no more of him, for all that they says* ' *'tis worse* not *to have him than 'tis to !* ' "

SPICK. Spar (*q.v.*), (for thatching.)

SPIKED RAMPION. *Phyteuma spicatum.* A rare plant bearing cream-coloured flowers, found only in Sussex.

Spiked Rampion

SPILE[1], w. *A spigot.*

SPILE[2]. A stake: a spile fence is one made of vertical stakes, pointed at the end, hammered straight into the ground and connected top and bottom and sometimes between both, with twisted wire. Also called "spale". (See S.S.&C. under Copse, Coppicing and Hedge and fence.)

Spile Fence

SPILE[3]. To put such stakes in the ground.

SPILE[4]. Spoil. (*Cf.* Spill.)

"He's spiled all his hay."

SPILL. Spoil; destroy.

"So full of artless jealousy is guilt
It spills itself in fearing to be spilt."
—*Hamlet*, Act iv. sc. 5.

SPILT. [Spillan, *Ang. Sax., to spoil.*] *Spoiled.*

"*She shod the milk all over her, and spilt her new frock.*"

SPILWOOD. Refuse of wood; wood split (or spoilt) by the sawyers. (*Cf.* Scutchett, or Scrutchell.)

SPINNEY. A thicket; a small plantation.

SPIRE. A tree not polled.

"One Oake pollard, 2 Spire Do. 23 Spire Elm Trees, 19 Pollard Elm Trees."—*Tompkins Diary Extracts. S.A.C. LXXI.* p. 27.

SPIRES. Upright spars at the end of the comb of thatch, sometimes ornamented with an onion or a potato.

SPIT[1], m. *As much earth as can be taken up at once with a spade.*

SPIT[2]. Likeness.

"The very spit of him"—just like him.

SPIT[3]. A pointed piece of wood.

Spit means a point; Spithead —a point of land.

SPIT-DEEP, m. *As deep as a spade goes in digging.*

SPITTLE. A kind of short, broad peel; used for turning oatcakes. It is 26 inches long, of which the handle is 15 inches.

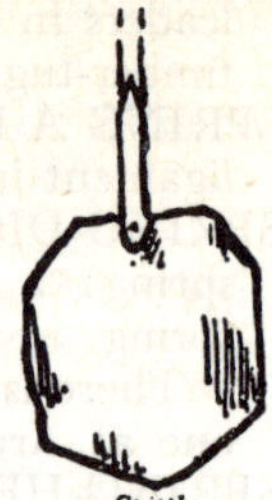

Spittle

SPLASH[1], m. *To bank up a hedge.* (See S.S. & C. under Hedge and fence.)

SPLASH[2], e., *or SPLISHER*, m. *To lay a live hedge.* Or rather to layer a live hedge. (See Layers, and S.S.&C. under Hedge and fence.)

SPLEAT.‡ A Clish.

SPLEATS. (Allied to splint and splinter, wood divided by cleaving.) The bars of a field gate, usually four or five; the broader top bar being the beam (*q.v.*)

SPLINTER-BAR. The front cross member of the Hounds of a waggon etc., to which the thills, or of a coach etc., to which the pole and the traces are attached. Sometimes confused with Pummeltree (*q.v.*)

SPLISHER. To layer a hedge. (See splash[2], and S.S.&C. under Hedge and fence.)

SPLIT[1]. Hogboat's foresail boom or bumpkin.

SPLIT[2]. Spoilt.

"Them maggots have split all my peas."

SPOLT. See Spalt.

SPONG[1], e. *To cobble; to work in a rough clumsy way with a needle.*

SPONG[2]. An irregular, narrow, projecting part of a field, whether planted or in grass.

There is a house in Lindfield High Street called "Spongs."

SPRACKISH, w. *Smart and active.*

SPRAY-WOOD. Faggots of brushwood used in the ovens.

SPREAD-BAT, e., or SPREADER. *A wooden bar used to keep the chains apart from rubbing the horses' legs and sides when drawing a plough or harrow*, or in any trace harness, as leaders in the team of a waggon, timber-tug, etc.

SPRING A LEADER. To strain a ligament in hand, foot, etc.

SPRING-DICK. A ditch fed by a spring: a stream running from a spring.

There is one at Shoreham, and one at Arundel.

SPRING-HEELED JACK. A practical joker who early in the 19th century terrified walkers by suddenly springing on them.

SPROCKET. A triangular piece of wood extending a rafter over the eaves of a house, and reducing the pitch of the roof there.

SPROG. A linch-pin.* Or lynsepin. Also called a prog.

SPRONG, e., *or SPRONK*, m. *The roots of a tree or a tooth.*

SPRONKY, m. *Full of roots.*

"Ah! I guv' old Muz' Tweazer the biggest job o' tooth-pulling ever he had! It took him purty nigh two hours! and he said he'd never seen such a tooth all his days, to goo so fur down nor yet to be so spronky."

SPROW. Short and brittle; as ash or elm grown in sand. Same as Spalt (*q.v.*) and Carroty.

SPRUG, e. *To smarten.* Sprug-up means neatly dressed.

"She was sprug-up for our outing last Sad'dy."

SPRUT. To jerk violently, as with a spasm: a sudden movement.

SPRY, e. *Gay; cheerful.* Vivacious.

A word frequently used in America, meaning "in good health."

SPUD. A light garden tool with a long handle for cutting up weeds. Also an ordinary garden fork.

Spud

SPUDDLE, m. *To use a spud.* To fork over without digging.

"*I be gettin' in years and can't do no more than just doddle about the ground and spuddle up a few weeds.*"

SPUNK. Decayed wood . . . touch-wood used for tinder.

Spurtle

SPURTLE. A small straight stick, slender, sturdy and wedge-shaped at one end used for stirring porridge, stews, sauce, etc., instead of a wooden spoon. Called also Theeval.

SQUAB[1]. A young unfledged bird.

SQUAB[2]. A well-stuffed cushion, usually long, used on a settee.

SQUACKETT, m. *To quack like a duck.*

"*I thought Mus' Reynolds was about last night, the ducks kep all on squacketting so.*"

SQUARING AXE. A small axe used by woodmen for squaring the trunk at the base before sawing. Properly, used for axe-squaring timbers which were never sawn.

SQUAT[1], w. *To indent or bruise anything by letting it fall.*

SQUAT[2]. A small, low beer cask.

SQUAT[3]. See Chucle.

SQUAT[4]. A more recent improvement on the squat-bat (*q.v.*), consisting of a small wooden roller hooped with iron at each end and attached to a chain fixed to the axle of a waggon and to the hub of the wheel. It was drawn along close behind the wheel to squat or hold the wheel when the horses rested on a hill. See S.S.&C.

Also anything used to effect the same result. (*Cf.* Trig[1].)

Squat-Bat

SQUAT-BAT, e. *A piece of wood used for stopping a wheel while the horses are at rest on a hilly road.*

SQUATTY, w. *Said of meal that has fermented.*

SQUEAKER. The swift. Called also Sreech, or Screech.

SQUEEZEGATE or SQUEEZER. A narrow opening between two

posts set out of the vertical with just room for one leg, with a sideways movement to pass through. Used instead of a stile on footways and generally from one field to another.

SQUENCH, or SQUENCE, m. [*Corruption of Quench.*]

Blacksmiths "squench" hot iron in the water.

SQUIN. A scallop.

SQUINNEY. To squint; to pry about.

SQUIRM. To wriggle like an eel.

SQUISH-SQUASH. The noise made by feet walking over swampy ground.

SQUR-RL. Squirrel. (Pronounciation similar to Bar'r for barrow.) Its nest is a Cage, Dray or Draw.

SREECH, SREECHER. Screech, Screecher, (*q.v.*) Both the Swift or Deviling and the Missel-thrush or Storm Cock are so called among many other names.

SRIMP. Deformation of shrimp.

STAB. A small hole in the ground in which the rabbit secures her young litter. A Stop, or Stop-hole.

This is not the rabbit bury, or collection of holes, but apart by itself and with only one entrance.

STABBLE, e. *To make a floor dirty by walking on it in wet or muddy shoes.* (*Cf.* Spannel.)

STADDLES. Another name for taller grown totts. (*Cf.* Stools and Tot[3]. See S.S.&C. under Copse —coppicing.)

STADE, e. [Stede, *Ang. Sax.*] *A shore where ships can be beached; a landing place.* A staith. This word is much used at Hastings.

STAFF-SHOVEL. A long-handled one with iron spiked haft used by charcoal burners.

STALDER. [Stælan, *Ang. Sax., to place.*] *The stool on which casks are placed in a cellar.*

STALLAGE, m. or STOLLAGE (*Same as Stalder.*)

STALLED, e. *Tired; satiated.*

"*Ain't you fairly stalled of waiting?*"

"*I think the old dog has stalled himself now, for he found a stab out in the field and eat the lot.*"

STAM. The stump of a felled tree.

STAMMERS. The fresh shoots of a tree which has been cut back. I.e., those that grow from the stem directly, not indirectly from the branches.

STAM-WOOD, m. [Stam, *Dutch, a stem; a trunk of a tree.*] *The roots of trees, stubbed or grubbed up.* (*Cf.* Stam.)

STANDING. A stall at a market or fair.

STANDUP. To take shelter from rain.

STANFAST. Stand fast; firm. The warning given by the carter to those on the wagon before he moves his horses when taking up hay or sheaves in the field.

STANLEY. Iron tripod to take the weight of horse's leg at shoeing. Also called Lazyboy.

STARK, e. [Sterc, *Ang. Sax., rigid.*] *Ground is said to be stark or starked up, when the surface has dried very quickly after rain.*

STARKY, e. *Flinty.*

"*The land is very starky.*"

START. An excitement; a fuss.

"*There's been a pretty start up at the forge this morning! Fighting and all manner.*"

When a Sussex man is at a loss for words to describe events or ideas of a somewhat discreditable nature, he gets out of the difficulty by using the phrase "all manner!" If he wishes to describe great profusion and plenty, he says "there was everything of something and something of everything, as the saying is;" but where he gets the saying from I have no idea.

STASH. Stash up, to destroy . . . end . . . as of a game interfered with; or a society broken up.

"You've no call to come and stash up our game."

STATESMAN, m. *An estates' man; a man who owns a few acres of land and farms them himself.*

The general condition of such persons is that their property is mortgaged, and with much harder work they are worse off than ordinary labourers.

STEALE. [Stela, *Ang. Sax., a handle.*] *The handle of most agricultural implements.*

STEAN[1]. *To pave a road with stones; to line a well or a grave with stone or brick.*

The Steine, at Brighton probably, derives its name from this word.

STEAN[2], m. *To mark out a field for ploughing, which is usually done by placing large stones to show the lines.*

STEDDLE[1]. [Stathol, *Ang. Sax., a basis.*] *The wooden frame-work placed on stones or other support, on which corn stacks are built.* See S.S.&C.

When made of faggots laid on the ground it is called a treddle (*q.v.*)

Steddle

STEDDLE[2], m. *A small side table, or a temporary arrangement of boards and trestles.*

STELL. To check as horses do a cart by pushing back against the breeching.

STENT[1], m. *A portion of work appointed to be done in a set time.*

STENT[2], or STINT. A period of running for a windmill or a watermill.

STEW. A pool in which fish are kept for the table.

STILE GATE. Same as Tumble-down gate (*q.v.*), or Clatterdown gate.

STILL. Quiet; respectable.

"*He's a nice still man.*"

STILL-WATERS. Distilled waters.

There is generally an old woman in every village who is a notable distiller of waters, which are in great request as domestic medicine. (*Cf.* Still-room.)

STILTS[1]. *Crutches.*

It is rather surprising to be told that a person is such a complete cripple that he can only walk with stilts.

If infirm and uses sticks he is said to "walk on two bats." (*Cf.* bat.) Or to Cuddle (*q.v.*)

STILTS[2]. The handles of a wooden plough.

STINT[1], e. *Shabby; undergrown.*

STINT[2]. See Stent.

STITHE, w., or STITHY. *An anvil.* See Pointing stithe.

"*If his occulted guilt*
Do not itself unkennel in one speech,
It is a damned ghost that we have seen;
And my imaginations are as foul
As Vulcan's stithy."
—Hamlet, *Act iii, sc. 2.*

STIVE. A straw hive or coop in which fighting game cocks were put to keep them warm.

STIVED-UP, m. *Crowded.* Cognate with stifling.

"*We were all stived-up in one room. There was four families, one in each corner, and a single man who slep' in the middle. I put up with it as long as I could, but when the single man began to take in lodgers I couldn't stand it no longer.*"

STIVER. To go vigorously.

"Look 'ow 'e stivers through the slub."

STIVER-ABOUT. (*The i is pronounced as in shiver.*) *To stagger.*

STOACH, e. *To trample ground as cattle do in wet weather.* Usually with poach (*q.v.*) An entry to a field in bad weather will be "all stoached and poached." (*Cf.* Stug and Paunch.)

STOACH-WAY, e. *An expression used at Rye harbour for the channel which runs through the sand lying between the pier-head and the deep water at low tide.* At Selsey and around there they would call that a "swatch-way." (*q.v.*)

STOACHY. Dirty; muddy.

STOCK. Fertilized; of a cow.

"She is stocked for September."

STOCK-CARD. A standing (or fixed) carding comb.

STOCK STILE. [*Stoccen*, Ang. Sax., made of stocks, tree trunks, stakes.] A stile made of stocks or logs of wood. The same sense is implied in the names Stockbridge, (Chichester) and Stock Ferry (formerly near Itford.)

STOCKY[1], m. *Strong; stout; well grown.*

STOCKY[2], m. *Headstrong; saucy; wilful; generally said of girls.*

> "*Since nought so stockish, hard, and full of rage,*
> *But music for the time doth change his nature.*"
> —Merchant of Venice, *Act v. sc. 1.*

STODGE[1], e. *Thick mud.* (*See Stoach.*) Also thick pudding. (*Cf.* Stug.)

"This pudden do be stodgy."

STODGE[2], m. *A fuss.*

"*He's always in such a stodge; if he's got to goo anywhere's he always wants to be off two hours too soon.*"

STODGED. Satiated with eating, especially of schoolboys.

"I'm stodged!"

STOKE. To stir the fire; hence the word stoker.

STOKOS. Oatmeal and water flavoured with lemon for a refresher insead of beer.

STOLIDGE. See Stallage and stalder.

STOLT, e. *Stout; strong; generally said of fowls.*

"*The chickens are quite stolt.*"

STOMACHY, m. *Proud; obstinate.*

STONE. A weight of eight pounds. Generally pronounced 'stun'. A nail (*q.v.*)

STOOD, m. *Stuck fast.*

An old man told me, "*I've seen a wagon stood in the snow on the road from Selmeston to Alciston, and they never moved it for six weeks.*"

STOOK. A collection of shocks or sheaves stood together as a protection against weather and for convenience of carting.

STOOL-BALL. An old Sussex game similar in many respects to cricket, played by females. It has lately been revived in East Sussex by the establishment of stool-ball clubs in many villages, which not only provide good exercise for young ladies who might otherwise become lazy, but also promote kind, social intercourse among all classes. The 'elevens' go long distances to play their matches; they practice regularly, and frequently display such perfection of fielding and wicket-keeping as would put most amateur cricketers to shame. The rules are printed, and are as keenly discussed and implicitly obeyed as those of the Marylebone Club. Boys often play stool-ball with the girls now.

The game is thus alluded to in Poor Robin's Almanack for 1740,—

> "*Now milkmaid's pails are deckt with flowers,*
> *And men begin to drink in bowers;*
> *Sweet sillabubs, and lip-loved tansey,*
> *For William is prepared by Nancy.*
> *Whilst hob-nail Dick and simp'ring Frances*
> *Trip it away in country dances;*
> *At stool-ball and at barley-break,*
> *Wherewith they harmless pastime make.*"

Also called Bittle-battle (*q.v.*)

STOOLS. Stumps. The roots of copse cut down nearly to the ground; Staddles; Tots or Totts (*q.v.*)

(See also S.S.&C. under Copse —coppicing.)

STOP, e. *A rabbit-stab; probably socalled because the doe stops up the entrance when she leaves her young.*

Sometimes called 'stop-hole.' (*Cf.* Stab.)

STORE. To store is to value.

"I stores that brooch, it belonged to my mother."

STORM-BOLT, *w.*‡ When only the lower part of the rainbow is seen it is called a storm-bolt; it is said to foretell a long spell of bad weather.

STORM-COCK, or SREECHER. The missel thrush. See Screech. Also called Grey-bird and Shrite.

STOT, w. *A young bullock.*

STOUT. Stout-fly, a fly that stings and bites. Cattle worried with them rush about with their tails raised:

"They've got the stout."

The gadfly; also locally known as the Goad fly.

STRAND, m. *A withered stalk of grass; one of the twists of a line.* See Heart-strand.

STRANGER. A stalk of tea floating in the tea-cup is called a stranger; applied to a visitor. Put on the back of one hand and smitten with the back of the other hand the number of smacks used to get it off tells the number of days to pass before the visit will happen. If a hard stalk it is said to be a male visitor, if a soft one a female visitor.

*STREALE.** [Stræl, *Ang. Sax.*] *An arrow.*

STREET. In Sussex a road is called a street without any reference to there being houses beside it; but I am quite unable to say why some roads should be distinguished from others by being so called. (*A street originally meant a paved road, from the Latin* strata via.)

The village Streat is on a Roman road. It has preserved its Latin name, although the road has been lost for centuries. Street, is generally used as High Street, a part of the High Road or principal thoroughfare, but not necessarily the most important street. *E.g.* Cart or Cat Street, now called Cade Street, Heathfield, part of the old Mid-Sussex ridgeway.

STREWERS. Persons who cast flowers, etc. before the Bride and Bridegroom. See S.S. & C.

STRICKLES. Made by smearing grease on a shaped piece of wood and embedding fine sand in it to give an extra fine edge after sharpening on the stone, to sickles, fag-hooks, swap-hooks and so forth. (*Cf.* Ripe-stick.)

STRIDE, m. *A long distance.*

"*I doànt exactly know the name of the place he's gone to, but I know 'tis a middling stride into the sheeres.*"

STRIG. The foot-stalk of any fruit or flower. As of currants, etc.

STRIKE. A smooth straight piece of wood used in measuring, to strike the loose corn which lies above the level of the rim of the bushel.

In old inventories "a bushel and strike" usually go together.

STRIKE-PLOUGH, m. *A plough used for striking out the furrows.*

STRIKER. A swiple or swingel; the beating part of a flail. Often made of maple, the handle being of hazel; the hinge part is of ash bent over and secured with raw hide which together make a swivel hinge. See Flail hinge.

STRIVES, m. *Rivalry.*

"*Sometimes I think those people must dress so for strives, to see who can be smartest.*"

STROD. A forked branch of a tree. A catapult strod, like the letter Y.

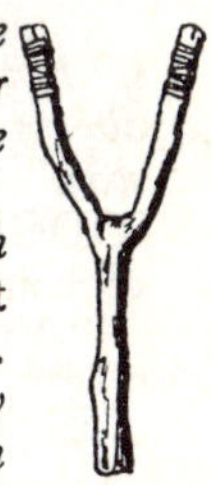

Strod

STROMBOLO. (*Possibly connected with the Dutch* stroomballen, *stream or tide balls.*)

"*Pieces of black bitumen highly charged with sulphur and salt, found along the coast. Called thus at Brighton, doubtless from the Flemings settled in the town. The stones have been used for fuel, and Dr. Russell applied the steam to scrofulous tumours.*"

—Durrant Cooper's Sussex Glossary.

STROWS. Waterways of the Pevensey and Romney Marshes. (See S.S. & C. under Wahztrew.)

STRUTH ! (God's Truth.) A mild oath of exclamation; of surprise, etc.

STUB[1], e. *The stem which is left standing out of the ground after a tree has been cut down.*

STUB[2], e. *To stub a horse is to lame him by letting him tread on stubs of underwood in a cover.*

STUB[3]. To dash one's foot against a stone, etc.

"In the dark I stubbed my toe agin' the bed leg."

STUB[4], m. *To grub up trees with their roots.*

STUB[5], m. *To pluck chicken clean after their feathers have been pulled off.*

STUCKLING. *An apple-pasty made thin in the shape of a semicircle, and baked without a dish.* An apple-turnover; a Flapjack; a Crowdie.

STUD, m; *STUDY*, e. *A state of thoughtfulness.*

"*He seems all in a stud as he walks along.*"

STUG, *e.* See Gubber; Paunch; Poach; Pug; Slab; Sleech; Slob; Slogh; Slub; Slurry; Stoach; Stodge and Swank.

STUGGY. Cledgy; Clodgy; Slabby; Slobby; Slubby; Smeery and Stoachy.

Sussex, being a notoriously muddy county, has many names for mud and muddiness, the fine distinctions of which can be appreciated only by close contact with the mud. (*Cf.* Garm; Gawm; Gorm; Hike; Ike; Slub-up; Spannel; Stabble.)

STUMP, w. *A stump of hay is an item frequently found in farm inventories in West Sussex. It means the remains of a round stack, most of which has been cut away.*

"Round" is an intrusion, that would be a corn rick, not hay. (*Cf.* Core.)

STUMP-OUT.‡ To tether cows for grazing. The cow needs some education for this method, otherwise she tangles up her chain.

STUPE, e. *Stupid; dull.*

An old schooldame thus described the progress of a pupil (aged 5):— "*He's that stupe that he can't tell 'A's' from 'V's', and he actually dòant know the meaning of 'Verily, verily!'*"

STUSNET. *A skillet; a small saucepan.* A Posnet.

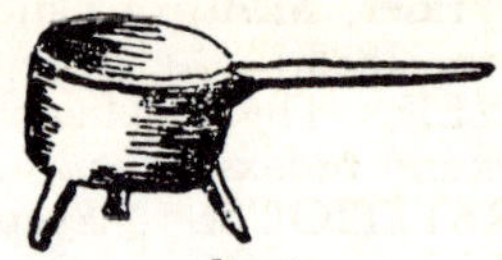

Stusnet

SUCK, or SUCKED-IN. Deceived.

"Yaas 'twere a fair suckin' fer me."

"Suck for you!" is the schoolboy's exclamation of triumph.

SUDDENT, m. Suddenly.

SUDDING. Suddingly for suddenly.

"Death be so sudding."

SUE, e. *To drain land; also a drain.* (See Sew, [1] & [2].)

SUENT, e. *Pleasant; agreeable.* Moving freely and easily whether of an animal or of a machine.

"'E be very suently inclined to 'er I reckon."

SUFRENS. Sovereigns. (Coins.)

SULFURIOUS. (Probably a confusion of sulphur and furious.)

"Did you see the northern lights last night?" "Ah! smelt most sulfurious it did!"

SULLAGE. [Souiller, *French to soil.*] *Any filth or dirt of the nature of a sediment.*

SUMMER[1], e. *The beam which supports the bed or body of a wagon.*

SUMMER[2] *AND WINTER*, w. *To have summered and wintered a person is to have known him at all seasons and under all circumstances, both good and bad.*

SUMMERINGS. The earliest apples and pears.

SUN 'DRAWING WATER'. Said when rays shew through and against cloud and fall straight to the sea.

SUNGREEN. House leek. *Sempervivum tectórum.* Also called thunderwort as it is supposed to guard against the house being struck by lightning.

SUN-HOUND.‡ A halo round the sun (but not parahelion—a mock

sun.) Generally a sign of rain.

(Note from Parish to the Revd. Jas. Fraser, M.A., of Chichester, August, 1882.)

SUNREEK. The evening mist on rivers and brooks.

SUPERSTITIOUS. Suspicious; inquisitive.

A flint-breaker at Kithurst, formerly a shepherd, said, "If anything comes fer me (*i.e.*, a parcel) they most gen'raly over-'auls it t'see what the old gen'leman (himself) got. They be terr'ble superstitious."

SUPPOSE, m. *This word is used not to express conjecture, but certainty.*

SURE, and NO-SURE. Certainly, and Certainly not.

"Sure as God made little apples."

"Mus Collins 'e sez 'Your runts was in my clover-lay. I suppose,' an' I sez 'No-sure they wus not'."

SURELYE. There are few words more frequently used by Sussex people than this. It has no special meaning of its own, but it is added at the end of any sentence to which particular emphasis is required to be given, and numerous examples of its use will be found in illustrations of other words in this dictionary.

Two syllables, both accented, the second very strongly.

SUSHY, e. [Séche, *French*, *dry*.] *In want of water.*

"*I never knowed such a dry time; we're as sush as sushy.*"

SUSSEL. A disturbance; an impertinent meddling with the affairs of other people.

SUSSEX CAP. The small pyramidal cap on a church tower, usually a Norman tower. Found occasionally in other counties but frequently in Sussex; North Lancing, Clayton and Slaugham are typical examples.

Sussex cap

SUSSEX DIAMONDS. Flints, especially knapped flints or broken flints as distinct from pitchers. (See S.S. & C. under Flint.)

SUSSEX MARBLE. See Winkle stone.

SUSSEX-MOON. A man sent on in front with a lantern fastened behind him. Also the large lanthorns used on the broad wheeled wagons.

SUSSEX-PUDDING. A compound of flour and water made up in an oblong shape and boiled. There is a moment when it is first taken out of the saucepan, when it can be eaten with impunity; but it is usually eaten cold, and in that form I believe that it becomes the foundation of all the ills that Sussex spirit and flesh are heir to. It promotes a dyspeptic form of dissent which is unknown elsewhere. It aggravates every natural infirmity of temper by the promotion of chronic indigestion, and finally undermines the constitution; for the first symptom of the decay of nature which a Sussex man describes is invariably that he can't get his pudding to set. It was often cut in slices and eaten when cold with treacle especially for breakfast. See S.S. & C.

SUSSEX WEED. Oak tree.

SWAB. Swab-hook. Same as Swap; Swap-hook.

SWAD, or SWOD, e. *A bushel basket, generally used in selling fish.*

SWADE. The leather strap of a spinning-wheel.

SWADING-IRON, w. *An instrument used in a blacksmith's forge.*

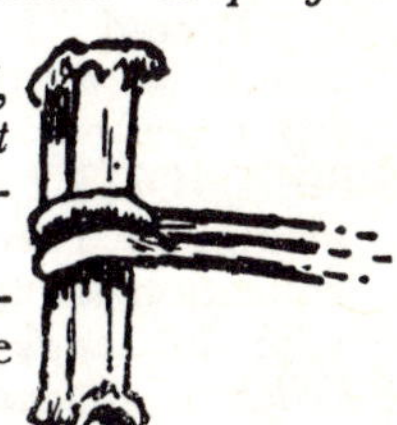

Swading-Iron

SWAFFLE-HOOK. Same as Swap-hook.

SWAITHE LAND. *w.* ‡ Heavy clay or gault land.

SWALE; SWALE FIRE. To burn off the old Fag (*q.v.*) and grass to allow new grass to grow better by fertilizing the ground with the ash. Swaling on the Downs is a common sight. Also called Denshering, and in the west country Burn-beking. (*Cf.* Sweal[1].)

SWALLOCKY, e. *A term applied to the appearance of clouds in hot weather before a thunder-storm.*

SWANK, w. *A bog; a dell or damp hollow.*

SWANKY, m. *Small beer* . . . . light ale at one time bought at village provision shops for twopence a quart.

SWAP, m. *To reap corn and beans* . . . with a hook *not* a sickle: a sickle has a long tapering point; but a swap-hook, or swob-hook is cut off obliquely. Also, to trim hedges, cut rough grass, brambles, hawth and the like operations.

SWAP-HOOK, m. *The implement used for swapping.* Also called Swab-, Swaffle-and Swop-hook.

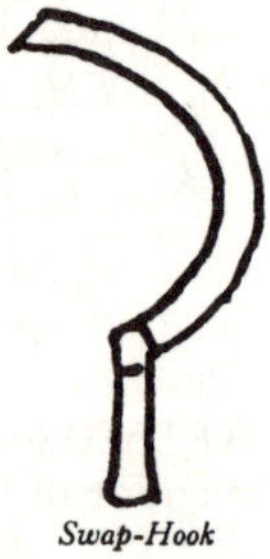

Swap-Hook

SWAP - MY - BOB. A kind of confirmative oath; a euphemistic rendering of "So help me God."

SWARLY or SWORLY. *Ill-tempered; usually applied to animals.*

SWARVE, e. *To fill up; to choke with sediment.* To silt up.

"*Our ditch is quite swarved up.*"

Various Sussex harbours are so swarved up as to leave the towns inland. *E.g.*, Rye, Pevensey, Lewes and others.

SWATCH-WAY. A small channel on a shoal coast by which one can get a boat to shore without going aground. (*Cf.* Stoach-way.)

SWATH. [*Pronounced swarth.*] *A row of cut grass or corn as it is laid on the ground by mowers or swappers.*

"*And there the strawy Greeks, ripe for his edge,*
Fall down before him, like the mower's swath."
—Troilus and Cressida, *Act v. sc. 5.*

SWEAL[1]. [Swélan, *Ang. Sax., to kindle.*] *To burn the hair; to singe a pig.* (Cf. Swale.)

SWEAL[2]. A thing that smells when burning like hair or feathers.

SWEEPS. The swifts, arms or sails of a windmill. The complete structure of spring or patent sail.

SWELT. [Sweltan, *Ang. Sax., to die.*] *Hot; faint.*

"*Like a swelt cat, better than it looks.*"

To swelt rice is to soften or slightly boil it before being baked in a pudding.

SWEYPINGS. Coarse refuse siftings of flour. (*Cf.* Pollard.)

SWIFT. A sheep bell giving a distinctive high note. See Sheep bells.

SWIFTS. Windmill sails; Sweeps, (*q.v.*); particularly the frames on which common (canvas) sails were rigged.

SWIMMERS. Flat discs of plain suet pudding boiled and then cut in two, with butter and sugar, or treacle, spread over them thus formed into half-circle sandwiches.

SWINGE. [Swingan, *Ang. Sax.*] *To flog.*

"*I will swinge him well when I catches him.*"

SWINGEL. [*Swing-el,* Ang. Sax., He who, or that which, beats or thrashes, from *swing* to beat, thrash, labour.] *That part of a flail which beats the corn out of the ear.* (The 'g' is soft.) Called also Swiple, Swipple, or Swingell. Usually made of maple.

(In an agricultural community, one who labours at beating or thrashing must surely be he who threshes with a flail.)

SWINGEL CAP. See Shuckle.

SWIP. Sweep—a windmill sail.

SWIPLE, SWIPPLE. [*Swip, Swipe,* Ang. Sax., a whip, scourge.] Swingel (*q.v.*)

SWISH[1]. Swiss. See S.S. & C.

SWISH[2]. Smart; swell.

"'E looked very swish w'en 'e come to that weddin'."

SWOD. A bushel basket for measuring fish. Also spelt swad.

SWORK. [*Corruption of Sulk.*] *To be angry and surly.*

SWORLE. *To snarl like a dog.*

SWYMY. [*Swimmy.*] *Giddy; faint.* A person who isn't seasick but feels bad is swymy or swymy-headed.

"*I felt so swymy that I was obliged to get up and go out of church.*"

T

TACHENERS.§ *Young men employed in the fishing boats.* (*Possibly so called from being* taken *to learn the trade.*) Or from teach. This is the same word as Takeners, (*q.v.*) The spelling Tacheners is from the Brighton Custumal of 1580.

TACK[1]. *A peculiar flavour; a strong, rank, nasty taste.*

TACK[2]. *A path or causeway.*

TACKLE[1]. *Working implements; machinery of any kind.* Ploughing tackle, reaping tackle, threshing tackle, sketching tackle, fishing tackle, etc.

TACKLE[2]. *Distasteful* or other *food or drink.*

"*I calls this here claret wine about the poorest tackle ever I tàasted.*"

Or used euphemistically as "proper tackle." Or as "This (viand) is pretty good tackle."

TAFFETY. Pernickety.

"She's that taffety you can't be upsides with her."

TAG. e. *A sheep of the first year.* A Teg.

TAIL-DOCKER. A wooden tool with a sharp rounded knife on a wooden handle used for shortening horses' tails.

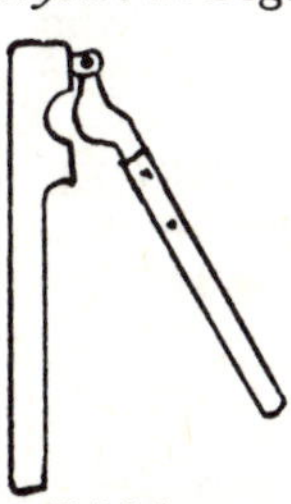

Tail-docker

TAILING IRON. A small spade-shaped iron on a rod with a wooden handle used for docking sheep's tails to ensure cleanliness.

TAIL-WHEAT, m. *The inferior grain which is left after the corn has been winnowed.*

TAINTER. Tenter; a linen finisher. See S.S. & C.

TAKENERS, m. *Persons taken to learn a trade; young men employed in fishing-boats at Brighton.* (*Cf.* Tacheners.)

TAKE THE GROUND. A boat is said to take the ground when she lies well on it without undue heeling.

TAKE UP. Of wood, to swell when wet and close open joints.

"She do leak above a bit, but she'll soon take up if you takes and sinks her."

TALK THIN. *To talk in a low voice.*

"*He talk so thin that no-one can't scarcely hear what he says.*"

TALL. At all.

"You've no need ter go in 'tall."

TALLYMAN. A door to door vendor of household things travelling to villages. Also another name for the Busheler who measures the hops from the bin. (See S.S. & C. under Hop drying.)

TALWOOD, w. [Tailler, *French, to cut.*] *Wood cleft and cut into billets for firing.*

TAN. Tan bark; the bark of trees (chiefly oak) which was formerly used for tanning leather. The bark was stripped in pieces about 3 ft. long, and stacked to dry before being sent to the tan-yard. (*Cf.* Healers.)

TAN-FLAWING. *Taking the bark off trees, the bark itself being called tan.*

"*If I can get a job of tan-flawing I shall make out very well.*"

(*Cf.* Rining and Slip[1].)

TAN-SCRAPER. A tool used for Hatching, *i.e.*, scraping off the lichen or moss from the bark of newly felled trees. (*Cf.* Hatch[2].)

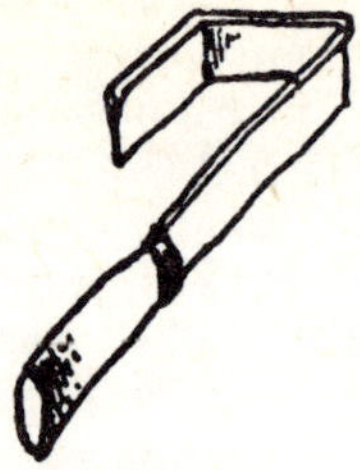

Tan-Scraper

TAN-SPUD. A flawing spud; a barking-iron, (*q.v.*); a tool used for Flawing or Rining trees.

TAPERING.‡ Temporary.

TAPSELL GATE. One working on a medial vertical pivot as at Friston Churchyard; Pyecombe, etc. Tapsell is a Sussex name and the gate seems to occur only in Sussex. (See S.S. & C.)

Tapsell Gate

TARBLE. Terrible. *E.g.*, Tarble Down where there was a battle. Turble has the same meaning. Both terms used to mean much, many, excessive.

TAR-BOY. Boy with tar pot at the sheep shearing . . . . the tar to dab on an accidental cut against fly or other pest. Sometimes lime is used instead. (See S.S. & C. under Ship.)

TAR CORD. Yarn dressed with tar used by fruit growers, gardeners and thatchers.

TARMINATION. Determination.

TARNAL or TARNEL. Equally well; very nearly.

" Master's bull would tarnal nigh go under that gurt ol' helefant."

TARRIFY. Terrify (*q.v.*)

TARRIFYER. One who worries; particularly a dog which worries or baits. It is probable that this sense of the word, modified to our usual terrier, has passed into general use.

TATER-DOG. Caterpillar or pupa of Death's Head Hawk Moth which frequents potatoes.

TAVORT. Half a bushel. (*See Tovet.*)

TAW[1]. A particularly choice large marble used in the game of marbles. Also known as an alley taw.

TAW[2]. A strap with a fringed edge for thrashing boys; used more in Scotland than in Sussex.

TAWER. [Tawian, *Ang. Sax., to prepare hides.*] *A fellmonger; a leather dresser.*

(" *Tawere*, a tawer," *Bosworth's Anglo-Saxon and English Dictionary.*)

TEAM[1], w. [Téman, *Ang. Sax., to propagate.*] *A litter, or a number of young beasts of any kind.*

" *I have got a nice team of young pigs here.*"

TEAM[2]. Horses' names. In a wagon team the horses are called thus:—

Wagon: 1. Thill horse, Thiller or Wheeler.
2. Body horse.
3. Lash horse.
4. Next to fore.
5. Fore horse or Leader.

TECK. Take. " Teck it away quick; 'tis bad."

TED, m. *To spread hay*; *to shake out the new mown grass.*

Nowadays the hay which has lain in swath until one side is dry, is " tedded " to dry the other side. Hence the implement used is the Tedder.

TEDDIOUS. Fretful; difficult to please.

TEDIOUS. Excessive; very. Pronounced ' Tejus.'

" *I never did see such tedious bad stuff in all my life.*"

" I come a tejus way."

TEGLEASE or TAGLEASE. Right to pasture sheep on the Down. See Leaze.

Tegleaze Common on Woolavington Down includes the highest point on the *South Downs* in *Sussex;* it is 837 feet above Ordnance datum.

TELL. [Tellan, *Ang. Sax., to count.*] *To count.*

" *Otherwhiles I be forced to tell the ship over six and seven times before I can get 'em right.*"

Shepherds tell their sheep letting the flock run through between two hurdles at a time. See S.S. & C.

TELLER, m; TELLAR; *or TILLOW*, w. [Telgor, *Ang. Sax., a branch.*] *A young oak tree.* A storer; one left in an underwood to grow into a timber tree. (See S.S. & C., under Copse—coppicing.)

TELL TALE TIT; BLOBTIT, or BLOBTONGUE. A tale bearer; a tell-tale.

TEMPERSOME. Hasty-tempered.

TEMPEST. When the wind blows roughly it is said to tempest.

" *It tempestes so as we're troubled to pitch the hay upon* (up on) *to the stack anyhows in the wurreld.*"

TEMPESTY, w. *A gale of wind.*

TEMPORY. [*Corruption of Temporary.*] *Slight; badly finished.* Tempory built—built badly.

" *Who be I? Why I be John Carbury, that's who I be! And who be you? Why, you aint a man at all, you aint! You be naun but a poor tempory creetur run up by contract, that's what you be!* "

TEMPTATIOUS. Tempting. When I took an apple without asking, my nurse said, " Apples be very temptatious to you don't they? "

TENANTRY-ACRE. Mr. Durrant Cooper gives the following account of this allotment:—" The proportion between the tenantry and the statue acre is very uncertain. The tenantry land was divided first into laines, of several acres in extent, with good roads, some sixteen feet wide between them; at right angles with these were formed, at uncertain intervals, tenantry roads, of some eight feet in width, dividing the laines into furlongs. In each furlong every tenant had a right to his proportion, which was set out for him, not by fixing any superficial quantity, but by measuring along the line of the tenantry road of each furlong a certain number of feet to each paul, the number of feet being the same, whatever was the depth of the furlong; thus, if the furlong, for instance, consisted of what is called a hatchet-piece, something like three-quarters of a square, the part where the piece was two squares deep would contain double the superficial contents of the portion at the other end, where the measurement next the road would be similar but the depth only one half."

—Sussex Glossary, *p. 65.*

See Furlong, Laines, Leakway and Paul and Hatchet-pieces.

TEND. To watch.

" *He can't sing in church no more, for he goos to work rook-tending, and he comes home of nights that hoarse that you can't hardly hear him speak.*"

TEN-SHILLING MEN. Those who helped smugglers land their goods and were paid 10/- per run.

—S.C.M., XXII, p. 168.

TERNATION. Frightfully; terribly.

" I cum away ternation crass (cross)."

TERRIBLE. Excessively. (Pronounced tarrible, or tarble, as below.)

TERRIER. [Terre, *French, land.*] A *survey and register of land.*

Two terriers were made at Brighton in the last (18th.) *century; the first in 1738, the second in 1792, by Thomas Budgen.*

TERRIFY. (*Usually pronounced tarrify.*) *To tease; to annoy.*

" *These here fleas tarrifies me tarrible.*"

TESSY, w. *Angry.* [*Probably a corruption of Testy.*]

TESTOWRAS. [*Testire*, Old French a head cover.] A tester bed.

THANKS BE. A common expression.

" I'm better now, thanks be."

THAT. So.

"*I was that tired I didn't know how to bear myself.*"

THATCHING NEEDLE. A long piece of iron, sometimes straight sometimes curved, with an eye, used by thatchers for sewing thatch when threaded with tarcord or binding. Occasionally made of wood. Used chiefly when thatching a sheepfold.

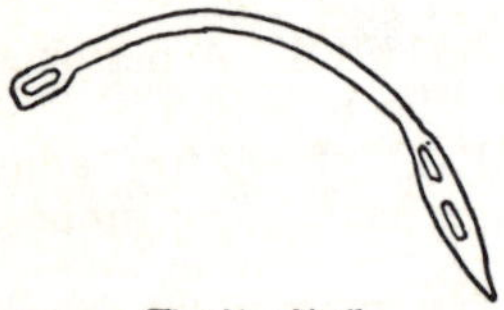

Thatching Needle

THEAVE[1]. Two stooks, equal to 24 shocks.

THEAVE[2]. Ewe of the first year.

THEEVAL. Another word for Spurtle, (*q.v.*)

THEIRN. Theirs.

"That stick baint yourn, it be theirn."

THERUM. Thereabouts.

" Well, it's at Lewes or therum.'

THICK-AS-GUTTER-MUD. Thick as thieves.

THICK-OF-HEARING. e. *Slightly deaf.*

" *Old woman, old woman, will you go a shearing?*
Speak a little louder, sir, I'm rather thick of hearing.
Old woman, old woman, shall I kiss you very sweetly?
I thank you very kindly, sir, I hear you quite completely.
—Old Sussex Rhyme.

THICK-MILK, m. *Hot milk thickened by the addition of a few spoonfuls of flour and sweetened.*

THILL-HORSE, w; *or THILLER. The shaft horse.* See Team.

" *What a beard thou hast got. Thou hast got more hair on thy chin than Dobbin my thill-horse has on his tail.*"
—Merchant of Venice, *Act ii. sc. 2.*

THILLS, w. [Thil, *Ang. Sax.*, *a plank.*] *The shafts of a wagon or cart.* Also called Rods and Sharps.

THIMBLE. That part of a gate hinge fixed to the gate with nailed wings. It ends in a ring that fits over the gate hook which is attached to the post.

Thimble

THINGS. Smuggler's term for tubs or kegs of spirit.

THRABY, *w.*‡ Untidy.

THREADDLE. To thread a needle.

" *Open the gates as wide as wide,*
And let King George go through with his bride.
It is so dark, we cannot see
To threaddle the tailor's needle."
—Children's Game.

THREE - FACES - UNDER - A - HOOD. The pansy. *Viola tricolor.* Also called Jump-up-and-kiss-me, (*q.v.*) etc.

THREE-PARTS, or THREE-PARTS GONE. Drunk but not incapable.

" 'E wuz allus three-parts."

THRO. Fro. To-and-thro is always used for to-and-fro.

"*He goes to-and-thro to Lewes every Tuesday and Friday.*"

THROT, m. *The throat.*

THROW[1]. [*Through.*] *A thoroughfare: a public way. The four-throws is a point where four roads meet.* (*Cf.* Carfax and Went.)

THROW[2]. *To cut down trees.* (*Cf.* Fall.)

THUNDERBARROW. The name of a long barrow-like Down between Shoreham and Edburton; the Hill of Thunder or Thor.

THUNDER BUG. The harvester.

THUNDER PILLARS. The piles of cumulus cloud seen in thundery weather.

THUNDER-WORT. House leek or Sungreen (*q.v.*)

THWARTLE. To crossplough.

" On March 24th, 1716, George

and May thwartled (*i.e.* cross-ploughed)" From *The Marchant Diary* edited by the Revd. E. Turner. —*S.A.C. XXV*, p. 175.

TICE. Entice; allure. A countryman explained that the ringing of handbells, banging of frying pans, etc. made when following a swarm of bees, really made to shew that bees are being followed and the followers are not trespassers—"'Tis for to tice the bees."

TICKLE-PLOUGH, w. *A plough with wooden beam and handles.*

TICKLER, e. *An iron pin used by brewers to take a bung out of a cask.*

TICK-SPIDER. Death watch beetle.

TIDE-WAITER or TIDE SURVEYOR. A preventive watcher against smugglers whose business had to be carried out when the tide was suitable for landing, irrespective of the time of day or night that might be.

TIDY[1], m. *A child's pinafore*, which keeps the dress tidy.

TIDY[2]. Considerable; as 'Tis a tidy step—a good long way. Tidy size—rather big. See S.S. & C.

TIFFY. Touchy; irritable. (*Cf.* a tiff, a slight quarrel.)

TIGHT. Drunk.

Either Sussex beer must be very strong or Sussex heads very weak, for however drunk a man may have been he will declare that he did not take more than a pint, and all his friends will make the same assertion.

TIGHTISH. Well in health.

"*I'm pretty tightish thank you*" *is not a very common expression, because it is not considered genteel to be in perfectly good health; and to say* "*How well you are looking*" *is by no means taken as a compliment. I suspect that the height of gentility is not reached till a person dies outright, and then of course it is only reflective, and the relations take credit for it.*

Folk never allow that they are more than middling, or "Fair to middling." (*Cf.* Middling and Common.)

TIGHT-UP. [Variant of dight, from *dihtan*, Ang. Sax., to dress.] *To clean; to put in order.*

"*To tight oneself up*" *is to dress or put on clean clothes.*

TILLOW, w. (*See Teller.*) Also S.S. & C. under Copse—coppicing.

TILTH, m. [Tilth, *Ang. Sax., culture.*] *The condition of arable land.* That which is tilled.

"*He's a man as always keeps his ground in good tilth.*"

TIMBER-TOES. A person with a wooden leg or legs.

TIMBER-TUG. An adjustable carriage for hauling timber, trees and logs.

TIME OF DAY, m. "*To pass the time of day*" *is to greet a person passing on the road.*

"*I dòant know any more of him than just to pass the time o' day.*"

TIMMERSOME, e. *Timid.*

A boy, who recently stated as a valid reason for not attending evening school that he was afraid that the pharisees would interrupt him on his way home, was excused by his mother on the ground that he was "*that timmersome that he couldn't abear to go out after dark.*"

TIMONEER. A helmsman—probably obsolete or nearly so.

TINKER, w. *To mend anything clumsily.* To botch.

TINKERBELL. Reflected light on ceiling, etc. from a teacup or suchlike.

TIPPÈD, m. *Pointed.*

TIPPYTOPPY. Easily overturned.

"I upset that stuff a dustin' I din' see it an' 'tis such a tippytoppy thing 'tis in."

TIP-STICK. The game tip-cat.

TIP-TEERERS, w. *Mummers who go round performing a sort of short play at Christmas time.* (*See Appendix.*) Or Tipsheers or Tipsteers.

TIP-TONGUED. To talk tip-tongued is to talk in an affected manner.

"*She talks so tip-tongued and gives herself such airs.*"

TIRE. Flax for spinning. (Probably obsolete, but frequently found in old parochial accounts.) Also spelled tyre. (See S.S. & C. under Tainter.)

TISSICK, m. *A tickling, faint cough.*

"*Punch cures the gout, the cholic and the phthisic,*
And it is agreed to be the very best of physic."—Old Song.

TITCHY. Anything small and attractive. "Oh, that is a titchy vase."

TIVER, w. *Red ochre used for marking sheep.* (*Cf.* Marking iron and Ruddle.)

TO-AND-AGIN, m. *Backwards and forwards.*

"*She doddles to-and-agin.*"

TOAR-GRASS. See Tore-grass.

TOAT or TOTE or TOT. A group of bushes or young trees that if left would soon form a thicket.

"I shall have some of them toats out and muck this piece of the old furze field." *E.g.* Toat Farm (near Pulborough), Toat Hill (near Slinfold). (*Cf.* Tot[1].)

TOATY. Said of land dotted about with small bushes, etc.

"You know, that old toaty field 'atween the two woods."

TOKEN[1], e. *A present.* From the old phrase: "A token of love."

"*My lad's brought me such a nice token from Rye.*"

TOKEN[2], m. *An apparition.*

A woman who had asked me to write to the War Office for tidings of her son, whose regiment was in India, came to me a few days afterwards to say that she was sorry she had given me so much trouble, as it was no use to make any enquiries about her son for he was dead, and she knew it because she had seen his token, which had walked across the field before her and finally disappeared over the stile. It was useless to reason with the woman, or to attempt to comfort her by reading her the reply from the War Office that her son was well. It was not till he returned home and in his own person refuted the evidence of the token that her confidence in it was at all shaken.

A picture falling down untouched, by cord breaking or for some reason unaccounted for, is a token, *i.e.*, of death.

"I sh'd take ut f'r a token."

TOLL or TOWLE. A clump of trees.

TOLLY. The shooting alley used by marble players.

TOM. Any cock bird, as a tom-turkey or a tom-parrot.

"*I bought two hens and a tom off old Mis Cluckleford, but I dòànt know as I shall make out much with 'em, for they dòànt seem none of 'em inclined to lay.*"

TOM-BACCA. Traveller's joy. Clematis vitalba; *also called boys'-bacca, because the boys cut the small wood in pieces to smoke like cigars . . .* and call it also "smoking cane."

TOMMY, m. *Bread.*

TOMPAIN. A boot besom at the doorway.

TONCEST. At once. Once is often oncet (wunst *q.v.*), sometimes 'To-wunst'.

TONGUES, e. *Small soles; probably so called from their shape.*

TONSERS. Tonsils.

"'E's better now 'e's 'ad his tonsers out."

TOOK-TO, e. *Ashamed; vexed.*

"*I was quite took-to when you come in, for I hadn't had time to tight-up all day.*"

TOOTERS. Tradesmen at sea-side places who watch the arrival of visitors to solicit custom. Much practised at Worthing.

TOP-AXE, *w.*‡, or TOPPING-AXE. A light axe, about 4½ lb., used for trimming felled trees. (*Cf.* Bough-spud.)

TOP-OF-THE-HOUSE. A person who has lost his temper is said to be up-a-top-of-the-house.

"*If you says anything to him he's up-a-top-of-the-house drackly minut.*" (*Cf.* Up-a-top-of-the-house.)

TORE-GRASS, m. [*Also spelt toar-grass.*] *Tare-grass.*

The long old grass which remains in pasture during the winter. (*Cf.* Fag².)

TORE UP.‡ (Taken up with.) Enthralled.

"She's quite tore up with 'r pony."

TO-RIGHTS, m. *Completely; perfectly.*

"*I had my little boy into Lewes to get his likeness taken a Saddaday, and the man took him to-rights, and you'll say so when you sees it.*"

"I give it him to-rights . . ." scolded him well.

TORRET. A persisting root-stock, hassock of grass like sedge, etc., that grows at the head waters of the Hammer ponds and lakes.

TORRETTY. Abounding in such.

TO-SHE-AND-FRO-SHE-GATE. A kissing-gate or cuckoo gate (*q.v.*)

TOSS, e. [*Tas*, Ang. Sax., a mow of corn.] *The mow, or bay of a barn into which the corn is put to be thrashed.*

*TOT*¹, m. *A bush; a tuft of grass.* Same word as Toat (*q.v.*)

"*There warn't any grass at all when we fust come here; naun but a passel o' gurt old tots and tussicks. You see there was one of these here new-fashioned men had had the farm, and he'd properly starved the land and the labourers, and the cattle and everything, without it was hisself.*"

*TOT*². e. *A brood of chicken; a covey of partridges.* And a small child that can only totter.

TOT³, or TOTT. A stool; a small staddle; the live stump of a coppiced tree from which the new growth will spring. A willow tott has a number of shoots that spring up after the tree has been cut down, these make the osiers. (See S.S.&C. under Copse—coppicing.)

TOTE. See Toat and Tot¹.

T'OTHER-DAY. *If pronounced t'-otherdy, means the day before yesterday.*

This expression is correct, because in Early English other invariably means second, and the day before yesterday is the second day reckoning backwards. It is remarkable that second is the only ordinal number of French derivation; before the thirteenth century it was unknown, and other was used instead of it.—Archæologia Cantiana, *vol. ix.* (Pegge's Kenticisms.)

TOTT. See Tot³.

TOTTY-LAND, e. [Totian, *Ang. Sax., to elevate.*] *High-land, frequently on a side hill; used at Hastings.*

TOURNATE. All worked up.

"She's got in a proper tournate."

TOVET, e. [*Two fats; a fat, or vat, is a peck.*] *A measure of half-a-bushel.* (*See Tavort.*)

TOWLE. See Toll.

TOWN-BULL. A tolerant term for a local libertine.

TOWN-CAGE. See Cage³.

TŌ-WUT, or TŌ-WOORT A! Said to a horse to make him incline to the left. 'To' means 'this' like the 'to' of to-wards expressing direction. The driver who walks on the near side saying, "Gee woort-a!" means the reverse, get over to the right.

TO-YEAR, w. *This year, as to-day is this day.*

TRACK. A pathway across a field.

*TRADE*¹. *Anything to carry; such as a bag, a dinner basket, tools or shop-goods.* "*He's a man as has always got such a lot of trade along with him.*"

*TRADE*², e. *Household goods; lumber.*

TRADES. [Treads]. *The ruts in a road.* When deep, "Rowts," and when low and very deep, lōces or lōwses. Trades might be only the part of a good water-bound road where the grass was prevented from growing by passage of wheels. Also called Rides. (*Cf.* Loast, etc.)

"*You will never get your carriage down that laine, for it can't take the trades,*" i.e., *it cannot run in the ruts.* In this case the trades must have degenerated to rowts or even lowses.

TRADING. Big business, or any large works.

TRAIN, m. *To boil down fat for lard.* (*Cf.* train oil.)

TRAMP, e. *Gin and water.*

TRAPE. To trail; to drag along the ground.

"*Her gown trapes along the floor.*"

TRAPES-ABOUT. To run about in an untidy, slovenly manner; to allow the dress to trail on the ground.

A Sussex maid describing to another servant how her mistress went to Court, said, "And as soon as ever they sees the Queen they lets their dress-tails trapes, because it ain't manners to hold 'em up."

"I can't go trapesing all over there."

TRAPOALIUM. *Trifolium.* (Trefoil and clover plants.)

TRAVELLER. A vagrant, a tramp. In the Lindfield Parish Church Registers there occur the entries; "Nicholas Calton a travailer was buried Feb. 14th, 1616" and "Lindfield the son of a traveller was baptised July 22, 1716."

TRAVERSE or TRAVASE, or TRAVIS. *The place adjoining a blacksmith's shop where horses are shod.* Also the partition between stalls in a stable.

Mr. Turner had an adventure in a traverse, which he thus records in his diary:—" 1758. Sept. 27. In the morn my brother and self set out for Eastbourne. We dined on a shoulder of lamb, roasted, with onion sauce—my family at home dining on a sheep's head, lights, etc., boiled. We came home about 10 p.m., but not sober. Being very drunk, my horse took the wrong way, and ran into a travase with me and beat me off."

From this it would appear as if Mr. Turner had entertained his horse as liberally as himself!

TREAD THE WHEEL. A desperate expedient for maintaining blast at a furnace in time of drought. See S.S.&C.

TREDDLE or TREADLE, *e.* A footing for a rick or stack made of faggots laid on the ground, as distinct from a steddle (*q.v.*), on which the stack is supported on a frame giving free access of air below the stack.

TREEN. Wooden. Implements and utensils made of wood are treen.

TREFT, m. *A trivet.*

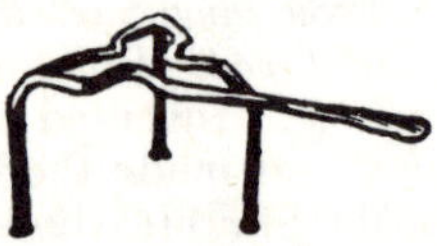

Treft

TREMEN'JEOUS. A superlative form of tremendous.

TRENAILS. Wooden pegs used in jointing timbers.

TRENCHER. [Trancher, *French, to cut off.*] *A wooden plate on which to cut up meat or bread.*

TRENCHERMAN, m. *A feeder.*

A good trencherman is a hearty eater.

"*He's a very valiant trencherman, he hath an excellent stomach.*"

—Much Ado About Nothing, *Act i. sc. 1.*

TRESSLES. The dung of sheep or rabbits, or hares.

TRIG[1], w. *To place anything behind a wheel to prevent a carriage from slipping back on a hill.* See Squat[4].

TRIG[2]. Neat and tidy.

"She looked wunnerful trig in her new gown."

TRIPET, w. *A wicket gate.*

TRO or TROW. Trough.

"Fill up the pig-trow John, it's empty." Also called Pat.

TROT or TROTLINE. A fishing line of stout cord with many short hooked lines at intervals of a yard or so.

TROUCHING. A scolding; a good talking to; a Nowling (*q.v.*)

TROUGH. A trow or tro. In Hastings Guide for 1794 the pieces of wood for launching boats on the beach are called troughs: elsewhere they are called skids.

TROW. See Tro.

TROWEL. Truant.

" 'E played trowel yesterday an' 'is master give 'im a trouching." *Heard at Henfield in 1916.*

TRUCK. Rubbish; odds and ends.

" *There's too much truck about the floor for the house ever to look tidy.*"

TRUG. [Trog, *Ang. Sax.*, *trough.*] *A strong basket made of split wood, used for gardening.* Invented at Hurstmonceux and made there by one family, the Smiths, who still make them.

Trug

TRUGG. A milk tray, or " Hastings basket."

TRUGGY. Term for " dirty " weather used by fishermen.

TRULL. [*Corruption of trundle.*] *To bowl a hoop.*

TRUNDLE. [Probably from *tryndel*, Ang. Sax., a circle; a sphere.] A round hill, as " The Trundle " at Goodwood.

TRUNDLE-BED, w. *A low bed on small castors, trundled under another in the day time.* A truckle-bed.

TRUNK, e. *To under-drain land.* Also the underground drain itself.

TRUSSING-BEDSTEAD, w. [Truss, *Old English, to pack up.*] *A camp bedstead which can be packed for travelling.*

TRUT. A hassock or footstool.

TUB. The usual term for casks or kegs of about 14 or 16 quarts, in which Brandy, generally 30 to 40 degrees above proof, was illegally imported by smugglers.

TUCK. A pinafore worn by children.

TUCK-APRON, m. *A long apron which is fastened round the neck and waist.*

TUCKERS[1]. The frilling worn round the sleeves and neck of a tuck or dress. " Best Bib and Tuckers " was, and is, a common facetious phrase for Best Clothes or Party Frocks.

TUCKERS[2]. § *Small boats of about three tons burden, used in fishing for plaice.*

TUCKNETT. A plaice-fishing net of unspecified size. Only two were used, they were owned with the boat as boat and nets together took four shares.

TUCKNETT FARE. Plaice fishery during February, March and April. Each Tucker carried 8 or 9 men, each man taking one share; none was to take more than one share and a quarter. This means that none of the men engaged in this fishery owned the boat or nets, the master would have one share " for his body " and a quarter of the tithe share; it is the only one where earning is specifically limited. (*Cf.* Fare and Shares.)

TUCK-SHELL. A tusk.*

TUG. A carriage for conveying timber. A Timber-tug (*q.v.*)

TUGS. Iron chains which fit into the hames and shafts.

TUMBLE-BAY. See Bay[1].

TUMBLE-DOWN GATE, m., or STILE GATE. *A gate on a towing-path so constructed that horses may pass over it while one end is pressed down. It recovers its position through being weighted at the opposite point.* Also called Clatterdown gate.

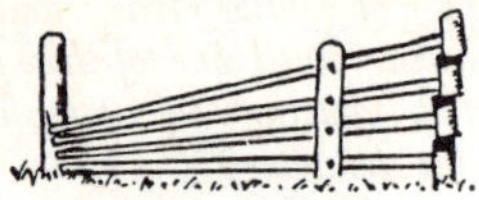

Tumble-down Gate

TUMBLING. Said of a mass of unsmelted coarse mine which falls to the bottom of the furnace and spoils the run. Also called a Loop (*q.v.*) (See S.S. & C. under Iron-working.)

TUND. [Latin, *tundo*, thump.] A School term for a kind of punishment of a schoolfellow by two others taking him one by the wrists and the other by the ankles and swinging him backwards against a wall or a tree.

TUNNELL, w. *A funnel.*

TURBLE, or TARBLE (*q.v.*) Terrible, meaning very or much. We had a dog named Tarble because he was mischevious.

TURF-CUTTER. A tool for cutting turf. Specially for cutting heath turfs for fuel.

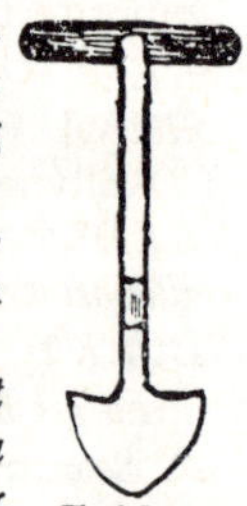

Turf-Cutter

TURMUT, m. [*Corruption of Turnip.*] Often "Durmut."

"*'Twas the worst year I ever knowed for a job of turmut-hoeing, for there warn't no turmuts for anyone to hoe.*"

TURNIP-BECK, or Pecker or Puller. A special fork like a light Canterbury hoe 4½ to 5 ft. long with two curved tines used for lifting turnips for sheep. The turnips were then quartered by the cutter.

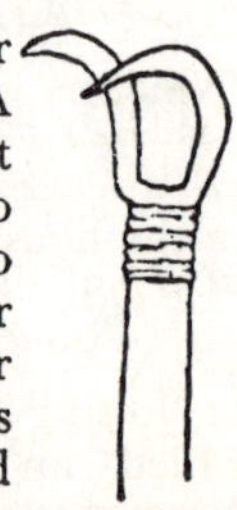

Turnip-Beck

TURNIP CUTTER. Used by the shepherd's boy to quarter the becked up turnips.

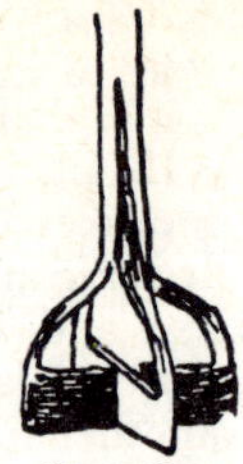

Turnip Cutter

TURNIP PECKER or TURNIP PULLER. A Turnip Beck. (*q.v.*)

TURN-OF-THE-WORLD. Time between dark and dawn.

TURNPIKE. "I shall miss you when you go." "Yes, miss me like a turnpike gate." *I.e.*, glad to be quit of me. In frequent use after the abolition of turnpike gates.

TURNRYST PLOUGH. [*Reost*, Ang. Sax., a ploughbeam.] or *TURN-WRIST PLOUGH.* [*Pronounced turn-rice, and sometimes so spelt in inventories.*] *A plough with a moveable mould-board, which turns up the second furrow on to the first.* The second part of the word should be spelt "reest"; it has nothing to do with wrist.

TURRET. Bell turret. The frame of horse-bells.

Turret

TUSHES, m. *Tusks; long teeth.*

"*O, be advised! thou know'st not what it is*
With javelins point a churlish swine to gore,
Whose tushes never sheathed he whetteth still,
Like to a mortal butcher, bent to kill."
—Shakespeare. Venus and Adonis.

TUSSICK, m. *A tuft of rank grass.* (*Cf.* Hassock.)

TUSSIE-MUSSIES. Small nosegays of mixed flowers such as children pick by the wayside.

TWEEN-STICKS, w. *Sticks which are used to keep horses' heads apart when working two abreast.*

TWELVE-MONTHING. A yearling calf.

TWET. Palpitation. (See Farisees.)

TWIBILL. A tool used in making mortices in the stakes of hurdles. It is a combination of a very small axe and adze, with long curved chisel blades set opposite one another like a very light pickaxe.

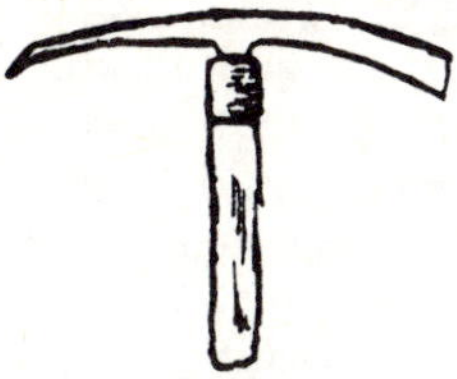

Twibill

TWIG-BEAN. Mountain ash; corruption of quick-beam. *Pyrus aucuparia.* (*Cf.* Serb.)

TWIST. To stir. A Sussex woman never stirred the tea in the teapot before pouring it out—she always "gave it a twist."

TWIT. To taunt; to tease.

"*And twit with cowardice a man half-dead.*"
—Henry VI, *Act iii. sc. 2.*

TWITTEN, w. (Now used all over Sussex.) *A narrow path between two walls or hedges*, or wall and hedge, usually leading from one street to another.

TWO, e. *To be at two is to quarrel.* (*Cf.* One[2].)

TWORT, e. [*For thwart, a corruption of the Ang. Sax.*, thweor, *perverse; froward.*] *Pert and saucy.*

"*She's terrible twort—she wants a good setting down she do; and she'll get it too. Wait till my master comes in!*"

TYE, m. *A common; a large open field.*

TYRE. Linen or flax prepared for spinning. (*Cf.* Tire.)

U

UCK. To pick out grass in walks with a knife.

"What's 'e doin' now?" "'E's ucking the bricks."

UN or 'N. One, for him or it. See One[3].

UNACCOUNTABLE. A very favourite adjective which does duty on all occasions in Sussex. A countryman will scarcely speak three sentences without dragging in this word.

A friend of mine who had been remonstrating with one of his parishioners for abusing the parish clerk beyond the bounds of neighbourly expression, received the following answer: "You be quite right, sir: you be quite right. I'd no ought to have said what I did, but I dòan't mind telling you to your head what I've said a-many times behind your back—We've got a good shepherd, I says, an excellent shepherd, but he's got an unaccountable bad dog!"

UNBEKNOWNST. Unknown.

"*All I can say is, if he comes here, it's quite unbeknownst to me.*"

UNDERBACK. A large open vessel in a brewhouse, which is placed under the mash-tun.

UNFORBIDDEN, e. [Unforboden, *Ang. Sax., undaunted.*] *Daring; disobedient.*

UNFRIEND. (Noun and adjective.) Opposite to friend; unfriendly.

UNKED[1]. [Uncwyde, *Ang. Sax., solitary.*] *Lonely; dreary; dismal.* (*Cf.* Ellynge.)

UNKED[2]. *Having the appearance of evil; betokening bad weather.*

UNLUCKY. Always in mischief.

UP. To get up.

"*Soonsever he comes in at the fore-door his missus she ups and pulls his hair.*"

UP-A-TOP-OF-THE-HOUSE. In a rage.

"*He's so hot headed, he's up-a-top-of-the-house in a minut.*" (*Cf.* Top-of-the-house.)

UPERDS. Up the country.

UPPING-STONE. A Horse block or Jossing block (*q.v.*), sometimes called an Upping-block, or a Mounting stone.

UPPISH. Pettish; out of temper; easily provoked.

"'E was that uppish I went out."

UPSET. To find fault; to interfere with; to attack.

UPSIDES. Stand up to it; difficult to get the better of; even or equal to.

"You cant be upsides with that chap, 'e seems ter know everythin'."

UPSTANDING. Upright; honourable.

"*They're such an upstanding, downsitting family, you won't find their match, search England through.*"

US. We (*q.v.*)

USAGE, w., or USUALS. *Provisions given to workmen besides their wages, called also 'lowance (allowance).*

USED TO IT, *m.* Used to do.

"Aah, I finds it tääkes me ever s'much longer to get up this 'ere 'ill than it used to it."

UTCHY. Cold, nippy, parky.

V

VACANCY CART. A cart for clearing up refuse in roadway, gutters, etc.

VADY. Bad, tainted.

"I cäänt eat this 'ere mate, ' tis vady."

VAGARIES.‡ Tantrums.

"'E bruk one o' my cups, an' I told him I wouldn't have naun of his vagaries here."

VAIL. A present given to a servant over and above wages (like the French pourboire). *The word is contracted from avail, and originally meant an advantage.*

"*Welcome shall they be;*
And all the honours, that can fly from us,
Shall on them settle; you know your places well;
When better fall, for your avails they fell."
—All's Well that Ends Well, *Act iii. sc. 1.*

VALIANT, w. [Vaillant, *French.*] *Stout; well-built.* Also very much.

"*What did you think of my friend who preached last Sunday, Master Piper?*"

"*Ha! he was a valiant man; he did just stand over the pulpit! Why you bèant nothing at all to him! See what a noble paunch he had!*"

VALLER[1], or VALLOR. A large wooden dish used in dairies.

VALLER[2], or VOLLER. To fallow; to plough but not sow.

"That field I vollered last year."

VALLERS, or VOLLERS. *Fallows. Spelt vallowes in Humphrey's inventory, 1697.*

VALLOR. See Valler[1].

VARMINT, or VARMUNT. Vermin; also used as scamp; rascal.

VARN. Fern; usually meaning bracken.

VEERING, *w.*‡ Setting out the lands or warps for ploughing.

VEINS. Finest iron mine. (See Mine, and S.S. & C. under Iron-working.)

VENT, e. *A place where several roads meet, generally pronounced went.* (*See Went.* Also Carfax, Crossways and Partways.)

VERT. [Vert, *French.*] *Green. Still retained in the names of fields, as The Lower Vert Field, at Selmeston.*

VETEL. See Fetel.

VIVERS. [Viviers, *French.*] *Fishponds.*

VLICK, w. *To smooth the hair.*

VLOTHERED, e. *Agitated; flustered.* Moithered.

"*I was so vlothered I did'nt know what to be at.*"

VOLLER, or VOLLOW, m. *A fallow field.* (*Cf.* Vallers.)

VOOR, m., or VUR. *A furrow. Contracted as barr for barrow.* See Sparrow.

VURZE. Plural of above Vur; Furrows.

"It was so clear you cu'd see the vurze on the hill 'smornin'."

Our companion thought he meant the furze bushes or clumps.

W

WAD. Woad.

WADMAN, or WADDER. A pedlar or dealer in woad; a grower of it.

WAGGON ROPE. Every Sussex waggon was furnished with at least two ropes. They were tidily coiled and hung from a stay, or from the winch at the rear.

Waggon Rope

WAHZTREW. A tidal sluice. See S.S. & C.

WALKER. A Fuller.

WALKER MILL. A fulling mill.

WALLET. [*Walt*, Old English, to swag; overhang; lean one way, from *wæltan*, Ang. Sax., to reel or stagger.]

The Wallet Oak at Twineham. *S.A.C.* ii. p. 123.

WAND. See Perch.

WANT, w. *An abbreviation of warrant.* "*He wunt give ye naun I want ye.*"

WANTY, w. [Wamb-tíge, *Ang. Sax.*, *a belly band.*] *The girth which is fastened to the thills of a cart, and, passing under the horse's belly, prevents the cart from tilting back.*

WAPPLE-WAY. See Whapple-way.

WAPS. [Wæps, *Ang. Sax.*] *A wasp.* (*Pronounced Wops.*) The plural is "wapses."

WAPSEY, m. *Spiteful*; *waspish.*

"*These bees of yours are terr'ble wapsey.*"

WAPS-HYME, w. *A wasp's nest.*

WARK, *w.*‡ Ache; as, head-wark, tooth-wark, etc.

WARN. Warrant. As bar'r for barrow. (*Cf.* Want.)

WARP[1]. *A piece of land consisting of ten, twelve, or more ridges, on each side of which a furrow is left to carry off the water.*

WARP[2], e. *Four herrings*, *i.e.*, in telling or counting them when landed two in each hand. Usually two fishermen "tell" at once from the pile of fish on the beach each calling out the next number to the last call by himself or his mate. After "score" they count one and twenty, two and twenty and so on up to sixty; then one two three four. That makes 64 warps or 64×4 herrings. Then a third hand who watches, shifts from one hand to the other or to his cap a pebble as a tally. He generally prepares at the beginning of the count by gathering a handful of small pebbles in his right hand and nursing his inverted cap on his left forearm.

WARREN.‡ A narrow path.

WASE. A small bundle of straw.*

WASTELLER.‡ (Wassailer.) A Howler (*q.v.*)

WATER-COWEL, w. *A large wooden tub.* A Cowell.

WATER-SCOT. Rate paid by occupiers of brooklands in respect of the upkeep of the River and Flood banks. Now paid by all riparian owners.

WATER-TABLE. A low part on the side of a road, or a small cutting across a hill-road to carry off the water.

WATTLE. [Watel, *Ang. Sax.*] *A hurdle.*

WAYBAT. A stake hitched on to the ploughbeam for striking the mould-board into position on starting a furrow on the opposite side.

WAYGOER. A tramp. Under baptisms in Lindfield Church Registers for 12th July, 1593, occurs "Elnor, A waygoer's child."

WAYGOOSE. A bean-feast or celebration particularly with blacksmiths on the day of their saint, Clement, (November 23) when at Brighton they enjoyed a roasted leg of pork, boned and stuffed with sage and onions.

WE. Us.

"Us'll take 'un along 'o we."

WAYWARDEN. A keeper of private roads. (*Cf.* Meresman.)

WEALD. [Weald, *Ang. Sax., a forest*] or the Wild (*q.v.*)

The name given in Sussex to the large woodland tract of country which extends from the Downs, with which it runs parallel to the Surrey Hills. It was formerly an immense forest, called by the Britons Coit-Andred, and by the Saxons Andredes-weald.—Durrant Cooper.

WEAN-GATE. [Wæn geát, *Ang. Sax.*] *A wagon* or wain *gate.*

WEAN-HOUSE. [*Pronounced Wen-hus.*] *A wagon shed.*

WEAN-YEAR-BEAST, w. *A calf weaned during the current year.*

WEED HOOK. A tool used for uprooting weeds.

Weed hook

WEEZE, e. [*Wæs, Ang. Sax., water.*] *To ooze.*

WELLY. Well.

"I was welly minded not to goo."

WENT, e., or VENT. A Partways (*q.v.*) *A crossway.* A place where several roads meet. By contraction from four-five- etc. -wents. Went strictly is a road or lane.

"*Just as gate (from the verb go) means a street in Old English, so went (from the verb wend) means a lane or passage.*"—Pegge's Alphabet of Kenticisms.

(*Cf.* Carfax, four roads coming together but not forming a cross: and Cross ways, Fourthrows or fourwents, which generally means two roads crossing one another directly.

Sussex roads, like Sussex ways of speech are often a little confusing to the "furriner.")

WEST-COUNTRY-PARSON, e. *The hake, so called from the black streak on the back, and abundance of the fish along the western coast.*

WET. To wet the tea, is to make tea. Or rather to infuse the tea in a little boiling water before adding the volume of boiling water required. *To wet the bread, is to mix the water in the flour.* To "wet the top brick" is a bricklayers' celebration; see Rearing feast.

WHAPPLE-GATE. A gate on a whapple-way.

WHAPPLE-WAY. A bridle way through fields or woods, where horses can go but carts cannot. Sometimes written Wapple.

WHEELS, m. *A hand cart.*

"*I can get my wheels through whapple-gate, and that often saves me a journey fetching wood.*"

WHIFFLE, m. *To come in gusts.*

"*I see there had been just rain enough to whiffle round the spire whiles we was in church.*"

WHILE. Till.

"I'll stay with you while Satterday."

WHILES. Whilst. As amonges has been corrupted to amongst, so whiles is the original and correct form of whilst.

WHILK[1], e. *To howl like a dog.*

WHILK[2], e. *To mutter to oneself.*

WHIMBLE. See Wimble.

WHIPPLE TREE, or WHIPPEL TREE. See Wippance.

WHIPS. Quantities; same meaning as Lashings.

"There's whips of elder berries round Camber Castle."

WHIST, m. *Silent.*

"*Bide whist! I hears un!*"

WHITE-HERRING. A fresh herring, as distinguished from a dried one, which is called a red-herring.

WHITE-MAN'S FOOTSTEPS. Plantains; so named because it is said that wherever white man has trod plantains will be found. *Plantágo media.*

WHITTLE. [Hwítel, *Ang. Sax., a white mantle.*] *A mantle of coarse stuff formerly worn by country women.* Usually fringed.

WHOLE. Conceited. A whole person is one entirely self-satisfied: open to no improvement.

"He's that whole you can't tell 'im nothing."

WICKS. The wretched maggots that attack sheep.

WIDDERSHINS. Going contrary to the course of the sun. At fairs and ceremonies country people marched round a tree from right to left.

WIDE-OF. Out of the direct road, but not far off.

"*Stone is a little wide of Rye.*" Generally lies or lays wide of, etc. (*Cf.* Broad.)

WIDOWS-BENCH. (See Bench.)

"*And that if any tenant having any land either fforrep or board die seized, his widow after his death sho'd have the said lands which were her said husbands at the time of his death by the custom of the said manor as by her bench dureing her natural life, altho she marry afterward to another husband.*"—Bosham Manor Customs.

Bosham was exceptionally generous to widows. (See S.S. & C. under Borough English.)

WIFFS. Withes; also the "spray" of twigs on the end of a lither wand or sapling used in making a withe.

"Ah you've spoilt un now, you've gone and cut the wiff off."

WILD. The Weald of Sussex is always spoken of as The Wild by the people who live in the Downs, who by the same rule call the inhabitants of the wealden district "the wild people." Or Willocks or Wildishers.

WILD FARING. Wild fruits, mushrooms, etc.

"Poor windy tackle wild faring be."

WILDISHER. An inhabitant of the Wild (Weald); a willock.

WILLICK. A guillemot. A nickname for an Eastbourne fisherman; also called Willicker. See Fishermen.

WILL-LED, e. *Led away or bewildered by false appearances, as a person would be who followed Will o' Wisp.*

WILLOCK. A wild man, one from the Weald; a wildisher. A mad man. A mad or wild (out of control) animal.

WILLOCKY. Mad. Willocky mad.

"Wat with one thing an 'nother 'tis enough to drive a man willocky mad."

"A willocky bull," is a mad bull. (*Cf.* Amakin.)

WIM. To winnow corn.

WIMBLE, WOMBLE or WHIMBLE. A hook usually with two handles, brace-like for twisting up hay and straw bands for tying. The bands were sometimes coiled round and sewn into door-mats.

Wimble

WIND. The wind is referred to as 'she.'

"Wind's all over the place, 'smorning she wuz down here, then at dinnertime she came up from the barn and now she's got right back here away." (S.W. to N.W.)

WIND-FANNER, or WIND-HOVER. Kestrel. So called because he fans or hovers. Also called Fanner, or Fanner-hawk.

WINDING. To make hay into haybands; to make a withe ready for binding.

WINDOGS. White clouds blown by the wind.

WINDROW[1], m. *Sheaves of corn set up in a row one against the other; a thin row of new mown grass raked up lightly so as to allow the wind to pass freely through it and dry it.* This grass also called leeks. See S.S. & C.

WINDROW[2]. *To put hay into windrows.*

WINDSHAKEN, e. *Thin, puny; weak.*

"*He's a poor windshaken creetur.*"

And said of timber that developes longitudinal cracks when sawn.

WINGS. Flanges of thin iron with holes for nailing them to the gate post to strengthen the thimble hinge. (*Cf.* Thimble.)

WINKLE STONE OR SUSSEX MARBLE. A conglomerate, mainly of shells, found in the Weald clay and capable of taking a blue-grey polish.

WINNOWING-FAG, w. *A rough machine for winnowing.*

WINT, e. [Windan, *Ang. Sax., to turn.*] *Two ridges of ground which are ploughed by going to one end of the field and back again. Arable land which is harrowed twice over is said to be harrowed a wint (or a turn); if three times, a wint and a half.* (See S.S. & C. under Cant.)

WINTER-BEAN. The Everlasting Pea. *Lathyrus latifolius.*

WINTERPICKS. Blackthorn berries . . . sloes. *Prunus spinosa.*

WINTER-PROUD. Cold.

" *When you sees so many of these here winterpicks about, you may be pretty sure t'will be middlin' winter-proud.*

WIPPANCE, w. *The bar on which the traces of a horse are hooked, and by which he draws his load. Also called whippel tree, or whipple tree.* (*Cf.* Splinter-bar, and Pummel-tree. Strictly, whippance is the assembly of two whipple-trees and one pummel tree.)

WIPPEN. Same as Wippance.

WISH. [Wesc, *Ang. Sax., a washing.*] *A damp meadow; a marsh, or low land in a nook formed by the bend of a river or stream, and liable to be flooded.* (*Cf.* Wish Wharf, Portslade.)

WITHE. A with or withy specially twisted for binding faggots: the wiff or spray end being twisted back round the withe to make an eye.

" He takes the withe and winds it
And lays it on the ground,
Around the faggot he binds it
Drink round brave boys. Drink round."

Chorus to the song *The Woodman.* A similar song is *The Jolly Woodcutter.*

WITHY. The Willow. Salix, *various species.*

WIVERING. Shaking, as a reed in the wind.

WOL. Will.

" 'E sez 'e wol, but I doubts it."

WOLF-CAMP. A valley earthwork: supposed to be a watch place against wolves.

WOMBLE. Same as Wimble or Whimble.

WOMENATED. Being fussed over by women.

An exasperated patient at Fairwarp said to our brother, " I carn't abide being womenated."

WONDRUS. Wonderous; very; very much.

" 'E wer wondrus worritted about them writings."

WORRITTED. Worried.

WOT. What; used also for that.

" 'E cāān see no better'n a man wot's bline."

WRASTLE[1]. When a pain shoots or burns it " wrastles."

WRASTLE[2]. Wrestle.

" John 'e do wrastle with them chicken bones."

A dinnertime remark heard at Uckfield.

WRATCH, or RATCH, e. [Hrǽcan, *Ang. Sax., to reach; extend to.*] *To stretch.*

WRING. Ache.

" Does your ear hurt ? " " Yes, it wrings a bit."

WRĪST, or RISE. [*Reost*, Ang. Sax., a ploughbeam.] *The moveable wing* (mould board) *of a turn-wrist plough.* (Always said with a long " i ".) See Turnwryst.

WRITINGS. Deeds. Title Deeds in particular. The Revd. Robert Hurst of Thakeham always so called Title Deeds.—*Circa* 1871.

WROCKLED, e. *Wrinkled.*

WULE. To cry.

WUNNERFUL. (Wonderful.) Remarkable.

WUNST. Once; at once; Toncest (*q.v.*)

WUTS. [*Corruption of Oats.*]

Y

Y. A yokel giving directions described partings of the ways as Y turns and V turns.

YAFFLE, e. *The green woodpecker.* Also called Yaffingale, Galley bird (*q.v.*), and Bargeboat.

YANGER, e. [*Corruption of Yonder.*]

"*I see an old yaffle in de 'ood yanger.*"

YANK. A long talk with an old friend chiefly of bygone times.

"I 'ad a good ole yank along of 'e."

YAPE, e. *To gossip.* (*Cf.* Helve and Nabble.)

YAR. *Aghast; frightened.*

YARBS, w. *Herbs.*

An old man in East Sussex said that many people set much store by the doctors, but for his part, he was one for the yarbs, and Paul Podgam was what he went by. It was not for some time that it was discovered that by Paul Podgam he meant the polypodium fern.

YARMOUTH FARE. Herring fishery from September to November off the East Coast. Boats, of 15 to 40 tons, carried 12 or more men; those from 15 to 24 tons took 3 shares, from 24 to 30 tons 3½ shares and from 30 tons upwards 4 shares. Every man had half a share, this implies that all the men engaged on this fare had nets; on the larger boats they took Norward nets 10 to 15 fathoms long and 5 Ranns deep, on the smaller boats Heaks 24 to 30 fathoms long, 4 Ranns deep; 4 Norward or 3 Heak nets taking a share. (*Cf.* Fare, Heak, Norward, Rann and Shares.)

This fishery was the cause of many minor bloody conflicts in mediæval, and later, times.

YAT, m., YET, or YETE. *A gate.*

YEAN.‡ To bring forth, particularly of a ewe.

YEASTY, m. [*Ang. Sax.*, yst., *a storm.*] *Gusty; stormy.*

"*A little rain would do us good, but we dòant want it too oudacious yeasty.*"

"*Though the yesty waves*
Confound and swallow navigation up."
—Macbeth, *Act iv. sc. 1.*

But that quotation and Longfellow's—

"The billows frothed like yeast," relate to the yeasty or foamy appearance only.

YEILD-IT, e. *Give up.*

A farmer took his team to harrow a piece of wheat, but finding it too wet he said to his carter "*Come along home, we'll yeild it.*"

YELM. To lay straw out in order for use by the thatcher.

YELMS. Straw so sorted and laid out for thatching.

YEST-KEELER. Yeast-keeler. The same as Keeler (*q.v.*)

YET, or YETE. A gate. See Yat.

YETNER. [Git ná, *Ang. Sax.*, *not as yet.*] *Not nearly.*

The reduplication of the negative is very common in Sussex.

"*I bèänt farty year old yetner.*"

YEO, or YOWE, m. [*Corruption of Ewe.*] *From the Ang. Sax.*, eowu. Ewe might more truly be termed a corruption of eowu, which better expresses the word used.

YOKE[1]. Of oxen; a pair of beasts, whether in harness or not.

"Took a yoke of oxen and slew them."—*I Kings*, xix. 21.

YOKE[2]. The harness:—Consists of the oxbeam which rests on the necks of the pair forming the yoke, together with an oxbow near each end, one surrounding the neck of either beast, and a shackle in the middle of the beam which takes the oxtights by which the load is drawn. See S.S.&C.

YORKS. Leather garters used below the knee to loop up trousers to prevent dragging. Called also knot leggers or nollegers. (*Cf.* Nims.)

YOYSTER, m. *To play about roughly and noisily*. Same as goyster.

YOURN. Yours. As hern, hers; hisn, his (*q.v.*), etc.

Z

ZACKLY. Exactly. (See Hedge carpenter, S.S.&C.)

ZEERS. Sneers.

"I dóánt want naun of your narsty zeers."

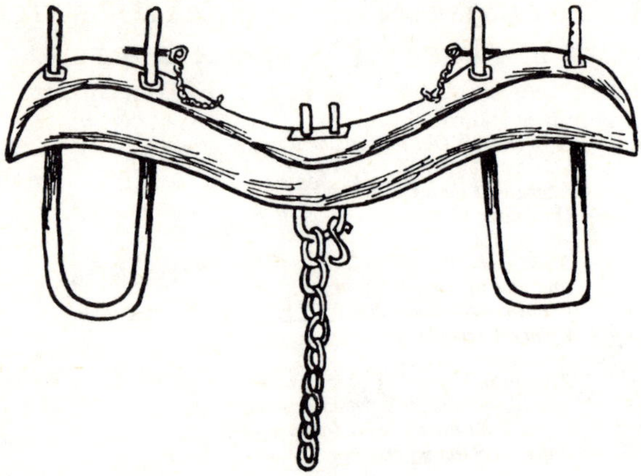

Yoke

APPENDICES

THE MUMMERS' PLAY.

Dramatis Personæ

FATHER CHRISTMAS.	*A TURKISH KNIGHT.*
ST. GEORGE	*A DOCTOR.*

Father Christmas.— *Here come I, Old Father Christmas.*
Christmas or not,
I hope Old Father Christmas
Will never be forgot.

Make room, make room here, gallant boys,
And give us room to rhyme;
We've come to show activity,
Upon a Christmas time.

Acting youth or acting age,
The like was never acted on this stage;
If you don't believe what I now say,
Enter, St. George, and clear the way!

St. George.— *Here come I, St. George the valiant man,*
With naked sword and spear in hand;
Who fought the dragon and brought him to the slaughter,
And for this won the King of Egypt's daughter.
What man or mortal dare to stand
Before me with my sword in hand?
I'll slay him and cut him as small as the flies,
And send him to Jamaica to make mince-pies.

Turkish Knight.— *Here come I, a Turkish Knight,*
In Turkish land I learned to fight;
I'll fight St. George with courage bold,
And if his blood's hot will make it cold.

St. George.— *If thou art a Turkish Knight*
Draw they sword, and let us fight.

They fight; the Turk is killed.

St. George.— *Ladies and gentlemen,*
You see what I've done,
I've cut this Turk down,
Like the evening sun.
Is there any doctor that can be found,
To cure this Knight of his deadly wound?

Doctor.— *Here come I, a doctor,*
A ten pound doctor;
I've a little bottle in my pocket
Called hokum, shokum, alicampane.
I'll touch his nose, eyes, mouth and chin,
And say, " Rise, dead man," and he'll fight again.

The Turk, having been carefully examined by the doctor, is restored and immediately indicates his readiness to renew the combat.

St. George.— *Here am I, St. George, with shining armour bright,*
I am a famous champion, also a worthy Knight.
Seven long years in a close cave was kept,
And out of that into a prison leaped;
From out of that into a rock of stones,
There I laid down my weary bones.
Many a giant did I subdue,
And ran a fiery dragon through.
I fought the man of Tillowtree,
And still may gain the victory.
First I fought in France,
Then I fought in Spain,
And now I've come to Selmeston
To fight the Turk again.

They fight again, and St. George is again the conqueror.

St. George.— *Where is the doctor that can be found*
To cure the Turk of his deadly wound?

Doctor.— *Hocus, pocus, alicampane,*
Rise Turkish Knight to fight again.

Ladies and gentlemen, our play is ended,
Our money-box is recommended;
Copper or silver or gold if you can,
Five or six shillings will do us no harm.

At Salisbury the Mummers used to be called John Jacks, and there was a fifth performer called John Jack, who was represented with a large hump-back, and concluded the play by coming forward and saying,—

Here come I,
Little Jack John,
With my wife and family at my back,
Roast beef, plum-pudding, and mince-pie,
No one loves them better than I!

God Save the Queen!

Much more elaborate versions of this ancient play have been published since Parish recorded the one above. He wrote down what was actually performed at Selmeston and many other places in Sussex during the latter part of the nineteenth century by tradition from time immemorial.

There were, of course, many local variations. At Lancing, in the years 1874 to 1886, the opening lines went:—

" In comes oi, ole' Fad'r Christmus,
An' ham oi welc'm or ham oi naht."

Sometimes there were various other characters, the most usual of these were the Dragon and Princess Saba (his intended victim). Others were the Valiant Soldier, Maid Marion, Robin Hood and Beelzebub.

In *The Wonderful Weald*, p. 373, Arthur Beckett gives a revived and much extended version.

ANGLO-SAXON NAMES IN SUSSEX.

The following Anglo-Saxon words will be traced in the names of almost all the towns and villages in Sussex:—

BECC. A brook. Beck. *Bexhill.*
BÚR. A cottage; a dwelling. Edburton.
BURH. A hill; a citadel. Burghersh; Bury; Pulborough.
BURNE. A stream; a river. Bourne. *Eastbourne.*
CEASTER. A camp. [*From Lat.* castrum.] Chester. *Chichester.*
COMB. A valley. [*From Welsh* cwm.] Combe. *Balcombe.*
COTE. A cot. Woodmancote; Coates.
CROFT. A small enclosed field. Wivelscroft.
DAL. A valley. Dell; del. *Arundel.*
DENU. A valley. Den; dean. *Marden; Westdean.*
DÚN. A hill; a down. Don. *Slindon.*
EA. Water; marshy place. Ea. *Selsea; Winchelsea.*
FELD. An open field; pasture; plain. Field. *Heathfield.*
FOLDE. A field. Fold. *Slinfold.*
GAT. A gate; or rather, a way; street. Gate. *Rogate; Eastergate.*
GRÆF. A grave; or a grove. Grove. *Boxgrove.*
HAM. A village; an enclosed place. Ham. *Beddingham.*
HOU. A hill. Hoe. *Piddinghoe; Houghton.*
HOLT. A grove. Wigginholt.
HURST. A wood. Nuthurst.
IG. An island. Ey. *Thorney.*
ING. A meadow. Angmering.
ING. Used as a patronymic; thus Wilming would signify the descendants of Wilm; whence Wilmington; Rustington, etc.
LEAG. A pasture. Ley. *Earnley.*
MERE. A pool or lake. Mare; mere. *Haremare; Tangmere.*
MERSC. A marsh. Marsh. *Peasmarsh.*
STEDE. A place; a station. Stead; sted. *Eastgrinstead; Horsted.*
STÓC. A place. Stock; stoke. *West Stoke.*
TÚN. A close; a field; a dwelling. Ton. *Alciston.*
WEORTHIG. A farm; an estate; a public way. Worth. *Fittleworth.*
WIC. A dwelling place; a village. Wick. *Wick; Terwick.*
WINCEL. A corner. Winchelsea. (*See* Wincel *in Bosworth, who gives this example.*)

This subject has been dealt with exhaustively by Professors Mawer and Stenton for the English Place-name Society in Vol. 1 part ii of their publications (1924) and in *The Place Names of Sussex*, Vols. VI and VII (1929/30).

SUSSEX SURNAMES.

(*Connected with Sussex words*)

The following names of families, now residing in the county, are derived from or connected with Sussex words which will be found in this dictionary:—

AKEHURST. [*Ang. Sax.*, ác, *an oak, and* hurst, *a wood.*]
ASHBURNHAM. [*Ang. Sax.*, æsc, *an ash;* burne, *a stream, and* ham, *a dwelling.*]
ASHDOWN. Æsc, *an ash, and* dún, *a hill.*
ASHENDEN. Æsc, *an ash, and* denu, *a valley.*
BALKHAM. Balca, *a ridge, and* hám, *a dwelling.*
BARTON. Barton, *a farm-yard.* [*Ang. Sax.*, bere-tún, *an enclosure.*]
BECK. Beck, *a brook.* [*Ang. Sax.*, bėcc.]
BENTLEY. Bent, *a tuft of grass, and* ley (*Ang. Sax.*, leag), *a pasture.*
BICKLEY. Beck, *a brook, and* ley, *a pasture.*
BINSTEAD. Bin *and* steddle, *a stand.*
BOURNE. *A stream.* [*Ang. Sax.*, burne.]
BOSTEL. *A hill path.* (*See Borstal.*)
BRACKFIELD. Brake, *a fern, and* field.
BROAD. *A common.*
BROOKSHAW. Brook, *a water-meadow, and* shaw, *a wood.*
BURTENSHAW. Barton (bere-tún), *a homestead, and* shaw, *a wood.*
BUTTERWICK. Butter, *and* wick, *marshland.*
BYTHAM. (*By the ham.*) Hám, *a dwelling.*
CALLOW. [Calo, *Ang. Sax., bald.*] *Smooth.*
COCKINGE. Ing (*Ang. Sax.*), *a son.*
COMBER. Coombe, *or* Combe (*Ang. Sax.*), *a valley in the downs.*
COMPER. *Comp* (*Ang. Sax.*), *a valley.*
COPLEY. Cop, *a ridge, and* ley, *a meadow.*
CROCKER. Crock (crocca, *Ang. Sax.*), *an earthen vessel.*
CROFT. Croft (*Ang. Sax.*), *a piece of pasture land near a house.*
CROWHURST. Crow, *and* hurst, *a wood.*
DYKE. Dike (*Ang. Sax.*, díc), *a ditch.*
ETHERIDGE. Ether (*Ang. Sax.*, éther), *a pliant rod, and* hedge.
FELDWICK. Feld, *or* field, *and* wick, *a town.*
FELSTEAD. Feld, *or* field, *and* stead, *a place.*
GILHAM. Gill, *a rivulet, and* ham, *a dwelling.*
GRIST. Grist, *a grinding; a week's allowance of flour for a family.*
HASLEHURST. Hasel, *and* hurst, *a wood.*
HATCH. *A gate. In North of England, a* heck.
HAYLEY. Hay, *and* ley, *a meadow.*
HAYWARD. *A hedge-warden; an officer of the lord of the manor.*
HEADLAND. *A part of a field.*
HEATHCOTE. Heath, *and* cote, *or* cot, *a cottage.*
HENTY. Hen, *and* tye, *a common.*
HIDE. [Hyd, *Ang. Sax.*] *As much land as could be tilled with one plough.*
HOCKHAM. [Hóh, *Ang. Sax., a heel, and* hám, *a meadow.*]
HOCKLEY. [Hóh, *and* leag, *Ang. Sax.*] *Both these words mean a field of a certain shape.* (*See Hocklands.*)

HOLT. [Holt, *Ang. Sax., a grove.*] *A small plantation.*
HOLTHOUSE. Holt *and house.*
HOOKER.
HOOKHAM. } (See *Hockham.*)
HUCKWELL. Huck, *to knock, or to spread anything about.*
HURST. *A wood.*
HYDE. (*See Hide.*)
INGS. [Ing, *Ang. Sax.*] *A common pasture.*
KELK. Kilk, *or charlock.*
KITTLE. Kiddle, *delicate; ticklish.*
LADE. *Part of a wagon.*
LANGLEY. Long *and* ley, *a meadow.*
LANGRIDGE. Long *and* ridge.
LANGSHAW. Long *and* shaw, *a wood.*
LANGTON. Long *and* ton, *an enclosed place.*
LEE.
LEIGH. } Leag, *a meadow.*
LINGHAM. Ling, *a heath, and* ham, *an enclosure.*
LONGBOTTOM. Long, *and* bottom, *a valley in the downs* (*the long valley*).
LONGHURST. *The long wood.*
LONGLEY. *The long meadow.* (*See Langley.*)
MEERES. Mere, *a marsh.*
NAPPER. Napery, *linen.* (Knapper ?)
PEART. *Lively.*
PECK. *An agricultural implement.*
PELLING. Pell, *a pool, and* ing, *a pasture.*
RAVENSCROFT. Raven, *and* croft, *a field.*
REEVE. *An officer of the manor.*
SHAW. *A wood.*
STEAD. *An enclosed place.*
SOUTHERDEN. *The south valley.*
WENHAM. Wen, *or* wain, *a wagon, and* ham, *an enclosure.* *The wagon-house.*
WENMAN. *The wagon-man.*
WHEATCROFT. *The wheat field.*
WOODWARD. *An officer of the manor; a wood-warden.*
WYNDHAM. Wynd, *a path up a hill, and* ham.

SUSSEX SURNAMES.

BOURNE. [Burne, *Ang. Sax.*] *A stream.*

Boorne *Bourne* *Bourner* *Michelbourne.*

BROOK. *A stream; a water-meadow.*

Brook *Brooks* *Brookfield* *Brookshaw* *Colbrook* *Westbrook.*

COMP. *A valley.*

Comper *Compton.*

COOMBE, or COMBE. *A hollow in the downs.*

Combe *Comber* *Anscombe* *Balcombe* *Dunscombe* *Ellcome* *Farncomb* *Farncombe* *Lipscombe* *Titcombe* *Whitcombe* *Witcomb.*

CROFT. [*Ang. Sax.*] *A small enclosed field near a house.*

- *Croft*
- *Crofts*
- *Horsecroft*
- *Longcroft*
- *Pycroft*
- *Ravenscroft*
- *Tredcroft*
- *Wheatcroft.*

DEN, or DENE. A valley.

- *Barnden*
- *Blagden*
- *Blunden*
- *Brigden*
- *Cobden*
- *Cruttenden*
- *Farenden*
- *Fogden*
- *Gosden*
- *Hebden*
- *Hepden*
- *Hobden*
- *Holden*
- *Norden*
- *Ockenden*
- *Pagden*
- *Pattenden*
- *Ramsden*
- *Rigden*
- *Standen*
- *Southerden*
- *Wickenden*
- *Wisden*
- *Witherden.*

HAM. (1) *A hamlet;* (2) *an enclosed place.*

- *Balkham*
- *Barham*
- *Bellingham*
- *Benham*
- *Bromham*
- *Clapham*
- *Cobham*
- *Coldham*
- *Cosham*
- *Gilham*
- *Grabham*
- *Gresham*
- *Grinham*
- *Hardham*
- *Higham*
- *Hockham*
- *Hookham*
- *Kingham*
- *Langham*
- *Lingham*
- *Lulham*
- *Markham*
- *Mepham*
- *Milham*
- *Needham*
- *Oldham*
- *Oxenham*
- *Packham*
- *Pelham*
- *Sandham*
- *Stoneham*
- *Stonham*
- *Stopham*
- *Southam*
- *Tatham*
- *Wenham*
- *Whapham*
- *Wickham*
- *Witham*
- *Woodham*
- *Woodhams*
- *Wyndham.*

HURST. [*Ang. Sax.*] *A wood.*

- *Hurst*
- *Brinkhurst*
- *Broadhurst*
- *Crowhurst*
- *Folkhurst*
- *Haslehurst*
- *Longhurst*
- *Luckhurst*
- *Medhurst*
- *Pankhurst*
- *Staplehurst*
- *Songhurst*
- *Ticehurst*
- *Wilmshurst.*

LEY. [*Ang. Sax.*, leag.] *A pasture land.*

- *Ley*
- *Bayley*
- *Bentley*
- *Bletchley*
- *Burley*
- *Cawley*
- *Copley*
- *Cowley*
- *Crutchley*
- *Ernley*
- *Graveley*
- *Handley*
- *Hawley*
- *Hayley*
- *Helmsley*
- *Hemsley*
- *Henley*
- *Hickley*
- *Hoadley*
- *Hockley*
- *Huntley*
- *Langley*
- *Lee*
- *Leigh*
- *Longley*
- *Lutley*
- *Medley*
- *Morley*
- *Notley*
- *Nutley*
- *Oakley*
- *Pelley*
- *Papley*
- *Ripley*
- *Stapley*
- *Wheatley*
- *Worsley.*

SHAW. *A small wood on a hill side.*

- *Shaw*
- *Bagshaw*
- *Brookshaw*
- *Burstenshaw*
- *Burtenshaw*
- *Buttonshaw*
- *Crawshaw*
- *Henshaw*
- *Langshaw*
- *Oldershaw.*

STEAD. [*Ang. Sax.*] *A place.*

- *Stead*
- *Felstead*
- *Grinstead*
- *Halstead*
- *Halsted*
- *Hempsted*
- *Isted*
- *Maxted*
- *Polsted*
- *Steadman.*

WICK. [*Ang. Sax.*] *A town.*

- *Wicks*
- *Butterwick*
- *Chadwick*
- *Feldwick*
- *Gratwick*
- *Hardwick*
- *Madgwick*
- *Markwick*
- *Padwick*
- *Rudwick*
- *Strudwick*
- *Wickerson*
- *Wickham*
- *Wickenden.*

SUSSEX SAYINGS AND CRAFTS

ANDREW MAC.

Mr. Charles Knight, Senr., of Brighton told us of an inn called "The Andrew Mac," with the sign of a man in Highland garb. On investigation he found that this sign was the result of deformation of the original name, quite meaningless to the present tenant, of Andromache.

ARTCHITEX.

In the early years of this century Mr. Ernest Black, R.I.B.A., had a week-end "cottage" made of old railway carriages at Holmbush near Henfield. One day, in the adjoining field, he heard two passers-by discussing the foreigners. "Well, 'oo be they ?" "Well, I doän't rightly know, but I do 'eear as 'ow they calls theirselves Artchitex."

BACON PUDDING.

There are two ways of making Sussex Bacon Pudding.

The simpler way is to make a dough—about 8 oz. of flour and 4 oz. of chopped suet mixed with a pinch of salt and a little water. Roll out and spread on it rashers of bacon, a chopped onion and a sprinkle of mixed herbs. Roll up, tie it into a floured cloth and boil for two hours. Serve with thickened gravy.

The other method is:—Make a dough as above, mix well one onion, some parsley and 3 or 4 rashers of bacon all chopped, a little salt and pepper, a teaspoon of mixed herbs, a beaten egg and a little milk. Put all into a greased basin, lined and covered with the dough and boil for two hours. Serve with thickened gravy.

BEEN AT 'ER.

A village woman at Lindfield was reported to be unwell and not able to attend the Women's Institute meeting. I asked the boy who spoke of her, "Is she very ill ?" He replied, "Well, Ole Miss Woolgar and Mrs. Dumbrell 'ave been at 'er for mor'n a week."

BEESKEP.

There are many superstitions about bees and their psychic relations with their owners: "Go and tell the bees" of any important event; death, birth, marriage, etc., otherwise they will not provide any honey.

In an article on Slaugham village in the *Sussex County Magazine* for 1948, p. 358, Margaret Cooper (nee Kensett) tells the story of one Mrs. Tompsett, who "always came to the shop for her goods on Saturday night wearing a beautifully clean, starched, white apron. She would calmly tuck this up and put all her goods, including flour, into her black skirt to carry them home. She was also the only one I ever knew who told her bees the news and put crepe bows on the skeps when there was a death in the family. She said one day: 'You know Mas Kensett, it don't do to be too out of the way honest, but you want to be a little near so.'"

" BENDING IN " DAY.

The old custom of this day, sometimes called Bendin' In or Brenchees-and-beer day, was prized by fishermen and is still remembered by some old men of Shoreham. At the beginning of the mackerel season in the spring, the master held a party on the beach near his smack to which the men with their wives and families came, ate much bread and cheese and drank his health in beer. The children had pop-ginger.

Since " Bending in " is a corruption of Benediction the custom may have started in early days when the priest went down to the beach to give Holy Communion and blessing to his people before they set sail.

BILBO.

The bilbo, bilboe or sheep-bow used on a Southdown sheep farm was a natural Y-shaped wooden strod, the long end being pointed to go into the ground. It was used by the shepherd at fair time or for any special show. He made a hole in the earthen floor of the sheep shed and rammed the pointed end into the ground, securing it firmly. Each of the two forked arms was bored at and near the top, with two or three holes. Through any pair of these holes an iron rod attached by chain and staple could be passed. Then by his crook he caught a sheep and made its neck fast in the Y, the iron rod securing the head. With his sharp shears any ragged lock was clipped off and other bits carefully trimmed. Finally the wool was softened with a heavy square carding comb. The sheep then looked its best.

The well known shepherd's crook consists of two parts—The curved top that fitted round the leg of the sheep to be caught is called the " barrel " and the long tongue with scrolled end is the " guide."

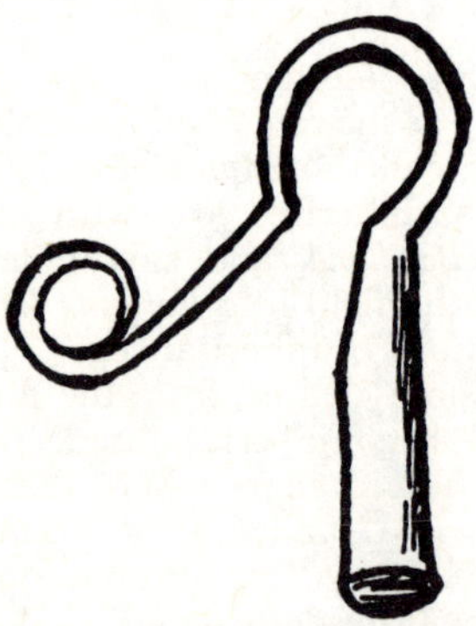

Shepherd's Crook

BLACKEYED SUSAN or POND PUDDING.

This pudding is not always made in the same way, but the following recipe is the one our cook used: 2 oz. of lard rubbed into ½ lb. of flour, a pinch of salt, 2 teaspoons of sugar and a few currants. Mix and make into a stiff paste with a little milk and water. Take off about a quarter of it and roll into a square, put in the middle a good gob of butter and make into a ball. Roll out the rest of the paste and gather it up round the ball. Put into a greased bowl and boil 1½ hours. Turn onto a dish, cut a round hole in the middle and stir in some home-made wine (or sherry would do) and some brown sugar. Replace the bit cut out and it is ready to serve.

BOOTLIGS.

Boot-legs are described by Parish as " Short gaiters, not reaching to the knee." But fellmongers, who tanned sheepskins, manufactured therefrom hedging gloves and bootligs, which were long leggings reaching nearly to the top of the leg. The trade was seen carried out at the old Dolphin Fair, essentially a pig fair, held on Muster Green, Haywards Heath, and is described by an old inhabitant, Mr. A. R. Pannett in an article in the *Sussex County Magazine* for April, 1942.

These bootligs, adorned with bright brass buttons, were " the pride of the maker and the glory of the owner." A good trade was done with them at the fair together with a brisk business in handbills, swaphooks, riphooks and other agricultural cutlery. Jeffery of Wivelsfield was one of the last of the fellmongers and with him departed the bootligs and other old-time crafts, together with the round frock and the chummy hat.

BOROUGH ENGLISH.

This remarkable Manorial custom, while not confined to the County of Sussex, is so much more prevalent here than elsewhere that it merits some mention. It was treated at length by the late G. R. Corner, F.S.A., in *S.A.C. VI*, p. 164. It is so involved that John Rowe (steward of the manors of Lord Bergavenny from 1597 to 1622) in his book, says of the tenants of the manor of Notborne (Nutbourne):—" . . . whose customes I finde so variable that I can not certainlye resolve myselfe thereof, much less satisfye others . . ." And if *he* cannot, who can ?

By this custom, various lands held by copy of the Manor roll, descended, not to the eldest son of the late copyholder, but most commonly to the youngest son. In some cases to a daughter or to a co-lateral younger son according to the custom of the particular manor in point.

Occasionally the widow had all her late husband's holding for her lifetime, but more frequently she had some kind of a jointure called her *Bench*, such provision lasting only so long as she remained a widow, or on remarriage she was liable to a fine or heriot, called a *Marchant* or in Bosham a *Marchet*, usually her best beast. Lands so inherited are, with specific condition of tenure and inheritance, called *Bondland*, and subdivided in Bosham into *Boardland* and *Cotland*, and in Rotherfield into *Farthing land* and *Cotman land*, which carried still further variations of inheritance.

As distinct from such lands, those cleared from the forest and cultivated *after* the manorial custom had become crystallised, were generally not subject to Borough English in those manors where that custom obtained, but descended to the heir at law. Usually called *Assart* or *Assert* land, in Bosham and Wadhurst they were *Forrep land* and *Soke-* or *Sook-land* respectively. Assarting was formerly a misdemeanour and subject to a fine which in time became an accustomed rent. The tenure probably originated as a squat right.

The peculiarities of tenure at Framfield were rehearsed in a Court of Chancery judgment (4 July, 4 James I, 1607), and those of Wadhurst are mentioned in Nelson's *Lex Maneriorum*, quoting Lord Justice Anderson. It is interesting to note how, in these matters of manorial usage, words of Norman-French origin predominate.

BUSTLING PART.

I was told an emigrant native wrote home to his folk living outside

Ditchling, describing the City of Durban where he was living. " There's a dunamany people always going about, mor'n you'd ever see in the bustling part of Ditchling." (That part would be by the Bull inn.)

CANT.

The word cant is used for a division of labour as well as a division of land; the amount of work going to the quantity of land in agriculture makes the words practically synonymous, and here the division of labour may be the primary meaning.

Landwarps are sometimes called cants, and it may be for the reason suggested. Land is seldom ploughed by cants or warps nowadays, the tractor ploughs so much more land in a day than the team, that the division is no longer a practical necessity.

In the days of the old half-swing plough and the earlier ox plough, both of which worked turning the furrow on one side only, the first furrow was struck at half the width of the cant from the side of the field. The plough was then turned on the headland and the next furrow cut to throw a ridge together forming the wint. The plough then followed up and down on each side throwing the turned earth together until the full width of the cant or warp had been ploughed. The next warp was then started and ploughed in a similar way.

A copse may be divided into cants for seasonal coppicing; and a harvest field for reaping.

CANTERBURY.

A Canterbury or Canterbury-hoe is a combination of hoe, mattock, rake and fork. It has two or three speens $\frac{1}{2}$ to $\frac{3}{4}$ inches wide about $\frac{1}{4}$ inch thick and 6 inches to 8 inches long. The two-speen tool is about 5 inches wide, and the three speen is about 8 inches. It could be used for digging—Chinese fashion—cultivating, drilling, raking, earthing up and many other purposes. It had the disadvantage of being heavy and back-breaking to use for long periods, which may account for its present unpopularity.

Of Kentish origin it was formerly much used in the hop gardens of the Sussex-Kent border, also for preparing the tilth, sowing and earthing up potatoes, and for other horticultural operations in that area. A gardener at Lindfield still uses his Canterbury-hoe (1957).

CART.

" He's left his mate in the cart "—*i.e.*, in the lurch, to take the punishment. The saying is from the cart in which the prisoner stood at Tyburn under the gallows, and which, being driven away, left the condemned man hanging.

CHARGER.

It may seem strange that the Revd. W. D. Parish included " charger " among Sussex dialect words, especially considering its Biblical use. But at the same time the dish used (generally on Sundays) for the family joint and furnished with grooves and a deeper dip at one end for the gravy, was always called a " charger ". It adorned the highest shelf of the kitchen dresser and I have heard our cook say, " Fetch me down the charger Jane will you."

CHEESE.

In days gone by it was customary for peasants to have cheese at every meal, even breakfast. Cheese was always eaten with apples and with apple pie. The old couplet runs:—

"Apple pie without the cheese
Is like the kiss without the squeeze."

CHICHESTER SLOE FAIR.

On the 20th of October there is held in Chichester a one-day remnant of the old Sloe Fair. In the past this fair was the most important in West Sussex, it was held on various dates and for different periods.

The origin of the fair, as well as the court of Pie Powder held in connection with it, goes back to time immemorial. The earliest record we have is a grant made by King Henry I to Ralph, Bishop of Chichester to hold a fair for eight days at a time to be fixed, and to receive tolls. The date selected by the Bishop was the Feast of St. Faith the Virgin, October 6th.

In 1204 licence was given (by King John) to alter the date to the vigil of Holy Trinity and eight days after. There is no record that it was actually so changed.

In 1582 there is record of the Pie Powder Court being held in the name of Queen Elizabeth, the See of Chichester being then vacant. This court was nominally held by the Bishop on the fair days in a room over the Canon Gate. Its function was to adjudicate on all matters arising out of the fair, and to levy the Bishop's Toll. Haydn derives the name from *pieds poudrés*, dusty feet, but Halliwell gives *pie*, a roll of bailiffs, (I Edw. VI, Rolls House, i–140.)

In the record preserved in the Chichester Cathedral Chapter, the conduct of the Court is fully set out and it is there described as the Bishop's Pavilion Court. (2 James II, 1686). It is specified that the Mayor's jurisdiction ceased during the eight days of the Fair called Sloe Fair, and that the Bishop then had liberty and jurisdiction of the whole City. At that time the fair ran from the Vigil of St. Faith the Virgin (October 5) to the Vigil of St. Edward King and Confessor (October 13). Later it is described as " the Antient Pavilion or Pyepowder Court."

In 1807 the Bishop's privilege was vested in the City Corporation.

COAGER CAKE.

There are more ways than one of making coager cakes, but each recipe is based on pastry left over from pie-making. They are a Sussex design and one method is to roll out the pastry in thin rounds about the size of the top of a breakfast cup. In the middle put quite a small gob (knob) of butter, a half-teaspoon of moist sugar and about four sultanas. Catch it all up round to the middle, press and put a little bit of pastry on the top and bake in the ordinary way. As well as at Lancing this same method of making coager cakes was used by Mrs. Pont, a native of Hellingly, but now living in South Africa where she still makes them.

COLLAPSE.

Old Mrs. Wells of Lyoth Lane, Lindfield, who had been away for a fortnight on a holiday visit, being asked about it said she had had a very pleasant time but could not say where she had been staying. At last she said, " Well I know it were a shilling the other side of Lewes." (about 1932). She attributed the wet weather in the summer to the " collapse of the sun " she had " 'eard tell on."

COPSE—COPPICING.

A copse is a wood which is coppiced, meaning that the underwood is cut at regular intervals. It is generally divided into *cants* which may be from two to five acres in extent, but refer to divisions for seasonal cutting rather than area.

The underwood is not cut down to the ground, but well-rooted *stools* called locally *Totts* or *Staddles* are left from which the new growth will break. These totts are not stumps (which are of trees cut close to the ground) but stand from eighteen inches or more high, and when staddles up to three feet and more. Many may have served up to ten coppicings.

Among the totts, Storers, called *Tellers* or *Tillows*, are left; they are young trees which will grow to size fit to fall for timber.

In Ironworking times coppicing was well understood and the bulk of the cordwood from which charcoal was made was coppiced. The prevalent idea that the iron trade died out because all the available fuel was expended is erroneous. Seaports, and in particular Rye and Winchelsea, were interested in a large export trade in firewood, and as a result of their outcrys various commissions sat.

The findings of these commissions were occasionally embodied in restrictive legislation, but the enactments seem to have been aimed at appeasing the shippers rather than at reducing the output of iron. One specified a minimum of thirteen years for coppicing, and the numbers of Tellers on each acre coppiced.

Large landowners and the ironmasters had their own ideas on coppicing, twenty-four years was usual, large trees were too valuable and *frith* a waste of time to cole, so it is probable that the regulation had little effect on the supply of fuel.

In the accounts of John Fuller, ironmaster, of Brightling, who spent hundreds of pounds annually on coppicing and coling at 1/4 per cord for cutting, 2d. per cord for stacking and 2/6 per load for coling, there is an item of £3 12. 0 for two trees to make the " Furnace wheel and frame."—*S.A.C. LXVII*, p. 28.

Latterly coppicing was largely concerned with growing hop poles, for which purpose Spanish or sweet chestnut is most suitable. Now that hop gardens are wired a new trade has come to the copses—the making of spile fencing.

CORDING AND CHARCOAL BURNING.

A quantity of wood was cut and corded, *i.e.*, cut to cord lengths, and placed in stacks called *cords*. The wood was mainly coppiced, but all trimmings from timber trees were included. These cords were latterly eight feet long, four feet wide and four feet high (128 cu. ft.). Formerly another cord was used, it was fourteen feet long, three feet wide and three feet two inches high (allowing the two inches for shrinkage, 126 cu. ft.). The *Cord bats* were nominally four feet—or three feet—long, but much wood of smaller dimensions found its way into the cord, the ends however being all nicely lined up on the long face of the cord.

The wood was then *coled* in the following way. The *collier* or charcoal burner, cleared a floor for the hearth, either in a customary place or just a clearing in the wood, the size of which was governed by the quantity of bats to be coled. These were first built up in a kind of triangular log cabin to form a *hole* and the remainder stacked on end in a circle round it: this stack was covered with turves, grass inwards, well beaten down to make it airtight and form the *pet*. A fire was started in the hole with live coals, the top sealed with turf and this completed the *clamp*.

Small vents were made in the clamp, and it was the office of the collier to watch the smoke from these vents and close them as the smoke got thin or *lait* appeared, for if the clamp is allowed to flame the coal will be consumed. He then made other vents as necessary until the whole clamp was coled, a process lasting from a week to a fortnight.

After the iron industry declined coling was carried on in the hop industry until the present time as hops require a smokeless fire to dry them as much as iron smelters needed a purely carbonised fuel for working the iron.

It is interesting to know that charcoal fires are still in use by some cooks for grilling, both in this country and in France. The Managing Director of Harlow Mill Restaurant in Harlow, Essex, tells me he has lately had a charcoal grill put in his country inn there. The result of cooking by this method is particularly good.

COSTS.

"Yes," said a farmer at Woodmancote, "'e 'ad ter pay the costes an' they do just nip it on ter yer."

CUCKOO PENNY.

An old custom observed in the spring was that on hearing the cuckoo for the first time you should turn a penny over in your pocket. If you did so you would never be without a penny until you heard the bird again. The custom was called "Cuckoo Penny".

DEVIL.

Formerly Oak trees were felled in the spring when the sap was rising. This was done in the interest of the tanning trade as it is easier to strip the bark when in that condition. There is a Sussex saying, "The Devil cannot creep between the oak and its bark."

DIBBLING-IRON.

The sowing of seeds by a dibbling-iron, or dibbler, was called drilling. The sower walked backwards with an iron in each hand to which he gave a sharp twist, thereby making a shallow hole in the soil to the right and left of his path. This double row of holes the whole length of his journey was known as a *rocket*. He was followed by a boy or a woman or by both, called *droppers*, who dropped the seeds into the holes by dexterously jerking thumb over forefinger, much like a boy playing marbles. In those days of song the droppers sang (although the words vary):—

> "Four seeds in a hole;
> One for the rook, one for the crow,
> One to rot and one to grow."

If used for sowing corn the iron had a smaller knap at the end, but a larger knap was easier for peas, beans, etc. Dibbled corn, especially wheat was said to grow finer than if sown by any other method.

It is recorded that Sir Hugh Platt explained that the origin of dibbling where was owing to a "silly wench" when sowing carrots and radishes accidentally dropped grains of wheat into some of the holes. The wheat thus sown grew so luxuriantly that Sir Hugh set thinking and in 1600 devised the method of dibbling or drilling wheat in a field.

DISEASED.

A peasant at Ditchling, reading aloud a notice of the death of a resident: —" The deceased (which he pronounced diseased) came to Ditchling about a decade (decayed) back." " Ah," said the reader, " I rac'n'd 'eed got summat a matter wid 'm, but I did'n allow as 'twer 'is back."

DITCH-HOOK and DITCH-KNIFE.

A ditch-hook was a special kind of rake used in the Amberley Wild Brooks. Latterly this tool was made from a flint spud with the two outer speens cut off and the remaining six speens further bent at the usual set and fitted to a pole handle ten to twelve feet long. The skill in setting the speens lies in giving a balance to the whole tool which enables the mud and weeds collected to be dropped on the bank by a rolling motion, which becomes automatic when the load is drawn up.

Formerly the tool was made with four broad speens of about the same overall dimensions, but much heavier. All the speens had diamond points, those at the outside had their outer edges sharpened for cutting the weeds.

A Ditch-knife had a broad blade like a hayknife about two feet long, and was set on a long pole handle for cutting the weeds under water. It also was used at the Wild Brooks.

DR. BUDDINGTON.

One weekday a-hunting at Ditchling, Parson Campion took a toss into a ditch. Dr. Buddington, half a field ahead, was hailed by riders, " Hi ! Doctor, come back ! Here's the parson thrown into a dick." " Oh, never mind him," shouted the Doctor, " we shan't want him till Sunday."

DOCTOR'S MEDICINE.

Our eldest brother, when practising at Uckfield was attending a patient at Fairwarp. When seeing him for the second time and enquiring progress the patient said, " That medicine you gave me Doctor, was much too physical for me."

DONE UP FOR THE WINTER.

An old man dressed with a queer assemblage of garments with pieces added here and there secured by safety pins, bits of string, bootlaces, etc. Asked if it weren't a good deal of trouble dressing and undressing he replied, " Well, ye see, I be done up for the winter."

DONKEY TEA.

Slices of bread toasted until well burnt, then broken into pieces and put into a teapot. Boiling water is poured over them and when cold makes a refreshing drink, the colour being the same as usual tea. In earlier days when tea cost 10/- a lb. poorer people used to drink donkey tea hot, sometimes adding a little sugar, but never milk.

DUMPLINGS.

Dumplings have always been a favourite dish with Sussex country folk. Two of the many different recipes are popular, one a Savoury-meat and the other a Currant-apple. For the Savoury-meat mix together ½ lb. flour, ¼ lb. suet, ¼ lb. any cold meat diced, a teaspoon of mixed herbs, pepper and salt to taste. Then add a well beaten egg and a little water to get the right consistency. Roll into dumplings, boil 15 minutes and serve with thick gravy.

For the Currant-apple mix ½ lb. flour, ¼ lb. suet, 2 oz. each of sugar and currants, one ripe apple peeled, cored and diced and a pinch of salt. After adding a little sour milk or water, roll into dumplings, boil 15 minutes, dust with moist sugar and serve with treacle.

ENTHRALLED.

" Enthralled " meant to be heavily in debt or bankrupt.

In the *Sussex Weekly Advertiser* for March 5, 1770, there is the following peculiar custom recorded:—

" Last Monday a Maltster in this town (Lewes) was married to a widow whose husband died enthralled; he therefore, to save himself from the obligation of paying her late husband's debts, took her in her smock only, she going across the street to his apartment, with no one thing on but her shift, which was witnessed by Cork Fig." In this eighteenth century a man who took a widow in her smock only, was not compelled to pay her late husband's debts.

FISH.

In addition to taking pride and interest in " Bending In " Day, fishermen in Sussex all along the coast as well as in the rivers, prized their fish, worked hard in all weathers and thoroughly enjoyed fishy compliments.

In his *Worthies of England* Fuller recalls an old saying, " He is none of the Hastings," spoken of a person who was slow or tardy in business, thereby conferring a compliment to the people of Hastings. Among the many " excellencies " of special fish, the Arundel mullet, the Chichester lobster, the Selsey cockle and the Amberley trout are well known and frequently quoted.

In an article on *Old Speech*, M. A. Lower records the Revd. Edward Turner's observation that very fine grey mullets were caught between Arundel Bridge and the sea, and though plentiful *below* it was a rare thing for the fish to be caught *above* the bridge, making them peculiarly Arundel mullets.

Chichester was the great mart for lobsters, which were taken in large numbers from the adjacent seas. Mr. Turner continues, " Selsey is still famed for its cockles and of the excellence of the Amberley trout I can speak from experience." *S.A.C. XIII* p. 232.

FLINT.

Flint working is by a very long way the oldest craft of the County, and the Cissbury flint mines and workings represent a highly developed, but by stone age reckoning, a very recent occupation.

Before the days of easy transport, local materials were always used for the majority of buildings, and the quantity of flint available in the downland country made its use obvious. The flints were used in a number of ways; very rough work in which they were laid at random in their natural state was easily improved to *snail-creep* work in which one face of each flint was struck off to give a flat face to the wall. The joints ran at random according to the natural outline of the surface, when well done they were comparatively narrow and gave a pleasing effect.

In *pitched* work large natural or sea-worn flints called *pitchers*, are laid in straight level beds, sometimes with brick quoins. The joints are wide, deeply pointed and often decorated with ironstone, broken flint or shingle *garreting*. Pitchers are also used for pitched paving.

In the most elaborate form the stones are all *knapped*, that is the faces of each flint are struck off to form a flat rectangular face for the exposed surface. They are called *Sussex diamonds*. One dimension is constant for the whole of each course, and frequently for many or all the courses of a building. They are laid in perfectly straight level beds with very fine joints, and are the ashlar work of flint. Sometimes knapped flint panels are laid alternately with blocks of the lower grey chalk to form Chequer work.

The craft of the flint knapper is now nearly dead in Sussex where it was formerly much practised, as witness the many buildings of knapped work. It is still carried on for the manufacture of gun flints in Norfolk.

FLOUSH-HOLE.

" Floush-hole " may mean any kind of spill-way for relieving flood water, but it seems to have originated with, and to be particularly applicable to, a kind of tumbling-bay of Sussex origin and mainly used in this county. It consists of a well weir standing in the pond with a tunnel passing through the pond bay. It has the advantages of keeping the falling water well clear of the puddled bay, and of providing a maximum length of weir crest for a minimum of masonry.

With the decline of the local milling industry and the abandonment of the mill ponds, floush-holes are becoming rare. Two good examples may be seen in Eridge Park near the footpath from Eridge Green to Frant.

Incidentally, the position of this path is indicated by some finger-posts. These were once plentiful in the County, but now are nearly obsolete. Even the word had been superseded by " signpost."

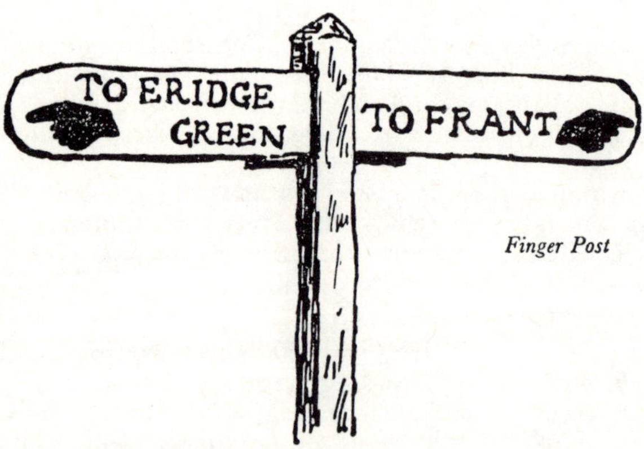

Finger Post

FROUDEN or FROUGHT'N'D.

" Well ye see, wen 'e 'eered the keeper a-coming, young Jesse e' tuk ter's 'eels an' charged slap froo the 'edge in the dark, 'en that frought'n'd ole mus' Dumbrill's runts (steers) t'other side o't an' one o' they goos splosh inter the dick (ditch) en that frought'n'd young Jessee an' 'e lets out a scritch fitter skeer the dead, en that frought'n'd t'other beasties en they all goos willocky (mad) en frought'n'd each udder, en they frought'n'd 'im wus en evver, en they all frought'n'd onenudder." Description of the finale of a little poaching affair at Holmbush, Henfield in 1890.

FUST.

In Lindfield churchyard, on the North-west side, is a tombstone to Richard Turner, who died in 1768, aged 21, bearing these words:—

" Long was my Pain, great was my Grief,
Surgeons I'd many, but no Relief
I trust through Christ to rise with the just
My Leg and Thigh was buried fust."

This is the Sussex way of saying ' first ' and so far as the Author is aware, it is the only example of a dialect word on any headstone in the County. The occurrence is so remarkable that she had the stone recut to save the word becoming illegible by weathering. The recutting was done most skilfully by John Skelton of Burgess Hill,who took infinite pains to preserve the words and lettering exactly.

GELDABLE.

The freemen or burgesses of Pevensey, described in the Custumal as being " of the franchise," had undertaken in respect of that privilege to pay scot and lot to the communal treasury. Other residents were liable to the usual king's tax or geld, and were described as " geldable."

This Custumal of Pevensey gives interesting light on the old habits of life in the towns of the County. Here is a modernised transcription of the form of execution.

" 8. And if a man be attainted of felony of the Crown and shall forfeit his life, the Portreeve, sitting as Coroner with the Steward beside him, shall give Judgment in these words.—' N. withdraw and axe for a Priest.' And if the condemned man be of the Franchise, he the same shall be had to the Town Bridge at high tide and shall be cast over the bridge into the Haven; and if he be of the Geldable he shall be hanged outside the Lowy at a place called Wahztrew." *S.A.C. IV* 217 & *XVIII* 51.

The liberty, a district subject to various jealously guarded privileges, was called in some Sussex towns the Lowy or Lawy. (See also under Wahztrew.)

GOOD FAULTS.

Dr. Habberton Lulham, speaking to a country wife of a connection who had recently died, remembered that the deceased was not a favourite and hastily added, " But she was not a member of your family really was she?" " No, that she warn't, 'twer like this Doctor, Marriage brought her in and death took her out;" replied the dame, adding magnanimously, " But there, I'll give 'er 'er doo, she 'ad 'er good faults as well as 'er bad ones."

GOTHAM.

To Andrew Borde, the original Merry Andrew, Friar, traveller, jester and royal physician to Henry VIII, are attributed the fables of the Wise Men of Gotham.

The Sussex Gotham is a farm having Manorial rights in the Pevensey marshes. In Andrew's time it was the property of the unfortunate Thomas, Lord Dacre, who, with others, was appointed to a commission to enquire into the obstruction of waterways by the setting of " nettes, pottes or innyances " (annoyances) by unauthorised persons, (24 Henry VIII, 1533).

The business of the marshes was conducted by a Last (court) of a Receyvour and twelve Shawers; these were appointed, three each from the four quarters of the liberty of the marsh. The proceedings of this body seem to have provoked Andrew. He is known to have spent much time there with his brother Richard Borde, who held the livings of Pevensey, Westham and Northey.

Possibly Andrew fell foul of the local judiciary in some way, he may even have set an " innyance " or in otherwise poached—The men of the Franchise of Pevensey, at any rate in the reign of Edward III, claimed right of free warren over the Liberty of the Marsh, even to the taking of game on enclosed land without permission from the owner—And he may have been one of those summoned before the Last, and have been subjected to one of the ingenious indignities to which Pevensey felons were liable.

In any case it seems that their proceedings inspired the fables, some of which are told against Pevensey to this day as Parish's story under Mesh (*q.v.*). Although "Andreas Perforatus " as he styled himself travelled widely, he was a native of Sussex, and so we may claim were the Wise Men.

Of course the best story against them has yet to be told. How they industriously walled and sluiced the tide water off the levels until there was so little tidal scour that the harbour silted up, and the Port of Pevensey ceased to exist.

GROMMET MAKING.

Gromets or grommets are made by the villagers of South Harting, and thousands were ordered by the Admiralty in World War II and made by them. Gromets are used for making joints in condensers etc., on warships, liners and other steam ships. An account of the work is given in *Secret Sussex* by Hardiman Scott.

HAYKNIFE.

At one time, when our eldest brother was a boy, he stayed at Latchetts Farm, Danehill. Early one Sunday morning a haystack was found to be on fire. (From spontaneous combustion, being stacked too wet.) The hayknife was then undergoing repair at the blacksmith's, a matter of some two miles away. The only means of transport available was a cart horse for which there was no saddle. Our brother, being at that time the lightweight, volunteered to ride to the blacksmith's and fetch the knife. The horse was " saddled " by placing a sack on its back, secured only by a pad girth. Thus equipped he rode the horse to the forge at the best pace it could manage, and after rousing the smith from his Sunday rest, returned with the knife, (a tool having a blade about thirty inches long and eight inches broad) newly set and sharpened, under one arm and urging the beast with his heels and the other arm. He arrived at the farm in time to save much of the stack.

HEDGE AND FENCE.

Hedging is a craft by no means confined to Sussex, nor are any of the particular methods. Good Sussex hedging is a joy to see, though the names a Sussex man gives to the objects of his work are mixed indeed. The same words means different things in different parts of the county, different words mean the same thing, and it is quite impossible to localise these differences with any degree of accuracy. On one farm the farmer and the hedger may use words differently.

In general, *rossel*, in the downland country means a wall, or a place in a wall, low enough to be used as a stile; in the eastern part of the weald it means a *raddle fence*, and in the north and west it means a *quick layered* hedge.

To *layer*, also sometimes called to *splash* or to *splisher*, is properly to construct a growing or *quick* hedge, by cutting at suitable intervals, stakes to hedge height still growing from the root. This is sometimes called the *binder*: the rest of the old growth is partly severed to enable them to be bent down and woven between the binders; these are the *ethers*, or *layers*, variously called *edder* or *heather* or *binder* or *quick*. This method can only be employed where an old overgrown hedge exists.

The *raddle fence* is a similar structure in which the headers and binders are completely severed from the root, and are therefore dead. When made from thin branches of trees they are sometimes called *rice* or *rice-headings*.

To *splisher* is also to bury the ends of completely severed ethers in hope that they may take root or to give the appearance of being quick. *Spile* was formerly used of a stake driven into the ground but not growing. Nowadays spile is almost exclusively used of wire woven chestnut paling fence. *Raddle* means any interwoven woodwork, whether of hedging or of building.

HEDGE CARPENTER.

An old hedge carpenter worked for our brother at Uckfield from 1888 to 1891. He was named Benjamin Tunks and used to aver " Ye cah't cut a board 'zackly square ye know Sir, and my motter's ' Let nigh enough bide '." A favourite phrase was " About so-ey." He made and inlaid a workbox for his bride with forty different kinds of wood including broom and ling. When we praised it the old man said, " Aah ! them wot knowed wot Oi cud do would'n beleef as 'ow Oi done it, (a pause) but them wot *seed* me do it *they* beleft as 'ow Oi done it."

When we praised an ash rail chair he said, " Aah, Oi made 'im meself an' Oi be only a hedge carpenter ye know Sir "—meaning he had not been apprenticed to the trade. Then he displayed the workbox. I have a pair of oak nutcrackers made by him for my brother in 1888 with his initials, W.H.H. and the date in brass pins. They are 4½ inches long.

HELP.

A letter sent by hand by a servant would be sealed. If sent by a friend or neighbour it would be unsealed and the friend or neighbour could properly consider himself insulted if the letter entrusted to him were sealed, for by sealing it was suggested that he had not the upbringing of a gentleman.

HERNE.

Herne or Jackearne. A heron. A young nephew, Philip, speaking to a woodman was told by him that he had " See old Jackearne out on the flats " that morning. Philip asked the meaning of jackearne and was told, " Those big grey birds wot stand in the water." " Oh, you mean heron," said Philip, to which the old man replied, " Naa, them's fish."

HIGH HURSTWOOD.

In 1888 our brother Hamilton Hall in practice at Uckfield had a patient who gave his address as " Iurstood." " Where is that ? " enquired the doctor. "Well, you wos ridin' up there yisterday," replied the patient. "But I was only at Buxted, Herons Ghyll and High Hurstwood yesterday." "That's what I said," was the triumphant reply, "Iurstood."

HOLLERING POT.

Hollering (hallooing) Pot was a custom observed at the end of harvest. On the last day, about 5.30 in the evening all the labourers employed on the farm gathered together, formed a ring and sang:—

> "We've ploughed, we've sowed, we've reaped, we've mowed,
> We've carried the last load and never o'er throw'd.
> Hip, Hip, Hurrah, Hurrah!"

Then every man had a pint of beer. This custom was never observed if a load had been overthrown, or if anything had gone wrong with the harvest work.

HOP DRYING.

Hop pickers are paid by the bushel for the hops picked. They are picked into the *hop-bin* which is a canvas trough arranged on poles for convenient transport about the garden. From it the hops are measured by the *tallyman* or *busheller* into the *poke* and taken to the *oast-house.*

They are there hoisted into the loft, and in due course spread over the *oast-hair* for drying. This oast-hair is made of horse hair and for the usual type of oast is twenty feet in diameter. It is loosely woven and although having the general appearance of a sieve, is in fact a carpet. It is spread on open joists at the point of the oast where the flare of the *roundel* comes out to the walls. The hops to be dried are spread thinly on the hair and the hot gases from the fire below pass through the hair and so dry the hops.

The art of drying is so to spread and turn the hop flowers and control the heat of the fire as to dry them out evenly and steadily, without waste of time, for as the hops are picked they must all be dried without delay, but without hasty uneven drying, which spoils the crop.

When dry they are raked back onto the floor of the oast loft, spread out to cool and a further batch is placed on the hair. The dry hops are shovelled into the *hop pocket*, a large sack, suspended through a hole in the floor of the loft for convenience of filling, and forced down with the hop press until the loaded pocket weighs from one and a half to two cwts., the exact weight being customary to the particular farm or district. The pocket is then sewn up and dropped through a hatch in the floor onto a wagon for conveyance to market.

ILE.

In his extreme youth my brother J. H. S. Hall was in the habit of consorting with those fishermen who at that time still did a little smuggling as a side line. One day, on the smack *Caroline*, he noticed that the octagonal clock above the cabin stove was badly charred. He said, "Your clock seems to be pretty badly burned skipper," "Ah! She aint no good. W'en her wunt goo I takes and iles her, and then I biles her, 'an one time w'en I biled her 'n then her wood'n goo, so I took an' frier 'er—'n the 'ole lot caught light."

IRON WORKING

Two methods were employed to work the Sussex iron. The first was by direct reduction or *blooming*, which was used from pre-Roman times to the end of the 14th century, and in some places for a good deal longer. The finest *mine* only, later called *veins*, was broken small and placed with the *coles* in a furnace which was small and originally worked by hand or foot operated bellows. It had a slightly concave hearth of stone, and on this stone the iron collected in a plastic state. The mass of plastic iron was taken, generally by total destruction of the furnace to the anvil and there beaten to remove the dross. A great deal of highly metalifferous *scoria* was left which was reworked and much prized by later operators. The finished product was a *bloom* of wrought iron. It is probable that water power was first used for these hammers.

The second process, which grew up during the 15th century, was of *founding* or making cast iron. By this process coarser *mine*, called *collour*, *pitty*, of various depths as *eleven foot pitty* and *bottom* could be used mixed with the veins and old scoria if available. The coarse mine was first *burned* (heated) in an open fire of small coles called *brayds*, to *mollify* it, *i.e.* to make it friable, it was then broken into small pieces to prevent masses of partly smelted metal *tumbling*, falling to the bottom of the furnace before it was fully fluid.

The broken mine was then placed in layers with coles in a *furnace*. This was much larger than the bloomery, and was when possible in blast for eight or nine months. This continuous blasting was effected only by working the bellows by water power. (But see Tread the Wheel.) A temperature of complete flux was attained and the molten metal was drawn off on *foundays*, which were usually at intervals of six days, and was run into open trenches in loam to make *sows* and *pigs* for refining into wrought iron, or into moulds for cast iron goods such as tombstones, firebacks and later cast iron cannon.

Wrought iron was made an an *iron mill* or forge, sometimes near the furnace on the same stream, sometimes elsewhere and in other ownership. Here the sow was first heated in the *finery*, a part called a *loop* melted off and the loop *shingled i.e.* drawn down under the hammer to make a *bloom*. This is John Ray's description. The bloom was re-heated in the finery, forged to a state called *ancony* and finished as bar iron in the *chafery*. These hammers were worked by water power.

JONNICK.

In the summer of 1896 my brother was sketching in Pepperscombe chalk pit, Steyning, when a workman came up with:—" 'Fraid you'll 'ave ter move outer that Sir, we be agoin' ter blast and it wunt be very jonnick sittin' theer." It would not have been for soon the site of his subject was blown over and the sketching position covered with masses of foreground some of a hundredweight or more.

KETTLE BENDER.

This dish was quickly made by filling a basin with pieces of bread, pouring on boiling water, adding a good gob of butter and a little pepper and salt. After a good stir it was ready to eat. Although the mixture sounds plain it is quite good, but butter is needed, not margarine.

LARDY-JOHNS.

These favourite little squares are easily made: ¼ lb. of flour, 2 oz. lard, 2 teaspoons sugar and a sprinkle of currants. Unless self-raising flour is used add $\frac{1}{4}$ teaspoon of baking powder. Rub flour and lard together, add the rest and a *very* little water to make a stiff paste. Roll, cut into squares and bake for about 15 to 20 minutes, turning over to brown the other side if necessary. This quantity will make about nine two-inch squares.

LIFTING.

In Hone's *Everyday Book* for 1827 under November 19 occurs " Lifting is a custom practised with hurdles among shepherds, in the South Downs, at their marriages. The bride and bridegroom are carried round a flock of sheep; a fleece is put for their seat, and may-horns made of the rind of the sycamore tree, are played by boys and girls."

LONG ROPE DAY.

On Good Friday it is the custom of Brighton fishermen to skip in the fish market. A rope is swung by two men and all and sundry are expected to run in and skip. Formerly every street had its own long rope. The practice is said to have a religious origin, the rope representing the one with which Judas hanged himself. The Priory of St. Bartholomew is known to have encouraged it.

MEMBER.

" There 'e was a-settin' with Stumpy Wood, you mind 'im? 'E'd 'alf a wooden leg and they was both on 'em more'n three parts and the winder smashed and all manner. 'E were a member an' no mistake."

Another " member " was Alfred Blaker, of Sompting, a very strong man, who singlehanded lifted a large pig into the cart when it was loose after the tailboard came out, and who nearly knocked over the wooden signal box at Lancing station when he lurched up against it when he was pretty well primed—about 1870.

MIDHURST BATHING PLACE.

At Midhurst a stranger asked " Where is the bathing place in the river? " and was told cheerfully, " You goos thro' the 'ood till yer comes to the post put up where the butler was drowned an' that's it."

MOLE'S FEET.

Old Tom Weller the wooden-legged cattle tender on Ditchling Common, said to one of Eric Gill's daughters who was suffering from toothache, " Ah, you wants a pair o' mole's feet." " Do you believe in them Tom ? " " Yus, why I've sold many a score on 'em sixpence a pair."

NETTLE BEER.

About two gallons of nettle leaves picked in the spring and the rind of a lemon with enough water to cover them. Boil five minutes and then strain. Add 1 lb. of loaf sugar to each gallon of liquor and the juice of the lemon. Spread yeast on a piece of toast, place it on the top of the liquid when it is cool and leave 24 hours. Lift off the yeasted toast, bottle, but do not cork down tight until working is finished.

ONE.

A smuggler told a tale of how he was overhauled on a small boat by a revenue cutter and ordered to lower his sail. He refused and hung on to the halliard. He went on, " The orficer sung out, ' if 'e don't lower, chuck 'im down in the bottom o' the boat,' " and continued quite impersonally, " 'n they chucked 'n too." 'n being the narrator himself.

OPTICS.

The " foreign " lecturer had come down to the village hall to lecture on optics. When the audience was assembled, the village worthies in support on the platform, and the lecturer clearing his throat to begin, a gaffer sitting at the back of the hall slowly arose from his seat and said, " We knows you come from Lunnon an' 'ad proper schoolin', but I wants to say that 'ere abouts us calls they 'op poles not 'op sticks."

PAD.

The Sussex Pad is a well-known inn at the Lancing end of Old Shoreham Bridge. The name comes from the pad bridge by which the river was crossed before the original Old bridge was built in 1782. This pad bridge is variously described as a faggoted causeway and as a raft ferry. It was in all probability a combination of the two. No doubt the inn was frequented by smugglers, foot-pads and other gentry on the windy side of the law, but the name has no reference to *their* use of it.

PICKING MINE.

In former times, when it was the custom to beach the coal ships at Bognor for unloading sea-coal, they were frequently ballasted with iron pyrites. This could make the return cargo more valuable than the coal, and was much more profitable than the usual shingle ballast. The pyrites occurs naturally in the London clay and at each low tide a certain amount was likely to be exposed. The collection of this was called Picking Mine, which is interesting because the use of the word is in its original sense of *that which I have secured.* " It is mine."

PITCH—PITCHER.

The word pitch has several meanings, principally to place anything in orderly array, the sense to throw being only secondary. Hay on the stack and on the wagon must be pitched carefully or it will be spilt and the stack might fall, hop-poles and hurdles for a fold are pitched in such order, and the tool with which it is done is called a *pitch.* The small hay fork is known as a pitch-fork, and the very large fork is the *rick-pitcher*; this was used by the strongest man, who was also called the *pitcher*, for placing hay on the nearly completed stack or rick.

Pitchers (stones) are large round flints suitable for use in *pitched* work, which is a particular method of building or paving. (See Flint.)

PLUM-HEAVY.

Usually called plumeavies and are made with ordinary plain pastry with a little sugar and some currants, sultanas or raisins mixed with it. It is then rolled out, cut into small rounds and baked for about fifteen minutes. It is well to turn them over to brown the other side. Another, plainer, way of making them and called Plum duffs was with flour, sugar, currants and water only, but treated in the same manner. Schoolboys liked them thus, because when they threw them at one another they did not break.

PUMPKIN PIE.

A favourite pie enjoyed at the " Harvest Home " supper. One method of making it was to fill a deep dish with diced pumpkin and sliced apple with a generous supply of currants and sugar. The whole was flavoured with ginger, mixed spice and plenty of lemon juice. After covering with pastry it was baked in a moderate oven to a golden brown.

PUTT.

" Pore old George 'e 'ad a fit or summat o' Sunday jess arter dinner 'e did, an' falls dowan on the flo-er an' they putts a piller unner 'is 'ead an' thur liddle boy 'e runs for the Doctor an' the Doctor 'e cooms an' taakes a look at un an' 'e sez " E be dead, 'e be; putt 'e on the sofy '."

ROUNDEL.

Parish does not give Roundel as being an East Sussex word in his time, but latterly it has had a much wider use there than elsewhere. An interesting sidelight on the variation of dialect within the county was given by the Amberly blacksmith, who said (1955) that in his youth as an improver he went into East Sussex to work. A customer came into the forge where he was employed and asked him to make a roundel. The young blacksmith, not knowing any usual article by that name, asked the customer to describe it. The man was unable to do so, and on a piece of chalk being produced was unable to illustrate his requirement, merely repeating his desire for a roundel. The blacksmith then chalked a circle on the anvil asking if that was what was wanted. The customer said, " Yes, that's it, a roundel." The blacksmith forged and welded a ring which met the customer's wishes and he left the forge satisfied, but probably deploring the blacksmith's inability to understand the Queen's English.

SHAKEN OAK.

Shaken Oak is the name of a house and of the district where some people lived who told us they found that there had been an inn formerly called " The Sheaf and Hook ". Sheaf would be vernacularly pronounced Shafe and the H of Hook would be omitted: hence the deformation to the modern romantic " Shaken Oak ".

SHEEP.

On one occasion my brother was painting a Downland scene with sheep in the distance. A countryman came up: not a word for 10-15 minutes. " Wot be them liddle white marks mister ? " " Sheep." 10-15 minutes silence. " Ah, ship, they be dearly loike."

On another occasion my brother was working on a dry-point when his landlady came into the room and said, " Oh you are clever, Mr. 'all, that is a nice picture. Represents fish ? " It was the South Downs.

SHEERE-MAN.

An old man when asked by a " foreigner " if he had ever been in Oxfordshire replied " Sheer ? I never seed a sheer except it was a plough sheer." The word shire, in spite of modern usage is properly confined to the old kingdom of Mercia which was divided into shires by King Alfred when he conquered it. It is held in contempt by the Saxon counties. A Sussex labourer accounting of a wastrel who had departed to places unknown said, " Oh he be gone to the Sheeres."

SHELL-SNEGS.

" My boy 'ad been put in plaster at the hospital, but the doctors could'n do 'un no good and he could'n move 'is neck. But a gypsy woman wot come to the door did 'im more good than the doctors. She tol' me, ' You take an git a lot of shell-snegs (snails) an' pum them all up on a flat stone an' make a poultice of 'em with brandy an' putt that to 'is neck ', an' that strengthened 'is neck more than anythin' an' 'e can turn 'is 'ead now. I tol' nuther woman of it for 'er liddle boy an' it done 'im good too, but that was for a bad leg.

SHIP.

Ship or sheep shearing was an event in days gone by and looked forward to by farmer and shearer alike. Every year parties of men went from farm to farm headed by a Captain with a lieutenant and a tar boy who both worked under him. The Captain wore a special hat with a gold band round it and the lieutenant had a silver band round his hat. The boy carried a pot of tar and dabbed tar on to any accidental cut or even a slight nick by the shearer as a safeguard against flies, or other such pests, attacking the wound. Woe betide the boy if he were not quick in applying the remedy ! " Spoiling the ship for a ha'porth of tar " came from the Sussex ship-shearers. They worked hard, both the skilled men and the learners who were called *colts*, and when all the shearing trips were over for the season a gathering called *Black Ram Night* was held at the village inn.

The captain of the gang arranged the final share-out, they had a good old-fashioned supper with their special toast and afterwards enjoyed singing and story telling.

The shepherd's toast is:—

" If I had store
By sheep and fold
I'd give you gold;
But since I'm poor
By crook and bell
I wish you well."

SHUCK.

A tale is rife of a former Sussex Major of Yeomanry addressing his troops apropos drawing swords. " When I cries ' drar ' yer not ter drar, but when I cries ' soords ' shuck 'em out smart like." Of the same officer is the legend that to get a good line in a review he got a noted ploughman to run a straight furrow or skidmark for the troops to line up to.

Brighton, c. 1880

SILLY SUSSEX.

Sussex people are descendants of those Saxons who came over from Saxony in the third and fourth centuries A.D. after the departure of the Romans. The Saxons rejoiced in the happy spirit of the natives, who to this day are truly fond of a practical joke, and nicknamed the county Saelig Sussex. *Sǣlig* is spelt several different ways—*selig*, *soelig*, *suelig* but all meaning happy, blessed. The word has been corrupted into " silly ", but true Sussex people only laugh at *that* meaning.

SMOCK.

Smocking was practised all over England. The Sussex women were very proficient at the craft, and their intricately worked white round frocks became a pride of possession for Sunday and holiday wear. They were known as smocks, a shortening of smocked round frock, and needed a good deal more time and material to make than the ordinary working round frock, usually shortened to frock. These were of grey or natural coloured material, and although smocked to some extent, were not so much worked as to merit the name " smock ".

SOULING.

On All Saints Day, November 1, men dressed in black paraded the streets asking for contributions for prayers for the dead, and money was given them for masses to be said on the following day—All Souls Day. Later on people went from house to house with a collection box, in theory for the same purpose, but in practice it was a social affair; bread, cheese and home-made wine being given in exchange for all the latest news and gossip. Still later the custom was kept up by children who were given hot spiced buns called soul-cakes and a drink of ginger-pop in return for singing:—

" Soul! Soul! for a soul cake
Pray, good mistress for a soul cake:
One for Peter and two for Paul
Three for Him who made us all."

Much the same custom was observed on St. Clement's Day, November 23, and on St. Catharine's Day, November 25, when children went Clemmening and Catterning for apples and beer.

The 30th November is St. Andrew's Day and then bricklayers took a holiday Andring. They cut short pieces from the handle of a broom and threw them at squirrels and other small game. When the hunt was over they enjoyed the usual big dinner prepared at the inn and afterwards a merry sing-song evening.

SQUAT.

To a carter who was hauling coal from a railway station it was remarked that railways always seemed to be in the valleys. He replied, " Ah, I shud like to see 'em goin' up hill an' down, skid-pan and squat."

STEDDLE.

Steddle, a Stand or Standing, was a framework to support a granery or corn rick and to keep it out of reach of damp and vermin, particularly rats and mice.

The frame was of bresummers on lines of stones like gigantic mushrooms, a pillar stone and a cap stone to each, with lighter timbers between. On this frame was built the granery or rick.

STREWERS.

The custom of strewing emblems and flowers at the feet of a bride and bridegroom is ancient; quite likely performed in pagan times and even today continued by aboriginals.

In the *Sussex Weekly Advertiser* (the first newspaper published in the county) for 1 September, 1771, is recorded a wedding in Lewes of a Lewes Woolstapler, Mr. Thomas Kemp to Miss Reed, the daughter of an eminent grazier in Romney Marsh, who " gave to the Poor Women of St. Michael's parish who strewed them, three guineas."

In *Country Life* for March 10, 1955, a writer says that many interesting details are recorded in the diary of John Rofe, for 40 years a bellringer of Cranbrook, one of the records being, " 1795 Feby. 17th. the Strewers 3 guineas." And that " as the bride and bridegroom left the church, the strewers threw emblems of the bridegroom's trade on the pathway—shavings of wood for a carpenter, straw for a hatmaker, pieces of oak bark for a tanner, iron filings for a blacksmith, pieces of leather for a shoemaker, and even sheep skins for a butcher." I find no record of when throwing special emblems ceased and no note is given of *what* was thrown at the Lewes wedding although the price paid was the same—three guineas.

The custom continued at country weddings in Sussex, for in June, 1885, when my elder sister was married at Lancing, a friend asked a village girl, "Are you going to the wedding, Annie?" "Oh, yes," she replied. "I be one of the strewers." There was then no payment given for strewing and among others the vicar's son, aged four, carried a trug from which he vigorously flung roses all down the nave at the feet of the newly wedded pair.

The custom expressed the wish for future health and happiness. On the pathway *outside* the church rice was scattered before them indicating the wish for material blessings.

SUSSEX PUDDING.

The usual and better recipe for Sussex Pudding is to boil a small plain oblong suet (not much suet) pudding rolled in a cloth. When done, cut it into slices about half an inch thick and place them under the meat to brown to serve with roast mutton. Sussex pudding with mutton is equivalent to Yorkshire pudding with beef.

SWISH—SWISS.

"'E was Swish I think—leastways a German sort of genilman with spartacles as smelt o' smoke."

TAINTER.

Flax was a crop formerly grown widely in Sussex, and with the scutching and hitchelling or itchelling (hackling) to produce a carded thread called tire, which was then spun, woven, fulled and tented, by which various processes it became linen, formed one of the more important local industries.

In the impoverished conditions of the 18th and early 19th centuries, spinning flax was a usual workhouse occupation, and mention of it frequently occurs in parish accounts. Whether the preliminary processes were also carried out by paupers is not stated, but in some cases it is said that the linen thread was sent away for weaving, so that at that time the trade had fallen on evil days.

That the whole process was formerly carried out is shown by the number of Fulling Mill farms and fields and of places named Fuller's. The finisher or tenter was, in Sussex, called a Tainter, and we have in Lindfield "Tainter's Meads", in Buxted "Tainter's Croft" and the name occurs elsewhere.

There is no record of the bleaching process and surviving local examples are generally so faded as to give no evidence, but the area of the Lindfield Tainter's Meads is such as to suggest that it was carried on there in conjunction with the tenting process.

TAPSELL GATE.

This ingenious gate is peculiar to Sussex, but nothing is known of its origin or of its designer. Its special use is to prevent cattle entering churchyards and to make room for coffin bearers to pass through easily. It is at the entrance to a churchyard that the gate is found today. It is made of light wood, well fixed into the ground and passing through the cross bars. It swings open with a slight touch and even at half way gives plenty of room for coffin bearers to walk through. A hook or spring catch at the end post secures the gate.

In the 18th century tapsell gates were probably common enough, but today there are only six in the county, most of them in the eastern part. They work well, are a joy to handle and may be found at the churchyards of Combes, East Dean, Friston, Jevington, Kingston near Lewes and Pyecombe.

The name is spelt several ways: Tapsell, Topsel, Topsayle and otherwise and is found distributed throughout the county. Nearly all members of the family *recorded* were bellfounders and on a bell at Chiddingly one may read:—" Robert Tapsell made me—1663 ". It is likely that the gate was devised by one named Tapsell, but whether or not he was a bellfounder is unknown.

In 1610 Edward Topsell was vicar of East Grinstead and in the late 16th century Henry and Roger Topstill, father and son, were bellfounders at West Tarring, Roger making four bells for All Saints Church, Hastings. John Tapsell, a carpenter, lived at Mountfield, near Robertsbridge, but no certain one has yet been identified as the inventor of the Tapsell gate.

TELL.

Shepherds count sheep—tell them—by letting the flock run through between two hurdles, two sheep at a time, counting the pairs. The numerals used are strange and the sets differ. One set runs:—

1. One-erum	6. Sath-erum
2. Two-erum	7. Wineberry
3. Cock-erum	8. Wagtail
4. Shu-erum	9. Tarry diddle
5. Sith-erum	10. Den.

Den means a score, or twenty sheep through the hurdles. The scores were recorded on nick-sticks or tally sticks. One shepherd said he used his crook-stick to cut the notches in so that he never lost his count.

TIDY.

Finding the gardener shutting up the entrance gates early one summer afternoon a son of the house said, " You're shutting up pretty early today, aren't you, Serle? " " Well, I 'ears there's a couple of willocky bullicks about the village an' a bullick soon makes a tidy 'avick in a garden."

TREAD THE WHEEL.

When a furnace is blown in (started) it must be kept in blast for a considerable period to make its use economic.

Sussex furnaces were commonly blown from November to May or June according to the seasonal water power available.

In very dry winters it was sometimes necessary to tread the wheel, that is for men to walk inside, or sometimes on the outside stepping from bucket to bucket, to keep it in motion and the bellows going to maintain blast.

In a letter from John Fuller the ironmaster of Heathfield, to Mr. Remnant, his London agent, dated February 4, 1744, explaining why delivery of guns must be delayed, he says:—

" I presume you are not ignorant of the fact that both Mr. Crowley's furnaces are blown out for want of water and as I previously stated they tread the wheel at Waldron, Robertsbridge and Beckley, which is an excessive charge, and is the same thing as if men should walk in one of your Capsterns, night and day for a quarter of a year together.

" If the weather continueth, want of water will blow out all the Furnaces in the County." *S.A.C. LXVII*, p. 44.

Whether some enterprising Sussex ironmaster had the bright idea of employing criminals for this purpose or perhaps only paupers, I have been unable to ascertain. But it was certainly the origin of the treadmill.

WAHZTREW.

Wahztrew, spelled alternatively Wahstrew and Wahztrewe, is the name given in the Pevensey Custumal to the place of execution of felons who were not freemen. It means wash-tro, a wash trough, and probably in its original sense the pool below a tidal sluice. (*Cf.* The Wash.)

The word trow or strow, a water trough or pool, formerly current in the East Sussex marshes, seems recently to have gone completely out of use. Parish does not mention it, but the late Revd. A. A. Evans uses it of a water course in general but not in any particular sense.

It is used as a terminal in the place names Sakevylestrow, Wyllyndonestrow and Ladytrowe mentioned in the findings of a commission held at Westham in 1396 (*S.A.C. LIII*, p. 46.) and Wartrow mentioned in the Pevensey rate books, in 1528 as being in the quarter of " Horsye," but in 1523 as " *Adhuc Horsy* " or further, or Farther Horsee. (*S.A.C. XLV*, pp. 176, 169.)

Sakeveylestrow and Wyllyndonestrow are specifically the places where the Sackville and Willingdon sewers respectively joined Hurst and Pevensey Havens; and Ladytrowe is where a formerly important sewer draining the Herstmonceaux marshes joined the Haven. The names of water courses were frequently appropriated to adjacent land areas as in the case of " A parcell of Land called Martines Gutt." (*S.A.C. XXIV*, p. 260.)

There is some likelihood that the Wartrow of Farther Horseye was the place of execution, and that it was at the extreme North point, and most remote, of the liberty of Pevensey where it abutts on Hailsham and Herstmonceux, and where the Whelpley and Puckeridge sewers join the Haven, at some time in the history of the Levels the head of tide water.

WINDROW.

The Revd. W. D. Parish likens a windrow to a thin row of new mown grass raked up lightly so as to allow the wind to pass freely through it and dry it. Other writers have a different opinion and think the letter " D " is an intrusion, because the word was intended to mean that the hay had been " won ", or gathered in and that the word should be simply winrow.

The drag rake used to form the windrows (which were often called leeks) was about four feet ten inches wide with some twenty-five or so iron or wooden tines twelve inches long. Sometimes the outside tine at each end of the rake was half as long again as the rest, and was curved forwards to slide along the ground and support the weight of the rake. The frame was of wood, often artistically chamfered.

YOKE.

The decline of the use of oxen yoked for ploughing was caused by the speeding up of agriculture. In the *Sussex Weekly Advertiser* for October 10, 1796, was a most interesting account of a ploughing match at Stopham Bridge, Petworth, where yoked oxen were tried against oxen in collar and harness and later against horses. These methods showed increasing speed. The case of oxen harnessed never gained much support and both were eventually superseded by horse ploughing. All are now lost to mechanisation.

A SHORT LIST OF ADDITIONAL WORDS

BIVVER

To quiver, shake or tremble. The expression is seen in the drooping lip before the tears fall.

BUFFLEN

In a child's game of cricket the jacket thrown over a stick, or a stump, to form a wicket.

COKELERS.

w. A religious sect founded in 1850 by John Sirgood, a London shoemaker, and named The Society of Dependents. All were abstainers, Sirgood drinking cocoa, little known in his day and being a novelty, he and his following were nicknamed cocoa-drinkers shortened to cokelers, Their number grew, stores were opened and communities established at Loxwood, Chichester, Plaistow, Kirdford, North Chapel, Warnham and Wisborough. Steady and industrious, always ready to help one another, they are respected and trusted by all who deal with them whether in business, farming or character. Although small it is hoped this purely Sussex sect will never die out.

DEW-STRINGS and LEATHER WASHERS.

Dew-Strings and Leather Washers are other names for Knee straps, Knee cords, Knot-leggers, nims, nollegers or yorks: sometimes of leather, sometimes of cord, but all used for the same purpose=to loop up trousers to prevent dragging on the knee, or unduly rubbing round the ankles.

DO.

e. Or, possibly from the French d'ou. " For pity's sake keep that oven door shut, do they cakes wunt plim."

DREANING.

m. A soaking. After falling in the pond and spoiling frock. " I went dreaning home to my mother wich gave me a good stripeing and confined me the rest of the day." From James Nye's Diary. (*Cf.* DREAN).

LET.

A leak. " Better not use that cup, it lets. Heard at Lindfield, 1957.

SOME-SENSE.

To-rights. " I'll give 'im some-sense when 'e comes home."

WICK.

Long ending. " Oh she gets my wick," *i.e.* goes on talking too long a time.

INDEX TO APPENDICES